# ASPECTS OF EDUCATIONAL TECHNOLOGY

# Aspects
# of Educational Technology
# Volume XV
# Distance Learning
# and Evaluation

*Edited for the Association for Educational
and Training Technology by*
**Fred Percival and Henry Ellington**

*General Editor*
**A J Trott** *Bulmershe College*

**Kogan Page London/Nichols Publishing
Company, New York**

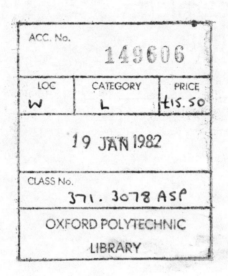
First published 1981
by Kogan Page Limited
120 Pentonville Road, London N1 9JN

**British Library Cataloguing in Publication Data**
Aspects of Educational Technology
    Volume XV: Distance Learning and Evaluation.
    1. Educational technology — Congress
    I. Percival, Fred    II. Ellington, Henry
    371. 3'07'8    LB1028.3

ISBN 0-85038-494-X (UK)
ISBN 0-89397-116-2 (USA)
ISSN 0141-5956

Printed in Great Britain by
The Anchor Press Ltd and bound by
Wm Brendon & Son Ltd,
both of Tiptree, Essex

Published in the USA by Nichols Publishing Company
PO Box 96, New York, NY 10024

# Contents

# Section 4: Reports on One-Day Symposia

# The 1981 Agecroft Trophy Competition                                    316

---

**Paper Not Included**
Owing to lack of space the following author's presentation has not been included
in this volume:

**J Morton**
*The Brick Development Association*
The Introduction of Educational and Training Courses for Professional Designers
on Behalf of the British Brick Industry

# Author Index

# Editorial

## Introduction

ETIC 81, the Fifteenth Annual Conference of the Association for Educational and Training Technology (AETT), was held in the Kepplestone premises of Robert Gordon's Institute of Technology, Aberdeen from 31 March to 3 April 1981. AETT has a policy of holding its conference in different parts of mainland Britain, and of trying to ensure that each of the 'four corners' is visited at least once every five or six years. The previous conference to be held north of the border was ETIC 76, which was hosted by Dundee College of Education. Since then, the conference venues have been Guildford, Pontypridd, Sheffield and London, so that a return to Scotland in 1981 was highly appropriate. Aberdeen was by far the most northerly location in which an ETIC conference had yet been held, and a number of would-be delegates residing south of Watford had expressed fears about 'falling off the edge' or succumbing to the permafrost. Despite this, there was an excellent attendance, the conference and its various associated activities attracting well over 300 people from 16 different countries.

## The Conference

Following successive conferences which had respectively reviewed progress in educational technology over the last 20 years, and looked forward to possible developments during the next 20, it was decided that ETIC 81 should concentrate on the contribution that educational technology was *currently* making to the *quality* of education and training. The overall conference theme was 'Educational Technology and the Learning Experience'; there were two major sub-themes, namely, 'Distance Learning and Broadcasting', and the 'Role of Evaluation in Educational Technology'.

In planning ETIC 81, a deliberate attempt was made to implement AETT's policy of making their activities relevant to teachers and trainers 'at the coal face' as well as to professional educational technologists. For this reason, it was decided to complement the conventional academic programme of papers and workshops with a number of events designed specifically for the former. This strategy proved highly successful, and resulted in roughly 100 people who would not normally attend an ETIC conference coming along for at least part of the programme.

## The Mainline Programme

Previous ETIC conferences have, as a rule, accepted a large number of paper and workshop proposals, a policy which has sometimes led to criticism on the following two grounds. First, programmes have tended to become overloaded with as many

as four parallel streams of papers, plus further streams of workshops and other
activities in some cases; this has resulted in delegate frustration with regard to
choice of activity, to poor attendance at some papers and workshops and, in a
few cases, to non-viability of participative sessions. Second, the non-too-stringent
selection procedures sometimes adopted have, on occasions, led to concern
regarding the quality and relevance of a number of the contributions.

In an attempt to overcome these problems, it was decided to limit the main
programme of ETIC 81 to two streams of papers plus a parallel stream of
workshops. This automatically restricted the number of papers and workshops to
just over 50, enabling the organizers of ETIC 81 to be much more selective than
in previous years (roughly 30 per cent of the proposals received were not
accepted).

To give the conference academic as well as logistical structure, the following
overall plan was adopted. Day 1 started with a keynote address on the overall
theme of the conference, followed by papers and workshops particularly relevant
to this theme. Days 2 and 3 were each devoted to one of the main sub-themes,
each day opening with an appropriate keynote address. Day 4 (the final day)
was devoted to further papers and workshops related to the overall conference
theme.

## Other Activities

In addition to the above programme, the conference included two one-day events
designed for specialist interest groups. The first, a symposium on 'Information
Retrieval in Educational Technology', was held on Day 2 of the conference, and
addressed itself to the question: 'How do we improve the accessibility and
usefulness of educational technology resources?'. The second, held on Day 3,
was a workshop conference on the educational applications of microcomputers;
this was organized in association with the Scottish Microelectronics Development
Programme. Both events aroused considerable interest, and were extremely well
attended; the micro-electronics conference, in particular, attracted over 30
Scottish teachers and lecturers who were not associated with the main conference.

Another innovative feature of the ETIC 81 was the inclusion of a programme
of skills workshops intended specifically for practising teachers and trainers.
These were run by the Scottish Council for Educational Technology (SCET) and
consisted of a full-day course on the use of portable video equipment and
half-day courses on the production of slide-tape programmes and overhead
projection materials (see Figures 1 and 2). These courses all proved extremely
popular, the first two being heavily over-subscribed; in all, they were attended
by over 50 teachers, lecturers and trainers.

Possibly the most unusual feature of ETIC 81 was the Agecroft Trophy
Competition, in which teams of senior pupils from three local secondary schools
played THE POWER STATION GAME over the last three days of the conference.
This involved each of the three teams preparing a detailed 'consultants' report'
on the feasibility of building one particular type of power station (coal, oil or
nuclear) in a given area and preparing and presenting a case supporting its
particular scheme. As well as having the opportunity of seeing the teams at work
on their cases, the delegates acted as judges of the competition during the
plenary session that constituted its climax; thus (to borrow a phrase from
Ian Morris) delegates had the chance of seeing educational technology 'on the
hoof'.

The conference also included a wide-ranging exhibition, containing both
educational and commercial stands (see Figure 3).

**Figure 1.** *Outdoor work on the SCET portable video course*

**Figure 2.** *Work on the SCET slide-tape course*

**Figure 3.** *One of the commercial stands at the exhibition*

**Figure 4.** *AETT Chairman, Mr John Sinclair (left), replying to the speech of welcome by Lord Provost Alexander C Collie of the City of Aberdeen\**

*\* The editors will be happy to award a bottle of malt whisky to the reader who comes up with the best alternative caption to Figure 4.*

## Social Events

In addition to a programme of local sightseeing tours for non-participants, ETIC 81 included three major social events.

On the evening of Day 1, an informal whisky/wine reception was held at the conference centre. The exhibition was open during this reception, giving delegates the opportunity to combine business with pleasure.

The Conference Dinner was held in a local hotel on the evening of Day 2. This again had a distinctly Scottish flavour, incorporating a traditional Burns Supper, complete with piper and address to the haggis.

The climax of the social programme was a magnificent Civic Reception hosted by the City of Aberdeen. This included a buffet supper, a cabaret featuring local entertainers, and a dance. Some idea of the spirit of the occasion can be gained from Figure 4.

## The Conference Proceedings

The Proceedings of ETIC 81, which constitute the remainder of this book, have been arranged in the following manner.

The book starts with the opening keynote address, delivered by Professor John Nisbet of the University of Aberdeen. The main body of the book is divided into four sections:

*Section 1* deals with the first main sub-theme of the conference, 'Distance Learning and Broadcasting'. It begins with a keynote address on the subject given by Mr David Butts of the University of Stirling; this puts into context many of the papers and workshop reports given later in the section. These are grouped in sub-sections, as detailed in the Contents.

*Section 2*, which deals with the second major sub-theme of the conference ('The Role of Evaluation in Educational Technology'), adopts a similar format. In this case, the keynote address that introduces the section is by Professor Tony Becher of the University of Sussex.

*Section 3*, entitled 'Educational Technology and the Learning Experience', contains those papers and workshop reports which, while relating to the overall theme of the conference, cannot be included under either of the two main sub-themes.

*Section 4* contains overview reports on the two one-day 'conferences within the conference', written by their respective organizers.

The book concludes with the closing remarks delivered by Mr Ian Morris, HMCI, of the Scottish Education Department, on the final afternoon of the conference. These consist of critical observations on the quality of the conference and the various activities that made up the programme.

*Fred Percival and Henry Ellington*
*Robert Gordon's Institute of Technology, Aberdeen, June, 1981*

# Opening Keynote Address

## Educational Technology: Its Current Impact

**Professor John Nisbet**
*University of Aberdeen*

### Introduction

I start by declaring a prejudice and making a confession. Perhaps the conference organizers invited me in the role of neutral commentator, or even sceptic: implying that if I can be persuaded that educational technology has made a contribution to the quality of education, then convincing the rest of the educational world will be relatively easy. If that is in your minds, you are wrong. For my prejudice is in favour of educational technology: I have a firm belief in its potential. I was involved in it in the early days. Together with Leslie Reid, I think I can claim to have been one of the first on this side of the Atlantic to receive a research grant for a programmed learning project. It was in 1960, when research money was even harder to come by then it is today: incredibly, the research grant (to develop a teaching machine) was for £100, and it was made by the Aberdeen Endowments Trust.

My confession also dates back to that period. In May 1959, David Finney, then head of the Statistics Department in the University of Aberdeen, wrote a letter to various colleagues:

> You are doubtless aware of the rapid development that has occurred in the design of electronic digital computing machines. A few years ago, the construction of such a machine was itself a major research project; now many different models are in standardized production, they have become indispensable to some types of investigation . . .

He asked a number of questions:

> Were we interested?
> Had we used computers?
> Did we expect to use them? and so on.

I keep this letter in a file marked 'Museum', together with my reply, a note in my handwriting, initialled by me:

> As far as I am concerned, the answers to all the questions in the letter are 'No'.

How wrong can you be? I keep that note of mine like the hair shirt worn by the mediaeval ascetics: whenever I begin to believe that I am right and some other person is wrong, one glance at that old correspondence is enough to make me feel very humble.

## Impact on Education

The theme which I was asked to develop in this address is the contribution which educational technology has made to the quality of education. It is not the old argument of whether eduational technology can demonstrate successful achievements, but rather the question of what effect it has had on education generally. In a paper to this conference in 1977, Elton (1978) distinguished between the influence of educational technology on what he called mass instruction, and its influence on individualized instruction. Of its influence on mass instruction, he said:

> The best use that educational technology can be put to is to make the average teacher a better than average teacher by helping him, not by in any sense replacing him.

Ignoring the statistical oddity of trying to make everyone above average, is there any evidence that this objective is being achieved? Looking beyond the tight group of committed enthusiasts, what wider effect has educational technology had on the world of teaching and learning?

As with other studies of the impact of educational research and development, we can distinguish two kinds of effects, the direct and the indirect; and the indirect effects are more important in the long term.

### Direct Effects

The history of educational technology is strewn with aberrations and dead-end developments, but so is the history of the evolution of life on this planet. In the relatively short period of some 20 years, educational technology can claim quite a creditable record of achievement. Though programmed learning and teaching machines are now obsolete, they have left their mark in individualized learning, distance learning, Keller Plan, tape-slide programmes and language laboratories. Computer-assisted learning using large-scale machinery is also obsolescent, but it paved the way for the current generation of microcomputers, which are already being used quite widely in schools and colleges. Games and simulations have flourished dramatically. My colleagues here in Aberdeen have been particularly energetic and imaginative in developing ideas for their application to science education (Ellington, Addinall and Percival, 1981), and in other fields such as management, military work, professional staff development and skills training, they have become almost standard techniques. More generally, basic ideas from educational technology have won wide acceptance in principle, such as the objectives model, resource-based learning, and a systems approach to syllabus construction and to assessment procedures. The applications of these ideas to education have resulted in a much more sophisticated approach to the design and practice of teaching and learning — really quite an impressive step forward from the crude programming of the 1960s.

But to what extent are these sophisticated ideas reflected in actual changes in the curriculum and methods of schools and colleges within the formal educational system? The answer is disappointing: changing a curriculum is as difficult as moving a cemetery (and sometimes seems rather similar). There are many instances of innovation, but relatively few of successful implementation and of final institutionalization. We should not be too pessimistic, however. In Scotland, for example, the six-year development programme for implementing the Munn and Dunning reports (Scottish Education Department, 1977a, b) is already producing some encouraging work in its pilot schools, even in the first year of the programme. Within 15 miles of Aberdeen there is a secondary school where the Foundation level course in science is already operating (apparently successfully) on a modular self-instructional design, and Foundation level is for pupils in the lowest performance band. Modern language teachers are usually thought of as traditional in attitude and method, yet they have taken readily to the use of the taperecorder: in the University of Aberdeen, the language laboratory last session marked up 20,000 student hours of use, and that was regarded as nothing out of the ordinary. Many primary schools incorporate new strategies in their teaching, like Breakthrough to Literacy and the SRA Reading Labs. But these are examples of innovations which were taken up because they fit existing practice: there has been no dramatic revolution in method. Educational practice is, as always, very slow to change. Ten years and more after the Plowden Report (Department of Education and Science, 1967), four major studies agree in showing that only a small minority of primary schools — about one in six, possibly — have adopted a 'progressive' style of working (Bennett, 1976; Galton, Simon and Croll, 1980; Department of Education and Science, 1978; Scottish Education Department, 1980). Even where teachers think they are applying educational technology principles and procedures, too often they are only grafting them on to traditional practices. Where this has happened, all that we can see as a direct effect of educational technology is that schools are littered with work-cards which pupils find just as boring as the old chalk-and-talk.

Unfortunately, we expect too much too soon. The innovator frightens people with his talk of rapid change; he threatens them by attacking the practices they are familiar with; and he antagonises even his potential allies by his posture of moral superiority. Avoid the temptation of thinking that you have exclusive possession of some divine gift to bestow on your fellow men. There are too many experts flitting round the fringes of educational institutions, saying, 'God sent me here to help others — what he sent the others for, God only knows'. At the 1979 conference, Kay (1979) warned us:

> Not everybody in education loves educational technology . . . I wish I could tell you that every time the subject of educational technology is mentioned, a warm glow of sympathy and support circulates . . . Alas, it does not.

I should like to see a history of educational technology written covering the past 20 years, as a warning on how *not* to bring about innovation.

## Indirect Effects

Thus, if you look around for direct evidence of the improvement of educational practice in schools and colleges as a result of educational technology, you will be able to find quite a number of examples. But you will find many more examples where traditional educational practice has not even been dented by the impact of educational technology. To adapt a comment by Lamke (1955), if research over the past 20 years in medicine, agriculture, physics, chemistry or biology were wiped out, professional workers would have to alter their present-day practices drastically, and our life would be changed materially; but if all the work on educational technology over the same 20 years were to vanish, educators and education would continue much as usual.

But perhaps, in looking for impact, we are using the wrong model. In a recent book (Nisbet and Broadfoot, 1980) on the impact of educational research on policy and practice, there is a quotation from an interview with the Chief Education Officer of Manchester which sums it up:

> The impact of research findings is not like a parcel being delivered to the post-room, neatly done up, which finds its way upstairs into the main building where different people can take the wrappings off. It is more like somebody releasing a canister of gas somewhere. It blows about, and at any one moment, if you were walking down the corridors you could sniff it but you wouldn't quite know where it had got to. You

might find somebody coughing and spluttering in a corner who had actually taken an enormous dose of it!

With this model in mind for examining effects, I was tempted to adopt one of these cryptic wordy titles for my address:

'Abjure military metaphors: try a whiff of gas'.

If you wish a more inspiring metaphor, there is a poem by Arthur Hugh Clough which Winston Churchill used on a more celebrated occasion:

> For while the tired waves, vainly breaking,
>     Seem here no painful inch to gain,
> Far back, through creeks and inlets making,
>     Comes silent, flooding in, the main.

Certainly, at the university level in the last 10 years there has been quite a change of attitude to methods of teaching and the design of courses, and the example of the Open University has had an effect on the quality of teaching in many universities, colleges and polytechnics throughout the country. My impression of other sectors of the educational system is that people nowadays have a better understanding of the principles of syllabus construction, and there is more sophisticated use of resources and more effective design of assessment systems. It used to be said of programmed learning that when eventually you had completed the laborious process of making up your programme, you could throw the programme away, because in the process of construction you have learned how best to teach the subject. In a similar way, educational technology has made some teachers think, and has given them a model for their thinking; and there is better teaching and learning as a result.

The indirect or long-term effect of educational technology is in providing a theoretical basis, a rationale, for the improvement of teaching. This effect operates through concepts and structures and theories and assumptions which are gradually absorbed into popular thought and discussion until they become a new climate of opinion. The paradox of innovation is that the criterion for successful implementation is when the innovation is no longer seen as novel, but is accepted as part of established and accepted practice. In time, successful examples of development create a public attitude or climate of opinion — Cronbach and Suppes (1969) call it a 'prevailing view', cumulatively built up until it becomes a dominant influence on policy and practice in education.

Of course, educational technology is not the only contributor to this 'prevailing view'. There have been substantial developments in cognitive psychology in recent years, parallel to and interacting with those in educational technology. I need not detail the work of Gagné and Ausubel, the many studies on memory and information processing, on learning styles and strategies, which have led to a new psychological theory of learning which is particularly well fitted to the educational technology approach. These developments have provided us with a vocabulary and a grammar for the discussion and improvement of educational practice.

If we glance back over the past 100 years, we can see how psychological theories of learning have affected educational practice. In the 19th century, failure to learn was seen primarily as a moral weakness and attributed to lack of effort and application. In the first half of the 20th century, the concept of ability was dominant: the amount and quality of learning depended on the amount and quality of intelligence which the learner brought to the task. Now at last, we have begun to look for an explanation within the process of instruction: learning is seen as a product of the interaction between the framework of concepts of the learner and the structure of the curriculum content presented to him. This is a much more optimistic gospel in that it implies that many can be 'saved' who would have been damned for ever, according to the old theory of intelligence. But the gospel can also be interpreted in an over-simplified way, to imply that if only we had enough research and resources for teaching, the right material, the right method, sufficient time, adequate training and so on, we could teach everybody everything. Bruner's brave suggestion was 'the hypothesis that any subject can be taught effectively in some intellectually honest form to any child at any stage of development'; but he put it forward as a hypothesis, not as an article of faith. Its value is that it directs attention to the subject-matter of instruction, its structure and form, and to the intellectual powers of the learner, his stage of development and his cognitive frames of references, and to the interaction between these, namely *The Process of Education* — the title of the book by Bruner (1960) from which that quotation is taken.

The growth of educational technology has tended to revive the old idea of a 'science of education', the belief that educational research, experiment and inquiry can build up a system of fundamental laws by reference to which any educational problem can be solved. This belief reached its peak in the 1930s, but it originated over 100 years ago, and one of the pioneers of the idea was Alexander Bain, a professor in the University of Aberdeen whose book, *Education as a Science*, was published in 1879. With the emergence of educational technology in the 1960s, we began to look again at those old experiments to decide whether a film was better than a lecture, television better than radio, colour better than black and white, the appropriate length of a talk, the best balance between exposition, example and question, and so on. We are still witnessing determined efforts to deal with educational issues by statistical tests, by indices, item banks, formulae, and so on. Technology needs a science as its base. If educational technology could create an educational science, it would indeed make a great contribution to the quality of education generally. But I think that development along these lines is fundamentally mistaken: the model of technology and science is the wrong model. The movement which this annual conference represents began as programmed learning, and then became educational technology; I suggest it may have to undergo a third change before it gets its metaphors right. Further examination of this issue in the concluding section of this address will not resolve the issue, but it may help to throw light on the achievements of educational technology and on the resistances which it has encountered.

## The Distant Drum

Why has progress in educational innovation been so slow? There is a whole field of literature on obstacles to innovation. MacDonald (1975) summarized it in his evaluation of the National Development Programme in Computer Assisted Learning:

> The citadel of established practice will not yield to the polite knock of a new idea. Instead, we must use the strategies of a pre-emptive strike, a wooden horse, a cunning alliance or a long siege.

Note the military metaphors. We talk of 'strategies' and 'barriers', and plan our campaigns as if the customer was an object to be assaulted and battered into submission. We use a centre-periphery model of change, asking how ideas developed centrally can be diffused to the periphery, and how to overcome the obstacles to effective communication of these ideas down the channels to the people below, who are optimistically assumed to be waiting eagerly for the gifts we send them. The error of this assumption is pointed out in the Australian Karmel Report (Australian Schools Commission, 1973):

> The effectiveness of innovation, no matter at what level it is initiated in a school organization, is dependent on the extent to which the people concerned perceive a problem . . .

Too often it is the experts who define the problems in their own terms, and it is hardly surprising if teachers have to be persuaded to accept the solutions offered. You have to start where the other person is, accepting his definition of his problems: you have to demonstrate that you can help him, on his terms. It is no use saying: 'You are doing it all the wrong way'. That is like the motorist who stopped to ask a fool the way to a nearby village. 'Well, if I were you', was the reply, 'I wouldn't start from here'. Criticizing your colleagues for being slaves of convention is hardly the way to win friends and influence people.

Part of the reason why educational technology has not had the success one might expect is that the metaphor is wrong: the term 'educational technology' implies a set of assumptions which lead us off in the wrong direction and then we follow the line of thought which the metaphor suggests. It is dangerously easy for innovators to set up a new orthodoxy. There is a paradox here in that for those who are engaged in innovation (as also in political revolutions) adherence to an ideology is necessary if they are to survive at all. The securely established society can tolerate divergence and turn it to advantage: the innovatory group demands commitment and loyalty.

Another title which I considered for this address was 'The distant drum'. This is a reference to one of Thoreau's sayings, that the divergent thinker 'is merely marching to a more distant drum'.

Some of you will say that there is no shortage of divergent thinkers in a conference like this. Yet my impression of educational technology, viewing it from a distance, is that it tends to impose rather rigid frameworks — demanding convergent thinking within an innovative framework. Thus some texts on educational technology (and even some conferences) are horribly predictable.

I cannot claim to have done more than touch on this fundamental problem. It might have made an interesting address if I had taken 'the distant drum' as my theme; but perhaps it would have taken us too far from the theme of this conference.

## Targets

To sum up, then, what are the targets which educational technology should now be aiming to achieve? (The word 'targets' reminds me how difficult it is to escape the military metaphor.) What do we expect as the contribution of educational technology to the quality of education generally?

Different kinds of claims have been made. Some adherents strive for a wholesale takeover of the educational system: let us rebuild the system on sound educational technology principles. A second group of advocates claim only a limited area: let us take over certain parts of the curriculum where we have most to offer, and we shall thereby allow the teacher to make his unique personal contribution all the more effectively. (The Learning Resources Centre of Dundee College of Education, for example, aimed to put 20 per cent of the curriculum on to an individualized modular basis. Is that the right proportion?) A third group of believers look forward to a quiet revolution, a gradual but steady absorption of the ideas of educational technology into the fabric of educational practice, so that they become part of what I earlier called 'the prevailing view', the established conceptual framework for tackling educational issues.

My guess is that most of those present belong to the second group, and a few to the first, but, as you will have guessed, I am in the third group, and it is by quiet revolution that I think educational technology can contribute most to the quality of education.

I do not much like the 'separate development' of educational technology as an 'alternative education'. I think it unnecessary as well as unwise, for you have many potential allies, among cognitive psychologists, educational advisers and many committed teachers, and you have plenty of willing listeners among those who are deeply concerned with the tedium of much conventional education — tedium both for teachers and learners. Recent developments open up new possibilities. The old-style computer was so massive, so expensive and so complex that it put the expert into a control position and the potential could only be exploited through a centre-periphery style of innovation. The introduction of the microcomputer changes the position completely: it can be fitted into the existing framework, and can be used by teachers and pupils in the way they choose to use it. With microcomputers the expert loses his position of control; some may see this as a danger, but to me it is a great potential strength. Admittedly, if people are allowed too much freedom, there is a risk that they may choose ideas other than the ones we want them to adopt, or they may only adopt those new ideas which leave their old prejudices undisturbed — innovation without change. This was a problem which Rousseau had in mind in 1762 when he wrote:

> People are always telling me to make *practical* suggestions. You might as well tell me to suggest improvements which can be incorporated with the wrong methods at present in use.

I admit that this is a real risk, but I think it is worth taking, because I believe that it is only by working along with existing practices, by incremental change, that we can achieve the quiet revolution by which educational technology can make its greatest contribution.

You see that I am arguing for a 'centre party', neither the hard-line traditionalist approach nor the radical left. The centre is where most of the votes are, but in education as in politics, we need the manifesto spelt out in greater detail.

## Conclusion

I do not pretend to be able to undertake that task. As a first step, I suggest an attempt to diminish the present intellectual isolation of educational technology. It seems to me to be a rather exclusive realm of educational research and development, perhaps because of that commitment to an idea which I spoke of earlier. Belonging to an exclusive group has attractions, but in the long run it is self-defeating. I should like to see educational technology develop greater flexibility. I should like to see it encouraging greater personal responsibility for decisions, and less emphasis (or less exclusive reliance) on objective data. I should like to see it more sensitive to the context of learning, especially the social context, for education is a social activity rather than a technology, one in which motivation and the sense of personal involvement are even more important than in industry where many of these lessons have already been learned.

In an address to this conference in 1977, Hooper (1978) argued for curriculum integration, 'to ensure that CAL or CML developments happen within a framework of broader curriculum or course design'. There is a lot of related work being done in curriculum development, and educational technology must come to terms with it, for it has much to gain from a closer integration. An address by Hubbard (1979) to the 1978 conference also stressed this point. His first proposition was:

> Educational technology is essentially one part, alongside curriculum development, staff development and the development of student learning, of the wider process that might be called 'educational development' and we need therefore to strengthen the links between these different aspects of the process.

So perhaps I am not saying anything new.

The time is ripe for educational technology to move out of its somewhat narrow enclosure. You will note that I am not using any military metaphor: it is not a matter of sending out raiding parties to capture strategic points. I would rather use a human metaphor. If we take Skinner's work as the birth of programmed learning — all the previous work, important as that was, can be regarded as the period of gestation — then I reckon that educational technology has now clearly passed the age of 21. It has reached its majority, and it is accepted as a mature and reputable member of the educational community. Its achivement during these 21 years has been to win that acceptance, to win its way into the perception of educational problems, to influence how these problems are perceived, and how they may be tackled. This is no mean achievement in the relatively short period we are talking about. Its effect on the quality of education has been indirect but nevertheless real and substantial, and I predict that its greater contribution will be made in the years immediately ahead.

## References

Australian Schools Commission (1973) *Schools in Australia* (Karmel Report). Australian Government Printing Service, Canberra.

Bennett, H (1976) *Teaching Styles and Pupil Progress.* Open Books, London.

Bruner, J S (1960) *The Process of Education.* Harvard University Press, Cambridge.

Cronbach, L J and Suppes, P (eds) (1969) *Research for Tomorrow's Schools: A Disciplined Inquiry for Education.* Macmillan, New York.

Department of Education and Science (1967) *Children and Their Primary Schools* (Plowden Report). HMSO, London.

Department of Education and Science (1978) *Primary Education in England: A Survey by HM Inspectors of Schools.* HMSO, London.

Ellington, H I, Addinall, E and Percival, F (1981) *Games and Simulations in Science Education.* Kogan Page, London.

Elton, L R B (1978) Educational technology — today and tomorrow. In Hills, P J and Gilbert, J (eds) *Aspects of Educational Technology* XI. Kogan Page, London.

Galton, M, Simon, B and Croll, P (1980) *Inside the Primary Classroom.* Routledge and Kegan Paul, London.

Hooper, R (1978) The dissemination and assimilation of educational innovation. In Hills, P J and Gilbert, J (eds) *Aspects of Educational Technology* XI. Kogan Page, London.

Hubbard, G (1979) Educational technology in a changing world. In Race, P and Brook, D (eds) *Aspects of Educational Technology* XIII. Kogan Page, London.

Kay, H (1979) Educational technology 20 years on — Sheffield revisited. In Page, G T and Whitlock, Q (eds) *Aspects of Educational Technology* XIII. Kogan Page, London.

Lamke, T (1955) Introduction. *Review of Educational Research,* June, p 192.

Macdonald, B (1975) *The Programme at Two: Evaluation Report on the National Development Programme in Computer Assisted Learning.* Centre for Applied Research in Education, University of East Anglia.

Nisbet, J and Broadfoot, P (1980) *The Impact of Research on Policy and Practice in Education.* Aberdeen University Press, Aberdeen.

Scottish Education Department (1977a) *The Structure of the Curriculum in the Third and Fourth Years of the Scottish Secondary School* (Munn Report). HMSO, Edinburgh.

Scottish Education Department (1977b) *Assessment for All* (Dunning Report). HMSO, Edinburgh.

Scottish Education Department (1980) *Learning and Teaching in Primary 4 and Primary 7: A Report by HM Inspectors of Schools.* HMSO, Edinburgh.

# Section 1: Distance Learning and Broadcasting

## 1.1 Keynote Address

### Distance Learning and Broadcasting

**David Butts**
*University of Stirling*

### Implications and Questions

It would be quite impossible, in the time available, to give a comprehensive account of current developments in distance learning or to provide a balanced view of the role that broadcasting can play within this context. In any case, you have a formidable collection of papers to take you through the rest of the day and it would be wrong for me to encroach on their territory. An opening address needs a perspective and a point of focus, and fortunately these have been provided by the main theme of this Conference. Our task is to concentrate on the contribution that educational technology is currently making to the quality of education and training. By choosing the effectiveness of distance learning and broadcasting as one of the sub-themes, the conference organizers are presenting us with a number of interesting implications and assumptions. Rather than settle back and take them comfortably for granted, I think we should at least examine and perhaps challenge them.

The two main assumptions, clearly implicit in the choice of this sub-theme, are:

1. Distance learning, including the use of broadcasting, is a manifestation of educational technology.
2. Distance learning is making some kind of positive contribution to the quality of education and training.

Both these assumptions raise questions which, to my mind, are worth pursuing. For example:

(a) Distance learning, in the guise of correspondence education, has been around for a very long time. It was never highly regarded; people thought of it as a second best. Cynics might suggest that if you want to boost your sales without altering the nature of the product you simply change the name. Is this fair comment applied to the phrase 'distance learning'? Is it just a new name for an old concept or does it mark a real difference of purpose and approach?

(b) Why have educational technologists made such a strong takeover bid for distance learning? Has it been simply a matter of buying up a bandwagon, putting a new horse between the shafts and painting your name on the buck-board? Or is the nature of distance learning such that it lends itself to the principles and practice of educational technology?

(c) How easily does broadcasting — traditionally a matter of scattering seed upon the air-waves, without being too sure of where it would take root or what would grow from it — adapt itself to the discipline of a systems approach?

(d) What exactly do we mean when we talk about 'quality' in education and training?

It would be easy to brush these questions aside as merely academic. You could argue that distance learning is a fact of educational life, whatever you choose to call it, however you decide to categorize it, so let us get on with the job of making it as good as possible and waste no time discussing changes of label or conceptual differences. However, I would maintain that the questions do matter, particularly at a time when there are proposals to bring the development of all open learning systems in this country under the aegis of some kind of central agency. Should this be realized, the philosophy and style of the new management system will exert considerable influence on the way in which open learning (including its distance learning components) moves forward from its present condition. Presumably the intention is that it should no longer be allowed to just grow like Topsy, but that it should arrive at its full potential through a more rational regime. If the philosophy is that of educational technology, this will inevitably affect the methodology of teaching and learning and the relationship between teacher and taught. What should be the gains in efficiency? What may be the loss of freedom? And what criteria will be applied in making judgements about the 'quality' of education that will result?

## Definitions

So the questions, in my view, are valid. But before we examine them in more detail, we should carry out the routine task of establishing definitions. First: *distance learning*. I am content with Professor Holmberg's (1981) definition of distance education as:

the various forms of study at all levels which are not under the continuous, immediate supervision of tutors present with their students in lecture rooms or on the same premises, but which, nevertheless, benefit from the planning, guidance and tuition of a tutorial organization.

although it would appear that Holmberg is concerning himself with educational *systems* and excluding that kind of self-initiated, exploratory learning which can, for example, set someone browsing through all the material that a local library has to offer on a particular topic.

It is important to note that distance learning is seen (by the Council for Educational Technology (CET) and the Scottish Council for Educational Technology (SCET), for instance,) as one type of *open learning*; and that open learning systems are defined as those which offer students a measure of flexibility and autonomy, to study the programmes of their choice when and where they wish, and at a pace to suit their circumstances. This nesting of distance learning within the larger concept of open learning may present problems for the educational technologist; problems which I shall be looking at later in this address.

The rapid adoption, over the past 10 years, of the phrase 'distance learning' to replace 'correspondence courses' would seem to reflect the incorporation of media other than print (and particularly the medium of broadcasting); the fresh impetus coming from research into individualized learning and self-instructional methods; the broadening of the social base for open learning systems; and the development of courses and qualifications designed specifically to meet the needs of distance learning students.

*Educational technology*, according to the most recent CET (1980) definition that I have read, is concerned with:

the design of learning systems, drawing upon all the available methods, resources and communications media, and integrating them with established teaching techniques in the most effective manner to achieve stated ends.

In the face of possible objections from those who would maintain that progressive teachers have always been concerned with just that, without feeling the need to invent new labels for their craft, I would prefer to define educational technology rather more narrowly as:

the application of scientific method and techniques to the design, implementation and evaluation of courses, with the aim of making the processes of learning more effective and efficient.

There is no time at present to pursue all the implications of this definition, but you will appreciate its general drift. It raises again the question of how far a technology of instruction is compatible with an approach aiming to provide freedom for the student to do his own thing in his own way.

As to the meaning of *quality in education and training*, I think we should agree in this context to define 'quality' in the broadest possible sense, to include not only the effectiveness of the learning process but also the extension of possibilities and the efficiency of learning systems in terms of cost. It would appear sensible to concentrate upon this second area when looking for evidence of contributions which distance learning can make to educational and training quality. But even here we should be on our guard. Who, for example, decides when distance learning provides the only or most practicable means of study? And by what criteria, educational, social or political, are such decisions made?

## Distance Learning and Educational Technology

On the basis of these definitions, I should like to look more closely at the relationship between distance learning and educational technology, and to examine the questions, 'How well does distance learning lend itself to the principles and practice of educational technology? Is its development thereby facilitated or constrained?'

We should remind ourselves again that distance learning is not a new phenomenon. It has a long tradition, reaching well back into the 19th century. Over the years, a great many people have studied successfully at a distance without the benefit of advice from anyone calling himself an educational technologist.

Nevertheless, those who maintain that the application of educational technology can give distance learning a new lease of more effective life have strong arguments at their disposal. Any form of distance study which is backed by a tutorial organization is essentially a learning system; and the design of learning systems, according to CET, is the basic concern of educational technology. Moreover, because of the relatively tenuous links between their elements, distance learning systems are prone to disintegrate, unless they are carefully designed, closely monitored and controlled, and adjusted as necessary. One of the perennial problems of distance learning course organizers is to discover what is happening to their students — how well they are coping, how hard they are working. To this end, so the argument goes, course objectives must be explicitly formulated and their achievement evaluated; and course materials must be meticulously planned and validated, to reduce to a minimum the risk of ambiguity. Pacing of the students is essential if a high drop-out rate is to be avoided; and, because the organizational infrastructure of a distance learning course is much more complicated than it would be if a similar course were offered on a residential basis, pacing is equally essential for the planners, involving the construction of networks, the identification of critical paths, and so on. Finally, in its search for effectiveness, a distance learning course should surely exploit the new technologies of communication as fully as may be compatible with keeping costs at a reasonable level.

Acceptance of these arguments does indeed suggest the need for the systematic application of scientific methods and techniques which, in our definition, are characteristic of educational technology; so why not rest our case at that and accept the benefits? Unfortunately, as many of us know from hard experience, distance learning systems do not lend themselves easily to the kind of 'here we go round the mulberry bush' model of course development and implementation which educational technologists used to characterize, rather naively, as the systems approach. You will recognize the model that I have in mind: formulation of objectives leading to specification of content, followed by selection of methods and media, then on to implementation succeeded by evaluation and so back full circle through revision to the point where you started. However, distance learning systems are beset by hard-to-control variables which can only too easily take you off course into the uncertainties of outer space. The fact that there are problems, that the system is complex and difficult to control, should not, to be sure, provide an excuse for not trying. But it is as well to be aware of the nature of the problems before we glibly assume that educational technology can instantly soothe the pain of our distance learning headaches.

## Problems of Distance Learning Systems

These problems were precisely described by Professor Lewis of the Open University's Institute of Educational Technology, in a series of articles published in the *British Journal of Educational Technology* from 1971 to 1973 (Lewis, 1971a, b, c; Lewis, 1972; Lewis, 1973). At that time, the Open University was still feeling its way with its first intakes of students; but in my experience the problems have recurred time and again in the intervening years, at all levels of distance learning systems, large and small, in higher and further education. So let me comment briefly on some of the main snags that Lewis and others have identified.

First, there are all the problems inherent in creating effective learning materials in a format about which most academics are uncertain and indeed suspicious. It is not just a matter of acquiring new skills of communication. Experience in this field is gradually being built up, and guides such as CET's recent *How to Write a Distance Learning Package* can be a help. The most intractable problem is the need to maintain a consistency of approach, a kind of educational house style, throughout the course. Typically, because of the length of time required to produce a distance learning study unit, a team of writers will be involved in the compilation of any one course. Lecturers are just not used to adapting their teaching style to achieve a common tone. Each writer has his own ideas about what constitutes effective communication, his own idiosyncracies which he is loth to give up. Moreover, teamwork creates problems in ensuring coherence from one unit to the next. The time span needed for course production would stretch out alarmingly if the writer of Unit 2 delayed the start of work until Unit 1 was completed and the writer of Unit 3 waited in turn upon the completion of Unit 2. Yet, to achieve coherence, the later units in a series should be shaped to take account of what has gone before; and this may involve rewriting, which an author is very reluctant to undertake. Ironically, the more carefully structured a unit becomes and the more precise its objectives, the less willing may its author be to agree to changes. The problem is aggravated if non-print media are used, since these take more time and money to produce, and modification may entail a major deployment of resources.

There are other problems, relating to design and administration, which appear to be inherent in the distance learning format and which make it difficult to exploit the principles of educational technology to the full. For example, the systematic course designer would wish to overcome the hardships of spare time, home-based study by varying the stimulus wherever possible, employing a wide range of instructional media. Unfortunately, the use of media other than print can significantly increase the cost of course production and can impose restrictions on the learner, in terms of when and where he can study.

Lewis (1971a, b, c) points out that the planning and production problems of a complex dynamic process, such as a distance learning system, would, in the context of industrial technology, be dealt with under headings such as production control and quality control, systems analysis and activity networking. He then proceeds to demonstrate how, in an academic setting, these admirable intentions can go astray. In part, the difficulties are attitudinal. 'The notion of production control', says Lewis, 'with its connotations of unthinking machine-like production, offends the academic's sense of professionalism. And the notion of quality control, with its watchdog connotations, queries his competence and threatens his personal autonomy'. Indeed, Lewis concludes that: 'some of the greatest obstacles to course team efficiency are psychological rather than logistical. In general, course teams are unlikely to feel committed to a planning and scheduling scheme that is imposed upon them from outside'.

A further range of problems, affecting the control of the system, arises from the needs and nature of distance learning students. I have already mentioned the difficulty for tutors in keeping sufficiently closely in touch with the process of distance learning as distinct from measuring its product. The strategies employed by students for studying, the time spent on the units, their reaction to and understanding of the separate components of the study materials all need to be constantly monitored if the course is to be properly adaptive to its target population. Seeking and providing such information can be laborious for the course organizers and wearisome for the students concerned. Even the task of assessing the students on a basis of fair comparisons can be tricky, especially if the marking is distributed among a number of tutors.

## The Role of Broadcasting

I have mentioned some of the problems — cost and inflexibility, for instance — associated with the use of non-print media for distance learning. Broadcasting (which is a specific part of my brief) provides a good example of the way in which the use of technology *in* education differs from the development of a technology *of* education. The first does not automatically lead to the second.

Radio as a medium for distance learning has been switched on for a long time; in New Zealand, for instance, to reach children too remote from townships to receive their primary education at school; in the United States of America, where educational radio broadcasting was seen as one of the functions of universities; and in Britain itself, since the British Broadcasting Corporation radio programmes for schools were in many ways a form of distance learning, with the classroom teacher playing a subsidiary role. Much of the earlier adult educational use of both radio and television was restricted to the dissemination of lecture material, largely failing to exploit the characteristics of the media. Not surprisingly, few significant differences were found in the amounts which students learned 'off-air' and in the lecture hall. Nevertheless, in the 1950s and 1960s, there was a rapid surge of belief in the potential of television to become a major force in education. Some of you will remember the sense of euphoria that extended from Plymouth to Glasgow by way of Inner London and Hull, and recall that in its early days the Open University was thought of as the University of the Air.

Most people, I think, would agree that the early promise has not been fulfilled. Broadcasting as a medium for distance learning presents us with two main categories of problems. On the one hand, it can be difficult to control in the way that the educational technologist would wish. For a start, radio and television producers (even those with good academic pedigrees) can be awkward people for educationalists to handle. They like to think of themselves as creative and are therefore reluctant to tie themselves down in advance to precise objectives. Moreover, particularly with television, the medium itself has a disconcerting habit of getting out of control, partly because of its technical complexities and partly because the power of vision may be distracting rather than helpful, so that, in Chaucer's terms, 'accident' takes over from 'substance' and the message received by the viewer differs from the director's intentions. Broadcast material, too, is difficult to evaluate in a distance learning context and even more difficult to modify, because of the long time-span and high costs of production.

As against all this, educational broadcasting can exert too much control on the home-based learner, reducing the open nature of the learning system. Broadcasts impose a lockstep on pace and response — unless you can record the programme, you cannot view or listen at a pace to suit yourself. Additionally, without the benefit of recording, broadcasts place severe restrictions on the time and place of learning and it can be difficult for the student to hold them in step with the other elements in his study programme. Broadcasting as a medium is thus relatively unresponsive to individual differences; a characteristic which must reduce its value in the eyes of the educational technologist.

However, we should acknowledge the great strengths of the broadcast media, particularly if they are used as elements within a diversified learning system and not left to do the whole job on their own. They can communicate more directly and personally than the printed word. They can provide a focus of interest, drawing scattered students together through a shared experience. And they can transmit rich resources of primary source material, evidence from the field, case studies and so on. Moreover, many of the objections that I have voiced relate to the use of broadcasting as we have known it up till now. If, in the future, we can assume that every distance learner will record and store broadcast material for use at his own convenience, then the style of production will change and the lockstep of pace can be broken. Programmes can be designed to be more interactive, more responsive to individual learning styles. As such, they may assume a more central role within the learning system.

## The Effects of Educational Technology Solutions

I have listed a number of problems inherent in the complex and dynamic nature of open learning systems. I am sure that educational technologists would insist that the problems are there to be solved. Indeed, a number of today's papers — for example, those by Gary Coldevin, Wyllie Fyfe, David Mitchell and Robert Zimmer — would seem to be concerned with ways in which an educational technology approach is effectively solving specific problems in particular contexts. What interests me is the effect that educational technology solutions may have on the nature of distance learning; whether the gains on the instructional swings are offset by losses on the educational roundabouts.

Let me give you some examples of the kind of questions I have in mind. I have mentioned six broad categories of problems displayed by distance learning systems. They are:

1. The achievement of consistency and coherence in producing course units.
2. The costs and constraints associated with the use of non-print media.
3. The paradox of broadcasting, hard to control yet apt to exert its own kind of dominance on the learner.
4. Restrictions on the logic of course design.

5. Difficulties in applying the types of management and control appropriate to industrial systems.
6. The unpredictability of distance students.

Faced with the task of dealing with these problems in a rational and scientific manner, the educational technologist might well decide on a general strengthening of control systems. 'Classical' educational technology solutions might, for example, include:

☐ Formulating the objectives of each course unit in a more precise form and testing their achievement at more frequent intervals.
☐ Establishing a formula or house style for the production of materials, carrying out rigorous editing where necessary, but discouraging idiosyncratic revisions of agreed plans.
☐ Being prepared to risk a sizable proportion of the capital budget on non-print materials, but thereafter insisting on their widest possible dissemination and recurrent use.
☐ Making sure that broadcasting problems stick closely to an educational brief.
☐ In terms of course design, favouring the logic of the subject rather than that of the learner, pinning faith whenever possible to a Gagnéan hierarchy of task sequences.
☐ Imposing a strict pacing system on the distance students and judging their success on the basis of product rather than process.

Now I am not trying to depict the educational technologist as a kind of severe Victorian nanny, forcing her purgative remedies down the unwilling throat of an impure system. I am, however, suggesting that the technological imperative points to control rather than freedom, towards closed solutions and away from open learning. In many cases this direction may be the right one to take. It is likely that distance learning will find its biggest market among students seeking vocationally-oriented training qualifications, and concerned not so much with academic speculation as with mastery of a defined syllabus. At this level, precise objectives and a tightly structured course design may be entirely appropriate. However, some would argue that, at least at the higher education level, a systems approach may be unduly restrictive. Kaye and Rumble (1981), for instance, looking at distance learning from the standpoint of the Open University, remind us that:

> once enrolled on a course, the student is programmed into a tight study schedule, paced by assignment return dates and broadcast times. Within this framework he has very little choice to exercise in selecting and rejecting material. In other words, for a particular course, it is the University course writers who have already decided, on the student's behalf, which ideas and content are relevant.

Certainly the educational technologist, working as a member of an academic course team, must always be alert to the danger of reducing the learner to a passive recipient of information, of imposing a common learning style, of restricting the cognitive level by insistence on measurable objectives and of making the whole system too autocratic. He must beware, too, of discouraging creativity for the sake of tidiness. Geese that are capable of laying golden eggs never take kindly to being treated like battery hens.

Of course these dangers are not inevitable, nor have they gone unrecognized. The paper by David Boud, for example, describes a deliberate attempt to involve distance learning students in the design, development and evaluation of their course. Nevertheless, efforts to resolve this tension have to face up to two major difficulties. Tailoring study programmes to the needs of individuals necessarily raises costs; and increasing the flexibility of pacing may, in some ways, reduce efficiency.

Talk of efficiency leads me to the broader question of quality. In what ways can distance learning be said to be contributing to the quality of education? In this connection, I would stress the criteria by which (in the view of CET) the cost-effectiveness of open learning systems should be judged. These are:

☐ Student achievement (taking both intrinsic and extrinsic factors into account).
☐ The flexibility of a system in meeting demands that cannot be catered for in other ways.
☐ Opportunity costs for the student and employer.
☐ Academic staff costs of operating the schemes.
☐ Other capital and recurrent costs.

On the evidence so far available, distance learning systems, by comparison with conventional systems, would appear to rate highly on ability to meet demand, to be low on opportunity costs, academic staff costs and use of plant, but to be costly in terms of learning materials. The evidence on student achievement is mixed. Those who stay the course are reported as doing at least as well as students following equivalent programmes in traditional classrooms; but the drop-out rate among the distance students is a good deal higher.

So in these terms it would seem that distance learning can fairly claim to be making an effective contribution. It would be an over-simplification, however, to suggest that the effectiveness of distance learning depended merely on the determination of strongly motivated students to make the most of the one chance that was offered them to study the subject of their choice. Evidence gathered from distance learning students at Jordanhill College of Education, for instance, indicated that, contrary to their expectations, studying at home was not just a second best. They rated the experience highly on two counts: first, they considered the learning materials to be more carefully prepared than many of the lecture-based courses which they had previously undergone; and second, the fact that they had not forsaken their own places of work for the verdigris towers of Jordanhill made it easier for them to apply the course theory to the practical content of their jobs as they went along.

But, as we move up the scale of higher education, the relationship between distance learning and 'quality' becomes more complex. Lewis (1973) saw the problem of defining and measuring 'quality' as posing:

> a very considerable challenge to the educational technologist. The challenge is partly conceptual, partly empirical and partly prescriptive. At the conceptual level, the educational technologist is being challenged to say what, in his opinion, quality in higher education *is*. At the empirical level, the challenge is to devise objective tests and measures of whatever he takes quality to be. At the prescriptive level, the challenge is to specify design procedures which will help to build his conception of quality into tomorrow's teaching materials.

Lewis went on to distinguish three relevant levels of problem-solving ability: recognition and recall, explanation and justification, leading onwards to the point where 'the quality student should be able to challenge and extend and even *transform* the knowledge he is given'. We know very little about the capacity of resource-based learning to enable students to reach this goal. Certainly, anyone who has experience of Open University summer schools, where the students, like Browning's grammarian, arrive 'soul-hydroptic with a burning thirst' to extend their understanding through debate and discussion, must question the adequacy of distance learning to do the whole job on its own.

At any level of education or training, I think it would be unwise to make uncritical assumptions about the benefits of distance learning. We should remind ourselves just how hard, lonely and tiring the business of studying at home can be. It is therefore essential to be wary of those who might use glib educational arguments to justify political decisions, seeing distance learning as a convenient way of providing education on the cheap.

## A Pattern for the Future

I should like to end by drawing the threads of my thinking together, to see what pattern emerges. First, there is no doubt that distance learning systems exist in a variety of forms, most of them complex, dynamic and potentially unstable. Sometimes, the distance learning component is itself a sub-system of a larger and even more complex educational system. It would seem logical, therefore, to suppose that the effectiveness and efficiency of distance learning would be enhanced by subjecting the system to analysis, control and evaluation; in other words, to the characteristic processes of educational technology.

Experience suggests, however, that distance learning systems typically involve a number of hard to control variables. It is arguable that, in attempting to meet this challenge, the educational technologist runs the risk of reducing the flexibility of the system, its open character, its responsiveness to individual needs; thus detracting from what some would see as the distinctive advantages which distance learning can provide. If one recognizes this problem, it follows that the tension between the controlling function of educational technology and the flexible nature of open learning must somehow be resolved. This task will become particularly important if the organization of distance learning is to be brought under some kind of national surveillance exercised by educational technologists.

I think that we have reached a critical point in the distance learning scenario, and I believe that we have a good fairy on hand to help with our problem. Like all good fairies, she is small — I refer, of course, to micro-technology. Always provided that we can escape the ogre of national bankruptcy, it seems likely that, over the next decade, rapid advances of technology *in* education will ease the difficulties besetting a technology *of* education, at least where distance learning is concerned. I see these technological advances as helping in two ways. First, the increasing availability of tele-software, linked to the development of specialist viewdata systems, should do much to make distance learning programmes more adaptable to individual needs and interests without incurring the very heavy increase in costs associated with personal tutoring. Second, the use of tele-conference techniques as a regular element of distance learning systems should help to break down the isolation of the home-based student and reduce the present high drop-out rate. Experiments along these lines currently being carried out by the Open University point the way ahead.

Given this kind of technological impetus, I foresee a new role for distance learning, not as an alternative to traditional residential education but as part of a broader system which combines residential and distance elements. At the adult level of vocationally-oriented education and training, both the logic of subject matter and the inclination of learners seem often to point towards this kind of integration. There are stages in most courses of study when the adult student requires the stimulus, guidance and encouragement which can be provided only through direct contact with his tutors and his peer group; but equally there may be other aspects of the course which, with the help of resource materials adapted to individual needs, can best be assimilated in the student's own home or at his place of work. If we can break down the boundaries of existing systems in this way, then all adult learning will become more open. In the process, we shall, I hope, cease to talk so much about either educational technology or distance learning. Both concepts will be taken for granted, assimilated into a new synthesis. Like the Cheshire Cat in *Alice,* they will fade from our sight, leaving only the warmth of their grins behind. It will be a metamorphosis which should add materially — or perhaps immaterially — to the quality of education.

## References

Council for Educational Technology (1980) *Open Learning Systems in Further Education and Training — A Discussion of the Issues and Recommendations to Government. Consultative Document.* Council for Educational Technology, London.

Holmberg, B (1981) *Status and Trends of Distance Education.* Kogan Page, London.

Kaye, A and Rumble, G (eds) (1981) *Distance Teaching for Higher and Adult Education.* Croom Helm/Open University Press, London.

Lewis, B N (1971a) Course production at the Open University I: some basic problems. *British Journal of Educational Technology,* 2, 1, pp 4-13.

Lewis, B N (1971b) Course production at the Open University II: activities and activity networks. *British Journal of Educational Technology,* 2, 2, pp 111-23.

Lewis, B N (1971c) Course production at the Open University III: planning and scheduling. *British Journal of Educational Technology,* 2, 3, pp 189-204

Lewis, B N (1972) Course production at the Open University IV: the problem of assessment. *British Journal of Educational Technology,* 3, 2, pp 108-28

Lewis, B N (1973) Educational technology at the Open University: an approach to the problem of quality. *British Journal of Educational Technology,* 4, 3, pp 188-203.

# 1.2 Approaches to Distance Education

## 1.2.1 A Typology of University Distance Education

**B Holmberg**
*Fernuniversität, West Germany*

**Abstract:** The thinking behind the practice and implications of three general types of university distance education are illuminated. The three types are (a) the distance study university (like the Open University, the Fernuniversität etc), (b) university extension (here the Australian New England model is particularly interesting), and (c) the service organization type (Hermods, Centre National de Télé-enseignement, National Extension College, etc).

## The Distance Study Concept — A Common Denominator

In distance study 'the learner is at a distance from the teacher for much, most, or even all of the time during the teaching-learning processes' (Sims, 1977). Whether the distance is considerable or negligible (as in on-campus independent study) is immaterial for the distance study concept, although it may influence practical procedures.

### Non-Contiguous Communication

The main characteristic of distance education is non-contiguous communication. This does not only mean that the presentation of study material is brought about in writing, by the use of recordings, or on the wireless, but also that there is constant two-way traffic between students and their tutors and counsellors. This takes place in writing and, whenever possible, on the telephone. The most common form of two-way communication consists of the students answering assignments set, solving problems and submitting papers which are corrected and commented on by the tutors.

### Self-Instructional Pre-Produced Courses

It is possible to base the two-way communication, in this case usually personal correspondence between student and tutor, on reading lists and set texts, but it is usually more helpful to provide printed courses (and/or radio and TV programmes) guiding the study. These should be as self-instructional as possible and argumentative in style, causing the students to identify problems and either follow the problem-solving paths of leading scholars or do their own problem-solving (Weingartz, 1980).

In principle, courses can be (i) self-contained providing all the information necessary, or (ii) study guides guiding the critical reading of relevant literature. In the interest of critical approaches and pluralism, the latter approach is usually preferable in university study, although the self-contained course has sometimes great advantages (for instance, in elementary language courses such as Hebrew, Arabic, Chinese or other languages where elementary courses occur at university).

## Types of Organization

The types of organization to be looked into are:

(a) Universities which exclusively enrol 'distant' students and use distance study methods for all or most of their teaching.
(b) Extension departments of conventional universities providing distance study facilities.
(c) Specialized bodies outside the university providing courses and tuition for university degrees, the role of the university being that of an examination board.

### Distance Universities

Universities set up for the special purpose of providing distance study occur in various parts of the world. The pioneer here was the University of South Africa (UNISA), which began this work in 1951. In the European context the British Open University, the German Fernuniversität, the Israeli Everman's University and the Spanish Universidad Naçional de Educaçión a Distancia (UNED), all products of the 1970s, provide material for study and comparison. In particular, the Open University has been very successful.

These universities themselves develop printed courses, audio and video tapes and/or radio and TV programmes, kits for laboratory work and other study materials. They organize and provide advisory and didactic two-way communication with their students in writing and on the telephone as well as some supplementary face-to-face tuition: counselling; examining; issuing certificates; guiding doctoral study; running research projects; etc. For their non-contiguous teaching and counselling special organizational units have been set up and procedures conducive to the administration of distance study have been developed. Their teaching represents an economical way of working, allowing both a kind of mass production and an industrial approach to course development, tuition and administration through a division of labour, which ensures expertise for all functions, inclusive of such things as copyright questions, illustrations, typography and wireless presentation, and also a good deal of mechanization and 'industrial' rationalization generally.

The potentials, advantages and problems of the distance study universities have been discussed at some length in various publications (Clennel *et al*, 1977; Graff *et al*, 1977; Holmberg, 1979; Perry, 1976; Valgañon *et al*, 1976).

### Extension Departments

Particularly in America, it is fairly common practice that extension departments of the universities provide distance study opportunities for their own extra-mural and on-campus students. Usually no attempt is made to cover whole countries or to cater for large populations, which implies on the one hand small-scale course development with modest resources for pre-producing study material, and on the other hand far-reaching parallelism with residential study.

This parallelism is particularly striking in a somewhat different form of 'external' distance study common in Australia. The University of New England in Australia is very consistent in this respect (Smith, 1975). Compulsory periods of residential study safeguard the parallelism. Even the same tutor-student ratio for distant and on-campus study is considered advantageous (Sheath, 1972) so that the individual student is seen as a member of a class, although this is geographically distributed. This view of the distant students is quite explicit in a Canadian distant study scheme: the cassette teaching of the University of Waterloo (Leslie, 1979).

These types of distance study are sometimes less professional than the Open University type, as specialists cannot be engaged for all the various tasks involved. Thus, no full division of labour takes place. On the other hand, students are supported in an individual way, which may make up for any deficiencies in pre-produced course material. For the internal educational development work of the universities concerned, the New England model can be very profitable, however, as discovered in activities of this type in Sweden, for instance.

### Specialized Distance Study Organizations Co-operating with Traditional Universities

Universities can also rely on specialized distance study institutes to develop courses and provide tuition preparing students for university degrees. In a very successful scheme of this sort starting in 1952, Hermods in Sweden, co-operating with individual professors and university departments, arranged distance study at the university level in a number of subjects, developing courses and providing distance tuition, supplementary residential courses, counselling facilities etc. The Swedish universities took over the examination duties.

This proved a successful scheme, relieving the universities of the necessity of organizing distance study at the same time as they retained the responsibility for standards. It made national coverage and a large-scale approach feasible.

This experience indicates a generally applicable economical possibility to organize university distance study of the large-scale type. What is required is a small specialized institution which:

☐ Engages course authors and other subject specialists from among the academic staff of existing universities.
☐ Provides editorial service and expertise on didactics, media and communication.
☐ Arranges course development inclusive of formative evaluation (developmental testing), printing and other technical production (not necessarily within the organization but also or exclusively through the use of commercial companies).
☐ Organizes and runs counselling activities, the commenting on and correction of student papers, tutoring on the telephone, as well as any supplementary face-to-face sessions found desirable.

☐ Keeps constant contact with co-operating universities, arranges examination opportunities, etc.
☐ Takes responsibility for distribution, warehousing and general administration.

Setting up an organization of this service type is evidently less complicated and much less costly than setting up a full distance study university. Whether it is an acceptable choice or not will depend on the general conditions of university education in the countries concerned.

Special distance study organizations co-operating with traditional universities are, for instance — apart from Hermods — the French Centre National de Télé-enseignement (CNTE) and, in some respects, the British National Extension College (NEC). The latter organization prepares external students for London University degrees on a highly individual basis. Whereas Hermods provides its university students with pre-produced courses, NEC does not, but allocates individual tutors to its students. The tuition occurs in writing, on the telephone and by means of face-to-face meetings (El-Bushra, 1973).

Other forms of co-operation between universities and specialized distance study institutions are to be found in the English Flexistudy system, whereby a college or other tutorial body buys pre-produced distance study courses from a course-producing organization and provides tuition on the basis of these courses (Green, 1979; Sacks, 1980).

Athabasca University in Canada is run in a way similar to distance study organizations of the specialized service type (Stringer, 1980).

## Applications Related to Types of Organizations

The three types of university distance education outlined above are based on rather different philosophies. The extension type, particularly the New England model, uses distance study methods merely as vehicles of distribution during the periods when students are not on campus. They are thus substitutes for face-to-face sessions only. The distance university type, ie the Open University model, and the Hermods model of the specialized service type, make extensive use of what Peters calls 'industrial methods' (rationalization, division of labour, mechanizing, planning, mass production, etc) (Peters, 1967). These and other approaches, for example the mediated didactic conversation (Holmberg, 1981; Holmberg and Schümer, 1980), ascribe to such distance study types special characteristics and potentials (Keegan, 1980).

These and other differences have some noteworthy consequences in the practice of distance education apart from those used in the above descriptions as delineations of the three types.

### Combinations of Non-Contiguous Study with Face-to-Face Sessions

Periods of residential study and face-to-face sessions in general appear considerably more important to the types of distance study referred to as the extension type than to the others. To these, on the one hand, the attention paid to course development and non-contiguous tuition (on the latter see Bååth, 1980) and, on the other hand, the special character of most distant students (professionally active adults with social and family commitments) makes the academic and socializing influence of tutors and fellow-students present in person seem less important than individual study. (For this discussion see Daniel and Marquis, 1979; Holmberg, 1977.) This is based on the knowledge that, for cognitive learning, distance study is in no way inferior to conventional types of study (Childs, 1971; Granholm, 1971).

### Course Development and Non-Contiguous Teaching

Whereas for the extension type, particularly the New England model, courses are usually developed for a small group of students, perhaps 50 to 100, the course writer often being expected to act as tutor of the course students, the industrial approach that characterizes the distance university type (and at least the Hermods model of the specialized service type) leads to courses being developed for large groups of several hundreds or even a thousand students. Course teams consisting of subject and media specialists, editors, illustrators etc are then often in charge of the course development, whereas the student body is usually divided into small groups, for each of which a tutor or tutor-counsellor is made responsible.

It is often expected of a course author that he or she should correct and comment on students' assignments belonging to his or her course. This brings valuable feedback and serves purposes of formative evaluation. Students probably appreciate the contact with the course author which occurs when he or she also functions as a course tutor. This would then seem to favour the small-scale extention type. The two large-scale types can (and frequently do) make use of partly parallel procedures in that a course author is made to act as one (of several) tutors of the course. This, of course, makes sense if there is *one* author rather than a team behind the course or in any case *one* author who is primarily responsible for the course.

The course team approach is usually considered an excellent innovation. The first Vice-Chancellor of the Open University, Walter Perry, described it as 'one of the most important and far-reaching concepts of the Open University which, it seems probable, will become more and more widely used all over the world'. (Perry, 1976).

There can be little doubt that a big course team for each course with a number of different specialists is advantageous in providing for the best expertise available for all the various tasks involved. However, it may lead to a de-personalized style of presentation contrary to the style of didactic conversation and may tend to support the presentation of learning matter as ready-made systems rather than as guides to problem-solving. To what extent these effects occur, or are avoidable, is uncertain, although there are signs that few of the courses created by course teams are based on problem-solving approaches. This has been shown by Monika Weingartz, who favours problem-solving approaches and is doing further study on this issue (Weingartz, 1980).

Evidently there is a possible conflict between two important aims of university distance study, the educational (problem-solving, personal guidance), and the administrative and economic (industrial procedures). One way to avoid this conflict in distance study of the large scale models is to appoint one main author for each course, give him or her decision rights and make the other course team members support him or her as advisers and assistants. Systematic use of the approach and style of guided didactic conversation can, in particular, help to overcome the conflict if one author (editor) writes (and/or speaks) in his or her personal style. This didactic conversation (referred to above) consists on the one hand of real communication, which is the answering of and commenting on assignments for submission and the telephone tutoring already referred to, and on the other hand of simulated communication. This simulated conversation is a style of presentation which implies asking the students to consider, compare and question matters of relevance and interest. In this way a kind of rapport is assumed to be established between the students and the author, whom the students feel they get to know in this way.

## Administration

The large-scale approaches referred to above require special organizations, in which the computer has an important role (Merup, 1968; Bååth and Månsson, 1977). Less of this is necessary when the student bodies are small.

The unit costs can be very low in a large-scale organization, whereas the basic institutional costs are considerable. Research has shown that, on the whole, small-scale distance study does not differ much in cost-benefit from traditional university study (Sheath, 1972), but that large-scale distance study can bring great cost-benefit advantages (Wagner, 1972; Wagner, 1977).

## Conclusion

The above presentation has shown that university distance study of at least three distinct types occurs. All of them have potentials for excellent academic education. Although most distance study has as its chief traget group mature citizens with professional, social and family responsibilities, full-time students on and off campus also make use of distance study.

The characteristics of the three types have been discussed above. Each of them has particular strengths. Weaknesses have been shown to exist in the distance university type in that there seems to be a latent risk to neglect problem-solving approaches and the style of didactic conversation in course materials. Weaknesses in the extension type concern unavoidable lack of professionalism on some points owing to small-scale and thus limited resources. The service type organization can be — but is not always — run in such a way that the weaknesses referred to can be avoided.

National, regional and local conditions as well as political, cultural and social circumstances normally constitute the criteria for a choice between the three types. Experience shows that rational considerations do not necessarily exert decisive influence on the basic organization of distance study. Maybe, however, a study of existing types of distance education can support rational applications of the principles chosen.

## References

Bååth, J A (1980) *Postal Two-Way Communication in Correspondence Education.* Gleerup, Lund.

Bååth, J A and Månsson, N O (1977) *CADE — A System for Computer-Assisted Distance Education.* Hermods, Malmö.

Childs, G B (1971) Recent research developments in correspondence instruction. In MacKenzie, O and Christensen, E L (eds) *The Changing World of Correspondence Study.* Pennsylvania State University

Clennel, S, Peters, J and Sewart, D (1977) *Teaching for the Open University.* The Open University, Milton Keynes.

Daniel, J S and Marquis, C (1979) Interaction and independence: getting the mixture right. *Teaching at a Distance,* 14, pp 29-44.

El-Bushra, J (1973) *Correspondence Teaching at University.* International Extension College, Cambridge.

Graff, K, Holmberg, B, Schümer, R and Wilmersdoerfer, H (1977) *Zur Weiterentwicklung des Studiensystems der Fernuniversität. Struktur und Ablauf.* Fernuniversität, Hagen.

Granholm, G (1971) Classroom teaching or home study — a summary of research on relative efficiency. *Epistolodidaktika,* 2, pp 9-14.

Green, B (1979) Flexistudy — further education college-based distance learning with face-to-face tutorials. In Page, G T and Whitlock, Q (eds) *Aspects of Educational Technology* XIII. Kogan Page, London.

Holmberg, B (1977) *Die Ergänzung des Fernstudiums Durch Nahstudium.* Fernuniversität, Hagen.

Holmberg, B (1979) *Das Hochschulfernstudium als Innovation am Beispiel der Fernuniversität.*
    Fernuniversität, Hagen.
Holmberg, B and Schümer, R (1980) *Methoden des Gelenkten Didaktischen Gespräches.*
    Fernuniversität, Hagen.
Holmberg, B (1981) *Status and Trends of Distance Education.* Kogan Page, London.
Keegan, D J (1980) *On the Nature of Distance Education.* Fernuniversität, Hagen.
Leslie, C D (1979) Doing it differently at the University of Waterloo: courses by cassette. In
    Wentworth, R B (ed) *Correspondence Education: Dynamic and Diversified 2.* Tuition
    House, London.
Merup, A (1968) *The Computer in the Administration of a Correspondence School.*
    CEC, Copenhagen.
Perry, W (1976) *Open University. A Personal Account by the First Vice-Chancellor.* The Open
    University, Milton Keynes.
Peters, O (1967) *Das Fernstudium an Universitäten und Hochschulen. Didaktische Struktur
    und Vergleichende Interpretation: Ein Beitrag zur Theorie der Fernlehre.* Beltz, Weinheim.
Sacks, H (1980) Flexistudy — an open learning system for further and adult education.
    *British Journal of Educational Technology,* 11, 2, pp 85-95.
Sheath, H C (1972) Integrating correspondence study with residence study. In Bern, H A
    and Kulla, F (eds) *Ninth International Conference on Correspondence Education.
    A Collection of Conference Papers.* ICCE, Warrenton.
Sims, R (1977) *An Inquiry into Correspondence Education Processes: Policies, Principles and
    Practices in Correspondence Education Systems Worldwide.* Unpublished ICCE-UNESCO
    Report.
Smith, K (1975) External studies at the University of New England. An exercise in
    integration. In *The System of Distance Education.* Hermods, Malmö.
Stringer, M (1980) Lifting the course team curse. *Teaching at a Distance,* 18, pp 13-16.
Valgañon, C M et al (1976) *Criterios Metodologicos de la UNED.* Universidad Nacional de
    Educacion a Distancia, Madrid.
Wagner, L (1972) The economics of the Open University. *Higher Education* 1, 2, pp 159-83.
Wagner, L (1977) The economics of the Open University revisited. *Higher Education,* 6, 3,
    pp 359-81.
Weingartz, M (1980) *Didaktische Mermale Selbstinstruierender Studientexte.* Fernuniversität,
    Hagen.

## 1.2.2 Evaluating Alternative Strategies for Allocating Limited Resources to Develop a Tele-Education System

P D Mitchell
*Concordia University, Canada*

**Abstract:** We consider the dilemma facing a department in a traditional institution which hopes to initiate a tele-education scheme. To do so we show that the paragon of distant study systems, the Open University, is not a model to emulate if one has insufficient resources. We develop a model that challenges some key tenets of educational technology yet promises to prove very useful. Systematic instructional design that proceeds from objectives to evaluation is a costly alternative to traditional instruction.

The alternative proposed — the KWIK systems engineering method — can be implemented gradually and at little additional cost. The resulting self-instruction system can be used for open study within an institution or at remote sites. Thus the cost-benefit ratio is improved by increasing efficiency of existing resources rather than by shifting to a new level of resources and hoping for increased benefits to follow.

## Introduction

Abundant evidence exists that we face a new reality in educational financing and therefore in educational technology. Few nations, if any, will escape the financial pressure caused by the fact that the cost of providing educational opportunities has been rising more rapidly than GNP and political pressure is mounting to curtail increases. Exacerbating this is the current perturbation in enrolments which has seen (in most industrial nations) a decelerating growth rate. Meanwhile the world's 'education' system grinds on, consuming even more resources while half the school-aged children in the world cannot attend school. What can be done to improve education?

On the one hand, educational technologists will be called upon to design and manage new systems for education and training. On the other hand, we must anticipate budgets below the level which we have come to expect. I know of one consultant's report which shows that the college system in an extremely wealthy section of the world will be bankrupt in a few years unless faculty members accept an increased workload or a salary decrease. And many school systems and universities are hard pressed to survive. Confronting this new reality can shift the practice of educational technology into the forefront of educational management. How can we cope?

## Tele-Education

One possibility that has been forced upon many institutions, including corporate training centres, is to increase productivity by shifting education and training from a service industry (relying upon teachers) toward a goods industry (relying upon instructional materials). Much greater emphasis on increased productivity is predictable (even though this comes from politicians whose productivity is arguably lower than that of teachers!)

By tele-education I mean a system of education or training in which the learner is usually separated in space or time from the subject matter expert for most of his instruction. Thus tele-education might occur over an extended geographical area through interactive information systems (eg Videotex, cable-TV, satellite broadcasts or microcomputers) or various self-instructional schemes. However, learning at a great physical distance is little different from learning on campus or in a corporate training centre using the same instructional resources. In either case the course designers prepare or select instructional materials and design instructional control algorithms to facilitate the instructional progress of students. Thus, much of our work in systems analysis, theoretical and practical foundations of individualized learning, instructional design and materials development, management of learning resources, and evaluation of systems, methods and media is applicable to tele-education.

## The Generating Problem: How to Develop an Open Learning System on the Cheap

This paper describes research undertaken to investigate the utility of systems analytic procedures in helping to determine and evaluate educational policy and actions when the decision-taker is confronted with multiple (and conflicting) objectives. In particular, how can we establish a strategy for developing a tele-education system given the following objectives and constraints?

1. We want to maximize the quality of the learning experience by avoiding total reliance on print-based instruction and introducing more interactive learning materials (eg simulations, games, CAL).

2. We want to introduce the learner to developments and possibilities in microelectronics by some sort of hands-on experience, if feasible.
3. Where necessary or desirable we want to use audio-visual communications for mass or individual viewing.
4. We have limited human resources in the form of instructional designers, subject experts and production staff.
5. There are different costs (in time and money) associated with the development of each type of instructional material.
6. We want to convert a one-year programme of study to a tele-education system such that we can maximize the effectiveness of our limited human, material and financial resources.

The problem is complex and usually is handled intuitively. However, it is almost certainly the case that intuitively chosen strategies will not be optimal, and that a better allocation of our resources or an improved set of outcomes, or both, can be realized.

We hope to provide a model for grafting a distant study scheme onto an existing programme. We ignore the possibility that you represent a new institution devoted entirely to (and funded for) distant study. The rationale for this orientation is the growing awareness of the possibilities for self-instruction in an open study system both within an existing institution and at remote locations. Seldom is the enthusiasm for developing a distant study system matched by the necessary resources to implement it *de novo*. So we consider whether it is feasible for a traditional institution to develop a distant study scheme and, if so, how. Moreover, we hope to reveal how a few like-minded instructors can shift the scope of their department's operation.

## Solving Problems Versus Exploiting Opportunities

It is not realistic in present conditions to assume that large sums of money will become available for expansion of departments in higher education institutions. Yet is is predictable that many educational engineers would attempt to analyse institutional problems and recommend solutions that may increase the system's output but also would demand additional resources. The implementation of standard recipes for producing carefully contrived instructional sequences using a variety of methods and materials suitable for distant study systems requires considerable time, effort and money.

Though it may suffice for military or corporate training (where priorities differ and trainees are paid), the currently available course team and instructional design model cannot be justified by the typical institution of higher education. This is because of the excessive additional cost. As a general estimate, 100 man-hours of labour are required to produce one hour of self-instructional materials for the average student. But this estimate can very considerably, ranging from 15 hours for print-dominated instruction to 1,000 man-hours for some media programmes. It also varies with complexity of subject matter and the key people's competence in subject matter, instructional planning and media production. I know of one 15-day training course which required 30 man-years to produce. However, several man-years to develop an OU type course is fairly typical. Contrast this with the typical institution where one instructor must both develop and teach *several* such courses annually (in addition to other duties). The ratio of resources consumed in these two situations is 20 or 30 to one. Only a comparable increase in income, reduction in operating costs or overriding national priority can justify switching to the OU model. But a 20-fold to 30-fold increase in income from short- or long-term enrolment seems unlikely, especially since effective income may not rise as rapidly as enrolment.

The consulting educational engineer is not so likely to be asked to design an 'open university' as he is to transform an existing organization into something more efficient or more effective.

## Can a Solution be Implemented?

It is obvious that an educational technologist or instructor working alone or with a few colleagues cannot possibly produce courses based on self-instructional modules using the standard approaches even if this person had no regular teaching obligations. In the absence of a course team with consulting educational technologists and media production specialists, what can be accomplished? Is there any hope?

The solution lies in challenging, rather than adopting, the prevailing mythology of instructional development. It also challenges a common maxim, 'If a thing is worth doing it is worth doing well'. In the realm of systems development many jobs are worth doing but few are worth doing well; beyond some point of diminishing returns it is preferable to do something else. Thus an acceptable solution might be produced for a fraction of the cost of an ideal solution, leaving time to do something else or (and this is the key point here) permitting a small group to accomplish the impossible.

## The Mistake of Starting with Instructional Objectives

The idea of specifying instructional objectives; identifying possible instructional strategies, media and materials; and selecting appropriate learning resources is ubiquitous in educational technology. Aside from buying suitable materials if they happen to be available, the best course of action is to:

1. clarify your *systemic*, not instructional, objectives;
2. evaluate your resources (including your own time and that of potential co-workers);
3. examine and account for pertinent constraints; and
4. then devise a *systemic* model suitable for meeting your objectives, given these resources and constraints.

Only then does it pay to spend much time on micro-systemic issues such as instructional objectives or materials. In practice, we seldom need to go through the laborious instructional systems engineering process of identifying all or even many objectives and possible strategies, media and materials before choosing something that will prove more than satisfactory.

What we are searching for is a procedure whereby almost any institution or a department can shift its operations to offer an effective distant study scheme and yet do so with little or no increase in resources consumed. Thus, we hope to increase cost-effectiveness.

## Systems Approach

The foregoing notwithstanding it may be possible to develop a respectable distant study scheme. Using a systems approach, we can analyse the objectives and operations of an educational organization, formulating our problem in broad terms. Then we can develop a scheme to express, and model to improve, this system's effectiveness in using its resources to achieve intended objectives.

Of critical importance is the question of how to increase the efficiency and therefore productivity of *current* resources. Expressed otherwise, how can the institution maximize the return on its investment in human and other resources?

Because recommended approaches to instructional development require a tremendous investment of resources, it is likely that the solution is *not* to invest more resources but to use existing resources more efficiently and more effectively, given the available time (and other constraints). (We do not preclude modest increases in resources, if necessary.) Therefore the OU model is not acceptable. Is there a better model?

Rather than dealing with the problem directly we ask: 'What opportunities exist that can be exploited?'; 'What is the capability of the resources presently available, if only they were used differently?'; 'What are we doing now that could be done better, or faster so that resources may be re-allocated?'; and 'What else could we do that would increase our educational organization's effectiveness?'

## Mitchell's KWIK Systems Engineering Method

A useful approach exists. I have developed this educational engineering method only after years of frustration at being unable to do what I had been led to believe was essential and not merely an ideal. However, it owes a great deal to many writers. If you hope to develop a self-instructional scheme, distant or not, and have access to few resources to do so, my KWIK planning method may be useful and perhaps a *sine qua non*. KWIK is an acronym for its essential ingredients: knowledge, wilyness, ingenuity, and a keynote systemic perspective (Mitchell, 1981a).

### Identify the System's Purpose

Clarify the reasons for the existence and function of this system and do so from different perspectives (eg societal, institutional, immediate client's, user's). For example, consider a distant study system for the preparation and professional development of educational technologists. Why should it be developed?

Society needs practitioners of educational technology in schools, higher education, corporations and elsewhere, and many potential beneficiaries are unable to leave their jobs to study on campus.

The institution, on the other hand, stands to both gain and lose with a distant study system. In addition to actual costs of development and operation there is a possible cost in prestige if the university were seen as a diploma mill, offering correspondence study without conviviality and close faculty-student contact. A university education implies something more than the mastery of what is taught. On the other hand, the institution might gain students (at a time of uncertain enrolment) and make a contribution to people who would benefit from whatever services are rendered. A reasonable academic view would involve a mixture of distant and residential study. However, it is worth noting that material developed for distant study can be used at the university too. In short, tele-education provides an organizing theme and it may be convenient to begin by developing an instructional system intended to serve both groups of students.

### Clarify Systemic Objectives

Clarify your *systemic* objectives. What exactly is the nature and scope of the problem you are trying to solve or the system you are to produce?

Let us assume that the overall objective is to develop a distant study system which will increase the efficiency of an existing educational technology training programme by shifting the burden of repetitive instructional communications from faculty to self-instructional systems thus permitting faculty to cope with more students and to do more research. The resulting delivery system would allow any student to study some portion of his programme using self-instructional materials (proceeding at his own pace), whether in residence or at a distance.

To guarantee essential elements of human contact it should not be possible to complete the entire programme without face-to-face contact with faculty or other students. The self-instructional materials should be selected so that any student can use them, whether by going to a local learning centre for costly equipment or by using inexpensive equipment at home (eg slide viewer, audio-cassette recorder). But how many students do we have in mind? I assume that we are talking about a few dozen or a few hundred at most.

### Prepare a Conceptual Systems Analysis

Knowledge in a given discipline can be analysed as a system of concepts, procedures, relations, criteria, etc; these may be thought of as sub-systems. Meaningful relationships exist between many of these sub-systems.and their relations. The subject matter representation may take a variety of forms (eg relational network, entailment structure). A curriculum can be constructed and content selected to exemplify the structure of knowledge and to help the student create his own understanding of the topics and their relationships.

The basic idea is simple: construct a conceptual systemic model of what may be known (or a problem to be solved) and determine whether the model contains component sub-systems that are already within the person's repertoire (Mitchell, 1981b, Mitchell, in print). If so, he may begin to study any lesson which is linked to a topic that he has mastered. If not, it is necessary to subdivide each component topic into related sub-topics and/or link it to other topics that are expected to bridge the gap between the target system and the individual's current capability state.

The interconnection of ideas is immediately obvious if we stop to think about any subject or topic with which we are familiar. In order to understand that topic we must understand other topics which in turn entail our understanding of further topics. By using a systemic representation of knowledge we stress the coherence amongst ideas whereby components are organized to form a meaningful whole and avoid the dilemma of the behavioural objectives movement whereby lists of objectives are created which are devoid of epistemological foundations and which destroy the sense of structure that a learner might have developed.

The system we must produce can be represented as a reticulated curriculum and instruction system in which some modules are compulsory, some forced choice, and others freely elected. (In practice, different meshes will be needed to describe each subject.) Some of these modules will be available for study at home or in a learning centre but others will require face-to-face contact with the instructor and other students. Eventually a majority of modules should be available for self-instruction.

### Analyze Constraints

Examine and account for constraints under which you or the system must operate, but beware of imagined constraints.

A common constraint is money: in its absence we may do less than is necessary. However, sometimes lack of money is an imaginary constraint. To illustrate, two groups working independently produced similar task analyses and performance objectives for a certain career; one group spent about $200,000 over two years to produce its competency chart, the other team spent about four days and $100 to accomplish the task. Similarly an educational television series was running for three months before the Director of Extension heard that the university had a feasibility report on file which said it was impossible to do it.

### Evaluate Available Resources

Evaluate the resources available to you. Such resources include knowledge, human efforts, material, space, money, time and knowledge.

What do you have and know *now* that will enable you to develop a distant study scheme? If you ignore other possible alternatives or special techniques, do you have the capability today to get started? If not, what knowledge or other resources are needed and how will you get them? Suppose that no additional funds are available, does your institution offer 'free' services, eg raw film, video-cassettes, access to media production facilities, free computer time, or limited duplicating facilities? Used judiciously but fully, such support might be sufficient for most material needs especially if the library can assist.

### Create a Model for a Feasible Tele-Education System

Create an idea for, or a model of, a *feasible* system or process which is suitable for achieving all or many of your objectives, given your resource constraints. Don't be a perfectionist at this stage. Usually it will suffice to accomplish about 80 per cent of your objectives because diminishing returns make further effort seldom worth while. If resources permit, try to identify several feasible models or courses of action and select the best in the commonly recommended manner.

Given the resources outlined how can you exploit them to achieve the system objectives? Expressed otherwise, what could be accomplished with available resources if you really worked at it?

Don't fret if you produce only one all-encompassing idea for an educational system — provided that the dominant systemic ideas are clear, that imagination has been used creatively, that your knowledge base is broad as well as deep, and that the resulting system can be described alluringly to clients and users.

At this point you should be in a position to move swiftly toward implementation of a tele-education scheme though it will be necessary to consult references for details on various activities, eg facilities planning for a learning resources centre. But if you understand the subject matter to be taught and have mastered the principles of instructional design for self-instructional systems there is little remaining except implementation.

## Systems Engineering Recommendations

In most organizations when there is a problem to be solved the organization responds not by using existing resources more effectively or more efficiently but by increasing the resources available, even though the activity is questionable. Sometimes it does so by decreasing standards or increasing waiting time on the part of students (eg to gain access to media or human resources or to receive graded assignments). In either case, the effect on the bureaucratic core of the system — but *not* on users — is similar to that created by an increase in staff.

The KWIK method should increase the efficiency of existing resources so that more can be accomplished with no significant increase in resources. Efficiency of an instructional system is seen as a ratio of academic productivity to capability. But the question remains: 'Of what are you (and your colleagues or institution) capable?'

In planning educational systems and materials, the educational engineer must try to allocate the limited resources available (ie knowledge, materials and facilities, educators' time, students' time, money) so as to maximize the probability of achieving intended systemic outcomes. It must be remembered that there is no unique solution to real problems such as this, regardless of theories and textbook solutions to simplified stereotypical problems. And what is seen as a creative use of resources today may be seen as inefficient and obsolete tomorrow.

## A Feasible Model

The solution which I propose is deceptively simple. It assumes a gradual transformation from an existing instructional system toward a tele-education scheme in which most of the work involves self-instruction whether on or off campus. It requires radical changes in the use of resources. Finally, it is out of step with much of the instructional design literature insofar as it aims to maximize productivity of existing resources rather than to show what could be done if adequate resources were available.

This model is predicated on the assumption that you now offer a course in the traditional manner which is to be transformed into a tele-education scheme over the next few years. Even if such a course does not exist the principles should prove useful, though their sequence need not be adhered to.

Unlike typical strategies for instructional systems development this model assumes that you begin with an existing system and will modify it to produce the intended state. It is simple and practical. It would be surprising if we produced the same operating system as might be proposed if the institution knew no constraints. Our aim is to provide a system for tele-education that exploits the existing classroom-based operation and relies on inexpensive approaches to extend the institution's services. We cannot replicate the Open University.

The model recommended is outlined below. (Details may be found in Mitchell, 1981a.)

Start with available resources for instructional communication and for preparing instructional materials. Record classroom and tutorial presentations. By the end of the year you should have accumulated a large pool of instructional resources, some of which will be useful for local and distant study. The ratio of instructional output to input will be higher already; next year it will expand further. This calls for relatively little effort or time beyond normal preparation for existing classes.

More sophisticated materials may be produced by taking a picture of the chalkboard, OHP screen or a flip chart at short intervals throughout a classroom presentation. The resulting photos or slides can be edited and incorporated either as part of printed study material, or as a slide-tape presentation. (Very cheap 35mm hand-viewers can be provided for students lacking a projector.)

Conduct a topic analysis to decide which are the essential, desirable and optional topics with which a student should be familiar. This should be undertaken with a general idea of available resources.

Select those topics which you think are so important that a student should master them in order to finish your course. Then select those that you consider sufficiently important that students should understand at least some of these topics. Prune off any topics that you consider totally unnecessary. The remaining topics may be important to some students and can be used to bolster individual freedom in selecting course content. Eventually you may want to have a self-instructional module for each. Prepare a curriculum and instruction network. Mapping topics in this way should yield a curriculum that provides a good overview of the structure of knowledge in this subject.

Transform the topic into a curriculum map. For each topic, prepare one or more intended learning outcomes. These may be expressed as fuzzy objectives, capability objectives, or successful completion of activity objectives (behavioural objectives may be too cumbersome). In practice it is often possible and simpler to state or imply 'master this topic' and let the topic map stand.

Recognize the need for human contact by identifying modules that *require* group activity, techniques to promote interpersonal relations or criteria and occasions for regular seminars or workshops.

Note that particularly difficult self-instructional modules might benefit from dialogue between faculty and students or between students to sort out confusion or obsolescence in skills and concepts. Attitudinal development, if an objective, may demand instructional conversation.

Prepare instructional modules to operationalize the curriculum and instruction network. Keep the modules simple. Begin with available resources supplemented by curriculum and instruction maps, assignments, course notes, progress records, etc packaged in a standard module format.

A principle worth following much of the time is: Keep it simple. Do not use computer-based instruction via satellite if a booklet and regular post will be as effective. Nor should you use complex video if a slide-tape presentation (or a printed reproduction of the storyboard) will work about as well. (If in doubt about the efficacy of this suggestion, conduct the research needed to settle the issue.) On the other hand, never take an ordinary text and redefine its chapters as a sequence of modules. In a *later* phase, when time and other resources permit, try to provide short AV sequences that capture students' attention and arouse interest.

## Potential Criticism

The finished products may be criticized by perfectionists. Your modules will not closely resemble those of an OU course team — nor will the cost. That is the whole point. But will they be less effective? This is an empirical issue, yet remember that the core of the OU instructional system is print. Disarm your critics by reminding them that you plan to serve a group of students not otherwise catered for.

## Implementation and Management of the Tele-Education System

What will be needed in the way of management planning, management information systems and other resources required to operate a self-instructional system? The answer depends upon the number of students, the kind of facilities required, and the volume of non-print material.

For a small number of students, intuition and common sense will suffice. For a large student flow and/or large volume of modules that require expensive equipment, a systems analysis of facilities needs will be useful or essential (Mitchell, 1981a). Computer simulation may be needed for optimal allocation of resources to produce media materials or to provide materials that meet the constraint of a preferred 'media mix' (eg minimum of 10 hours TV, five hours simulation/gaming, but maximum of 50 hours print, etc) (Vazquez-Abad, 1980). Vazquez's model takes into account differential costs (time or money) associated with development of materials.

## Guidance Control Model

What kind of guidance control to use will depend on many factors such as whether pacing is to be synchronized or individualized, whether you want to help stragglers to complete the course by a target date, and whether you want to provide personal attention to people with poor assignments or low rates of progress. A course progress chart can be prepared which reveals at a glance which modules have been mastered by each student.

## Conclusion

I have presented an explicit model-building approach to formulate a strategy for implementing a tele-education system on the cheap, showing how different strategies can be identified and evaluated. Although the specific details used and the strategy selected are idiosyncratic, and are being tested by the writer in his own course, the general systems analytic and model-building methods are generalizable to other problems of a similar nature where the educational technologist needs either to economize or to maximize output. As such, the KWIK systems engineering method should prove useful for the theory and practice of educational technology.

## References

Mitchell, P D (1981a) *Systems Analysis in Planning Self-Instructional Systems.* Croom Helm, London.

Mitchell, P D (1981b) *Representation of Knowledge in CAL Courseware.* Presented to CAL 81 Conference, University of Leeds.

Mitchell, P D  *Conceptual Systems Analysis.* Cybersystems Publishing, Montreal (not yet published).

Vazquez-Abad, J (1980) *Simulation Analysis of a Model for Planning the Transformation of an Educational System from a Conventional into a Tele-Education Scheme.* MA thesis, Concordia University, Montreal.

# 1.2.3 The Impact of Independent and Open Learning on UK Libraries since 1970

**C S Hannabuss**
*Robert Gordon's Institute of Technology, Aberdeen*

**Abstract:** Developments in adult education and new strategies for learning and teaching have encouraged British libraries to adopt more adventurous roles *vis-a-vis* user groups than hitherto. Self-directed and distance learning systems depend on access to learning resources, and libraries are important access points.

## Introduction

Open learning is about access. It is concerned with enabling participants to develop independence through learning and consequently exercise such independence in decision-making. It is about giving groups in the community which lie outside formal full-time teaching an opportunity to acquire education, Open learning is geared towards students remote from traditional study centres, unable to attend formally structured institution-based courses.

Such learning systems require flexible uses of resources (buildings, staff, learning materials), and close attention to the needs of the learner — what information, advice and counselling are needed to support the programme of learning or study. The first part of this paper will be directed towards British public libraries and the efforts they have made through the 1970s to develop and encourage resource use (particularly use by students in the Open University), and the second part will be devoted to open learning systems organized by, and in, academic institutions, and ways will be considered whereby academic libraries have attempted to play a part.

## Public Libraries and Resource Use

Public libraries have been fully accessible in principle to everyone since the days they legally started in the middle of the nineteenth century. Even so, they have been accessible to some more than others right up to the present time, for largely social and educational reasons. The 1970s were important in highlighting the need to reach out to groups not using the library effectively (or indeed at all). The 1970s was the decade for the disadvantaged, as laws and outreach programmes on both sides of the Atlantic, in libraries as well as social and educational services, have revealed. Particular emphasis was given to adults who had missed out on educational opportunities: the adult literacy scheme directed itself to those whose loss was greatest, and public libraries played a part in this as referral points, advisers and resource providers.

The large numbers of adults for whom educational opportunity had been restricted were picked up by the research and investigation carried out in the early 1970s which materialized, *inter alia*, in the Russell and Alexander Reports on adult education. The value of learning resources, in libraries and arts centres and community centres, was stressed. Social mobility and the need to retrain were incentives for development in this area of education and resource provision. Increasing emphasis can be seen in statements made by librarians throughout the 1970s concerning the precise role they should play *vis-a-vis* those involved in adult education. The traditional, and passive, role of providing books was not thought to be enough. It did have the advantage, of course, that students all over the country could be reached (an essential factor in distance provision), but it was too diffuse a role, unco-ordinated with adult educators, and not personalized or individualized. Policy statements and guidelines began to appear, and statements as to how libraries might help local organizations with information handling skills (eg in the field of consumer information) suggested concrete help. Links were formed between librarians and educators, such as the East Midlands Joint Committee on Libraries and Adult Education (set up in 1969) which was responsible for considering how the two bodies could best collaborate. A range of services for adult education was developed by Derbyshire County Libraries: book lists for tutors; links with the extra-mural libraries in local universities and with WEA tutors; current awareness services; special pre-stocking for class use. Other services, like Leicestershire County Libraries, manned an adult education information desk annually at enrolment times (September, in this case). Systematic information and research is building up on such services, in particular, the report on the involvement of public libraries with adult learners prepared for the British Library (Allred and Hay, 1979). The report sees five roles for public libraries: (i) common carrier (of resources); (ii) back-up service (eg to an extra-mural library); (iii) self-help service (where the library directly uses skills for packaging etc but gives no face-to-face guidance); (iv) direct service (where the library actively helps users to achieve learning goals); and (v) network organizer (organizing or taking part in a network of agencies providing information and even acting as broker for educational opportunity). The report recommends that public libraries develop a more specialized role and play a larger and more pervasive part in continuing education, and there is plenty of documentary evidence in the report that, despite cuts in both library and adult education services, this is being done and will continue into the 1980s.

An American example proving influential in Britain is the Adult Independent Learning Project (1973-76), which started as a scheme for people lacking college education to take tests so that they could gain admission to college. In the libraries taking part in the scheme a Learners' Advisory Service grew up. This was for self-directing adults who wished to study independently, and took the form of librarian and learner working together, the librarian acting as adviser and facilitator and providing support by means of information.

The learners were of all ages and classes, and were encouraged to take responsibility for their own learning programme. Their educational goals varied widely, as did their learning styles. Much of the activity was not credential-based. Many had personal development or community work as their incentives. Such library services entail a change in professional attitudes and are very staff-intensive, and consequently, despite publicity in UK library circles (eg Dale, 1979; Bowen and Surridge, 1977), saw only limited implementation during the 1970s.

The area of independent learning in which public libraries have been able to play a significant part throughout the 1970s has been that of the Open University. The structures, media, materials and control systems of the OU have been widely discussed (eg MacKenzie, Postgate and Scupham, 1975; Kaye and Rumble, 1981) and so have the activities of regional centres, tutor-counsellors and OU students. The provision of resources at local (indeed at individual) level was considered essential for the start. Developments in the media and in technology (especially microelectronics) enabled such an open system to operate as it did. From the beginning, television and radio were used to relay programmes, and open learning systems stand to benefit in the future with developments in teletext and viewdata systems in homes, post offices, libraries, etc (Council for Educational Technology, 1978; Anderson, 1980; Martyn, 1979). With the increasing interest in automation for housekeeping management reasons and for enhanced information retrieval facility, libraries seem likely to become sources of information about courses — information which will help both students and developers of learning materials. Such a scheme has started at Bradford Public Library in conjunction with OU staff and with a British Library grant of £2,700. The project is to last six months (it started in 1980) and investigates the ways in which local adult education opportunities can be stored and exploited by the use of an on-line database. It was much influenced by the *links to learning* statement on the mediation of such information by agencies such as libraries issued by the Advisory Council on Adult and Continuing Education in 1979. A similar but more ambitious scheme has been started under the auspices of the OU in the Yorkshire Region, again with a British Library grant. American work in this field, like the VICS (Vocational Information through Computer Systems) project, is more advanced, but it is clear that UK libraries have become involved in schemes which have much practical promise for the future.

Libraries have been active throughout the 1970s in supporting the OU in other ways. Early in the decade, many libraries built up stocks of central course books and recommended reading. Research into attitudes towards using public libraries and on actual library usage has been carried out (eg Cameron, 1973; Jack, 1979; Green, 1976; Wilson, 1978; Marsterson and Wilson, 1975). These researches reveal what kinds of material were most used and most useful to OU students, whether advice from librarians was required, what course levels made most intensive use of libraries, and links between broadcast and printed materials. A 1973 pilot project recommended that more information should be prepared by libraries for two reasons: (i) information about libraries and resources was necessary as *general* information for students; and (ii) such information would help students acquire skills in locating and using *special* resources in their specialist studies. Remoteness compounded many students' ineffective use of libraries. Towards the end of the 1970s, the regional centres of the OU actively gathered together information and many resources guides, and lists of library facilities are now available, often showing details of stock, staff contacts, course materials, and so on.

## Academic Libraries and Open Learning Systems

At the same time as public libraries were giving attention to serving the adult learner in the forms discussed above, the academic libraries too were growing conscious of social and academic changes in their parent organizations which made similar adjustments essential. Universities have been moving more and more into the field of continuing education and non-traditional degrees. This growth of part-time continuing education presented challenges to teaching resources: in particular, a more flexible use of resources for individual need was required. Traditional resource provision, for example through extra-mural department libraries, had to be improved (Library Association, 1978), and a case was put by the Extra-Mural Librarian of Birmingham University (Fisher, 1971) for the formation of regional libraries for adult education, based on existing extra-mural libraries and responsible to regional liaison committees. A role for the university extra-mural department as a resource centre, linking society to academic skills and playing an active role in community education networks, heralded a wider interpretation of academic institutions and the community at large (Ellwood, 1976; Stephens and Roderick, 1978). For students, resources and information were essential: such needs varied widely, some courses might be non-credit and so make extraordinary demands on stock and readers' services; off-campus students might impose special demands on borrowing systems (Fisher, 1979).

So far the discussion of academic libraries has concentrated on their role in relation to broader or more open courses rather than traditional full-time credential-based courses. Yet considering the openness of open learning systems means we have to consider also traditional courses for students of the traditional age group and qualification band (that is, entry to courses). The influence of the OU and the development of technology have been part of the cause of a large shift of emphasis over recent years, from teacher-centred to learner-centred educational routes. Evidence on drop-out rates, motivation and attendance has encouraged change. More than that, there has been a change in educational assumptions, based on new ways of developing the curriculum and assessing student performance. It has been a change in which *the use of resources* and *the kind of resources used* have come to play a crucial part (MacKenzie, Eraut and Jones, 1970). In a so-called integrated teaching and learning system, the library can no longer be merely a collection of printed materials. It has to be an instructional resource centre, handling a wide range of print and non-print resources, and guiding independent inquiry (Hills, 1976).

At the start of the 1970s, librarians showed that they were faced with change. Fothergill (1971) discussed the need for libraries to develop as an integral part of the learning process, accommodating *and* helping to design structured or packaged learning materials, providing flexible individual learning facilities, and employing professional library skills to co-ordinate and exploit multi-media resources. The same message pervaded another important work of the early 1970s (Enright, 1972), which picked out the following courses of action for libraries: to organize library documentation so that information about materials should be made readily and intelligibly accessible to users; to assess the implications for library staff of student-centred learning, of how materials should be used by students working individually; to make efforts to understand the educational assumptions on which courses operated; to develop programmes to assist students handle and control information for problem-solving and decision-making. All this illustrates the climate of reaction among librarians in the early 1970s. Throughout the decade, the thinking and approach of librarians in school and college libraries have been influenced by two other main areas of thought, psychology and educational technology, and, before going on to consider *actual* responses to independent and open learning, some brief details about the impact of these two areas need to be recorded.

Librarians in academic libraries have, in many cases, made systematic attempts to learn more about the learning process itself. The conditions of learning outlined by Gagné, the educational objectives of Bloom, and the ways in which young people conceptualize are just three outstanding examples of this. Such ideas have become more thoroughly internalized in the thinking of librarians over the years, and now find creative expression in many studies of resource-based learning (eg Lattimore, 1978; Ford, 1979a, 1979b). The area of educational technology, too, has proved very influential in helping librarians define their role more clearly: definition of course objectives, desired outcomes of learning (Rowntree, 1973) and instructional goals, the preferred learning environment and the design and use of learning materials, have all been taken on board enthusiastically as useful measuring rods of the larger situation in which librarians work. An interesting complementary role between librarian and educational technologist is explored by B H Gill (Gill, 1975), where he argues that the heuristic and 'individualized' free-ranging approach of the resources centre contrasts with and complements the prescriptive and structured approach of the educational technologist.

But the complementarity of these roles, and indeed the contribution of librarians to open learning systems generally, needs some actual examples. UK libraries have progressed less far than those in America, and transitions, mergers and cuts have slowed down change. Nevertheless, the involvement of libraries/ resource centres with self-teaching systems is significant. Supportive materials for self-teaching systems in universities are described by Hills (Hills, 1971), while accommodation for video-tape facilities is provided at Brunel (Noordhof, 1974). The learning resource facility at St Albans Programmed Learning Centre (Davies and Needham, 1975) describes an on-demand learning resource facility for individual students and the necessity to assess individual need and assist with retrieval of data. A close partnership between resource centre and teaching staff in the design and production of learning packages at Bath University is described by Black (Black, 1974). Perhaps best documented is Dundee College of Education Library, planned from the start as an environment for self-instruction and equipped with carrel facilities for the individual reproduction of media by a dial-access system. This 'library college' concept nearly came into being, although cuts and reduced student numbers finally constrained the enterprise (Gill, 1975; Clarke, 1973; Clarke and Hutchison, 1972). Associated with resource provision is user education, a field in which libraries have made important advances in recent years. The kind of resources to which a learner, in a traditional or open learning system, gets access depends heavily on ways in which he or she can use them effectively. As can be seen from the Adult Independent Learning Project, such assistance is intensive, and at the same time it is an area receiving increasing attention from library organizers (Fjallbrandt, 1974; Stevenson, 1973; Lubans, 1974). Challenging interconnections will develop with computer-assisted learning: user education programmes can help users understand library systems and layout, and retrieval of library documents (perhaps in order of anticipated usefulness) will be integrated with learning programmes (Brown, 1975). Like the use of Prestel in The Information Skills in the Curriculum Research Project, these are schemes for the 1980s.

Looking back on the 1970s, and on the generously documented subject of open learning (eg Davies, 1977; Coffey, 1978), in an academic context, there are gaps in the literature which suggest that libraries and resource centres need to do more and tell more. The impact of independent and open learning on them, however, has been irreversible and profound, part and parcel as it is of the larger sea change of teaching and learning methods in the UK throughout the 1970s. This change has influenced public libraries just as much. The 1980s could prove both a period of imaginative collaboration and consolidation, if money and self-confidence are in good enough supply.

## References

Allred, J and Hay, W (1979) *A Preliminary Study of the Involvement of Public Libraries with Adult Learners.* School of Librarianship, Leeds Polytechnic.

Anderson, D (1980) The hollow tree syndrome: the implications and applications of new technology in education. *Times Educational Supplement,* 14 November, p 14.

Black, J (1974) Libraries and the learning process in higher education. In Wood, J (ed) *College of Education Libraries and Higher Education.* ATCDE, Bristol.

Bowen, J and Surridge, R (1977) *The Independent Learning Project: A Study of Changing Attitudes in American Public Libraries.* Public Libraries Research Group, London.

Brown, W C (1975) Computer-aided learning for all. *Programmed Learning and Educational Technology* 12, 5, pp 255-64.

Cameron, K J (1973) The Open University student as library user. *Library Association Record* 75 2, pp 23-4.

Clarke, J (1973) The implementation of educational technology at Dundee College of Education. *Programmed Learning and Educational Technology* 10, 1, pp 6-12.

Clarke, J and Hutchison, I (1972) The development of procedures for the production and distribution of resources in a college of education. In Austwick, K and Harris, N D C (eds) *Aspects of Educational Technology* VI. Pitman, London.

Coffey, J (1978) *Development of an Open Learning System in Further Education: A Report.* Council for Educational Technology, London.

Council for Educational Technology (1978) *Microelectronics: Their Implications for Education and Training.* Council for Educational Technology, London.

Dale, S (1979) The Adult Independent Learning Project: work with adult self-directed learners in public libraries. *Journal of Librarianship* 11, 2, pp 83-106.

Davies, K and Needham, M (1975) Running a learning resource facility for individuals. *Programmed Learning and Educational Technology* 12, 5, pp 181-5.

Davies, T C (1977) *Open Learning Systems for Mature Students.* Council for Educational Technology, London.

Ellwood, C (1976) *Adult Learning Today: A New Role for the Universities?* Sage Publications, London.

Enright, B J (1972) *New Media and the Library in Education.* Bingley, London.

Fisher, R K (1971) Regional libraries for adult education. *Journal of Librarianship* 3, 4, pp 228-36.

Fisher, R K (1979) Academic libraries and part-time adult students. In Stueart, R D and Johnson, R D (eds) *New Horizons for Academic Libraries.* Saur, New York.

Fjallbrandt, N (1974) *Library Instruction for Students in Universities in Britain.* Chalmers University of Technology, Gothenburg.

Ford, N (1979a) Cognitive psychology and 'library learning'. *Journal of Librarianship,* 11, 1, pp 25-38.

Ford, N (1979b) Towards a model of 'library learning' in educational systems. *Journal of Librarianship* 11, 4, pp 247-60.

Fothergill, R (1971) *A Challenge for Librarians? A Report on the Joint NCET/ASLIB Audio Visual Group Conference.* National Council for Educational Technology/ASLIB, London.

Gill, B H (1975) Educational technology in the academic library. *Programmed Learning and Educational Technology* 12, 3, pp 151-62.

Green, H R (1976) The OU and public libraries. *New Library World* 77, pp 189-90.

Hills, P J (1971) Self teaching systems in university courses. In Packham, D, Cleary, A and Mayes, T (eds) *Aspects of Educational Technology* V. Pitman, London.

Hills, P J (1976) *The Self-Teaching Process in Higher Education.* Croom Helm, London.

Jack, M (1979) A special type of borrower. *Scottish Library Association News* 152, pp 337-43.

Kaye, A and Rumble, G (1981) *Distance Teaching for Higher and Adult Education.* Croom Helm/Open University Press, London.

Lattimore, M I (1978) The learning resource centre. In Jefferson, G and Smith-Burnett, G C K (eds) *The College Library.* Bingley, London.

Library Association (1978) *Standards for University Extra-Mural Libraries.* Library Association, London.

Lubans, J (1974) *Educating the Library User.* Bowker, New York.

Mackenzie, N, Eraut, M and Jones, H C (1970) *Teaching and Learning: An Introduction to New Methods and Resources in Higher Education.* UNESCO, Paris.

Mackenzie, N, Postgate, R and Scupham, J (1975) *Open Learning: Systems and Problems in Post-Secondary Education.* UNESCO, Paris.

Marsterson, W A J and Wilson, T D (1975) Home based students and libraries. *Libri* 25, 3, pp 213-26.

Martyn, J (1979) Prestel and public libraries: an LA/ASLIB experiment. *Aslib Proceedings* 31, 5, pp 216-36.

Noordhof, G H (1974) The development of self-replay videotape facilities at Brunel University. *Programmed Learning and Educational Technology* 11, 1, pp 10-15.

Rowntree, D (1973) Which objectives are most worthwhile? In Budgett, R and Leedham, J (eds) *Aspects of Educational Technology* **VII**. Pitman, London.

Stephens, M D and Roderick, G W (1978) *Higher Education Alternatives.* Longman, London.

Stevenson, M B (1973) *Problems and Evaluation of Reader Instruction in British University Libraries.* MA thesis, University College London.

Wilson, T D (1978) Learning at a distance and library use. *Libri* 28, 4, pp 270-82.

# 1.3 Descriptions of Distance Learning Schemes

## 1.3.1 Independence and Interdependence in Distance Education: Responsive Course Design

**D J Boud**
*University of New South Wales, Australia*

**Abstract:** A major problem in distance learning courses is that of developing ways in which students can learn without continual dependence on prescribed study guides and correspondence from a tutor. It is not sufficient for a student to be able to master the objectives and content of a course; it is also necessary to develop skills of independent learning.

The aim of this paper is to explore ways in which distance learning courses can be made more responsive to student needs, develop skills of independent learning, and provide a climate of co-operative enterprise in which students, while isolated by distance, conduct themselves as part of a group of learners engaged in a common task. These issues are illustrated by reference to a distance learning course conducted by the author in Western Australia which operated under severe geographical constraints.

The example given demonstrates the problems faced by the tutor and course designer when an attempt is made to translate a co-operatively (staff-student) designed course to an external setting. It indicates that it is possible to involve students in decisions concerning the total design, development and evaluation of a course in which they are enrolled as distant students and that, through this, they can develop educational skills which are fundamental for distant learners.

## Introduction

Many important educational goals which can be pursued in campus-based courses have not been seriously considered or developed in the distance teaching mode, except in the non-distant component of summer schools and the like. Amongst these goals are those of independent and autonomous learning (Boud, 1981), of working co-operatively with peers (Goldschmid and Goldschmid, 1976), of planning and constructing one's own learning objectives and programmes (Knowles, 1975) and of monitoring and assessing one's own learning (Boud, 1980; Heron, 1981). Some of these goals are pursued by default when the planned system breaks down or becomes inefficient — when isolated learning becomes independent learning — but they are not usually given attention in conventional distance courses.

In the past, distance teaching has lent itself to some of the worst excesses of didacticism. Teachers have tended to closely prescribe material for students to learn and students have responded by completing tests and assignments which could easily be checked by a tutor not involved in setting the questions. Courses remained unchanged for many years and were often passed on to be administered by those far removed from the original intentions of the course. External students are already disadvantaged through their location; why should they also be disadvantaged through the provision of stereotyped courses?

The influence of the Open University has changed this somewhat but, even within that substantial institution, the emphasis is on the production of 'well-designed instructional materials' to which students respond: staff set the assignments and students complete them. There are some interesting innovations at the Open University which attempt to move beyond this, but many of these changes do not affect the core of the system.

It is possible to design and conduct courses in the distance learning mode which do address the goals which have been outlined. However, in order to do so, it is necessary for a perspective to be taken other than the content-centred one which so often predominates in distance education. If courses are to develop skills of self-directed learning and working collaboratively with peers in students, then they must be explicitly designed to do so and they must exemplify these aims through their structure and content. The course design must be one which is responsive to the needs of the students enrolled at any given time. It must be sufficiently flexible to accommodate a wide range of needs and objectives, but it must also offer tangible forms of support and encouragement to help maintain morale and commitment during what can be difficult times.

The ways in which those elements can be incorporated in a course design is best illustrated by an example. The one chosen is one component of a postgraduate diploma in science education offered by the School of Applied Science in 1977 at the Western Australian Institute of Technology. It is nominally equivalent to a campus-based course of four contact hours per week for 15 weeks and represents the first element of the core programme in science education for experienced science teachers in high schools, technical colleges and higher education.

## Case Study

### Geographical Constraints

The major constraint is one of distance and accessibility. Students were drawn from the non-metropolitan area of Western Australia and were dotted over a state with a similar area to that of Western Europe, approximately 1,000,000 square miles. The total population available were those science teachers required to serve a population of approximately 250,000. The numbers enrolled are small (five in 1977) and the students are isolated from each other by distance (1,000 miles plus), and by cost (the cost of a phone call to a large part of the state is approximately half the cost of calling the UK). Students are not able to attend the campus during any given unit of the course and therefore the only normal form of communication is by post.

### Course Rationale

The course is normally available as a campus-based course and there is free transfer between the external and internal units. Therefore the external version must have the same objectives and must broadly run in parallel with the internal version.

The course is based upon an explicit rationale which defines the characteristics of an educated professional in the field and is at once both a description to which students can aspire and also one which they can identify as already being partly achieved:

They are self-directing and self-motivating; that is, they are able to specify clear goals for their activities, they can design a programme of learning activities drawing upon all the necessary resources to pursue their goals, and they are able to evaluate their performance of the tasks they have established and judge the extent to which their goals have been met. Such people do not act in isolation but can draw upon the resources they need wherever they may be found both within and outside educational institutions (Boud and Prosser, 1980).

The course is designed on the basis of this description and includes students setting their own objectives, planning their own programme, identifying and using the resources of others and evaluating their own performance. The course is jointly designed and conducted by staff and students and the students are involved in teaching and learning from each other.

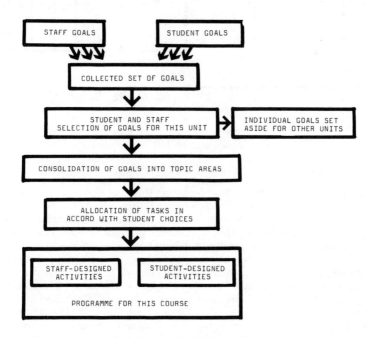

**Figure 1.** *Course design process*

**Course Design Process**

Figure 1 represents the process schematically. Basically, staff goals and student goals are identified. They are collected and ranked and those which are sufficiently common are used as the basis for the first unit of the course. Other goals are pursued elsewhere in individual project units and in other more formal courses. The common goals are divided into coherent groups and each student takes one of these and develops a set of learning materials which can be used to instruct the others. Through this, students learn by teaching others. A very detailed and systematic set of procedures has been created to facilitate this process. During the course design phase, in which there is considerable waiting time as goals and objectives and outline plans are passed to and fro by post, students complete a course on working through the packages designed by their peers and providing each other with feedback on their experience. The course ends when these packages have been studied and have been revised by each author in the light of this feedback and a summative self-assessment procedure completed — see Figure 2.

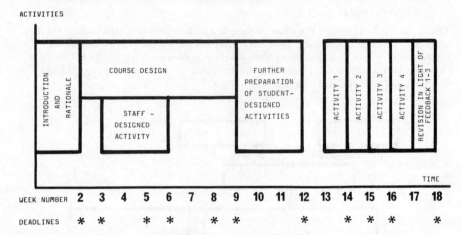

Figure 2. *Schematic outline of the course*

## Particular Features

If a course representing such a radical departure from the norms of a distance learning course is to be successfully implemented, then it must be carefully planned to support the desired process and to recognize both the educational and personal needs of those involved. The most important feature is the maximum use of the limited forms of communication which are open. In this case, use is made of *taped commentaries* by the tutor on each stage of the process, discussing the contributions of all the students, presenting himself in a human and accessible manner, giving emphasis to crucial aspects of the process and, most important of all, giving encouragement, support and reassurance to the students and assuring them that their anxieties are not unique. Students are also encouraged to make their own taped commentaries, but generally they prefer the written word.

Written correspondence is the most frequently used channel of communication. Students are required to provide a written *process commentary* in response to each mailing. The aim of this is to give immediate feedback to the tutor on any matter — unrealistic deadlines, obscure procedures, inappropriate tasks — and for students to express their personal reactions to the experience. Part of the tutors' taped commentary involves reviewing these process sheets. For urgent matters, a 24-hour automatic phone message recorder is available with a guarantee that the tutor will respond on each occasion.

## Deadlines

Deadlines for completion of various tasks are negotiable, but once agreed they are immutable — the whole system rests upon compliance with deadlines. However, they are fixed to take account of the normal vagaries of the postal system.

Various other forms of support are available. These include assistance in identifying on-site advisers, access to library facilities by post, and help in duplicating and mailing learning packages for use by other students.

## Assessment and Evaluation

The prime form of assessment is that of self-assessment mediated by peers — see Figure 3. Students complete an extensive self-assessment schedule which they submit, along with their final revised learning package. This, in essence, consists of a series of stages in which students list their learning objectives, set priorities for these objectives, relate these to learning activities, make judgements concerning their own level of achievement for each objective, identify causes and make action plans for how they will address each outstanding objective in subsequent units of the course.

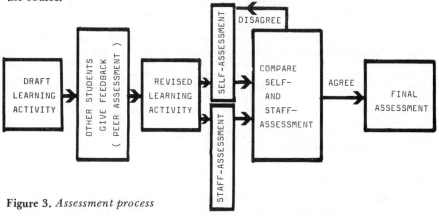

**Figure 3.** *Assessment process*

A wealth of evaluation data is collected: a set of process commentaries from each student, a summative commentary, the completed self-assessment schedules and statements from individual students. The conclusions which were drawn from this data in the 1977 study can be summarized as follows: students found the course challenging and demanding; they had difficulty initially in accepting the concept and methodology of the course as it was in great contrast with their previous experience. However, they did adjust successfully to the new procedures and found the detailed structure very helpful; they had problems in accepting the use of self-assessment at first, but they came to see the value and purpose of it; finally they did report that experience of the course had helped them gain confidence in working independently. Of course, various specific components and activities were criticized and suggestions were made for revisions. The course was constructed to be self-regulating and many of the usual difficulties of courses run for the first time had been corrected during the course itself.

The experience of the tutor is very different from that in a conventional distance course. In addition to being a subject authority and guide, the tutor has to adopt the new roles of peer, facilitator and exemplar. He has to be active in creating a supportive climate for the course and in responding to the full range of students' concerns. It is an exciting role, but one which demands more than the usual routine of marking and commenting on assignments. With each intake of students the course is created afresh and the tutor needs to adapt to meeting new requirements.

## Implications

The course described provides but one example of many designs that could be implemented to foster independence and interdependence in distance learning. It was constructed to fit local constraints and a particular clientele. This particular model could not be adopted elsewhere without appropriate modification. It was developed in the context of a favourable tutor-student ratio, but aspects of it could be used with larger classes if students were divided into smaller groups with about six students in each.

It provides a methodology which is relatively content-free and it could therefore be used in many different disciplines. However, it assumes a degree of maturity on the part of students which might not be found in some contexts.

## References

Boud, D J (1980) Self and peer assessment in higher and continuing professional education: an annotated bibliography. Occasional Paper 15. Tertiary Education Research Centre, University of New South Wales, Sydney.

Boud, D J (1981) Toward student responsibility for learning. In Boud, D J (ed) *Developing Student Autonomy in Learning*. Kogan Page, London.

Boud, D J and Prosser, M T (1980) Sharing responsibility: staff-student cooperation in learning. *British Journal of Educational Technology* **11**, 1, pp 24-35.

Knowles, M S (1975) *Self-Directed Learning: A Guide for Learners and Teachers*. Association Press, New York.

Goldschmid, B and Goldschmid, M L (1976) Peer teaching in higher education: a review. *Higher Education* **5**, 1, pp 9-33.

Heron, J (1981) Assessment revisited. In Boud, D J (ed) *Developing Student Autonomy in Learning*. Kogan Page, London.

## Acknowledgements

The methodology of the course was jointly developed by Dr Thomas Heffernan, formerly of the School of External Studies, Western Australian Institute of Technology (now of the University of Southern California) and myself.

I wish to thank my colleagues in the Centre for Educational Practice, University of Strathclyde for their hospitality whilst I was writing this paper.

# 1.3.2 Distance Learning for Technicians

J Twining
Guildford Educational Services

**Abstract:** Guildford Educational Services Ltd is investigating a system for distance learning for technicians, on contract to the Council for Educational Technology and with the involvement of the Training Services Division of the Manpower Services Commission and the Technician Education Council. A paper at ETIC 80 gave the background to the project and a workshop ensured that participation took place to solve one of the major issues. This paper will describe progress since April 1980.

By the end of March 1981 the feasibility of distance learning in a range of technician subjects had been considered in relation to a number of specific issues including (i) availability of learning material, (ii) expert subject tuition at a distance, (iii) credibility of non-expert counselling, (iv) provision and marketing of tests which contribute to the award, and (v) practical (hands-on) requirements.

The paper describes the principles involved in tackling these issues in the context of UK technician education. Where possible specific examples are given.

## Introduction

Guildford Educational Services (GES) is undertaking an investigation into distance learning for technicians, on behalf of the Council for Educational Technology (CET), the Training Services Division of the Manpower Services Commission (MSC) and the Technician Education Council (TEC). This project has been described in general terms (Twining and Ward, 1980), when reference was made to the feasibility of a 'network' system involving existing technical colleges. Since then a statement in the House of Commons on 26 November 1980, by the Secretary of State for Employment, has given added importance to this concept:

> I am convinced that we need more open opportunities for technical training. By 'open' I mean that there should be no formal pre-entry educational qualifications, and that such opportunities should be available to people irrespective of whether they can join with others for structured classes at set times in working hours . . . That is why I am asking the MSC to come forward with a scheme of distance learning — what I call 'open tech' — in conjunction of course with existing technical colleges and colleges of further education. (Hansard, 1980)

## Characteristics of Technician Education in the UK Context

While the characteristics of distance learning are common knowledge, and have been widely written about, the characteristics of technician education, especially those which will affect distance learning, are less well known. Some of these are discussed below.

### Characteristics Relating to Learning Material

Compared with general or business education, technician education has large numbers of subjects each with comparatively small numbers of students. It has been estimated that a distance learning system covering existing TEC standard units would be equivalent to the total target provision (not yet achieved) of the Open University undergraduate programme. One consequence is that, unless acceptable short cuts can be found, the capital cost for providing learning material for a comprehensive system of distance learning for technicians will be very high, and in most cases will not be recoverable from student fees unless these are also very high indeed. The calendar time required would also be very long.

Much of the subject content of technician education is susceptible to rapid technological change, which not only reduces the shelf life of the learning material and so makes the recovery of the original cost even more problematic, but also requires the material to be kept under constant review.

The relationship between the quality of learning materials and the quantity of tuition has been described in very general terms by Spencer (1980):

> To obtain as an output any given quality of learning from a given (large) number of students, the quality of the materials is related to the volume of tutorial help required . . . as the quality (and one may assume the cost) of learning materials falls, so the cost of tutorial help rises.

Presumably, the converse would also be generally valid:

> If more frequent tutorial help is available, lower quality learning material will suffice for a given educational output.

These statements are not absolutes, and would not necessarily be valid in the same way for all types of subject content, or for all groups of students.

Nevertheless it may follow that if the major barriers (from the point of view of both time and cost) to the introduction of distance learning is the special production of good quality self-learning material, it may be more profitable to make do with mediated text books, or (in the smaller subjects where text books are not available) with college-produced worksheets and reading lists, supported by more frequent tutorials. Some minimum level of standard would be required.

## 'Hands-On' Requirements

An 'armchair' technician is a contradiction in terms. Within technician education there are wide variations (depending on the nature of the work the technician is being prepared for) in the balance between theory and practice and in the nature of any 'hands-on' work. Different approaches (type of learning material; frequency, duration and nature of face-to-face sessions; links with current employment etc) are likely to be required for different subjects.

Figure 1 illustrates three alternative approaches to meeting such requirements: credit; infrequent opportunities; and frequent opportunities. Which is most appropriate will depend on the circumstances of each case, but it does appear likely that, where credit cannot be given, frequent opportunities are likely to be more effective for learning than infrequent ones, and hands-on experience may be easier to obtain at a college than in employment, unless the student's job matches his course very exactly.

| Credit | Infrequent opportunity | Frequent opportunity |
|---|---|---|
| Previous educational attainment | Summer school | Local college |
| | Residential weekend | |
| Previous work experience | Special arrangements by employer | Concurrent work experience |
| | | Home kit |

**Figure 1.** *Practical (hands-on) requirements of TEC programmes —*
*alternative approaches*

## Technician Students

Technician education attracts a wide range of students in terms of conventional measures of ability, previous academic attainment and learning styles. This adds to the problem of learning material design if the high capital costs involved mean that only one learning package can be produced for each TEC unit (or other 'parcel' of content). Evidence from the British Telecom Telecommunications scheme (Twining, 1980) also suggests that it cannot be taken for granted that all adult students following distance learning studies will be highly motivated. If distance learning becomes a major mode of study in a wide range of courses, the effect may be to introduce less highly motivated students. This will particularly be the case if younger students study by the distance learning mode. The Telecommunications scheme provides some evidence to support the hypothesis that less academic students (in terms of technician education) are likely to be less motivated in the more theoretical subjects — while such subjects are more easily provided by distance learning.

It now seems fairly well accepted that one of the main requirements of a distance learning system is good counselling to deal with the students' general (not subject-specific) study problems. There is a doubt, however, whether counsellors who are not also credible in the subject matter of the course, would be acceptable to technician level students, however well-trained or expert such counsellors may be in counselling. There is no hard evidence on which to base this assumption, but it would be unwise to base a distance learning system on the expectation that general counselling of adult technicians by non-subject expert counsellors would be effective. The alternative is to combine the roles of expert tutor and of counsellor, which requires a greater geographical spread of expert tutors.

**The Technician Education Council (TEC)**

TEC's policies and procedures already have particular implications for distance learning, including:

(a) A unit/credit system, enabling a high degree of individualization and self-pacing.
(b) The ability to take a complete programme, or individual units, or possibly a coherent collection of units less than a programme in length, thus meeting varied personal requirements.
(c) The opportunity of obtaining partial exemption from units (perhaps for life or work experience).
(d) The use of learning objectives to define unit content.
(e) Validation procedures which enable there to be some policy direction over the spread of distance learning.
(f) Moderation procedures to provide constant monitoring of the system.
(g) Registration and other student procedures (payment of fees, transfer of students, student unit reports) adaptable for distance learning, thus making it unnecessary to create any special central system of student records.
(h) Existing statistical procedures usable for the monitoring and evaluation of distance learning.

TEC's assessment requirements (particularly phase testing), which previously appeared to reduce the degree of self-pacing quite considerably (Ward and Twining, 1980), have now been amended to include a mode more suitable to distance learning (TEC, 1980). Although tests can be banked and provided on demand, unless all tests are objective, the problem of marking them (or of marking assignments) remains. One solution in the technician field is that adopted by British Telecom with banked tests and marking schemes but with the marking actually done by the students' expert tutors.

**Existing College Provision**

England and Wales are well served with technical colleges. Some 450 are concerned in some way with technician education.

TEC has approximately 100 subject headings (counting Certificate and Higher Certificate levels as a single heading). Over 50 are offered by under 20 colleges and only about 10 by over 100 colleges, but these 10 include the majority of the face-to-face students and probably the potential majority of distance learning students.

**Towards a Network**

All these factors point to there being a 'best buy', where there can be a wide national spread of expert tutors and specialist physical resources. These can be used by students on a learning-by-appointment model, with the 'centre of excellence' single-college model being used only where the necessary expertise and resources in sufficient colleges cannot be mobilized.

Naturally, the availability of a large number of colleges will not in itself guarantee that a distance learning network system can be established. In the early days, at least, there are bound to be gaps where colleges or authorities are not able, or do not want, to take part. And very frequent availability of tutors does not remove the need for there to be some minimum standards of learning material. There will be a need for planning and for staff training. Some injection of outside funds seems likely to be necessary. Nevertheless, a wide spread of expert tuition and resources appears likely to help solve many of the more difficult problems of distance learning.

## The Geographical Approach

The basic principle derives from a rough calculation made by Collier Macmillan Schools. That is, if it were possible to choose colleges in the right geographical location, only 15-20 colleges would be needed for 80 per cent of the population of England and Wales who would be within 40 miles of one of the chosen colleges.

Experimental mapping indicates that it is likely that most of the population of England and Wales lies within a radius of:

(a)  30 miles of 30-40 colleges
(b)  20 miles of 60-70 colleges
(c)  15 miles of about 100 colleges.

A radius, of course, is less than the actual travelling distance. A possible rule of thumb would be to add 25 per cent.

The question of what is reasonable travelling distance (for tutorials, practical work or other use of college facilities) is likely to be a matter of considerable debate.

Guildford Educational Services have tentatively identified the variables which seem likely to influence the effectiveness of national coverage. Their possible effect is shown in Figure 2.

| Distance | longer | shorter |
| Frequency | less often | more often |
| Time of day | earlier | later |
| Employer's assistance | generous | none |
| Students' perception of relevance of tutorial | high | low |

Compulsory/voluntary is not seen as a major variable in this context. If the circumstances are unfavourable (eg distance too great, employer assistance not forthcoming) compulsory attendance may lead to drop-out, while voluntary attendance will merely be less frequent.

**Figure 2.** *Variables affecting perceptions of 'reasonable' travelling distance*

There are two ways of increasing the number of suitable colleges:

1. By using those offering similar, although not identical technician subjects (eg telecommunications for electronics);
2. In subjects where there is a strong national craft base (eg printing), by using those which have the equipment and expert staff (because they run Part II or advanced craft courses) but cannot attract sufficient face-to-face students to warrant submitting a programme for validation.

Maps 1, 2 and 3 illustrate the coverage available (at different radii) in electronics, fabrication and welding, and industrial measurement and control.

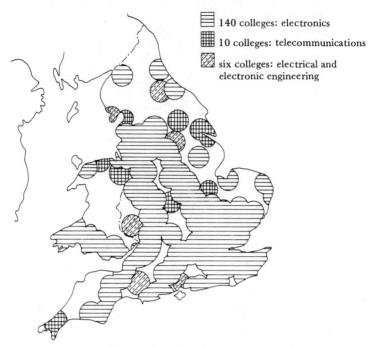

140 colleges: electronics

10 colleges: telecommunications

six colleges: electrical and electronic engineering

**Map 1.** *Electronics: 15-mile radius*

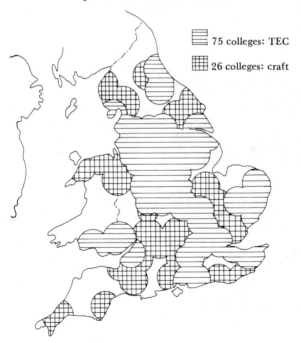

75 colleges: TEC

26 colleges: craft

**Map 2.** *Fabrication and Welding: 20-mile radius*

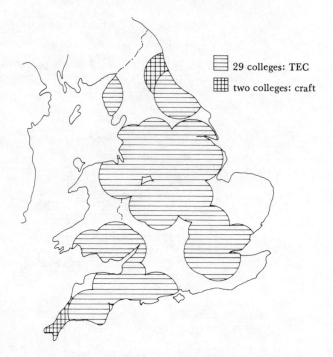

29 colleges: TEC

two colleges: craft

**Map 3.** *Industrial measurement and control: 30-mile radius*

## Pilot Studies

Pilot studies in these subjects are now taking place with some 18 colleges to test the theory and to identify any difficulties which might arise in implementing a system. These studies include a number of organizational issues for individual colleges, the implications of the potential national coverage in each subject, the nature of local demand, the availability of learning and assessment material, the extent and nature of the two-way communication required, and the 'hands-on' requirements and possible means of meeting them.

The colleges undertaking the pilot studies have been asked to tackle the planning of distance learning provision as a real, rather than a theoretical, exercise, leading to the introduction of distance learning in those subjects (and perhaps others if the colleges so wish) in the Session 1982/83. The view of Guildford Education Services is that real planning has to be undertaken in specified subjects by those who will have to implement provision, in order to identify the real issues to be tackled in introducing a national system, and to discover which are the difficult, time-consuming ones and which are those to which solutions are readily available. Colleges will be proceeding at their own pace, and in their own way, and indeed that pace and methodology are part of the reality. Feedback will take place during this coming summer, and we expect to learn as much from colleges which have difficulties with problems as from those which find the going easy.

## References

Hansard (1980) *House of Commons Official Report*, **994**, 5. 26 November.
Spencer, D C (1980) *Thinking About Open Learning Systems*. Council for Educational Technology, London.

Technician Education Council (1980) *Supplement to Guidance Notes* 8. TEC, London.

Twining, J P (1980) Preliminary survey of the educational effectiveness of the Post Office Telecommunications Scheme. (Unpublished report.)

Twining, J P and Ward, C M (1980) Distance learning for technicians. In Winterburn, R and Evans, L (eds) *Aspects of Educational Technology* XIV. Kogan Page, London.

Ward, C M and Twining, J P (1980) Distance learning for TEC: pacing and assessment aspects. In Winterburn, R and Evans, L (eds) *Aspects of Educational Technology* XIV. Kogan Page, London.

## Acknowledgements

The tables and maps are reproduced by kind permission of the Manpower Services Commission.

# 1.3.3 A New Development in Distance Teaching – The Cranfield Management Resource

M Cameron, A Fields, S H Kennedy and G S C Wills
*Cranfield School of Management, Bedford*

Abstract: The specific aim of the Cranfield Management Resource is to enable company trainers to provide company-specific courses on management subjects from a basic core of information provided by Cranfield School of Management. In a nutshell, Cranfield is offering the subject matter of its courses, combined with tuitional guidance to enable a trainer to produce his own adaptation of the material, including the expertise of his company management, to provide a course suited to the needs of his own company.

## The Concept

Cranfield School of Management has produced a development in the concept of distance teaching called the Cranfield Management Resource. This allows industrial trainers to devise programmes which offer the benefits of business school teaching methods as well as in-company training expertise and facilities.

The target market of the Cranfield Management Resource is the company trainer who wishes to present management training programmes which encourage participants to observe and analyze their own organization's situation. This kind of in-company training is felt by many training managers to be more suitable for most junior and middle management than attendance at public programmes at business schools.

In providing material which forms the basis of company-specific training, a number of teaching features which differ from those of conventional distance teaching have been introduced in the Resource. These features are:

☐ The teaching material has been prepared by Cranfield School of Management for use by the tutor who is training the student.

☐ The training course is designed to be presented by a tutor to a group of students who are working together.

☐ Tutor and student are encouraged to compare the course material with their own organization's situation and constantly to relate theory to practice. Tutors are encouraged to use in-company subject matter experts to lead sessions where specialist knowledge is particularly helpful.

☐ The teaching material can provide courses covering the needs of very different groups of students.

☐ There is two-way communication between tutor and student and between Cranfield faculty and the tutor.

☐ The course material contains both items written for direct assimilation by the student (the text and case studies) and for the tutor's use (the teaching notes contained in the tutor's guide).

In short, in the Cranfield Management Resource, Cranfield offers the subject matter of its management courses, combined with tutorial guidance, to enable a company trainer to provide a variety of programmes suited to the particular needs of different groups within his or her own company.

The training resources themselves (which are eventually to be built up within the Cranfield Management Resource as a Library of Resources) will constitute development materials for all the major management topics. The prototype Resource, described in this paper, is 'Effective Marketing Management'.

## The Background

The concept of the Cranfield Management Resource developed from market research work carried out by Cranfield faculty into the problems and needs of industrial trainers. This research showed:

☐ Considerable consensus amongst training managers about the challenges encountered.
☐ Most training managers agreed that organizations would benefit from increased training.
☐ However, the shrinking training budgets made it impossible for trainers to send more prople to business schools on public programmes.
☐ Many trainers were reluctant to use public programmes because:
  (a) the timing of the programme was often inconvenient;
  (b) the emphasis of the programme was often inappropriate to the organization's requirements.
☐ In addition, there was a constant demand from senior management for company-specific training. It was felt that junior and middle management benefited from working with company-specific material. Public programmes were thought appropriate only for very senior managers, those requiring very specialist training, or for high-fliers who were being groomed for the most senior positions.
☐ The increased demand for in-company training increased the trainers' workload, but reduced budgets prevented trainers from recruiting staff to help them.
☐ In addition, many trainers disliked presenting specialist programmes outside their own area of expertise.
☐ Many trainers wished to have training material which enhanced and complemented their role — to receive help in unfamiliar areas but also to be assisted in making full use of their teaching expertise.
☐ These research findings led to work on the Cranfield Management Resource.

## Why is 'Effective Marketing Management' Called a Resource?

The main difference between the Resource and conventional distance teaching concerns the *flexibility of use* designed into it. This flexibility arises from two major features:

☐ The variety of types of course that can be presented.
☐ How a particular course can be made to a greater or lesser degree company-specific by a particular company trainer, by using specialist tutors, project work, in-company case studies and application questions.

**The Range of Courses**

☐ Using 'Effective Marketing Management', a wide variety of courses can be taught to specialist and non-specialist managers. Course durations range from one-and-a-half to 60 hours. Course types range from appreciation level to in-depth studies of particular aspects of marketing.

☐ Both training managers and specialist managers can teach on training programmes developed from the Resource. Often, participants will derive the greatest benefit if both types of manager are involved in teaching.

☐ Tutors can select the combination of Resource components which are most suitable in meeting different training needs.

☐ Tutors can incorporate company-specific material into Resource programmes.

☐ Tutors can incorporate elements of the Resource into existing in-company training programmes.

**Using Specialist Tutors**

Specialist tutors will play a particularly important role in:

☐ Class discussions of the application questions in the text.
☐ Leading case study discussions.
☐ Developing company-specific case studies.
☐ Developing and supervising project work.
☐ Leading sessions with experienced marketing practitioners.

**Working with Cranfield**

Another distinctive feature of the Resource is that on-going discussion between trainer and Cranfield about the suitability of the teaching material is not only encouraged but expected.

Use of the Resource — and therefore membership of the Cranfield Management Resource — involves close collaboration between member organizations and Cranfield faculty.

Although it is not envisaged that Cranfield faculty will teach on the Resource programmes, the faculty will train tutors to use the Resource and provide assistance while the programmes are being designed and presented.

## What Does a Resource Contain?

The following description refers to the prototype Resource, 'Effective Marketing Management'. Future Resources may differ from this in the number and type of components involved.

The Resource provides two major types of inputs to fill a trainer's needs:

☐ Training materials of various types.
☐ Instructional advice explaining the alternative uses of the Resource.

The training materials consist of:

☐ *A text* (192 pages, 37 illustrations) specifically written for those wishing to learn about marketing in a practical business context. An overview is given of the different aspects of the marketing function. Examples from a wide range of organizations in the industrial, consumer and service sectors illustrate the concepts. The book is divided into seven units, each of which answers several important questions about a particular aspect of marketing. In all, 32 questions are posed and answered.

Application questions at the end of individual questions encourage readers to relate the concepts to the actual practice of their organizations. Tutors are shown how these application questions can be used to lead classroom discussion.

□ *Twenty case studies.* The case narratives have been selected from the case material used by Cranfield faculty in teaching marketing. For each of the seven units of the text, the case narratives illustrate key issues and offer a basis for structured classroom discussion. The real-life situations described have been encountered in a wide range of European organizations from the industrial, consumer and service sectors.

The case narratives are accompanied by detailed guides for tutors on their use in the classroom.

□ *Three colour video films* ('The role of marketing', 17 minutes; 'Marketing decisions', 23 minutes; 'Marketing planning and control', 11 minutes). The video films illustrate the internal and external situations encountered by three companies from different industrial sectors in their attempts to rationalize their marketing activities. The films both support the other components of the Resource and contribute a first-hand idea of the complexities involved in marketing decision-making.

Documentary synopses of the three films are provided so that tutors can use these situations as case studies.

□ *Seventy-one overhead transparencies.* Carefully designed to support the main teaching points of the text, case study discussions and films, the transparencies can be used in any length of type of teaching session.

□ *A two-volume tutor's guide.* This offers detailed teaching guides for individual teaching sessions based on the Resource. It assumes that the trainer understands the different elements of the Resource and the methods of combining them to meet specific training needs. How to include company-specific material into a programme is described in detail.

## Thorough Training for Tutors in the Nature and Use of the Resource

This includes:

□ *A two-day induction session* at Cranfield when the tutors are made familiar with the Resource contents and its various uses.

□ *A further three days' work within the tutors' own organization* — identifying the different training needs and how the Resource might meet these; discussing how company-specific material might most effectively be accommodated within the Resource.

## A Comparison of the Teaching Model of the Resource with the Conventional Distance Teaching Model

Holmberg (1981) lists 10 points through which he evaluates a conventional distance study system. They are:

1. The rationale of distance education.
2. The goals and objectives of study.
3. Target groups.
4. Contents and structure.
5. Organization and administration.
6. Choice of methods and media.
7. Two-way communication in distance study.
8. Course creation.

9. Evaluation.
10. Revision.

We now evaluate the Resource against these points to show the similarities with, and the differences from, the conventional distance teaching models.

1. *Rationale.* Holmberg (1981) shows that the characteristics of distance education which appeal primarily are:

   (a) 'the applicability of distance education to large groups of students as a kind of mass communication, particularly attractive at times when educational institutions are overburdened;
   (b) the possibility of improving the quality of instruction by assigning the best subject specialists and educationists available to produce courses for large groups of students;
   (c) the effectiveness of the method, proved by the students' acquisition of knowledge and skills;
   (d) the economy of the large-group approach and the facts that the need for residential teaching is eliminated or diminished and that study can take place during leisure time;
   (e) the possibilities for individualization of study pace and (to some extent) of study content;
   (f) the student's habit-forming experience of working on his or her own which is felt to develop independence and lead to greater autonomy than other types of study.'

Most of these characteristics interest company trainers — and the Resource exhibits most of them. The 'quality of instruction' characteristics will interest the company trainer, particularly if they are taken here to refer to the desirability of modifying the training material to reflect a particular company's situation.

2. *Goals and objectives.* The general goals and objectives of the Resource for the student do not differ from those for conventional distance teaching methods. Both seek to increase student subject knowledge, using the most appropriate educational techniques. For the trainer, the Resource provides flexible training material available immediately at an economic price per student, and usable at a date to suit the company's needs.

3. *Target groups.* The target customer identified by the market research is the company training manager who is dissatisfied with public courses and wishes to use company-specific material. The target consumer is the company executive for whom the training manager wishes to obtain training.

4. *Contents and structure.* The Resource contents follow the same principles of logical subject structure that conventional distance teaching does. The modular structure of the Resource enables a range of courses to be provided from one-and-a-half to 60 hours, using varying amounts of company-specific material.

5. *Organization and administration.* The detailed organization of the Resource material, pre-course administration, teaching the courses and the post-course evaluation are contained in the tutor's guide which parallels the organization and administrative procedure of conventional distance teaching.

6. *Choice of methods and media.* A wide choice of teaching methods and media is provided. The Resource can be used, for example, to develop programmes which make extensive use of the participative type of classroom sessions common at Cranfield. On the other hand, 'coaching' sessions can be developed in which a senior specialist manager instructs and trains small numbers of his line managers. In addition, the Resource can allow the learner to undertake a great deal of private study, only asking for tutorial help and

guidance when it is needed.

7. *Two-way communication.* Communication in the Resource is more complex than Peters (1973) suggests for conventional distance teaching. It covers two areas, between trainer and student in the company, and between trainer and Cranfield faculty for evaluation and support work. This is shown in Figure 1.

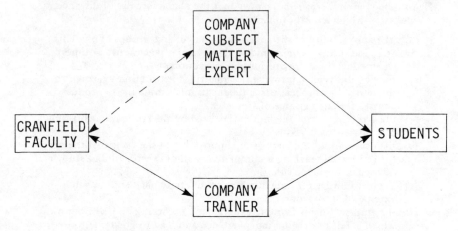

**Figure 1.** *The communication links of the Cranfield Management Resource*

The communications between the company trainer, company subject matter expert and students take place in a conventional instructional environment, and those between the company trainer and Cranfield faculty occur at the annual evaluation of the Resource or on an *ad hoc* basis.

8. *Course creation.* The material is not intended to be self-instructional. It follows the standard development procedures required to produce the student and tutor's material necessary for a teacher-student classroom instructional situation, and for material capable of being modularized into a number of alternative courses.

9. *Evaluation.* Evaluation procedures and their use are described in the tutor's guide and parallel those for conventional distance teaching.

10. *Revision.* The manner in which the method of presentation of the teaching material, the content of the material, and the communications between Cranfield faculty, tutor and students, is proceeding is reviewed as a formal mechanism at the annual meeting of users, together with the continuous evaluation of course teaching results with Cranfield.

The Resource therefore achieves most of the objectives of conventional distance teaching (for individualized instruction) identified by Kaye (1977) for face-to-face instruction.

'Systems . . . cover a wide spectrum of designs and functions. Most of them combine a relatively dispersed student population and a minimum reliance on (or a significant change in the role of) formal teaching with:

1. Concerning students
   (a) A degree of independence of the learner as to the pacing, timing and location of his study activities.
   (b) An enlargement of educational opportunity by providing new target populations with access to education.

2. Concerning learning materials and methods
   (a) A flexibility in the content and curriculum of the learning materials . . .
   (b) The provision of learning materials specifically designed for a self-instructional mode . . . and containing provision of feedback from students to learning system and vice versa.
   (c) The bringing together of learners and skilled people at a local level.
3. Concerning logistics and economics
   (a) Centralized production of learning materials.
   (b) Optimal use of available infrastructure.
   (c) Significantly lower recurrent cost per student.
   (d) More rapid time scale of implementation.'

## The Present and Future of the Resource

The concept of the Cranfield Management Resource represents a new development in management education and distance teaching. The prototype Resource is currently being launched on the market, and therefore no account of its performance in the hands of company trainers can be given. The material on which 'Effective Marketing Management' is based has been proven over a number of years on Cranfield courses, and therefore Cranfield faculty are reasonably confident that it will succeed in the new environment. The Resource is aimed at a known gap in the product market, and this gap also shows potential demand for courses of this type on other management topics. Cranfield therefore intends to follow this marketing prototype with other Resources in other management areas.

## References

Kaye, A R (1977) The Open University's developing role in international collaboration. *Educational Broadcasting International,* pp 98-100. June.
Holmberg, B (1981) *Status and Trends of Distance Education.* Kogan Page, London.
Peters, O (1973) Die Didaktische Struktur des Fernunterrichts. Untersuchungen zu Einer Industrialisierten Form des Lehrens und Lehrers. PhD thesis, University of Tubingen.

# 1.3.4 The Relational Glossary: A Tool for Effective Distance Learning

R S Zimmer
*The Open University*

Abstract: When a subject has a rich and intricately connected conceptual structure, students all too easily get lost and confused while trying to learn it — no matter how good its presentation. When the subject is taught at a distance, this problem is greatly exacerbated. There is no one the student can turn to immediately for help.

This case study describes how this problem was anticipated and tackled during the design of an Open University third-level course on relativity and cosmology ('Understanding Space and Time'). The strategy adopted was to try to enable any student to trace and put right, by himself, his own inevitable non-apprehensions and misapprehensions of parts of the subject, once he had noticed these by becoming 'stuck' in his learning.

As a means to this end, a device was developed to display, with extreme linguistic precision, all the logical interrelationships that the course writers could think of in the subject's conceptual structure, and the format of the device was designed to permit both random and logical access. The device was christened a 'relational glossary', and each student received a printed copy as an integral part of the course.

Follow-up evaluation showed that students found it extremely useful not only for getting 'unstuck' but also for general reviewing. In addition, the course writers themselves reported it to be very helpful for clarifying their own thinking and for co-ordinating their contributions to the course.

## Theory: What a Relational Glossary Is

According to Gordon Pask (Pask, 1975), a topic which is understandable and capable of being remembered is distinguished by two properties of the relations that make it up: they are consistent, and they are cyclic. A third property helps as well: he calls it 'cognitive glue'. I shall define these properties shortly.

Pask has developed a way of interrogating a subject-matter expert and recording his responses, so that the expert's topic, as expressed, acquires these properties. (Usually it does *not* already have them.) The topic as expressed is then in a very good state, structurally speaking, for someone else — a student, say — to try to learn it. Pask does this job with an enormous amount of help from a computer which his group has developed. Most people therefore cannot do the job as he does it.

In this paper, I shall discuss a way of doing the Paskian job with a subject-matter expert *without* recourse to a computer. Of course, the job then is not done as thoroughly as Pask can do it. But it is done *well enough* to give students help they appreciate, to find their way around complex topics on their own. This method for doing the job was developed by myself, in collaboration with members of a course-writing team at the Open University, during production of a third-level science course called 'Understanding Space and Time'.

To begin doing the Paskian job without a computer, one has to have a way to represent the relational structure of *any* topic with pencil and paper, no matter what is *in* the topic. Moreover, this method of representation must be capable of displaying the three properties of consistency, cyclicity and 'cognitive glue' whenever these properties are present in the relational structure of the topic, so that one is alerted when they are *not* present.

Before anything further can be said about this kind of representation, these three properties should now be defined.

☐ *Consistency*. Once one has named a concept in the topic, one never gives it another name, and one never uses its name for any other concept in the topic.
☐ *Cyclicity*. One can explain any named concept in the topic in terms of other named concepts in the topic, without recourse to concepts *outside* the topic (except for those in the 'everyday language' of the learner).
☐ *'Cognitive glue'*. A thorough explanation of any concept in the topic presents *several* aspects of its meaning, in terms of *several* other concepts in the topic. That is, the topic has a high degree of internal 'connectivity'.

Henceforth, I shall refer to 'cognitive glue' by the more technical name of 'connectivity'.

These three definitions create a need for three supporting ones. First, all three refer to something called a 'topic', which I shall define simply as an agglomeration of concepts that are meant to be coherently interconnected.

Second, all three refer to something called a 'concept', which I shall define, purely operationally, as anything that one can name as a noun.

Third, the definitions of cyclicity and connectivity also refer to something called an 'explanation', which I shall define (again purely operationally) as one or more sentences (or paragraphs) in which the name of the concept being explained appears as the grammatical subject.

It must be said that the first three definitions above, of consistency, cyclicity and connectivity, are very free paraphrases of Pask's own definitions. And the three supporting definitions, of topic, concept, and explanation, depart from his lines of thinking altogether — but with an immediate practical pay-off, since they create in themselves the basic format for a relational glossary, ie:

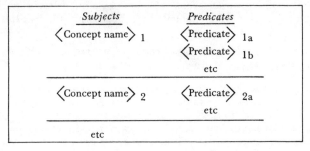

A page from an actual relational glossary displaying this structure is reproduced in Figure 1.

| TERM | RELATIONSHIPS | UNIT | SECTION |
|---|---|---|---|
| **SYNCHRONIZED CLOCKS** at rest in any particular **inertial frame of reference** | can be thought of as all running at the same rate and reading the same **instant** in **time** no matter where they are. That is, they would all appear to read exactly the same instant in time for a hypothetical, *non-physical* being who could stand next to each and every clock at one and the same instant (i.e. who could be everywhere at once!). They are therefore exactly the same in concept *both* in Newtonian mechanics and in **Einstein's special theory of relativity**, *provided that* one thinks about them only within a *single* chosen inertial frame of reference. | | |
| | in **Einstein's special theory of relativity**, will *not* appear to be synchronized when observed by an **observing system** which is moving relative to the frame in which they are at rest. (See the **relativity of simultaneity**.) | 5 | 4.2 |
| | in Newtonian mechanics, are *assumed* to appear synchronized *regardless* of the frame of reference from which they are observed. | | |
| | in **Einstein's sepcial theory of relativity**, are embodied in a **space–time diagram** by the very *existence* of an x-axis or an x'-axis, i.e. by the fact that a straight line (the axis) can be used to represent the same measurable **instant** in **time** at all possible measurable **positions** in **space** within any one single inertial frame of reference $S(x, ct)$ or $S'(x', ct')$. | 5 7 | 7 4 |
| | can be set up, in **Einstein's special theory of relativity**, by a simple procedure which allows for the finite **speed of light** as it travels from one clock to another. This procedure makes use of the fact that the speed of light is always the same under all conditions within a given inertial frame of reference, i.e. is absolutely invariant. | 5 | 4.3 |
| | *presumably* can be obtained, in Newtonian mechanics, by a procedure which allows for the finite **speed of light** as it travels from one clock to another. This procedure would be complicated on account of the assumption that the speed of light would depend on the motion of the clocks with respect to the 'aether' and therefore also on the direction of propagation of light from one clock to another. | | |
| | in *both* **Einstein's special theory of relativity** and Newtonian mechanics, will actually appear *unsynchronized* at any given **instant** in **time**, to a *physical* data taker at rest at a *single* **position** in **space** in the given inertial frame. In both theories the **speed of light** is finite, and therefore the synchronized clocks will appear to him to read earlier and earlier instants in time, the farther away from him they are. | 5 | 6 |
| **A TEST CHARGE** | is a particle bearing a known *small* **charge** (usually called charge $q$) which is used to measure the **electric field** at a point in **space–time**. (The charge on it must be small so that its effects on the charge distributions or current distributions that give rise to the fields being measured can be considered negligible.) | 4 | 2.2 |
| The **THRESHOLD ENERGY** for a reaction | is the minimum **energy** required to start the reaction. This energy is usually supplied by the **relativistic energy** of an incoming particle. | 7 | 6.5 |

**Figure 1.** *A page from a relational glossary (copyright © 1980 The Open University)*

From the example in Figure 1, it can be seen that any definition of a concept is given in a relational glossary, just as it would be given in an ordinary glossary: usually it is flagged by the verb 'is'. But many other aspects of meaning also appear as part of its explanation, and these cannot be regarded as definitions. Instead, they set the concept into the context which is created by all its fellow concepts in the topic — all those concepts whose names appear in bold print in its explanation.

## Applications: What a Relational Glossary Can Do for Students, And How

For students who are *revising* a course, a relational glossary can provide all the information they need, in order to decide whether they have understood the topic thoroughly. All they have to do is to read through the glossary. If they find anything which they cannot understand, then they know that they have a gap to fill, and they can set about filling it using the glossary's auxiliary references to the course text.

Now consider students who have become *stuck* in trying to understand the topic from the course text. All they know for certain is that there is something that they have not understood. Beyond that, they may *feel* stuck because they cannot find an explanation that they think they want, or perhaps because they cannot even decide what explanation to look for at all. Or they may *be* stuck because the explanation they think they want is not actually the one they need — that is, they have misunderstood something without realizing it.

For a 'stuck' student, a relational glossary can provide the information he needs in order to decide what explanation he really does need, and then to find this explanation.

To use the glossary in this way, he has to take two steps. First, he must formulate a question whose answer he thinks will help him to get unstuck. Then, second, he has to look up in the glossary those concepts which he has mentioned in his question. At this point, either he finds the explanation he needs straightforward or he does not. If he does not, he begins working back and through the cross-referencing until he does. And he *will* find it, provided the topic has been made properly consistent, cyclic and well-connected in the glossary.

One might well then ask what happens if he finds an explanation which seems, judging by the cross-referencing, to point at the heart of his difficulty, yet which he cannot understand. If this does happen, although he is now stuck in reading the glossary itself, he now at least knows exactly what questions to ask of his tutor — so he is still ahead.

Later on, I shall discuss what a relational glossary can do for course-writers themselves as well as for students.

## Limitations: What a Relational Glossary Cannot Do for Students

There are, of course, limitations as to what can be expected of a relational glossary. I have just touched on the major one, namely that a student might find an explanation which he can see to be crucial yet which he cannot understand. He may understand all the concepts used in the explanation yet not grasp the way they are being put together, or (worse) he may be caught in a circle of definitions which use concepts he does not understand at all. Both of these phenomena are possible in theory, because a relational glossary is a *retrospective* instrument. It is the subject-matter expert's completed and refined representation of his topic to *himself.* So it is written in language which assumes that a student already understands all of the concepts out of which any particular explanation is being constructed. Such language is no respecter of learning sequences.

Nevertheless, a student is unlikely to get caught in a circle of this kind in practice, *provided* that the topic *has* been made highly cyclic and connected in the glossary — an extremely demanding task for the subject-matter expert. When this has been achieved, the topic looks like a finely-woven 'string bag', to use Pask's own analogy, and so there is generally a large number of ways out of any definitional circle which the glossary may contain.

The retrospective nature of the glossary does, however, impose a limitation that cannot be avoided, namely that a student cannot easily use it to explore material that he has not yet encountered in the course text. And there is, of course, the further limitation that the glossary can only *explain* concepts. It cannot give a student practice in using them — except for using one concept to explain another.

## Construction: Standards, Time and Effort

To make one of these glossaries on a topic requires a significant investment of time and effort. One course unit author with whom I worked said that he considered the time and effort required for the job increased by 25 per cent. And that was in a subject area — physics — which is devoted to clarity and precision to begin with. The major difficulty is always to find ways to express relationships simply and clearly — very often relationships that were not thought through, or perhaps not even noticed at all, before the task of making the glossary was begun. In Figure 1, the first, third and sixth relationships are examples of these: they have no auxiliary references to the course text. The first, in fact, is the ordinary language definition of the concept being explained — 'synchronized clocks'. In the course text, only a mathematical definition is given, which is much harder to understand.

One particular feature of the clarity of thinking which is required to construct one of these glossaries is exemplified in the left-hand column in Figure 1, in the subject phrase for the term 'synchronized clocks'. Often a concept cannot even be talked about at all, much less explained, unless it is embedded in a particular context. Figure 1 shows that the concept of 'synchronized clocks' cannot even be discussed unless the clocks are all considered to be at rest within a single 'inertial frame of reference'.

A secondary but still significant difficulty in constructing one of these glossaries is proof-reading. It is much more complex than the proof-reading of ordinary text and requires many more readings through the material. Errors invariably slip through (eg line 15, Figure 1).

Perhaps the biggest question of all in constructing one of these glossaries is: How does one know when the job is done? This question has a very complicated theoretical answer, but in practical terms the answer is simple: the job is done when the subject-matter expert's topic has become *clear* to the interrogator-analyst. All that talk about consistency, cyclicity and connectivity is just an operational way of saying that the topic is clear — clear enough to become a single coherent pattern in itself. Once this has happened for the interrogator-analyst, there is nothing further he can do. He *has* no further questions. It helps, therefore, if the interrogator-analyst is *not* a subject-matter expert to begin with, so that by the time he stops asking questions, the topic is likely to have acquired clarity for students as well as for himself.

## Pay-Offs

Because of the extreme clarity that the exercise of making a relational glossary gives to a topic, I think that the major pay-off of the extra time and effort it takes is simply easier learning for the student. I am willing to wager that a relational glossary reduces a student's learning time and effort on a topic by at least the same amount that it increases these for a course writer. However, I cannot prove this.

| *For the purpose of* | | *Of these* | *and similarly* | *More importantly* | *and similarly* |
|---|---|---|---|---|---|
| | of the students turned to the relational glossary for help | rated the help they received *at least as satisfactory* | considered it to be *at least as good* as any help they received from any other source | rated the help they received as *good* or *excellent* | considered it to be *better* or *far better* than any help they received from any other source |
| (a) getting unstuck from a learning difficulty along the way (usually 3-4 times per Block) | 54% | 85% | 88% | 58% well over half | 56% well over half |
| (b) reviewing and consolidating along the way (usually 4-6 times per Block) | 67% | 91% | — | 71% well over two-thirds | — |
| (c) final revision for the examination | 85% | 80% | — | 49% nearly half | — |

(a)(b) **Sample:** 282 students (of 406 who went on to sit the examination) who responded to a questionnaire about the relational glossary for a Block they had just finished studying. (The course was made up of six Block topics, with a relational glossary of about 80 concepts for each of the first five.)

(b) **Sample:** 262 students (of 406 who sat the examination) who responded to a post-examination questionnaire about all five of the course's relational glossaries taken together as a final revision aid.

**Table 1.** *Summary of results from questionnaire*

What *can* be demonstrated, however, is that almost all the students who finished the course 'Understanding Space and Time' and who turned to its relational glossaries for help in learning along the way, rated the help they recieved at least as satisfactory. Most in fact rated it good or excellent. In addition, the use of the glossaries as aids in final revision before the examination was rated good or excellent by nearly as many.

The evidence comes from an evaluation which I carried out by questionnaire, in collaboration with the Open University's Survey Research Department. The results are summarized in Table 1, which can be read as a continuation of this text.

In addition to these encouraging results, nearly two-thirds (64 per cent) of the students who referred to the glossaries said they considered them to be an *essential* part of the course, and 80 per cent thought such glossaries would have been helpful to them on other Open University courses they had taken.

## Conclusions

The major conclusion that can be drawn from this evaluation is that the students regarded the relational glossaries as very useful aids for learning and revision.

But students were not alone in appreciating them; the subject-matter experts did themselves. Several, on two separate course-writing teams, reported to me that the glossaries — and the exercise of constructing them — increased their course-writing efficiency in one or more of three ways. First, the exercise imposed a very strict intellectual discipline on each course writer individually, and if the glossary was constructed before writing began, the writing itself was then found to be easier. Second, if the course writers acted as interrogator-analysts for one another, they learned one another's languages and sorted out differences in their thinking right from the beginning, differences which otherwise would have lain hidden and plagued their course-writing efforts as a team for months to come. Third, once constructed, the glossaries provided a concise and easily accessible record of *exactly* what material each author was covering, so that all the authors together could co-ordinate their efforts efficiently.

So it appears that not only are relational glossaries a boon to students, but they also actually pay back to course writers themselves, in terms of enhanced clarity of thinking and ease of writing, all the time and effort that is required to produce them. Everyone gets a pay-off: both the students and the course writers.

## Reference

Pask, G (1975) *Conversation, Cognition and Learning.* Elsevier, Amsterdam.

## Acknowledgements

I wish to express my thanks to Peter Davey of the Survey Research Department (Institute of Educational Technology, The Open University) for his help in preparation of questionnaires, to Professor Brian Lewis for many discussions which led to this work, and to The Open University for kind permission to reproduce material from the course S354: 'Understanding Space and Time'.

# 1.4 Educational Technology Courses at a Distance

## 1.4.1 Teaching Educational Technology at a Distance

**G Manwaring**
*Dundee College of Education*

**Abstract:** This paper describes a course in educational technology taught at a distance. From the students' point of view, the course has four main aspects: (i) wallets of study materials; (ii) intensive college blocks; (iii) a tutorial system; and (iv) assessment.

General comments are made about distance education as a mode of instruction. These include the needs of distant students, activities of the staff involved, the format of study materials, tutoring/counselling, assessment, and evaluation. Some typical problems occurring as a result of this type of course are considered.

## Introduction

I remember a paper about individualized learning on 15 reasons *not* to use the Keller Plan (Green, 1972). Many of these can be transferred to distance education. Thus, do not consider running a course at a distance if:

- ☐ You have a large number of students, no help, and no time to prepare materials.
- ☐ Your institution requires you to lecture face-to-face.
- ☐ You cannot specify objectives for your course.
- ☐ You do not have the energy!

However, there are three good reasons to use distance learning methods:

- ☐ It may be the only way some students can receive training or education.
- ☐ It may be the preferred and chosen way for some students to learn.
- ☐ In the current financial climate, it may be the only way for an institution to get students.

It was these three reasons that led us to turn our existing one-year full-time course in educational technology into a distance learning version. A pre-course survey indicated there was a demand for such a course and told us how much time per week a student would be prepared to spend studying.

This paper will give a case study of that course and also make general comments about the implications of distance education.

## Needs of Distant Students

The obvious way to start planning a course in distance learning is to consider the needs of the potential students. These are likely to include those listed in Figure 1.

## Staff Activities for Distance Learning

In a distance learning course, the academic staff will have many tasks to do. Some of these may require special help or training. The major activities are listed in Figure 2. Different activities may be carried out by different members of staff, or the same people may do them all.

1. self-paced flexible course
   — student's career and family take priority over studies

2. relevant and meaningful content
   — mature students want to see the application of their course

3. clarity of instructions

4. interaction and feedback within study units
   — active learning is essential

5. tutoring/counselling
   — help, advice and encouragement

6. rapid turn-round
   — assignments should be marked and queries answered immediately

7. study advice

8. peer contact
   — someone to talk to

9. facilities, eg libraries, laboratories
   — use of those belonging to the institution nearest to a student

**Figure 1.** *Needs of distant students*

1. planning the course

2. writing/preparing the study materials

3. course administration

4. marking students' work

5. tutoring students (on course content, project work, etc)

6. Counselling students (on study advice; discussing problems; giving encouragement, etc)

7. monitoring and recording students' progress

8. revising study materials

9. running intensive face-to-face sessions (eg summer schools, local seminars)

10. course evaluation

**Figure 2.** *Staff activities for distance learning*

## Case Study of a Course

I now want to describe the advanced diploma course in Educational Technology by Distance Learning at Dundee College of Education. The course is designed for teachers, lecturers and trainers and it covers all aspects of educational technology such as evaluation, assessment, use of media, design of instructional materials, psychology, curriculum development, etc. The students receive wallets of study materials by post. These contain structured learning units in a variety of media. They are studied in the students' own time. The minimum length of the course is two years; the maximum is four years. Each student is allocated a general tutor who will help him throughout the course, though other tutors may also be involved at certain times. Twice a year an intensive study week is run in college. These are now optional but students are encouraged to attend and they find them very valuable. Assessment is by assignments and a project, which can all be completed at a distance and may be discussed with a tutor before submission.

When we decided to plan the course, we built in and allowed time for all the activities listed in Figure 2. We drastically underestimated the time that items 4, 5 and 6 would take. The time we spend writing detailed comments on students' work and discussing items with them over the phone is enormous. However, we are convinced that it is essential and that even a brief call just to say hello is important to keep a student going.

### Study Materials

The actual study materials are one of the key parts of the course. It was relatively easy for us to adapt existing individualized learning units and production procedures for distant study (Fyfe, 1981). The materials conform to a basic house style and normally contain the elements listed in Figure 3.

1. Identification
   - title and author
   - date, edition, reference number
   - publisher or source (and copyright statement)

2. Instructions
   - pre-entry requirements
   - approximate time required
   - contents list
   - instructions for use

3. Introductory aids
   - aims, objectives
   - pre-test
   - overview, summary of content
   - advance organizer (to set it in context)

4. Text of unit
   - style: informal, lots of examples
   - layout
   - emphasis
   - audio-visual elements

5. Interaction within unit
   - questions and answers
   - activities and comments
   - experiments and creative work

6. Summaries and review sections

7. References
   - reading
   - follow-up activities

8. Post-test
   - marked by student
   - identifies student's problems
   - helps author revise unit

Figure 3. *Parts of a study unit*

We have noticed some tendencies in writing distance units beyond our normal style for individualized units. We are careful to provide an advance organizer to set the scene and lead the student through the package. This may be written, on audio tape, or given face-to-face during a college block. We make it clear when there are links to other study units and other activities — past or future. We add more examples to explain a generalization and our style is more informal and conversational. The activities built in to the units are now broader and more relevant to the students' interests.

It may be true that all these aspects ought to apply to all good individualized units whether used at a distance or not. But it was when we were writing for distant students that we became particularly aware of these points.

## Tutoring

We are very conscious that distant learners may feel isolated and insecure, and we provide tutors to minimize these feelings. The tutor develops a friendly relationship with the student, giving encouragement yet telling a student clearly where he may be going wrong and making constructive suggestions.

It is important for the tutors to respond to students' needs quickly. An efficient course secretary can help here by answering administrative queries and reminding the tutors about unmarked work. Nothing is likely to dampen a student's enthusiasm more than to struggle with an assignment, send it in on time and then wait and wait. If it eventually comes back marked 'pass', the student may have already lost interest. If it comes back marked 'fail, please rewrite', the student may have to repeat much of the background work which is no longer fresh in his mind.

Distance tutoring is a new skill for many of us and excellent advice is now available (Lewis, 1981). The wording of a letter and the tone of voice over the phone can be crucial. Well-timed contact by the tutor can often persuade students to remain on the course in spite of severe difficulties (Lewis, 1980).

## College Blocks

Twice a year we run intensive sessions in college. These are organized rather like conferences, with a choice of activities at any one time. A list of typical sessions is given in Figure 4. For some students, the main advantage is to use the facilities or to work in a group event, for others it is the chance to talk to like-minded people. For all it seems to be a refreshing and stimulating part of the course.

---

1. practical work, eg audio-visual techniques

2. group activities, eg discussions, workshops, simulations

3. team work, eg television production

4. lectures, eg advance organizers; guest speakers

5. individual tutorials

6. use of facilities, eg library, laboratory

7. informal contact with staff and students

---

**Figure 4.** *College-based activities*

## Assessment and Evaluation

These two processes are very much part of the learning system and are built into the course. We use them to monitor the students and the course.

Study units contain some self-tests with answers provided. These allow the student to assess his own performance and understanding. Some open-ended post-tests may be sent to the college for marking. The student is under no obligation to complete post-tests. If he does, they will be used to help him but never to grade him. Post-test performance is also used to help authors revise the units. Course assignments must be completed and each is marked as pass or fail. If it is a pass, the work is still commented on. If it is a fail, the student is given appropriate help and guidance and eventually resubmits the assignment. Assessment occurs regularly throughout the course. This is important in maintaining motivation and keeping up the student work rate.

The items used for the purposes of assessment and evaluation are given in Figure 5. It will be apparent that some items serve more than one function, ie to teach the student, to grade the student, and to improve the course.

| Assessment | Evaluation |
|---|---|
| self-test in unit | post-test in unit |
| post-test in unit | unit evaluation form |
| draft course assignment | course assignment |
| course assignment | assignment evaluation form |
| project | feedback sheets on college-based activities |
| rate of work | rate of work |
| | comments and discussions |
| | committees |
| | end-of-course questionnaire |

Figure 5. *Items used in assessment and evaluation*

## Problems

There are a few problems — as yet unsolved — that have developed in our course which may easily occur in other courses taught at a distance.

### Selection of Students

Each year so far we have been in the fortunate position of having more applicants than places available and thus having to select. What criteria should we use? Applicants should 'normally' have a degree or equivalent. If applicants do not have such a qualification we give them an entry test preceded by a study unit. If they pass the test we regard them as being on a par with those who have the standard qualifications. Then the most important factor is motivation and staying power. Up to now we have used personal references, interviews both by phone and face-to-face, previous history, knowledge of their institution, age, qualifications, career prospects, etc, and none has been a successful predictor. We seem able to select those who are intellectually capable of completing the course but to have no way of predicting those who will actually do so.

### Authenticity

We decided (rightly, I believe) to avoid formal examinations and to assess the students by more realistic assignments which were mostly carried out at a distance. This leads to the problem of never being sure if that student did the work. [I hasten to point out that similar problems are known to exist in traditional examination systems!] Many of the assignments on our course are likely to be better (and more relevant if we are training them for life) if the students discuss them with their colleagues or their tutor. However, it is still ultimately the student who decides which advice to take.

### Relevance

We try to make our assignments useful to the student, and not just to set pieces of work. For instance, if we ask him to design a course, make a tape-slide programme, or plan an assessment instrument, we would hope that these would actually be used. However, sometimes there is a conflict between the demands of the course and the needs of the student or his institution. For instance, a college may resent a student wishing to evaluate any of its teaching, although we may require such an activity.

### Student Deadlines

One often has two conflicting desires in distance education: to allow students a flexible timetable; and to ensure that they do complete the course. If we impose deadlines for the submission of work to persuade students to work regularly, should we penalize them for failing to meet them? My feeling is we should encourage students to meet deadlines, but if they do not have the time they should be allowed an extension. This, however, means that the deadlines cease to have any power.

## Conclusion

I think the distance learning mode, along with other open learning systems, has much to recommend it. But to run a course by these methods is a decision not to be taken lightly. If an institution desires such developments, it should show appropriate support. In particular, the following three items are needed:

(a) *Time.* Staff need appropriate time allowances to write study materials and to tutor distant learners.
(b) *Money.* Some money (though not necessarily a great deal) will be needed to provide certain essential resources, for example production and duplication of learning materials, postage and telephone costs, good secretarial support, etc. But overall there may be savings on staffing and accommodation costs, and in the end distance learning may be cheaper than conventional education.
(c) *Help.* Staff may need seminars, courses or consultancies to train them in new teaching/learning strategies.

But it is not all bad news. Materials written for distant study can be used for college-based courses. Staff development may show dividends in traditional teaching too. Greater collaboration between institutions and between teachers may occur. Both staff and students may find the new approach stimulating and enjoyable.

## References

Fyfe, W (1981) The production and evaluation of materials for a distance learning course. In Percival, F and Ellington, H I (eds) *Aspects of Educational Technology* XV. Kogan Page, London.
Green, B A (1972) *Fifteen Reasons Not to Use the Keller Plan.* In Education Research Centre, Massachusetts Institute of Technology.

Lewis, R (1980) *Counselling in Open Learning.* National Extension College Reports, London.
Lewis, R (1981) *Broadsheets on Tutoring at a Distance.* Council for Educational Technology, London.

# 1.4.2 The Production and Evaluation of Materials for a Distance Learning Course

W Fyfe
*Dundee College of Education*

Abstract: This paper is concerned with the staffing and procedures required to produce and evaluate the materials used on the distance learning version of the Dundee College of Education's Diploma in Educational Technology.

## Individualized Learning at Dundee College of Education

Dundee College of Education was specially funded in 1972 for individualized learning. The Learning Resources Department, which was set up as a result, was given the task of producing sufficient individualized learning materials to cover the equivalent of 20 per cent of the full-time students' timetable. This meant working with the college teaching departments and the establishment of production procedures to meet their needs.

### The Form of Individual Learning Units

All units which we have produced have one common denominator, namely printed materials, usually a booklet but in some cases an information leaflet or instructions card. The text is composed rather than typed, since we believe that the presentation of individualized learning materials should be at the highest possible standard, given the constraints of the institution.

In the better versions of face-to-face teaching, stimulus variation is used to keep learners motivated. As well as using a variety of media, we attempt to do this in individualized learning by providing a number of activities or questions requiring response from the students — hence the term 'response booklet' for our printed materials.

The final major component is the post-test which is used entirely in a formative sense, its prime functions being the provision of feedback to the student in his progress towards achievement of the unit objectives, and feedback to the author on the effectiveness of the unit.

(Other media employed include audio-tapes, slides and video-tapes, although nearly one-half of the units involve printed materials only.)

### Evolution of Production Procedures for Learning Units to be Used by Full-Time Students

Between 1972 and 1974, we identified about 70 different sub-stages which could be involved in the production of learning materials, although no single unit required quite that number! Analysis of these sub-stages revealed three major stages: namely:

1. Discussion/script production/editing (ie planning).

2. Preparation of the dummy unit (ie unit in physical form but still a 'draft').

3. Final production.

1. *Discussion/script production/editing.* This stage is almost entirely the concern of the author and the producer/editor who is a member of the Learning Resources Department. The author provides the basic idea and is responsible for shaping the materials, eg clarification of objectives, suggestions regarding question and answer sequences, or advice regarding media.

2. *Preparation of the dummy unit.* The balance of control at this stage moves away from the author towards the producer/editor, but the bulk of the work is carried out by the sub-editor and technicians in the Learning Resources Department.

The route followed by a particular learning unit will depend on the media involved, but for every unit the sub-editor produces a dummy response booklet. Sub-stages can include the preparation of artwork slides, textual slides, 'real-life' photography, recording and editing sound commentaries, and the production of video-tapes.

3. *Final production.* During this stage the main concern is the setting and printing of the response booklet but multiple copies are also made of slides, audio-cassettes and/or video-cassettes where appropriate. Control lies here with the sub-editor and the production manager.

Although this stage is described as 'final production' it is only final in the sense that it is the last of the three production stages. The unit has still to be used by the students and, following this use, has to be evaluated by the author. In practice, not all authors have returned to the Learning Resources Department, following the use of a unit, for the production of a revised version. This can be for one of three reasons:

(a) The unit has already been tried out before it is passed for 'first' production to the Learning Resources Department.

(b) The unit has attained its goals.

(c) The unit has not been evaluated by the author.

This was the current practice in 1977, on which was based the production of some 60 distance learning units for a course which was due to begin on 1 January 1978.

## First Decisions Regarding Distance Learning Materials

Six decisions were made which would influence the forms of the materials:

1. Materials should be attractively presented.
2. They should involve active learning.
3. Teaching should be as personal as possible.
4. The functions of different types of material should be clear, eg course information, teaching materials, course assessment.
5. Media input should be simple.
6. Each unit should represent about three hours to three-and-a-half hours of work.

The first three decisions were related to the need to keep students motivated when they were isolated from their tutors and from their fellow students. The need for the fourth arose because we envisaged a mass of paper descending on the unfortunate student who required some means for sorting it out and filing it. The availability of equipment, the problems of compatibility of materials and equipment, and the cost of production and postage made the fifth decision inevitable. A survey of potential distance learning students confirmed this view and at the same time provided the data which related to the final, sixth, decision.

## The Production of Distance Learning Materials

An attractive wallet was designed to contain all the items in a given unit. For the first intake of students, each of the 60 or so units in the course had its own wallet. As far as its contents were concerned the first question was 'Can we make use of any of the existing college materials or are additions or amendments required?' The college materials met three of the criteria stated previously. They were well presented, they involved active learning and the teaching tended to be in the first and second person rather than the third. However, we felt that this was insufficient and as a result an additional print component was born. This was christened the 'purple', this being the colour of paper it was printed on.

It was felt desirable to include this additional element to fulfil one or both of the following functions:

1. An overview or advance organizer for the materials in the unit.
2. A linking device relating the constituent parts of the unit together and/or pointing to its relationship with other materials in the course.

This element was printed on purple paper quite simply because we had over-purchased a supply of this colour! However, as it was such a striking colour it also served as a very useful signpost to the student saying: 'read this first'. Often these purples were quite short, eg one side of an A4 sheet of paper, but on occasion they were booklets of several pages. Colour was used more generally to aid identification, for example assignments were printed on red paper which seemed appropriate!

Students were expected to purchase a number of prescribed textbooks but if an author thought additional reading was necessary, we produced chapters or extracts from a number of unprescribed texts. We assumed that not all of our students would have ready access to libraries. Needless to say, copyright clearance was always sought first!

It was therefore comparatively easy to convert existing printed materials into distance learning materials by adding these supplements to college units. However, in a number of cases, the college units made use of media other than print and in others the materials did not yet exist.

Our decision to limit media input to the simpler forms meant that television was ruled out on the grounds of expense and the certain knowledge that we could not produce in the variety of formats which were likely to exist in the students' home institutions. The lack of compatibility also prevented us from producing *synchronized* tape-slide units which was a very popular format among the college units. The pre-course survey showed that all students were likely to possess, or have access to, an audio-cassette player and a filmstrip-slide viewer. Relevant college units which existed in television or tape-slide form were therefore converted to unsynchronized filmstrip and audio-cassette units. Where possible, the filmstrip frames were identical to the slides in the tape-slide units in order to save additional expense.

Completely new units were written to cover the gaps among the existing college units. This proved to be a double blessing. Every new distance learning unit meant new material for full-time college courses was also produced. Where a new filmstrip unit had to be produced for distance learning, the simultaneous production of a synchronized tape-slide unit for college use also took place.

In a few cases, rather than writing a completely new unit, the addition of a purple to material already in existence outside the college saved some time. If the external material was not completely relevant, it was an easy matter to inform the student, in the purple, to miss out the irrelevant sections.

**Practical Production Problems**

Production of the first units was begun about nine months before the course was due to start, and a production schedule drawn up with two dates for each unit, namely:

1. Manuscript deadline, ie the end of stage 1 of the existing production procedure.
2. Posting deadlines, ie the completion of all three stages.

'The best laid schemes of mice and men. . .' — despite the forward planning, quite a number of units only just met this schedule and on one occasion the course timetable had to be altered slightly when it became clear that a particular author was not going to deliver the goods on time.

For every author, including those from the Learning Resources Department, this was a part-time activity. It is therefore true to say that commitment to the course varied, with authors drawn from 11 different teaching departments whose first priorities very often lay elsewhere.

The overwhelming importance placed on these deadlines was justified. In traditional face-to-face teaching it is possible, although not desirable, for a tutor to start teaching less than totally prepared, or having prepared at the last minute. For distance learning, if the author has not produced the final draft well in advance of the posting date, the teaching may not take place at all. For this reason, distance learning materials, once designed, were given the highest priority possible within the production system.

The existence in Dundee College of Education of individualized learning materials, and the procedures for their production, meant that the conversion of a college-based course to a distance learning course was comparatively without trauma. Conversely, the need to produce materials for a distance learning course, helped to add to the Library Resource Centre stock of units to be used in college.

## Evaluation of Distance Learning Materials

The use of post-tests for the evaluation of materials was already part of the college system and this continued for distance learning materials. Other aids to evaluation included:

1. Informal feedback during in-college sessions.
2. The course co-ordinating committee which consisted of members of the course team and representatives of each student intake.
3. Unit evaluation forms which students were invited to send in. For the first intake of students, every wallet contained an evaluation form. For later intakes, students were given a supply of forms at the beginning of the course.
4. Meetings with the whole group at the end of each in-college session.
5. An overall questionnaire at the end of the course.

The evaluation revealed specific flaws in some of the units but usually the general form of the units was praised. Following the first intake's time on the course, two changes were made. We decided ourselves that it was not necessary to use one wallet for each unit (and it was certainly less expensive). Instead, each wallet contained a group of related units (as many as four or five), the purples acting as useful unit separators. A new standard layout was adopted for printed materials following student complaints that, for some units, there was just too much print per page. The students themselves selected the new style from six layouts which were less packed. The most popular style involved a narrowing of the printed area with a right-hand ruled margin.

The revision and production of new units for the second, third and fourth intakes required a similar schedule to that for the first intake, with one additional element. As our previous experience of college units had shown that not all authors would evaluate their own materials, we assigned a course tutor to each author to ensure that evaluation would take place. This also helped to make the deadline issue less of a problem!

## Three Evaluation Case Studies

Three unit evaluations are examined in more detail, the first of which was atypical but produced a result which may have a more general application. The other two evaluations of a 'good' unit and a 'bad' unit are treated comparatively.

### Media for Distance Learning?

One unit which consisted of two modified college tape-slide units was fairly universally criticized by the students on the grounds that the filmstrip was unnecessary. Apart from this flaw, it was regarded as a successful unit. The author was well aware that the photographic element was superfluous but had designed the original college units in tape-slide form because much of the content was mathematical. He felt that the inclusion of slides would motivate students, many of whom were not mathematically inclined. Used as synchronized tape-slide units in library carrels by full-time students, his hypothesis was confirmed. Why then were essentially the same units rejected by the part-time distance learning students?

The answer would appear to lie in the differing psychological 'sets' of the two populations. For the full-time student, regularly working in a well-equipped resource centre, using a carrel is almost second nature and there is the time to use it. A distance learning student who is studying part-time in the evenings, having just completed a day's work as a teacher or lecturer and probably being distracted by the television set next door, may have a more penetrating view of the learning materials which have arrived a week or two previously and which he really should be studying but that television programme does seem to be interesting . . .
It is also more difficult to use a filmstrip while travelling on public transport.

### Comparison of Two Units

This analysis compares two units, informal feedback relating to the first (unit A) suggested that this was one of the least acceptable.The response of the students to the second (unit B) suggested that it was among the best in the course.

The unit evaluation forms included student ratings for each of the units (see Table 1).

The two units could not be differentiated on dimensions 1, 2, 6 and 7. On each of these dimensions both units are at the preferred position.

In particular, the student view that both units had an appropriate number of activities provides some support for our view that distance learning should be active, since both had a large number of such items.

B's higher rating on the 'interest' and 'relevance' dimensions could have been due to its less theoretical slant. However, improvement along the 'explanation' dimension was required for A, and more specific student comments in response to other more open-ended questions in the evaluation form formed the basis of the revision.

Two general comments can be made:

1. Although the ratings for A were not entirely satisfactory, they were far

| | 1 | 2 | 3 | 4 | 5 | |
|---|---|---|---|---|---|---|
| 1. too short | | | A/B | | | too long |
| 2. too easy | | | A/B | | | too difficult |
| 3. badly explained | | | A | | B | clearly explained |
| 4. very boring | | | | A | B | very interesting |
| 5. totally irrelevant | | | | A | B | extremely relevant |
| 6. too few activities | | | A/B | | | too many activities |
| 7. too early in course | | | A/B | | | too late in course |

Table 1. *Position of median student for each unit*

from disastrous for a unit which was regarded as being one of the poorest on the course.

2. The overall student view of unit A, although mixed, tended to be on the positive side. This was somewhat better than the informal feedback had suggested, and sresses the importance of basing an evaluation on systematic data.

## Conclusion

Given the production base and the individualized learning materials which were already in existence in the college, the production of satisfactory distance learning materials, although time-consuming, was comparatively straightforward.

# 1.4.3 Academic Staff Development Through Distance Learning

L R B Elton
*University of Surrey*

Abstract: Over the past year, the Institute of Educational Technology at the University of Surrey has been developing a course for a Diploma in the Practice of Higher Education, to be taught by distance learning methods and aimed at academic staff at universities in South East Asia. In the attempt to achieve staff development through distance learning methods, this course is unique. This paper presents the rationale and genesis of the course, the methods employed in the writing of the course materials, first experiences of the course in operation including feedback from course members, and an outline of the methods to be employed to evaluate the course.

## Introduction

It may be perverse to suggest that academic staff development (an activity which might be expected to have a strong interpersonal element) may at times be more successfully carried out at a distance, but there are cogent arguments for this suggestion. Inevitably, any process of staff development puts staff into the role of learners, as is evidenced by the regularly occurring comment in post-course evaluations: 'It was interesting to be a student again'. But unlike those in other professions, such as doctors or industrial managers, who merely revert to an earlier student role, academics in staff development suffer a role reversal — from teachers to learners. Furthermore, the staff developers, who are normally their colleagues, temporarily become their teachers. This role change in staff developers is one of which they are very conscious and which they often find difficult to carry out.

It may be hypothesized that, in general, such role conflicts produce more stress, the closer those undergoing a staff development process are to the staff developers and the further they are from their own student days; also, that when they are actually substantially senior to the staff developers, the security which comes with the position of relative seniority may provide safe conditions for a temporary role reversal. All this has been observed in practice, although it would be difficult to provide conclusive evidence to verify the hypothesis since the very act of investigation is likely to accentuate the stresses.

It is reasonable to assume that these stresses are lessened by, and that the reduction in stress may compensate for, the absence of face-to-face contact. The present paper will describe early experiences with some attempts at staff development at a distance.

## Information By Post

This scheme, which started in 1978, is based on an idea originally due to Moss (1977) to send informational material on teaching and learning through the internal mail to academics who requested it. This 'information by post' scheme has proved popular and has by now been used by about two out of every five staff in the University of Surrey. It was started by sending a questionnaire to all academic staff in the University, inquiring what topics they might like to have information on. The topics requested were predominantly of the kind which are directly relevant to teaching. At present, the following titles are available:

1. On lecturing
2. Overhead projector
3. Assessment
4. Tape-slide programmes
5. Small group teaching
6. Multiple choice and short-answer questions
7. Computer-assisted learning
8. Essays
9. Laboratory work

How the material is being used is not easy to establish, particularly since there are indications that the privacy of receiving the materials in plain brown envelopes is one of the attractions of the scheme. Nevertheless, we are evaluating it at present and the first finding to emerge is that the materials are rarely referred to again, once they have been read, and that after some time recipients have only a very general memory of what they contain. If this finding is confirmed, then it would be desirable to add reinforcing features to the scheme, such as staff seminars based on individual titles. More ambitiously, perhaps, the information by post scheme should become available as a course which used distance teaching methods. I therefore now turn to our experiences with such courses.

## A Pilot Scheme for a Distance Learning Course

This scheme came about primarily for a very simple reason, ie that those taking part could not all be in the same place at the same time. I had been assisting, together with Dr Gaye Manwaring, in a staff development programme at the Universiti Sains Malaysia (Elton and Manwaring, 1981) and we wanted to provide continuity between two visits in summer 1978 and 1979 respectively. We did this by providing a short course on Individualized Learning, using distance learning methods, during the period March-July 1979. Improved versions of the course have since been used as part of on-campus courses on two occasions. The latter experience has confirmed to us the acceptability of the distance learning mode as part of on-campus staff development, while the original experience with Universiti Sains Malaysia mainly drew our attention to some of the logistic problems concerned with a course taught over a distance of 13,000 km.

## Diploma in the Practice of Higher Education

The experience of the course just described, together with that of the information by post scheme and of a Postgraduate Diploma course which had been taught face-to-face in this country (Gilbert and Cryer, 1979), encouraged us at Surrey to start a Diploma in the Practice of Higher Education, which used distance learning methods and was aimed in the first place at academic staff in South East Asia. The course started in October 1980 with 18 members, from all five of the ASEAN countries: Thailand, Malaysia, Singapore, Indonesia and the Philippines. We had hoped to be able to provide local tutors, but this has proved possible so far for only eight members, all of whom are from Thammasat University, Bangkok. This University, which was clearly committed to staff development, had previously sent two of its staff on a three-month course to us and one of these is now acting as tutor. The other 10 members come from nine different universities and enrolled on the course on their own initiative.

The production of the course materials has been, and still is, the responsibility of a course board, which consists of all those contributing to the course, with myself as editor. Materials are written by pairs of staff, so that one can always act as writer and the other as critic. These roles are shared as evenly as possible by each writing pair. Because we expected to learn a great deal about how best to present the materials after the course had started (and also because of time pressures) our production schedule was such that the first two modules were to be ready at the beginning of the course in October 1980, three further ones by February 1981, and the final four by June 1981. So far (February 1981) we have kept fairly closely to this schedule.

The course at present consists of the following modules:

|  Core: | Options: |
|---|---|
| (a)  Introduction to course | (a)  Communication and media |
| (b)  Teaching and learning methods | (b)  Individualized learning |
| (c)  Course design | (c)  Staff development |
| (d)  Assessment | (d)  Research in teaching and learning |
| (e)  Students and teachers | |

Course members must complete all core modules, at least one optional module, and a project.

By now we have received the first assignments from course members and are able to report on early experiences.

### Language

The course is conducted in English which, for most of the course members, is not the first language. This has not presented problems so far, but the fact that some members and their institutions are oriented more to Britain, and others more to the United States, is showing up conceptually, organizationally and culturally.

### Study Guides

However hard one tries to make these clear, some obscurities and errors only become apparent through feedback from course members. Thus, for instance, one member asked: 'What is the difference between purpose and aims?', when both had been used, but only the latter had been defined.

### Assignments

These should indicate understanding of what has been learned, and not mere knowledge of it. That students sometimes fail to do this, as is indicated for instance by the uncritical reproduction in the assignments of material from the study guides, may be at least in part due to the cultural tradition of Asia which tends to overvalue the mere possession of knowledge. It is interesting that course members, who are aware of this tradition and wish to change it in their students, may find it difficult to change it in themselves.

### Reading

We recognized that local libraries would not have appropriate books for the course and this has proved to be so. The study guides are accompanied by extended extracts from relevant books but, even so, it is to be hoped that the books will in due course become locally available. It may be noted that, so far, we have obtained all copyright permission for the extracts free of cost, and we are grateful to authors and publishers for their generosity. Naturally, the permission is restricted to reprinting within the course materials which are sent to members.

### Postal Delays

So far nothing has been lost, but transit times by airmail can vary from a few days to (the worst at present) eight weeks! As yet, we have not found any way to overcome this problem. Pigeon post, perhaps?

### Costing

Educational costing is a notorious minefield, as is well argued by Fielden and Pearson (1978) and by Mace (1978), but the balance of fixed costs proportional to student members is a comparatively safe part of it. While in the Open University this balance is about 3 : 1 (Wagner, 1977), our balance is almost exactly the other way round. The reason for this discrepancy is revealing. Compared to the OU, we spend a much lower proportion on the initial preparation of course materials, and expect to improve the materials very quickly in the light of feedback from the assignments of course members. We also use the assignments for continuous assessment and have no formal examinations. For both these reasons, all assignments are read, commented on and marked by the staff who have designed the course. While this is expensive, it is sensible for the small number of students on our course, while for large numbers, the OU procedure of using part-time tutors and computers is more appropriate.

## Conclusion

This article has presented a rational argument for the importance of distance learning as one of the methods to be used in academic staff development and has given an account of early experiences with this method. At this stage, it is not possible to provide more than a progress report, but this is appropriate for presentation at an international gathering where a presenter hopes to learn much from the reactions to his presentation, while the ventures presented are still at a formative stage.

I wish to end where I began. A number of staff from within the University of Surrey have by now seen the first of the course materials for the Diploma and have expressed both praise and interest. Perhaps this is an indication that staff development within an institution through an *on*-campus distance learning course might prove acceptable.

## References

Elton, L and Manwaring, G (1981) Training and education of teachers in higher education in developing countries. *Higher Education* **10, 5.**

Fielden, J and Pearson, P K (1978) *Costing Educational Practice.* Council for Educational Technology, London.

Gilbert, J K and Cryer, P (1979) CHS: a major development within the in-service training provision for higher education teachers in the United Kingdom. Conference of the European Association for Research and Development in Higher Education, Klagenfurt.

Mace, J (1978) Mythology in the making: is the Open University really cost-effective? *Higher Education* 7, pp 295-309.

Moss, D (1977) Staff development by post or 'the mountain to Mohammed'. *Impetus* 7, pp 26-9.

Wagner, L (1977) The economics of the Open University revisited. *Higher Education* **6,** pp 359-81.

## Acknowledgement

My thanks are due to Gaye Manwaring for help, encouragement, and sound advice.

# 1.5 Broadcasting

## 1.5.1 An Inter-College Research Project on School Broadcasting

**A McIntyre and R H Richardson**
*Jordanhill College of Education, Glasgow*

**Abstract:** This paper reports on the aims, methodology and results of a research project which is funded by the Scottish Education Department and involves researchers from all 10 Scottish colleges of education.

## Introduction

### The Research Personnel

The research project, begun in October 1978 and ended in April 1981, was investigating the use of school broadcasting in Scottish schools. Funded by the Scottish Education Department, the project was established by the National Inter College Committee on Educational Research (NICCER) and involved all 10 Scottish colleges of education (the first research project to do this). Each college had a representative on the steering committee and it was the college representatives who carried out the actual research in schools. They also participated in the design of the questionnaires and observations schedule used in the schools and in the analysis of findings.

In addition to the project director (R H Richardson), the chairman of the steering committee (M Roebuck, HMI) and the research assistant, the committee had various members who were there in an advisory capacity. They were the representatives of the broadcasting organizations (BBC, Scottish Television, Grampian Television), the Scottish Council for Educational Technology, and the Educational Television Association.

### The Structure, Aims and Methodology

The project was in three stages.

*Stage 1* attempted to identify the factors which inhibit or encourage broadcast use and the awareness teachers have of what broadcasts are available. To this end, 100 primary and 100 secondary schools in Scotland were selected, half of the sample selected being high users of broadcasting. A questionnaire (or *aide memoire*) was drawn up for use in these 200 schools and researchers visited the schools to interview members of staff: head teachers, assistant head teachers, principal teachers, class teachers, AV technicians or auxiliaries depending on which was appropriate.

The information in the 200 questionnaires was then tabulated to facilitate further analysis.

*Stage 2* had two aims:

1. to study the match between available broadcast materials and the school curriculum; and
2. to select teachers and schools where apparently worthwhile use of broadcasting was being made for further investigation in Stage 3.

This part of the project was carried out on a subject basis, with different colleges examining different aspects of the curriculum. Guidelines for discussion were drawn up for use by researchers in discussion with teachers. Practical difficulties forced the adoption of a variety of approaches: some meetings of groups of subject teachers were held; some researchers visited schools for individual interviews with teachers; in some cases questionnaires were sent to schools. Each of the researchers then wrote reports on the basis of their findings in each subject of the secondary curriculum and in each curricular area of the primary school.

*Stage 3* attempted to examine 'good use' of school broadcasts and further examine the context of this use. The pupils' responses to broadcasting were also investigated at this stage. The sample of schools at this stage was much smaller than at stages 1 and 2: 24 primary schools and 18 secondary schools.

A questionnaire, observation schedule and pupil-response questionnaire were drawn up for use in schools. Members of staff were interviewed, teachers were observed using broadcasts in the classroom, and pupils were asked questions about their attitude and response to school broadcasts.

## The Findings

The picture of broadcasting use revealed by this three-stage investigation is complex; a tapestry of interwoven factors involving the broadcast output itself, the knowledge and attitude of teacher-users, the organizational and pedagogical policies of head teachers and principal teachers, levels of equipment and design of buildings, the provision of auxiliaries and AV technicians, and the attitudes and responses of pupil-receivers. No single strand can reveal the whole picture, but an attempt will be made to examine a few of the principal threads which weave together to form the picture of broadcasting use in Scottish schools.

Broadly, there are three main aspects of our findings arising out of the different stages of the research, namely:

1. Factors facilitating the effective use of broadcasting.
2. Factors pertaining to the effective use of the broadcast within the classroom.
3. The pupils' response to broadcasting.

## Factors Facilitating the Effective Use of Broadcasting

These are the factors which *allow* effective use to be made of school broadcasts, principally the attitudes of school personnel, the facilities existing within schools, and the translation of these into an organizational structure.

### THE MATERIAL AND PHYSICAL RESOURCES OF THE SCHOOL

*Equipment*
Examining the secondary schools of our first stage sample (100 schools) reveals that the 10 schools which made the most frequent use of broadcasts were twice as well equipped with video recording equipment and colour television as the 10 schools which used fewest broadcasts.

When members of staff interviewed in the Stage 1 schools were asked to 'comment further about broadcasting' in their schools, in 19 of the primary schools and 24 of the secondary schools the desire to have video recording equipment was expressed. (In most of these secondary schools this wish was for additional equipment.)

### THE SCHOOL BUILDING AND ITS CONSTRAINTS

Schools on a split site, or with different levels, or with viewing rooms which also served other purposes (eg dining hall), presented problems for the use of broadcasting. The need to move classes some distance to a viewing room, or to share a viewing room with other classes, or to vacate a room immediately after viewing were not conductive to the use of broadcasts and, in the latter two cases, could also affect the quality of the use and its follow up.

### THE ROLE AND ATTITUDES OF SCHOOL PERSONNEL

*The Head Teacher*
In more than half the first stage sample of primary schools, the head teacher was considered to be in charge of broadcasting use. In 11 of these schools, the head teacher actually chose the programmes to be used by class teachers and in other cases vetted their choice. In a number of primary schools (15) the head teacher laid down specific guidelines about the maximum number of broadcasts to be used in a week with a class: this was most commonly two radio and two TV programmes per week. There was a clear link between the attitude of head teachers and the level of use of broadcasting. Among primary schools which used a lot of broadcasting, comments were often made about the head teacher's positive attitude: enthusiasm regarding broadcasting, conviction of its value, and encouragement of its proper use were all mentioned.

Of the 24 primary head teachers interviewed in Stage 3, two-thirds considered broadcasts sufficiently important to determine the timing of work in the course of the school year, and all believed that the curriculum benefited from the use of school broadcasts.

This contrasts with the secondary school where the head teacher, while setting cash limits on expenditure on broadcasting materials, generally delegated the responsibility for distribution of information to a deputy or assistant head teacher and left the principal teachers to make decisions about how much and in what way broadcasts should be used. These principal teachers, however, could profoundly influence the extent of use of broadcasts and their recognition as a valuable educational resource.

*The Class Teachers*
Through all stages of the project, 'teacher attitude' towards broadcasting emerges as a key factor in determining use. 'Knowledge' and 'enthusiasm' were frequently

mentioned, particularly in association with schools which used a lot of broadcasts. Attitude affected not only the amount of use but the quality of use and its educative effect on the pupils. One of the Stage 3 primary schools exemplified this, where a teacher 'inherited' a mathematics broadcast on taking over the class. She did not wish to use the broadcast and the success of its use was very limited. The same broadcast used by another teacher in the same school, but with enthusiasm which 'was transmitted to the class' was very much more successful, with the children 'gaining in knowledge and experience'.

A strong preference for TV over radio in both primary and secondary schools emerged. The exception to this was with broadcasts for primary schools in religious education, music and movement, and drama where strong 'series loyalty' was demonstrated. In secondary school modern language broadcasts, radio was more highly regarded as making a serious contribution to the subject than television. The ease of use and accessibility of radio (its general convenience) was noted in both primary and secondary schools, but teachers often said that pupils lacked the appropriate listening skills to capitalize on this. Perhaps this lack of skill was a reflection of teacher attitude and demonstrated a need for training of pupils in listening skills (some schools did take positive steps to do this).

A need clearly emerged for more training for teachers (pre-service and in-service) in the use of broadcasting, both in how to use the hardware and in how to make the best educational use of broadcast materials. The lack of provision of this in colleges of education pre-service courses was demonstrated in our preliminary investigation into the college use of broadcasting, and reinforced by the Stage 3 interviews with teachers. Two-thirds of these teachers had no training at all in the use of broadcasting. Those who had had formal training described it as 'very limited'.

*Auxiliaries and AV Technicians*
The use of broadcasting was greatly facilitated by the presence of an auxiliary in the primary school, or an AV technician in the secondary school. About half the primary schools in the Stage 1 sample had an auxiliary, and four-fifths of the secondary schools had a technician with responsibilities for broadcasting. The auxiliaries were principally responsible for recording radio broadcasts and the technicians responsible for recording and replaying TV broadcasts. In the secondary schools, where there was no technician with responsibilities for school broadcasting, broadcasting equipment was used less often and, when it was used, it was more apt to develop faults.

**Factors Pertaining to the Effective Use of Broadcasts**

INTEGRATION OF BROADCASTS INTO THE CURRICULUM
The reason most frequently given by the Stage 1 teachers (both primary and secondary) for using the broadcasts they did use was 'curriculum match', eg 'because programmes fit the syllabus', or 'because programmes fit the requirements of the curriculum'. Secondary teachers gave this reason seven times, while primary teachers gave it twice as frequently as any other reason.

In general it could be said that secondary teachers viewed broadcasting as a reinforcement, fitting itself round teachers' requirements, consolidating the existing syllabus. The secondary curriculum was not organized in the light of available broadcasts as was sometimes the case in primary schools, where broadcasts were often seen as a starting point, a springboard for an extensive centre of interest work.

PREPARATION, USE AND FOLLOW UP
We were concerned in the third stage of the research to observe the use of broadcasts

in the classroom and, particularly, to draw conclusions about what constituted 'effective' use. Asked what they considered good and effective use, teachers' responses revolved round the concepts of preparation by the teacher, preparation of the class, the viewing/listening conditions during use, and the generation of follow up activity.

*Preparation*

In practice, preparation by the teacher consisted of reading the teacher's notes, previewing (in secondary schools), and preparation of materials, eg worksheets and questions for discussion. Preparation of the class consisted of the recapitulation of previous programmes, an explanation of vocabulary where necessary, and the direction of pupils' attention to key points in the programme.

*Use*

In the *primary schools*, the TV broadcasts were taken live, due to lack of video recording equipment. In general, it was observed that pupils' attention to the TV broadcast was high. The radio broadcasts were usually recorded, and the facility of stopping and starting the tape mostly used. This was always the case with the 'music and movement' broadcasts, where intervention by the teacher was greatest. More mention was made of inattention among pupils with radio broadcasts, sometimes attributable to the poor quality of the recording.

In the *secondary schools*, all the use observed (both radio and TV) was of *recorded* broadcasts, and the stop/start facility was often used. This was the case with most modern language broadcasts, while English, maths and science broadcasts were more likely to be played through without interruption. The facility of replaying sections of the tape was rarely used: this was only found twice, once in modern languages and once in mathematics.

*Follow Up*

In the *primary schools*, the kind of follow up generated by broadcasts varied from the extensive, lengthy, centre of interest approach, embracing all aspects of the curriculum, to the brief discussion immediately after the broadcast.

In the *secondary schools*, discussion, completion of worksheets or blackboard questions, question and answer sessions covering the major ideas of the broadcast, all featured in the follow up observed.

Such generalizations about how the broadcasts were used do not convey the reality of some of the excellent and imaginative use observed. A more effective demonstration would be to see some actual examples which are available on video-tape.

**Pupil Response**

In general terms, pupils in the *primary schools* Stage 3 sample enjoyed watching television in schools, considered that programmes helped them learn, liked it when the teacher prepared them before the programme, and enjoyed follow up work. To quote the children themselves:

1. With regard to help in learning things: 'you are shown, not just told'; 'teaches you songs and gives you ideas for dressing up'.
2. With regard to preparation by the teacher: 'teacher helps you to understand what the programme is about'.
3. With regard to follow up activities, where younger children put more emphasis on drawing than writing or discussion: 'you get to do good things afterwards'; 'drawing, talking, puzzles, making things, thinking how it would be'.

One young child, however, deplored the fact that in spite of the post-programme art work, his drawing had not improved. Hard to categorize was the response of the infant who complained that he did not get to see 'Wonder Woman'!

With *secondary* pupils it was also found that they enjoyed radio and television programmes in school. Given the opportunity, they would like to listen to more radio 'sometimes' and were in no doubt that they would like more schools' television. However, a direct relationship between the use of broadcasts and pupils' subject preferences was difficult to substantiate. Using school broadcasts would be unlikely to improve pupils' liking for a particular subject.

Television had a more immediate appeal than radio for most of the pupils taking part, perhaps because teachers usually spent longer in preparing and following-up television programmes, and because pupils were, on the whole, exposed to more television than radio in school. Preparation and follow up were, for the majority of pupils, enjoyable ingredients of programme use and they would have liked more time devoted to them.

Both secondary and primary pupils also brought to television a critical faculty, expressing preferences about series, programmes and even aspects of programmes they had followed in class.

### Note

It must be stressed that the picture of broadcasting use described here is simply a sketch endeavouring to outline in broad strokes the main concerns and findings of this two-and-a-half-year study. For all the colour and subtle detail, reference must be made to the full report, shortly to be completed.

## 1.5.2 Use of Television Equipment in Scottish Secondary Schools

C F J Waters and N L Lawrie
*University of Strathclyde*

Abstract: During the past 10 years the increased use of video-cassette recorders has allowed much more flexibility in the use of television programmes within schools. An extensive study has been carried out by the University of Strathclyde to examine quantifiable factors affecting the use of TV in Scottish secondary schools. The main objectives of this research are: (i) to discover what provision of television equipment there is in schools, how this equipment is used, and how much it is used; (ii) to identify relationships between use and quantifiable factors such as size of school, number of VCRs and cassettes, availability of a resource centre, services of a technician, etc; (iii) to estimate the maximum feasible use of equipment; (iv) to examine the cost of provisions including the use of resource centres; and (v) to identify good practice in the use of VCR equipment. To achieve these objectives, detailed observations have been made of TV use in a number of schools, the operation of resource centres, financing arrangements and equipment provision. A questionnaire and survey data have been analyzed to give more general information. The present stage of the research is nearing completion and results obtained to date are presented.

### Introduction

In the Hayter Report (Hayter, 1974) it was suggested that education in schools would benefit considerably if teachers made more effective use of schools broadcasts and if there were a realistic increase in the supply of audio-visual equipment and material. By 1980, more than 90 per cent of secondary schools in Scotland had facilities for replaying recorded television programmes; even so there are problems about the quantity of equipment which should be provided and its organization. This is particularly so at a time when advances in technology, and shortages of money, are forcing the BBC and education authorities to reappraise their policies for educational TV.

The study described in this paper has attempted to answer certain questions about the level and organization of use, equipment, movement, technician staffing, and about the relations among these factors in Scottish secondary schools. It has run in parallel with a more extensive study undertaken by the Scottish Colleges of Education (McIntyre and Richardson, 1981).

The research began in 1977 with a series of brief visits to a number of local schools to observe equipment and the organization of its use. In the following year, visits were made to a large number of schools and more detailed data were collected. Each of these brief studies was reported on (Lawrie and Waters, 1977; Lawrie and Waters, 1978) and recommendations were made for action and for further research, some of which has been undertaken in a recently completed project funded by SSRC. This third phase has been carried out during the 18-month period ending in February 1981. Its main stages have been:

1. *Further visits to schools.* These were intended to provide information at first-hand about a wider sample of schools. They made the SSRC-funded research assistant familiar with the use of television in schools, and have provided material for case studies which will shortly be made available to schools which took part in the study.
2. *Further analysis of the SED/School Broadcasting Council for Scotland (SBCS)/IBA* Annual Survey of Listening and Viewing in Scottish Schools. This work also was partly to enable familiarization to take place, but was primarily preparation for the next stage.
3. *The main data collection and data analysis stage of the research.* A questionnaire, pretested in late 1979, was sent out in January 1980 to a sample of 100 Scottish secondary schools, chosen from schools with one or more video-cassette recorders (VCRs). Questions were asked about school role, staff and buildings; general aspects of audio-visual organizations; equipment and its organization; recorded material; and details of VCR use over the fortnight from 28 January to 8 February 1980 or over some other fortnight convenient to the school. Eighty-three schools returned the main questionnaire, and 75 of these returned the form providing details of VCR use over a fortnight.
4. *Visits to and data collection from resource centres.*
5. *Data collection by questionnaire from local authorities.* Both 4. and 5. have supplemented the data collected by the main questionnaire. In particular, data from resource centres have allowed an approximate costing of them to be made and also a comparison with costs of recording in school.

The remainder of this paper describes some of the results of the study.

## Some Results from the Study

Almost all television programmes used in schools are now recorded, with half of schools questioned saying they never viewed live programmes and only 20 per cent viewing more than 20 live programmes a year. The latter figure may be made up of schools which watch programmes live at the same time as recording them.

Results obtained confirm that there are substantial differences in both the amount of equipment available and the amount it is used. The number of VCRs per school ranged up to 11, with clear regional variations. For example, Highland, Grampian and the Lanark division of Strathclyde had an average of about 2.5, while Fife and Dumfries and Galloway had an average of under 1.5. From both SBCS and Strathclyde data it appears that schools in island authorities are less well equipped. The averages quoted are from schools with VCRs. Similarly, the number of uses per school per week ranged between 70 and three, and the number of pupils watching in a school ranged between 1,500 and 50 per week.

From the questionnaire and the SBCS data there is evidence that the amount of use a school makes of television is positively correlated with the number of pupils and the number of VCRs, colour television sets, and cassettes. The evidence from the questionnaire also suggests that technician support, a clearly defined booking system (preferably allowing booking some time in advance but with sufficient flexibility to allow for late requests), the size of the stock of tapes, clearly advertised BBC and IBA schedules, the number of programmes kept on tape from a previous session, the reliability of equipment, the use of a resources centre from which to borrow, a procedure for continuing television use when the technician is absent, and administrative support from, normally, an assistant head teacher are positively associated with the level of use. However, given staff commitment, even unpromising situations can be made to work effectively. Several schools have been visited where high use of television is achieved in what seem to be extremely difficult circumstances.

There is no clear relationship between level of use and shortage (or surplus) of teachers and shortage (or surplus) of space. It is clear, however, that the organization of television use must allow for more movement of equipment and pupil exchanges in schools which are short of space.

Two further comments about the relation between level of use and number of VCRs are worth making. One is that, for the fortnight observed, average uses per school were about 30, 50 and 60 for schools with respectively one, two and three or more VCRs. Thus, while average use per school increases as the number of VCRs per school increases, the intensity of use, ie number of uses per VCR, falls markedly. The other is that the number of using departments per school shows a distinct increase from an average of five in schools with one VCR to over seven in schools with three or more VCRs.

## Movement Associated with Television Use

Overall, there is a large amount of movement associated with the use of television. During the two-week period of observation, over 3,000 VCR uses (comprising 850 recordings, 2,100 playbacks and 50 other uses) were recorded on the questionnaire. With hindsight, it is clear that the part of the questionnaire concerned with recording the use of TV was too complicated and asked for too much detail. Some forms were filled in incorrectly (requiring correction), while others were clearly incomplete. The estimates of movement quoted below are therefore likely to be under-estimates.

For the replays, it was reported that in 56 per cent of cases the class met elsewhere and moved to another room to watch the programme (involving about 1,300 groups moving), while six per cent required classes already in the viewing room to move out. About 10 per cent of classes then left the viewing room before the end of the period. In the extreme case there were 18 examples quoted where all three of these movements occurred for a particular programme. These figures perhaps illustrate the lack of dedicated space for television use in most schools, and the problems involved in overcoming this. One school reported moving 600 yards to watch a television programme. While the average distance moved is 80 yards, distances considerably greater than this are not uncommon. About one-third of movements involve a change of building, another one-third change floor, while the remaining one-third moves to another room on the same floor.

This amount of movement appears to decrease slightly with the amount of equipment a school has. For schools submitting records for one VCR, 60 per cent of replays involve classes moving to a different location, while these figures are 55 per cent and 51 per cent for schools with respectively two and three or more VCRs. Similar decreases in the movement of the equipment itself were noted. Schools submitting records for one VCR moved it for 31 per cent of uses, while this figure had dropped to less than 24 per cent for schools with more equipment. Part of this reduced movement is a direct consequence of the different organization of additional machines. Roughly 40 per cent of schools with two VCRs used both machines in the same way, while the other 60 per cent used one machine as the major source of recordings. This trend was even more apparent in schools with three or more VCRs, where 83 per cent of schools used some machines for recording and others primarily as playback machines.

There is a marked difference in the amount of use made of equipment in these two circumstances. For schools submitting records for two VCRs, the average use fell from 29 per week, for specialized use, to 20 for non-specialized use, and for schools submitting records for three or more VCRs the average use fell from 32 to 12 per week. These can be compared with 15 uses per week for schools with one VCR.

For schools with one VCR, 72 per cent of all uses were in one location, whereas for schools with two or more VCRs an average of 85 per cent of uses of each VCR were in one location. This difference becomes less well marked when those machines which are used for recording only in one location are removed from the analysis.

## Technician Support and the Organization of Use

One item in the questionnaire asked about the number of technicians (including auxiliaries) whose main work or some of whose work was in the audio-visual area. The answers reveal that technical support for audio-visual systems varies markedly from region to region and school to school, with apparently no relation between the amount of equipment and the number of technicians. There is, however, a positive relation between the number of technicians a school has and its use of television, particularly in schools with three or more VCRs, but less clearly in schools with less equipment. This tends to support the common sense view that the more television equipment a school has, the more need there is for technicians to support it.

A number of questions were asked about general aspects of audio-visual organization, the booking procedure for recording and playback, rooms used for these activities, and the main difficulties experienced by teachers in using television programmes. The answers to these questions, together with the details of VCR use, build up a picture of a variety of types of organization which have clearly evolved to suit different situations. Organization of use may be in the hands of a technician or the head teacher; it may be centralized (with booking lists in a staff common room) or decentralized (with separate diaries for each VCR); VCRs (in schools with more than one VCR) may be specialized in use; they may operate in different parts (on different floors) of the school and in some schools some are departmental rather than school machines.

One conclusion which accords with common sense is that decentralized systems work better in schools with little or no technician support. In general, too, it is clear that VCRs in departmental control are not very fully used.

It is interesting to note here that 11 schools reported no problems with television use. Reported concerns of schools were lack of suitable space (in 19 cases), heavy use of equipment producing clashes (21 cases), unreliable equipment (15), and the need to move classes (18). Only five schools reported lack of suitable material as a problem.

## Other Analyses

Data on resource centres and their use has been collected, and an approximate costing suggests that the cost of providing tapes from resource centres is about £5 per tape per use, a figure closely comparable to the cost of recording in schools. Some study has been made of piped distribution systems, although of the 11 in the sample with such a system, only eight schools used it.

## Concluding Comments

As a result of this research, extensive data has been collected about the level and organization of use of television in schools. Some of the results from analysis of this data have been reported here, and a more detailed report will be written and sent to local authorities, to participating schools, and to other interested bodies. Further work on the data remains to be done, for example on costs and on the relation between the use of television made by departments and their ease of access to rooms where playback can take place.

The research was stimulated in the first instance by certain administrative questions about the most economic means of organizing the use of television in schools. What has been done so far has been largely descriptive of the organization of use and provides the essential background against which the study of alternative modes of organization may be made. Some of these alternatives, such as block transmission of programmes, are in the power of the broadcasting authorities to change. Some, like the development of video discs and the provision of more advanced equipment, are in the hands of the competing manufacturers.

Again, some alternatives, such as the level of equipment provided in schools, the policy towards technician support and the running of resource centres, are largely in the hands of education authorities, while much remains in the hands of the school and the individual teacher. It is at this last level or at the departmental level that quality of educational use is set. At the level of the school as a whole, organizational aspects are dealt with which should be designed to simplify the teacher's task in using television and to provide a suitable environment for its use.

## References

Hayter, C G (1974) *Using Broadcasts in Schools*. Joint BBC/ITV Publication, London.

Lawrie, N L and Waters, C D J (1977) *The Use of Television in Schools*. Department of Operational Research, University of Strathclyde, Glasgow.

Lawrie, N L and Waters, C D J (1978) *The Use of Television in Schools — A Second Report*. Departmental Note 24, Department of Operational Research, University of Strathclyde, Glasgow.

MacIntyre, A and Richardson, R H (1981) Inter College Research Project on School Broadcasting. In Percival, F and Ellington, H I (eds) *Aspects of Educational Technology* XV. Kogan Page, London.

## Acknowledgements

The authors are grateful to the SSRC for their financial support, and to Catherine Hessett, research assistant on the project, for her major contribution to the work.

# 1.5.3 Learning from Television:
# Effects of Presenter Delivery Style

G Coldevin and R M Bernard
*Concordia University, Canada*

Abstract: This paper describes the background, methodology and preliminary findings of a research project designed to investigate some relationships between learning from television and aspects of presentation style. It is concluded that the methodology of the study offers considerable promise as a diagnostic process to improve the choosing of a presenter for a specific set of educational or informational objectives.

## Introduction

This article outlines portions of the preliminary results of a study, currently under way at Concordia University, which is concerned with delineating varied television presenter delivery styles through *attribute clusters* resulting from factor analysis of semantic differential scale ratings. Attribute clusters in turn are examined in relation to their influence in stimulating information acquisition and attitude change. The end product of the research is directed toward predicting a given performer's effectiveness for a particular set of programme objectives.

Background literature in the area is scarce and reflective of the stage of television production variable investigation in general and presenter variable research in particular. The questions of 'who' and/or 'what' constitute an effective ETV presenter, at least from the available evidence, is very poorly defined. Studies so far have examined the effects of:

1. Uniform or rank of instructor in teaching US Air Force students (Calkins, 1971).
2. Body type on source credibility and interpersonal attraction (McCain and Divers, 1973).
3. Age and appearance on information recall and attitude change (Coldevin, 1977).
4. ITV instructor versus trained communicator on cognitive achievement (Wardell, 1976).
5. Eye-contact levels on learning, interest and attention (Westley and Mobius, 1960; Connolly, 1962), and presenter ratings (Coldevin, 1979; Baggaley, 1980).
6. Prior knowledge of performer (Baggaley, 1980).

Salient findings from the foregoing survey include the following:

☐ A typecast presenter selection across varied age groupings may have limited use when attitude modification is the primary thrust of a given production (Coldevin, 1977). The degree of homophily (perceived similarity in value structures and beliefs) between a speaker and a viewer also plays a major role in fostering attitude change;

☐ A professional newsreader generated significantly higher learning scores than an ITV instructor (Wardell, 1976);

☐ Low, medium or high eye-contact levels do not appear to affect learning, interest and attention (Westley and Mobius, 1960; Connolly, 1962); presenter ratings, however, are enhanced when readers work from a desk script (medium eye-contact) as opposed to reading from an autocue and exhibiting high eye-contact (Coldevin, 1979; Baggaley, 1980).

While studies such as these may be useful generally, and indeed should be encouraged as contributors to communication theory building, they offer only limited insight to selecting or grooming an effective ETV presenter, particularly outside North America. What is rather more important is a *methodology* which is efficient to apply in virtually any research setting and which might be undertaken by a wide cross-section of the viewing population. Some very promising work in this connection has been forthcoming from Liverpool University (see Baggaley, 1980). After a variety of experimentation with varied population samplings, Baggaley concluded that a presenter's performance, as evaluated through semantic differential ratings, may be principally defined by loadings in one or more of the attribute clusters or factors illustrated in Figure 1.

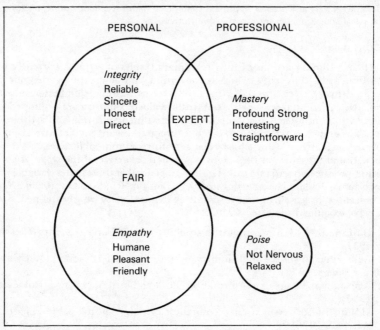

**Figure 1.** *Factor rotated attribute clusters according to Baggaley (1980)*

Whether these clusters will transfer to other cultural settings has yet to be determined as has also the influence of each factor (or attribute within each factor) on information acquisition and attitude formation.

## Methodology

### Presenter Selection

Two professional newsreaders from both sexes were engaged for the study and separated for analysis on the basis of the perceived ages by the sample. One female presenter was perceived as being in her mid-20s (hereafter referred to as Young Female), with the other in her late 30s to early 40s (Mature Female); one male presenter was perceived as being in his mid-30s (Young Male) with the other perceived as being in his 40s to early 50s (Mature Male). Age plus sex hence formed integral components in analyzing the principal variables under consideration.

All presenters were currently or previously television anchor newsreaders for regional Montreal broadcasts.

## Production Objectives and Execution

For the initial study, it was decided to simulate a 'local news' broadcast format. Scripts were developed from wire service copy concerning real stories; background visuals and cutaways were either prepared or selected from released footage. Newsreaders worked from a desk script format. The target timing of the complete production was 12 minutes with seven minutes to be devoted to news (proceeding from an international to national and local/regional focus), one minute to commercials, approximately three minutes to an editorial, and one minute to the 'intro', 'recapping' the top stories, and the 'extro'. The productions were intended to approach professional broadcast standards and to this end their execution was undertaken by a professional television director. With the exception of one of the four speakers, all news presentations were identical in every respect. (Editorials, however, used only male speakers to conform to current practice.) All final productions were within 30 seconds in length with the average timing being 11 minutes 50 seconds.

## Testing Instruments

The testing instrument consisted of four major sections, in addition to questions eliciting demographic information, television viewing habits, and perceived ages of newsreaders and editorial presenters: (i) an 18-item, 7-point semantic differential set of scales assessing viewer reactions to the newsreader (eg Confusing . . . Straightforward); (ii) a 28-item multiple-choice information recall test (KR-20 reliability of .90); (iii) an additional 18-item semantic differential scale inventory assessing viewer ratings of the editorial reader(s); and (iv) a Likert-type 7-point attitude inventory which probed reactions to the content of the editorial. (*Note:* only the initial semantic differential scales used to rate the newsreaders and the information test are included in the present analysis.)

## Sample

The sample consisted of five classes of second-year English literature students drawn from a local community college. All participants were English speaking from middle to upper mdidle class backgrounds. One class each was exposed to one of the video-tapes featuring one of the four newsreaders with an additional class serving as a control group. Individual randomization of Ss to treatments was precluded by random assignment of students to classes. Intact groups were hence used throughout the sampling. Class sizes ranged from 16 to 26 students (see Table 1). The average age of Ss was 18 with the sex distribution being virtually evenly split (50.5 per cent male and 49.5 per cent female).

# Results

Table 1 shows the mean information acquisition scores generated for each of the news presenters and the control group. When subjected to a one-way ANOVA, significant differences were found between all presenter scores and the control group, $F (4, 104) = 19.65$, $p < .001$. Mean comparison tests revealed no significant differences among the male presenters nor between both male and female scores. Differences between the scores accruing to the two females, however, were significant ($p < .05$) with the Mature Female being superior (Figure 2).

Further interesting differences were revealed when a two-way ANOVA was run comparing sex of presenter with sex of subject. Male subjects in this case learned significantly more from both female and male presenters than female students, $\underline{F} (1, 89) = 8.69$, $p < .004$. Figure 3 shows the distribution of scores.

| Group | X | S D | n |
|---|---|---|---|
| Mature Male | 17.38 | 3.35 | 21 |
| Mature Female | 18.48 | 4.19 | 21 |
| Young Male | 18.15 | 4.41 | 26 |
| Young Female | 15.40 | 3.30 | 25 |
| Control | 8.82 | 3.31 | 16 |

**Table 1.** *Mean information acquisition scores for treatment and control groups*

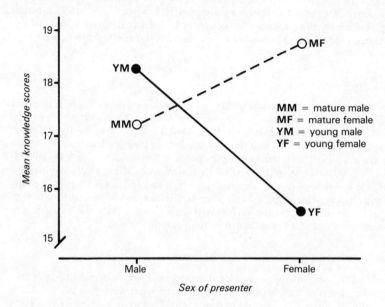

**Figure 2.** *Interaction of presenter age and presenter sex*

Analysis of the means accrued to the performers on the scale ratings pointed up many significant differences between males and females and among the females, but not among the males *per se*. In general, both males scored consistently higher across the majority of indices used. Our central focus in the study, however, was not to evaluate the differences in semantic differential ratings as an end in itself, but rather to determine the effects of the salient appeal characteristics among the presenters as rated by the total sample. To accomplish this end, the semantic differential scales were first subjected to a Varimax Factor Rotation (Nie *et al*, 1975). The common appeal factors which resulted are displayed in Figure 4.

A further analysis was performed to select the discriminating attribute(s) between the four presenters through discriminant function analysis. This test brings into relief the distinctive function(s) in which the groups are expected to differ. Each function is composed of attributes among which one emerges to define that function. In the present case, the function Honest accounted for some 77 per cent of the total sample variance. The attribute *honest* in turn accounted for 55 per cent of the total function variance and was the single most discriminating variable describing differences between the performers.

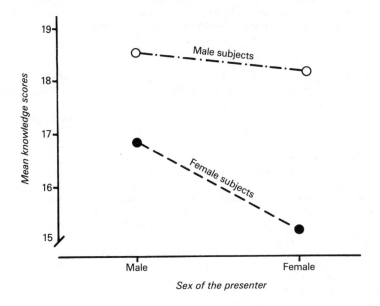

**Figure 3.** *Sex of the subject compared with sex of the presenters*

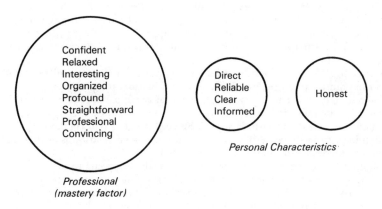

**Figure 4.** *Common appeal factors identified among presenters*

In returning to our analysis of the semantic differential scale ratings, we found that the Mature Female had the highest positive individual score on the Honest-Dishonest continuum ($\overline{X} = 6.00$). When subjected to two-tailed t-tests, this score was not significantly higher than either of the scores generated by the males ($\overline{X} = 5.52$ for the Mature Male and 5.84 for the Young Male), but was significantly stronger than the mean of 5.24 produced by the Young Female ($t = 2.26$, df = 44, $p < .003$). And, as noted earlier, the only significant information score differences were found between the Mature versus Young Female presenter.

The pattern which emerges from this sample, therefore, is a decided preference for 'honesty' which is reflective of the *personal* dimensions of a speaker's performance. This in turn appears to facilitate optimal information retrieval.

## Summary

Although the results obtained should be viewed within the context of the exploratory nature of the study, several tentative conclusions may be drawn. The more salient of these concerns the discrepancy between the attribute clusters found during Baggaley's research and those recorded here. Much of this may be due to the differing cultural environments (Baggaley's research was carried out in England). A corollary reasoning suggests that each stratified sample draws differing inferences from a speaker's performance dependent upon the prevailing consensus formation mechanism at the time of testing. The late adolescent, middle to upper middle class sample included in this study, for example, may change substantially in 'value attachments' over a relatively short period of time. Testing should therefore be consistently carried out over a wide cross-section of the population before any reliable profile of common appeal factors is formulated. It is anticipated that, while differing attribute appeal factors will accrue to various population sectors, a pool of overlapping characteristics may extend throughout each. Mass television programming could hence concentrate on the overlapping appeal factors, with specific target audience groups such as those receiving formal instructional television, profiting from the narrowly focused profiles.

The connection between the discriminating attribute selected by the total sample and the significant knowledge gains made by the group viewing the presenter with the highest mean rating on this attribute merits considerably more attention. It may well be that the general appeal attributes determined by the factor rotation analysis may only serve as a 'presenter enhancement surround' with the primary effective qualities of a given speaker residing in a small number of key variables. Much more research is needed to validate this supposition but the potential for predicting a performer's effectiveness in advance of production makes it worthy of concerted effort.

Significant differences found between the majority of semantic differential ratings run counter to a previous study in sound broadcasting, comparing professional male and female newscasters (Whitakker and Whitakker, 1976). It is apparent that the qualities associated with voice may constitute only a small portion of a television presenter's appeal. Since this paper reports the first television inquiry in the area, it is evident that more investigation is needed before any definite recommendations may be advanced.

In summary, the methodology applied in this study appears to offer considerable promise as a diagnostic process to improve the choosing of a presenter for a specific set of educational or informational objectives. It becomes particularly attractive in view of newer developments in evaluation techniques such as PEAC (Program Evaluation Analysis Computer) based on microcomputer technology. These modern 'tools' can provide an enormously reduced turn-around time between sampling and final results and can virtually assure a day-to-day data base for production decisions if such are required. It is recognized that this process may take much of the intrigue out of the time-honoured 'intuitive' approach in presenter selection. The matching of performers with predictable outcomes, however, should convince even the most sceptical of practitioners.

## References

Baggaley, J (1980) *Psychology of the TV Image*. Saxon House, Farnborough.
Calkins, D R (1971) Cognitive dissonance: effect on adult learning when incongruous

instructors teach through the medium of television. *Dissertation Abstracts International* 32, pp 103.

Coldevin, G (1977) Factors in ETV presenter selection: effects of stereotyping. *British Journal of Educational Technology* 8, pp 45-53.

Coldevin, G (1979) The effects of placement, delivery format and missed cues on TV presenter ratings. In Sullivan, A (ed) *Research in Video-taped Instruction.* Memorial University Press, St John's.

Connolly, C P (1962) *An Experimental Investigation of Eye-Contact on Television.* MA thesis, Ohio University.

McCain, T A and Divers, L (1973) *The Effect of Body Type and Camera Shot on Interpersonal Attraction and Source Credibility.* ERIC Document Reproduction Service, order number ED099 1917.

Nie, N H, Hull, C H, Jenkins, J G, Steinbrenner, K and Bent, D H (1975) *Statistical Package for the Social Sciences.* McGraw-Hill, New York.

Wardell, D (1976) Which is the better presenter, an ITV instructor or a trained communicator? *Educational and Industrial Television* 8, pp 41-3.

Westley, B H and Mobius, J B (1960) *The Effects of Eye-Contact in Televised Instruction.* University of Wisconsin.

Whitakker, A H and Whitakker, R (1976) Relative effectiveness of male and female newscasters. *Journal of Broadcasting* 20, pp 177-84.

# Section 2:
# The Role of Evaluation in Educational Technology

## 2.1 Keynote Address

### Evaluation and Educational Technology

**Professor Tony Becher**
*University of Sussex*

### Introduction

The two components in my title — evaluation, and educational technology — will
be familiar enough in the present setting to need no definition. However, they
share one major disadvantage when one attempts to use them as elements in a
general discussion, as this is intended to be. Each is a very broad concept,
embracing a variety of different but interconnected meanings, and designating a
miscellany of diverse but interrelated activities. In endeavouring to make some
sense of this complexity, it may be useful to begin with a modest venture in
logical mapping. By this I mean no more than the drawing of a few internal
boundaries within each concept. The outcome should be at least a minimal frame
of reference within which to organize our subsequent observations.

Accordingly, in the first part of this paper I shall set out to distinguish three
main forms of educational technology. In the second part, I shall similarly aim to
delineate three main forms of educational evaluation. These exercises, in what
I earlier denoted as logical mapping, can then be followed by an attempt to
identify matches and mismatches in the superimposition of the two patterns.
That is, I shall look at the various types of evaluation, and the various forms of
educational technology, and ask what does and does not seem to make a useful
fit. In the final part of the paper, I shall follow up some of the implications of
this analysis.

### Varieties of Educational Technology

My first self-imposed task is to mark some distinctions — intended to be useful for
subsequent discussion — within the overall notion of educational technology.
I have opted for three broad categories, partly because these seem to be based on
fairly obvious logical boundaries, and partly because I am reluctant to go into
finer detail. To make many more demarcations would involve a more complex
mapping exercise than it seems useful to undertake within the constraints of a
relatively brief analysis.

The three groups of activities will be labelled — for reasons which I hope will
soon become evident — as *product-oriented*, *process-oriented* and *organization-*

*oriented* forms of educational technology. I have no intention of suggesting that the frontiers between the three are in practice clear-cut and precise, or that borderline cases cannot be found. The distinctions I am making are conceptual, in rather the same way that the equator is. Although many countries are either north or south of it, there are a number through the middle of which it passes. The existence of these equatorial countries does not render less useful our references, for purposes of classification, to the northern and southern hemispheres. I am not, then, claiming that any application of educational technology must belong to only one of the three categories. All I want to suggest is that each of the groups marks off distinguishably different sets of properties, some or all of which may be possessed by any particular case in point.

One way to visualize the three groups is to think of a set of three concentric circles, marking off three identifiable domains. It is to the innermost of these – what might be called the hard core of educational technology – that the first of my distinctions refers. By *product-oriented* educational technology I mean that cluster of activities which is centred on pre-defined objectives. What is often called the 'objective model' of learning or training (Tyler, 1949) is central to so many developments that it scarcely merits further description. The whole notion of a systems approach in education is predicated on the idea that intended learner outcomes can be specified in advance, in behavioural terms, that their degree of achievement can thus be measured, and that any deficiencies identified in practice can be compensated by suitable remedial action.

Hard-core approaches in educational technology, then, take the characteristic form of basic training systems (sequences, for example, on how to check the electrical circuit of a car); or straightforward learning systems (eg how to solve algebraic equations); or even 'off-the-peg' testing systems (eg batteries of tests of reading proficiency). In all such cases, the acceptable responses at each stage are clearly determined in advance, and are amenable to direct measurement of a kind which aspires to be neutral and non-subjective.

In this category of activities, the emphasis is on the acquisition of fairly straightforward skills or factual information which does not allow any ambiguity or room for interpretation. The label 'product-oriented' seems appropriate because attention is focused on the product of the exercise – the success of the training or the learning or the testing sequence – rather than on the process by which that outcome is attained in any given case. Allowing that the desired outcome is achieved, no questions need be asked about the nature or the means of its achievement. To that extent, the quality of any individual participant's learning experience is regarded as a 'black box' whose contents are inaccessible to legitimate inquiry.

If we turn to the next of our three concentric circles, we see this hard-core domain of product-oriented developments as surrounded by an atmospheric layer of *process-oriented* approaches (Bruner, 1966; Stenhouse, 1975). These comprise instances of educational technology in which the outcomes are neither very specific nor clearly pre-determined. In other words, they do not subscribe to the philosophy of behavioural objectives, and are not usually categorized as educational or training systems. Their concern is rather with the promotion of improved teaching or learning techniques, the enhancement of motivation and the enrichment of the context of learning.

Examples of the process approach in educational technology would include a wide range of non-traditional modes of presentation, including television and other visual media; simulations, ranging from the sophistication of the flight trainer to the simplicity of role play exercises; learning games; and the use of the computer both for modelling hypothetical situations and for heuristics of the kinds pioneered by, for example, Seymour Pappert (Pappert, 1980) and Gordon Pask. What these very diverse examples have in common is a readiness to cope with the uncertainties and unpredictabilities associated with exploratory learning, despite the lack of definition of outcomes and the associated difficulty of measuring achievements.

Developments within process-oriented educational technology tend, understandably, to justify their effectiveness in terms of the positive experiences to which they give rise, as well as of the complex, high-level competences which they help to develop. Their emphasis is on understanding and adaptable skills, rather than on factual knowledge and routine techniques. In contrast with product-oriented activities, developments in this second category are directly concerned with what actually goes on in the process of teaching and learning. Indeed, they are designed to contribute positively to that process, in the expectation that if only its quality can be improved, the end-products will take care of themselves.

Now for the third and final category — the outermost of the three concentric circles, which might be thought of as a stratosphere enveloping the process-oriented atmosphere and the product-oriented core. I chose the label *organization-oriented* educational technology because the strategies I have in mind are all concerned to promote fairly generalized developments at the level of major institutions, local authorities or the education service as a whole. Their concern, in other words, is not so much with helping the individual in a specific learning or training context as with the management of the larger enterprise in which acts of individual learning are intended to take place (Schramm, 1967; Mackenzie *et al*, 1975).

Illustrations of an organization-oriented approach might include mechanisms for distributing information (such as television satellites and CEEFAX); computer-managed learning networks; the use of testing techniques for student diagnosis and allocation; and system-wide procedures for accountability. None of these examples can be comfortably accommodated within the categories of product-oriented or process-oriented developments, though it would I think, be generally agreed that they constitute legitimate instances of educational technology.

The main emphasis of developments in this category is on promoting system-wide efficiency, or effecting substantial cost savings, or enhancing existing forms of quality control. Organization-oriented schemes address themselves to a different, more generalized, set of questions from those we have previously considered. Their validity is established neither in terms of individually measurable learning products, nor in terms of the quality of individual learning processes, but rather in terms of the net financial gain or aggregated performance statistics.

These categories could of course be elaborated in considerably greater detail. I hope, however, that the very brief thumb-nail sketches I have offered are adequate for the present purpose. As I have already emphasized, although I hope that the distinctions may be useful for the purpose of analysis, they are not intended to be mutually exclusive in practice. Indeed, a number of significant developments — perhaps most noticeably the Open University — can be seen to encompass elements of all three domains.

## Varieties of Evaluation

In looking next at the concept of evaluation, I shall continue the attempt to identify some useful internal boundaries. Again, my distinctions will be threefold. There is no particular magic in the number three, but, as previously mentioned, it provides a conveniently small framework of analysis, and happens to match the main distinctions I propose to draw. That is scarcely surprising, in that the categories of evaluation I would like to explore happen to correspond exactly with those already marked out for educational technology.

In other words, I want to argue that the broad field of educational evaluation can be divided into the three groups of *product-oriented, process-oriented* and *organization-oriented* activities. Again, the notion of three concentric circles may be helpful in picturing the different domains of evaluation.

The inner core comprises *product-oriented* approaches. The intellectual tradition behind such forms of evaluation is that of psychometrics. The effectiveness of any educational enterprise is determined, on this approach, solely in terms of students' terminal scores on some appropriate (and properly standardized) objective test. The reliance on predetermined outcomes is obvious. In every instance, the evaluation measure has to be defined in terms of the anticipated end-point of the learning process (Glaser, 1970).

Product-oriented evaluation can appear in a number of different guises. Perhaps the most familiar is based on the notion of matched experimental and control groups, where the experimental group of learners is given a special educational diet, as against the control group's normal fare. Here the difference in educational performance is taken as a measure of the success or otherwise of the experimental programme. This approach, which has rather unkindly been labelled 'the agricultural-botany model' (Parlett and Hamilton, 1976) has tended to fall out of favour in a climate in which innovative developments no longer share many common aims with traditional ones. An alternative which meets this difficulty of incommensurable end-products is the input-output approach, in which an innovative programme is assessed in terms of its own stated (and behaviourally measurable) objectives, its success being gauged by the mean student gains between pre-test and post-test performance. A further variant is 'factor evaluation', in which one element in a complex situation is isolated for scrutiny, and its contribution to the eventual learning outcome appraised. An example of this approach is a recent study by Elihu Katz (Katz, 1977) of the comprehension of broadcast information, in which 'half of a random sample was asked to sit with their backs to the television screen in order to see what difference the picture makes for recall, understanding and emotional arousal'.

The salient features of evaluations of this type are, first, that they tend to concentrate on straightforward quantifiable gains in factual knowledge or performance skills; and, second, that they do not attempt to take into account the quality of the actual process of learning or the broader context in which it takes place. That is to say, they share the characteristics which were earlier attributed to product-oriented educational technology.

The same correspondence holds, broadly speaking, between *process-oriented* evaluation and its counterpart in educational technology. The type of study in question here is anthropological rather than psychometric, with an emphasis on qualitative factors relating to learning experiences and the environment in which they occur (Hamilton *et al*, 1977). There is no particular concern with pre-defined quantifiable outcomes, since the most significant elements in the educational process are considered to be both unpredictable and unamenable to measurement.

Investigations in this category may be found under a variety of brand-names — illuminative, naturalistic, and responsive perhaps being the best-known. Some process-oriented evaluations are virtually indistinguishable from ethnographic case studies, and have helped to prompt a resurgence of interest in case study research (Stake, 1978). The typical methods employed are observation and loosely-structured or unstructured interviews, as against the performance tests which feature largely in product-oriented evaluation. The emphasis is on the appraisal of the attitudes and concerns of participants in the teaching-learning process, on the characterization of key events, and on the depiction of the wider setting in which that process is embedded.

*Organization-oriented* evaluations are concerned with developments at a higher level of generality than the product-oriented assessments in our first domain, or the process-oriented exercises in our second domain. Their emphasis is on studies of managerial policy at the level of the system as a whole, or one of its sub-systems.

The concern here is not so much with assessing the learning process of individuals or groups as with gauging the overall effectiveness of broad educational policies and programmes (Fielden and Pearson, 1978).

Examples of evaluation techniques in this genre include cost-benefit and cost-effectiveness studies, programme-analysis review, and other comparable procedures introduced sporadically into departments of central and local government since the late 1960s. The aim of such techniques is to evaluate priorities and monitor and control the implementation of policy decisions on a systematic basis. The main data for organization-oriented studies are economics, statistics and quantitative information based on indicators of performance.

As before, in emphasizing the differences between these conceptual categories of evaluation, I have no intention of implying that every actual instance must fall neatly into one and only one of them. Real life is not as tidy as logic. The point is amply proved by the evaluative component in the National Development Programme for Computer Assisted Learning, which shared features of all three.

## Matches and Mismatches Between Categories

It may be useful at this point briefly to review the two parallel sets of distinctions I have drawn within the concepts of educational technology and evaluation. The first category, labelled in each case as *product-oriented*, has to do primarily with measurable objectives. It emphasizes the need for predictability and objectivity. It also reflects an analytic approach, based on the principle that any complex situation can be disaggregated into separate, relatively simpler, components which — once they are satisfactorily dealt with — can be recombined to help make sense of the whole.

The second, *process-oriented*, classification differs from the first in a variety of ways. It is not much concerned with outcomes, whether or not these are defined in behavioural and measurable terms. The emphasis is on means rather than ends, and on the wider context in which learning is intended to take place. Behind this approach lies a belief in holism rather than analysis — that is, a view that reality cannot be dissected into separate elements without a serious cost to both meaning and validity.

The third, *organization-oriented*, element is different again. It might be described as the application, at a more global level, of the systems thinking which lies behind the product-oriented approach. It, too, is concerned with objectives and with the measurement of performance. However, its ends tend towards the needs of managers rather than of teachers and trainers; and, its predominant emphases are on the techniques of large-scale resource provision and distribution.

The purpose of making such distinctions is, as I suggested at the outset, to clarify the relationships between evaluation and educational technology. It is now time to put them to work by exploring the matches and mismatches between categories. To do the job exhaustively would require nine distinct comparisons — an exercise likely to provoke more tedium than enlightenment. Instead, I shall select only a few examples to illustrate my conclusions.

One might begin by asking what happens when non-corresponding elements are paired. What, for instance, can be said about product-oriented evaluation as applied to process-oriented educational technology? The answer is, in this case, straightforward enough. The evaluation is doomed to failure, because the activity being evaluated is not defined in terms of measurable objectives. It is indeed not concerned with the promotion of the kinds of knowledge, or the acquisition of the kinds of skills, which can be identified in advance and quantified at the point of achievement. So the product-oriented evaluator has no definable products on which to exercise his psychometric techniques, and must therefore find it virtually impossible to come to any clear conclusions.

It might be argued that the same difficulties need not arise in applying process-oriented evaluation techniques to product-oriented educational technology. Evaluators in the illuminative tradition would maintain that context is no less important in the case of such developments than it is in those which directly stress the process of learning. One well-known case is the study by Smith and Pohland of a computer-assisted instruction (CAI) programme in the rural Appalachian highlands (Smith and Pohland, 1974). Their evaluation report is particularly informative about the difficulties of communicating the developers' intentions; the multiplicity of agents involved; effects of cuts in funding; problems of the location of terminals; erratic functioning of hardware; difficulty of integration with the rest of the curriculum; and the wide variability of practice between participating teachers. None of this important information would have emerged in a purely product-oriented evaluation. But with this said, one is left with a sense of a task which remains incomplete. Although some attention is given to pupils' reactions to the CAI programme, there is no indication at all in the evaluation report whether or not the children in question learnt any mathematics, and, if so, whether they were in any way better off than children given conventional teaching. Since this was the central purpose of the whole exercise, an evaluation report which makes no mention of it must be judged oddly deficient.

Perhaps, then, the ideal match is one of direct correspondence between evaluation strategy and style of educational technology. If, as we have seen, a process-oriented evaluation of a product-oriented scheme is liable to leave out of account the crucial question of learning gains, would it not be better simply to concentrate in such a case on a matching product-oriented evaluation? Before one leaps too hastily to any conclusion on this point, it may be worth considering the case of IMU, the Swedish individualized mathematics project for secondary schools (Becher and Maclure, 1978). This was in its time — the late 1960s — a remarkably sophisticated learning system in the best product-oriented style. It provided a common core of mathematical content for pupils at three distinct levels of aptitude, and a series of diagnostic tests which allowed periodic transfer from one level to another. The evaluation study which accompanied it was designed with considerable care, providing formative information which helped with the revision of materials and summative information which recorded, for potential adopters, pupils' learning gains relative to those following traditional courses. Because they were based firmly on the product-oriented tradition, the IMU evaluators deliberately excluded any consideration of what teachers and pupils thought about the new scheme or the political context in which trials were taking place. As it happened, the teachers soon became restive with their changed role from dispensers of knowledge to managers of learning, and the pupils became bored with long periods spent working at mathematics on their own. The project developers, realizing this, wanted to alter radically the pattern of presentation. The evaluators, whose whole elaborate design was based on the existing structure, resisted any such change, claiming that their initial data would then become valueless. The stalemate was eventually resolved by the appearance of a rival scheme devised on more flexible lines, and the IMU programme itself was quietly abandoned by its official sponsors.

What this cautionary tale suggests is that contextual data, of a kind that process-oriented evaluations specifically set out to provide, are indispensable in any attempt to appraise even the most emphatically product-oriented developments in educational technology. Put alongside this, the Smith and Pohland case study serves to emphasize that such an approach, though necessary, is not sufficient to constitute a complete evaluation. It begins to look as if the best answer might be a combination of product-oriented and process-oriented inquiries, the first evaluating the success of the development in its own terms, and the second checking its impact on the people, institutions and policies it most directly affects.

Arguing along much the same lines, I would want to suggest that organization-oriented developments are best appraised by a combination of organization-oriented and process-oriented studies. First, simply to get the question out of the way, it may be remarked that the frames of reference of product-oriented and organization-oriented styles, whether of development or of evaluation, are so far apart from one another that there is little possibility of fruitful interaction. That is, it is difficult to conceive of an organization-oriented evaluation, couched at a very general level and seeking gross cost and performance data, being applied to the very specific and down-to-earth setting of a product-oriented application of educational technology. Equally, it is hard to see how a product-oriented evaluation, designed to quantify a limited range of measurable learning gains in a closely-defined context, could be of much relevance in assessing the overall effectiveness of an organization-oriented educational technology programme.

But if we consider such a programme — an educational television satellite, let us say — it seems to make good sense to evaluate it in a matching style, by employing the techniques of organization-oriented investigation. In considering whether the service deserved to be continued, any policy-maker would be likely to ask not only about overall costs, but about the comparative economics of alternative systems. He or she would also clearly want to know about the generalized impact of the development on the educational levels of the target audience, as indicated (for example) by changes in national examination results over a period of time. Evaluation data at this global level seems more appropriate than other types of evidence in the appraisal of organization-oriented educational technology. Once again, however, a niggling doubt suggests itself. Whatever the broad social indicators show, and whatever the economic calculations indicate, there must remain the question of whether what is happening on the ground bears any relation to what was originally envisaged. Are the resources provided by the scheme being used as intended? Are the local managers of the scheme in touch with its developers, or with its recipients? Are the teachers enthusiastic or hostile? What is the pupils' conception of what is happening? Such contextual questions need to be asked, and answered, if the evaluation is to be anything other than narrowly and dangerously blinkered. As in the case of product-oriented developments, the best buy seems to be a matching — that is, an organization-oriented — evaluation, supplemented by a process-oriented one.

When it comes to process-oriented developments in educational technology — the group typified by non-traditional presentation media, simulations, computer modelling and the like — we have already seen that product-oriented evaluations are inapplicable. So, in general, are organization-oriented ones — how could cost-effectiveness techniques be applied to business games, or computer modelling be assessed in terms of performance indicators? Here the matching evaluation strategy is the only one which seems appropriate. That is to say, process-oriented developments are best assessed by process-oriented evaluation, alone rather than in conjunction with other strategies.

## Concluding Comments

To sum up, this analysis, based on three broad categories of educational technology and three parallel categories of evaluation, suggests that process-oriented evaluation is in something of a privileged position as against its counterparts. In each case, we have seen that a particular type of development in educational technology seems to call for a matching type of evaluation. But product-oriented and organization-oriented developments, so the earlier arguments suggest, appear to call for a complementary process-oriented study as well. Thus process-oriented evaluation figures against all three broad types of educational technology, while the other two forms of evaluation appear only once, in matching their counterpart styles of development.

On the face of it, this lack of symmetry is peculiar. However, the reason for it becomes, after further consideration, clear enough. The acquisition of definable knowledge and measurable skills does not occur in total isolation from other human activities. No more does the development of high-level adaptive techniques, or the distribution or monitoring of educational facilities through sophisticated management systems. That is to say, within the field of educational technology, product-oriented, process-oriented and organization-oriented developments cannot in practice be confined within the tidily aseptic atmosphere of a psychology laboratory, a design studio or a planning office. All such activities have to be played out in a complex and largely uncontrollable social environment. Sometimes as in home-based learning systems — the contextual factors may become less obtrusive, though by the same token the demands on individual motivation may be greatly increased. In the main, however, what people learn at any given time is affected, for better or worse, by what is happening in the rest of their learning context. Considerations related to other aspects of the curriculum, to one's relationships with one's teachers, to external expectations, to one's level of self-esteem — all these and more can assume an important place in educational performance.

It follows that educational technology, whatever style it adopts, cannot simply be plugged in and expected unfailingly to meet its designer's specification. The main implication, as I see it, of the arguments developed in this paper is that evaluation should help to bridge the gulf between the ideal and the actual. One of its central purposes might be to unravel the contextual complexities which are an inevitable consequence of putting ideas into practice. Another key task might be to enhance the educational technologist's understanding of what does and does not seem likely to function harmoniously in a particular range of settings.

In advancing these conclusions, I have to demonstrate a final paradox. I have put forward a largely theoretical argument: to be consistent, I must acknowledge that the real world of evaluation is of necessity far less tidy than the conceptual world I have here created for it.

## References

Becher, T and Maclure, S (1978) *The Politics of Curriculum Change.* Hutchinson, London.
Bruner, J S (1966) *Toward a Theory of Instruction.* Harvard University Press, Cambridge, Mass.
Fielden, J and Pearson, P K (1978) *Costing Educational Practice.* Council for Educational Technology, London.
Glaser, R M (1970) Evaluation of instruction and changing educational models. In Wittrock, M C and Wiley, D E (eds) *The Evaluation of Instruction.* Holt, Rinehart and Winston, New York.
Hamilton, D *et al* (eds) (1977) *Beyond the Numbers Game.* Macmillan, London.
Katz, E (1977) *Social Research on Broadcasting.* BBC, London.
Mackenzie, N *et al* (1975) *Open Learning.* UNESCO, Paris.
Pappert, S (1980) *Mindstorms.* Harvester Press, Brighton.
Parlett, M and Hamilton, D (1976) Evaluation as illumination. In Tawney, D (ed) *Curriculum Evaluation Today.* Macmillan, London.
Schramm, W (ed) (1967) *New Educational Media in Action.* UNESCO/IIEP, Paris.
Smith, L M and Pohland, P A (1974) Education, technology and the rural highlands. In Sjogren, D (ed) *AERA Monograph Series on Curriculum Evaluation No 7: Four Evaluation Examples.* Rand McNally, Chicago.
Stake, R E (1978) The case study in social inquiry. *Educational Researcher,* February.
Stenhouse, L (1975) *An Introduction to Curriculum Research and Development.* Heinemann, London.
Tyler, R W (1949) *Basic Principles of Curriculum and Instruction.* University of Chicago Press, Chicago.

# 2.2 Evaluation Processes and Strategies

## 2.2.1 Evaluating the Process of Learning

C J Lawless
*The Open University*

**Abstract:** Evaluation based on the information processing or cognitive model of learning focuses on the learner's processing skills and cognitive structure. The purposes of instruction are viewed in terms of the knowledge and skills that lie behind particular performance. Evaluative efforts need to be directed at how well students process, structure, and retrieve information. Ways of identifying and assessing deficiencies in these stages are reviewed and related to areas of remedial action. At each stage comparisons are made with the 'test-measurement' and 'illuminative' models of evaluation.

Any model of evaluation (and Eraut, 1972 identifies eleven) represents explicitly or implicitly a view of the nature of learning, what influences it, and how it can be investigated. The traditional 'test measurement' model has close links with the stimulus response approach of behaviourist psychology, while, at the other end of the scale, the 'illuminative' model (Parlett and Hamilton, 1972) represents a wider approach from the social sciences. By its very nature the basic information processing model of learning provided by cognitive psychology focuses attention on the actual process of learning, seeing 'the learner, and his cognitive stages and information processing strategies, as the primary determiner of learning with understanding and long-term memory' (Wittrock, 1974).

Figure 1 illustrates the features of a basic information processing system and the three basic stages into which it can be divided for the practical purpose of evaluation (see Lawless, 1979, and Lawless, 1980, for discussion of its implications for the design of instruction as a whole, and for assessing student performance). In this approach the learner actively processes information received through the senses, encodes it, and stores it. Effective application of knowledge depends on the way it is stored (or 'structured') and the quality of the individual's retrieving or problem-solving skills.

Even though supported by experimental evidence, such a representation of 'the complexities of human mental processes' (Neisser, 1967) is essentially an analogy or model in the sense used in the physical sciences 'to unify limited aspects of a particular reality' (Elton and Laurillard, 1979). This concept of a model has several advantages when used as a basis for the design of instruction, of which evaluation must be seen as an integral part. First, it allows essentially integrated and continuous processes to be divided into stages for practical investigation. Second, it allows other models with different emphases to be used alongside it. Third, it is not put forward as a definitive explanation of learning and covers both controversies and alternative approaches, eg Weil and Joyce (1978) identify six information processing models. Finally, the use of an approach as a model allows techniques from other, even rival, backgrounds, to be used where relevant.

If evaluation is broadly taken to mean investigating learning situations and materials with a view to improving them, then a cognitive approach appears to pose three basic questions. What are the stages of the learning process? How can they be evaluated? What types of changes is it likely to lead to? The main contrast

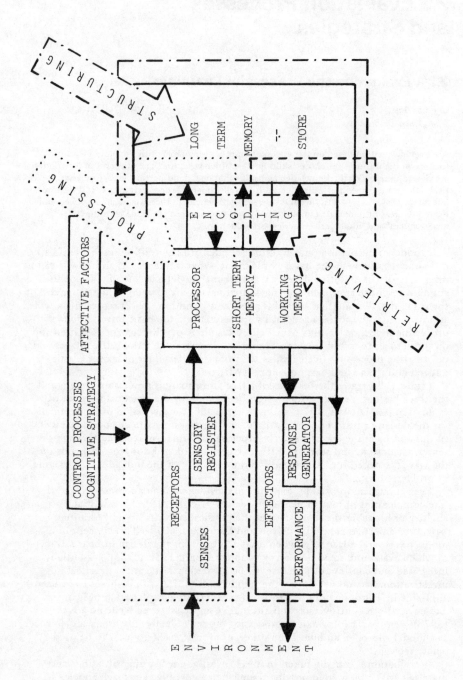

**Figure 1.** *Stages in the information processing model*
*(after Lawless, 1979)*

with other approaches to evaluation is that investigations are carried out *during* learning, rather than just on the results of learning.

The first task of this approach to evaluation is to look into the purposes, stated or otherwise, of instructional situations and materials. Since the cognitive approach is concerned with knowledge and mental procedures, evaluation must be focused on the knowledge and skills that lie behind a specific performance. It is important that students should be right for the right reasons. A learner may give correctly 0.15 as the answer to 0.3 x 0.5, but reveal deficient knowledge if he goes on to give 0.9 for 0.3 x 0.3. Where purpose is stated in performance terms, as a 'behavioural objective', it needs to be asked whether the stated task or behaviour is in fact the objective of instruction or whether its function is rather to sample the student's knowledge. If the performance is the actual objective (eg 'to be able to solve quadratic equations') then the knowledge required to do it needs to be clearly set out. Even the most mundane and apparently repetitive task can require complex procedures for deciding when and when not to perform it. On the other hand if, as is usual in higher education, part, at least, of the purpose of instruction is that the student should acquire knowledge (usually allied, implicitly, to certain mental skills), then performance has a sampling function. The nature of the knowledge to be sampled needs to be probed to see if the performance really does sample what it is claimed to; that it involves using procedures, not just recalling facts. The contrast between these two (rather artificial) positions brings out the need to come to terms with variety in learning. There are different types of purpose, involving different types of learning often within a single course or unit of instruction, and to try to force them into the straightjacket of a single format like the behavioural objectives approach will be counterproductive.

The information processing model is concerned with meaningful learning in which the learner successfully incorporates new facts and skills into his existing cognitive structure. Hence the need to examine the knowledge component, the content, of instruction for potential meaningfulness (see Ausubel *et al*, 1978, for a full discussion of meaningful learning). Where do the concepts or elements come from? What do they mean? How are they used? How do they interrelate? In what ways do they relate to other areas of knowledge? This is an aspect which, as Lewis (1974) has shown is usually totally neglected. Knowledge is not just made up of concepts, but of procedures for using them. Are these procedures set out? What is their origin? How are they applied? These are the sorts of question which need to be asked about statements of aims or purposes of instruction. Where high level procedures are specified, eg that students should think and operate as physicists or historians, it is important to be clear about what exactly is expected of students who are operating in a 'second hand' situation. Are they expected to display the skills or to recall and demonstrate an expert's display of those skills? The results of analysis using these questions have direct implications for both the type of tasks set for assignments and, in some degree, to the sequencing of teaching itself.

Meaningful learning involves building up the cognitive structure, incorporating new concepts and developing richer patterns of relationships. This facilitates further learning particularly when allied to explicit development of learning skills. In evaluating the aims of instruction an important issue is whether the knowledge is really going to lead to further and better learning and, if so, whether it is the type of learning required.

Evaluating the nature of purpose in this way contrasts with the 'test-measurement' model which accepts specified objectives and then investigates the extent to which students have achieved them. The illuminative approach goes in the opposite direction and purposely ignores objectives completely.

Although the working of the information processing system is essentially integrated and continuous it is useful to divide it into stages. In the 'input' stage, attention, selection, and perception prepare the material for encoding and then storing in the structure of the long-term memory. It is usual, though misleading, to refer to this part of the whole system as 'processing'. What this means in practice is well summed up in this description of a particular processing deficiency.

> Most students entering an introductory college physics course do not possess the learning skill of gaining an understanding of a new relation presented to them in a text (although the text discusses this relation at some length). Furthermore, most students do not acquire this learning skill merely as a result of ordinary instruction in a physics course (Reif, Larkin and Bracket, 1976).

Similarly, deficiencies in processing skills have been found by Abercrombie (1960) in medical studies, by Richards (1929) in English literature, and by Perry (1977) in basic reading skills. Thus right at the start of the overall process students are failing to get at the real meaning of the information in the way that it is presented to them.

Evaluating the process of learning requires investigation and sampling *during* the process in order to isolate these learning skill deficiencies. Conventional tests and attitude questionnaires have been used to identify problems in processing, but more limited and direct questioning is needed to identify specific problems. Of particular value in identifying processing problems are interview or 'teach back' techniques (Laurillard, 1979, Pask, 1976, Marton and Saljö, 1976). Since answers to assignment questions tend to be vague rather than right or wrong, Lewis (1974) suggests that students should be asked to explain their answers.

How then are improvements to be made when processing deficiencies are revealed? The first point is that traditionally, and particularly in higher education, such aspects are ignored or it is assumed that learning skills will be acquired by exposure to teaching. The experience of Reif *et al* (1976) that students do *not* acquire effective learning skills without explicit teaching, is more likely to be the case. The cognitive approach focuses attention on changing the learner. This does not, of course, rule out changing and improving instructional materials, but it recognizes that developing processing skills is a long-term educational goal. Particularly in higher education, materials causing problems are often the very subject matter of learning. Practical considerations may preclude revision of teaching materials. This concentration on the learner contrasts with the 'test measurement' approach which assumes a direct link between teaching and learning, and so looks to change the teaching. In complete contrast, the illuminative approach is largely unconcerned with either improving the learner's skills or revising instructional materials.

In looking at how students' processing skills can be improved, two issues need to be faced: the general or specific dichotomy, and the question of individual differences. It would be easy, but mistaken, to assume that what is needed are general learning skills, but as Gibbs (1977) has shown, such 'cook book' approaches rarely succeed because they do not relate directly to students' actual learning experiences and difficulties. Developing processing skills needs to be integrated into the mainstream learning experience both because an improvement in general skills such as reading needs to start with the student, and because some skills are specific to particular subject areas, such as the physics learning skill mentioned earlier. Reif *et al* (1976) identified the skills required and integrated their treatment into a 'Keller Plan' physics course. Abercrombie (1960) and Gibbs (1977) both made extensive use of small group discussions (integrated into regular teaching programmes) which focused on particular learning problems. Sticht (1978) demonstrated the integration of literacy and learning skill training with basic army training, relating 'reading to do' to 'reading to learn'.

Cognitive psychology holds that each individual's cognitive structure and processing skills are unique and there is considerable evidence to show that individuals have different 'cognitive styles' or patterns of learning skills. This is a vast area, but the main issues are whether such differences are relatively fixed traits, ie 'serialist' or 'holist' learning patterns (Pask, 1976), and whether they are qualitative differences, ie 'deep' or 'surface' processors (Marton and Saljö, 1976). Laurillard (1979), however, found that students changed their styles of learning in terms of both Pask's and Marton's approaches, according to their perceptions of the demands of a particular learning task. This highlights the need to take processing skills seriously, at the very least alerting students that this is an important issue.

Processing and structuring are essentially a single process, and separating them, though convenient, is artificial. In looking at students' cognitive structures we are asking firstly whether they know enough to understand the new information; at one level it is as simple as asking if the language is understood. In terms of the information processing approach the following questions need to be posed: Is the student's cognitive structure extensive enough to receive new concepts? During instruction, does cognitive structure develop sufficient complexity to represent the subject matter? Is the structure sufficiently well organized to allow for easy retrieval? Each person's cognitive structure is unique, but there must be sufficient resemblance to the knowledge structure as a public entity to allow for communication with other individuals.

How to test for cognitive structure is a problem. A considerable amount of work has been carried out using word-association tests (see, for example, Shavelson, 1974). Stewart (1979) has highlighted the shortcomings of this approach and in a subsequent article (Stewart, 1980) reports the use of a 'concept-map line labelling task' and a very similar 'tree construction line labelling task'. Basically, students are required to arrange concept labels in a pattern and describe the relationships between the different concepts. This is using the information processing approach very much as a model or an analogy since such a basic representation cannot be said to have more than a basic connection with the complexities of cognitive structure in the brain, but it does reveal understanding and misunderstanding of subject matter. Where it is supported by interviews and analysis of normal testing procedures, a detailed picture of students' cognitive structures can be built up. Structure, like processing, is unlikely to be entirely absent, but it can lack the connections which make application possible.

Where there is evidence that students' cognitive structure is inadequate, two courses of action can be followed. The structure of the teaching material can be examined and where necessary made more explicit. There is evidence that improving the structure of teaching improves student learning (Anderson and Lee, 1975, Trindade, 1972). This may not be as easy as it sounds because academic subjects tend to be studied, researched and taught as narrow, fragmented, specialisms with little or no attempt to relate to other academic areas. There is, however, a world of difference between improving the structure of a lecture or a chapter, and work carried out by cognitive psychologists under laboratory conditions. A more fruitful approach is that of encouraging students to take an active attitude to learning, to seek out and develop links between concepts. 'The ability to think creatively will presumably depend on the extent to which the memory has developed a multiplicity of unusual, but valid, interconnections' (Entwistle and Hounsell, 1975). How material is stored will, to a large extent, determine the ease or difficulty with which it can be retrieved.

Most teachers will have had the experience of receiving a piece of work from a student, an essay or an attempt to solve a problem, which shows an almost total lack of understanding of the subject matter. Yet a couple of simple questions put to the student may reveal that he or she has the knowledge and skills but has failed to use them. In terms of the model, the student failed to retrieve information even though it was in his/her cognitive structure, and it is from this position that the question of retrieval will be considered. As with processing, the general/specific issue has to be faced. A considerable number of articles on how humans solve problems have been written by cognitive psychologists, notably Newell and Simon (1972), and a number of studies have investigated the effectiveness of free-standing problem-solving courses (eg Whimbey, 1977). In spite of the benefit claimed for such general problem-solving approaches, it seems probable that development of problem-solving abilities needs to be embedded in the subject matter of the course. For example, given the specification of the skills of a physicist, social scientist, or historian, as part of the goals of a course, and the identification of that part of those skills which students will be expected to practise, it is important for this to be explicitly explained and opportunities for practice given. Reif *et al* (1976) shows that necessary cognitive skills are not acquired merely by exposure but that 'general cognitive skills necessary for effective performance in a science *can* be taught and should be considered a proper subject for explicit instruction'.

Course assignments, by themselves, rarely provide sufficient detail to establish the extent to which students have mastered the retrieval or problem-solving skills. There remains the risk of the student being right for the wrong reason. In a quest for a test of the quality of learning, Lewis (1973) proposes a three stage assignment in which the student is required to solve a problem, explain the solution and justify his explanation. Requiring students to explain how they solved a problem by presenting them with a structured test will reveal whether their solution has been arrived at in a valid way. There is a circular element in this, since problem-solving has to begin with processing information about the nature of the problem!

By focusing on internal processes which underlie learning skills, the cognitive or information approach emphasizes an area which, traditionally, is ignored by academics. Hence the first result of such an evaluation is to turn the light on dark corners of the educational process. Although there are undoubtedly specific skills to be learned, the raising of awareness of the importance of the issue is the vital first step for both teachers and students. Mistaken perception of the demands of a learning task rather than skill deficiency may be the cause of learning problems (Laurillard, 1979), and while such misconceptions may result from outside influences, eg personal problems or exam pressures (Miller and Parlett, 1974), they may equally well result from simple lack of awareness of the demands of the subject matter. This is what Broudy (1977) calls 'knowing *with*' (to go with 'knowing *how*' and 'knowing *that*'), and links with the need to back skills and knowledge with the ability to select and apply them correctly for a particular situation (Greeno, 1976). To return to the model in Figure 1, this involves the development of the control processes, and the improvement of the ability to learn.

## References

Abercrombie, M L J (1960) *The Anatomy of Judgement.* Hutchinson, London.
Anderson, O R and Lee, M T (1975) Structure in science communication and student recall knowledge. *Science Education* 59, pp 127-38.
Ausubel, D P, Novak, J D and Hanesian, H (1978) *Educational Psychology: A Cognitive View.* Holt, Rinehart and Winston, New York.
Broudy, H S (1977) Types of knowledge and purposes of education. In Anderson, R C, Spiro, R J and Montague, W E (eds) *Schooling and the Acquisition of Knowledge.* Lawrence Erlbaum, Hillsdale, NJ.
Elton, L R B and Laurillard, D M (1979) Trends in research in student learning. *Studies in Higher Education* 4, 1, pp 87-102.
Entwistle, N and Hounsell, D (1975) How students learn: implications for teaching in higher education. In Entwistle, N and Hounsell, D (eds) *How Students Learn.* Institute for Research and Development in Post-Compulsory Education, University of Lancaster.
Eraut, M (1972) Strategies for the evaluation of curriculum materials. In Austwick, K and Harris, N D C (eds) *Aspects of Educational Technology* VI. Pitman, London.

Greeno, J G (1976) Cognitive objectives of instruction: theory of knowledge for solving problems and answering questions. In Klahr, D (ed) *Cognition and Instruction*. Lawrence Erlbaum, Hillsdale, NJ.

Gibbs, G (1977) Can students be taught how to study? *Higher Education Bulletin* 5, 2, pp 107-18.

Laurillard, D M (1979) The processes of student learning. *Higher Education* 9, pp 395-409.

Lawless, C J (1979) Information processing: a model for educational technology. In Page, G T and Whitlock, Q (eds) *Aspects of Educational Technology* **XIII**. Kogan Page, London.

Lawless, C J (1980) Student performance: product of process. In Billing, D (ed) *Indicators of Performance*. Society for Research into Higher Education, Guildford.

Lewis, B N (1973) Educational technology at the Open University: an approach to the problem of quality. *British Journal of Educational Technology* 4, 3, pp 188-204.

Lewis, B N (1974) *New Methods of Assessment and Stronger Methods of Curriculum Design*. The Open University, Milton Keynes.

Marton, F and Saljö, R (1976) On qualitative differences in learning. *British Journal of Educational Psychology* **46**, pp 4-11, 225-27.

Miller, C M L and Parlett, M (1974) *Up to the Mark: A Study of the Examination Game*. Society for Research into Higher Education, London.

Neisser, U (1967) *Cognitive Psychology*. Appleton-Century-Crofts, New York.

Newell, A and Simon, H A (1972) *Human Problem Solving*. Prentice-Hall, Englewood Cliffs, NJ.

Parlett, M and Hamilton, D (1972) *Evaluation as Illumination: A New Approach to the Study of Innovatory Programmes*. Centre for Research in the Educational Sciences, University of Edinburgh.

Pask, G (1976) Styles and strategies of learning. *British Journal of Educational Psychology* **46**, pp 128-48.

Perry, W G (1977) Studying and the student. *Higher Educational Bulletin* 5, 2, pp 119-57.

Reif, F, Larkin, J H and Bracket, G C (1976) Teaching general learning and problem solving skills. *American Journal of Physics* **44**, pp 212-17.

Richards, I A (1929) *Practical Criticism*. Routledge and Kegan Paul, London.

Shavelson, R J (1974) Methods for examining representations of a subject matter structure in a student's memory. *Journal of Research in Science Teaching* 11, pp 231-49.

Sticht, T G (1978) Cognitive research applied to literacy training. In Lesgold, A M, Pellegrino, J W, Fokkema, S D and Glaser, R (eds) *Cognitive Psychology and Instruction*. Plenum, New York.

Stewart, J H (1979) Content and cognitive structure: critique of assessment and representation techniques used by science education researchers. *Science Education* 63, 3, pp 395-405.

Stewart, J H (1980) Techniques for assessing and representing information in cognitive structure. *Science Education* 64, 2, pp 223-35.

Trindade, A L (1972) Structure in science teaching and learning outcomes. *Journal of Research in Science Teaching* 9, pp 65-74.

Weil, M and Joyce, B (1978) *Information Processing Models of Teaching*. Prentice-Hall, Englewood Cliffs, NJ.

Whimbey, A (1977) Teaching sequential thought: the cognitive skills approach. *Phi Delta Kappan* 59, 4, pp 255-9.

Wittrock, M C (1974) Learning as a generative process. *Educational Psychologist* 11, 2, pp 87-95.

# 2.2.2 Evaluating the Process of Evaluation

P Lefrere
*The Open University*

Abstract: Current alternatives to 'systematic' approaches to designing and evaluating instruction may have limitations that are generally unrecognized by their users.

For example, evaluators who adopt only a single approach to evaluation may find there are mismatches between their conceptions and teachers' conceptions of education and evaluation.

Even evaluators who avoid such mismatches should benefit from examining the literature, briefly described here, on how individuals and groups process information and make decisions. Evaluation tools and procedures may therefore change, especially if it proves possible to make teachers' and evaluators' decision procedures more explicit and less intuitive.

## Introduction — Changing Views of Evaluation

A decade ago, educational technology was generally seen as a systematic, prescriptive and objectives-based way of designing, carrying out and evaluating the total process of learning and teaching (eg Tickton, 1970). The methods of evaluation were thought to be similarly systematic, unproblematic and straightforward. Thus, for Popham and Baker (1970), evaluation consisted of just five basic operations: establishing specific goals; developing a measuring device; pre-assessing students; implementing an instructional plan; and measuring and interpreting evidence of student achievement. Their approach represented the general view, for it favoured the method of evaluation, now called 'congruent evaluation' (Stufflebeam *et al*, 1971), which is concerned with measuring the degree to which the stated educational objectives for a course are congruent with what is achieved. Growing awareness of the limitations of that method — and of the prescriptive stance — is indicated by the many other models of evaluation and types of evaluator which have been identified and adopted since then; in 1972, Eraut was able to write of 11 such, while by 1978, Hawkridge had been able to raise this total to 30!

This diversity led to some uncertainty and 'role-reappraisal' by educational technologists, as evidenced by a description of evaluation as the '. . . unifying activity in which all those calling themselves educational technologists can join together. There is something for everyone [from]. . . participant observations of human interactions [to] . . . the empathetic "students'-friend" [who] can vet the course materials in advance . . .' (Rowntree, 1976).

Of course, one could modify the old prescriptive stance to make it more informed by evaluation, but this is not what was advocated. What was advocated was its rejection in favour of evaluation — which unfortunately does not guarantee that students' learning will improve.

## The Students'-Friend

As with any professional role, both the purely evaluative and purely prescriptive roles, to be filled successfully, require access to reliable tools and procedures. But how reliable *is* the educational technologist's professional 'box of tricks' (Lewis, 1980)?

1. Are opinions presented as facts?
2. Do arguments loop and change?
3. Are there digressions or irrelevancies?
4. Are assertions grounded in theories?
5. Are ideas fully developed or related?
6. Is the material consistent?
7. Is the material presented systematically?

This list contains some rather arbitrary self-evaluation criteria which I tried to keep in mind when writing the present paper; different criteria might emerge for readers with a different reading purpose. It is not clear to me whether a single such check-list would be used by a 'students'-friend' in trying to anticipate readers' difficulties, or whether the 'students'-friend' would have several models of readers, and so several sets of criteria to apply. The former seems more probable, to judge from one study where a group of 'experts' (actually teachers and student teachers) were asked to vet course material. Yet in this study, not only did they sometimes fail to identify problems experienced by students, but they also often detected supposed problems which created no difficulty (Frase *et al*, 1974).

## The Professional Evaluator

Whatever type of evaluator we try to be, and no matter how good our procedures, certain questions seem to recur. For example, in negotiating with teachers, should we present them with evaluation *options*, and, if so, how should those options be presented? Again, once an option has been selected, how should subsequent evaluation reports be presented? These questions hide other problems, of which four will be considered now.

1. Choosing an appropriate sample size.
2. Resolving apparent contradictions in evaluation findings.
3. Recognizing and allowing for mismatches in conceptions of education.
4. Reconciling ease of evaluation with ease of implementation of findings.

Professional evaluators should be able to cope with such problems with assurance, yet, as reported elsewhere (Smith, 1980), there is still no consensus in the literature on the question of sample size: most advice assumes that you need statistically significant evaluation data, and justifications have been given for sample sizes from as low as 10 to as high as 3,000, each of which meets some form of that statistical criterion! (Incidentally, if your intended sample size seems too small or not fully representative, Smith's own advice is to ignore the statistics and '. . . ask authors whether they will accept conclusions based upon the [group] . . . that you would like to use'.)

The literature is similarly vague on the second problem: how to deal with apparently inconsistent evaluation data, which may have been collected in different ways. The evaluator's report has to synthesize these findings in a systematic way (see the first list, point 7), a problem that is still unresolved in the possibly simpler context of synthesizing research findings from different investigators (Pillemer and Light, 1980).

## Whose Perspective?

The remaining two problems illustrate another point, to which I shall return: that the evaluator may not share the teacher's perspective, so mismatches may occur. The first possible mismatch I shall consider concerns one's conception of education. Even if a 'students'-friend' can identify difficulties in advance, this may not be seen as any reason for action: although conventional wisdom might indicate that problems, once revealed, should be eliminated before students encounter them; others contend that — in higher education at least — some should be left. The argument runs that 'real', rather than 'perfunctory' learning involves surmounting difficulties, becoming a critic, etc; also, it is said that a learner's initial confusion is not necessarily a bad thing (Northedge, 1976). Clearly, if an author holds such a view, and the evaluator does not know this, but goes off to collect 'objective' immediate-performance-based evaluation data, some disappointment will ensue. That would be an extreme example, with at least one obvious cause, of evaluation data not being fully accepted by an author or lecturer. I must emphasize here that I am not advocating an unquestioning acceptance by an evaluator of a teacher's expressed aims, even though this may represent a change in role. The difficulty is that, particularly with courses which are experiential rather than didactic, the evaluator may be under pressure to adopt informal methods (Duchastel, 1976).

Yet those methods do not, by themselves, assure use of evaluation findings. As Heilman (1980) has observed, people who do not like evaluation results often want to reject them, and the use of soft and informal methods can provide grounds for doing so. As he notes, if goals and perceptions shift, then 'Even the most sincere [teacher] . . . can find, in the end, that the "evaluation" answered the wrong question or missed the main point. When that happens, the active-reactive-adaptive evaluator is deprived of the principal rationale he or she had . . . [the teacher's approval]'.

Because of this difficulty, there has been a tendency at the Open University for large-scale evaluations to be of another type: *empirical developmental testing* (Henderson and Nathenson, 1976). In the past, that testing has been in the form of 'piloting' mimeographed drafts of our teaching material, before it is printed. In some ways, it is reminiscent of the older 'congruence' evaluation, since the variables which contribute to collecting useful and implemented feedback are seen as being: the relationship between performance data and other types of student feedback; the use of feedback in making revisions; the selection and motivation of testers; the development of data-collection systems; and the implementation of revisions. It has therefore been criticized as being '. . . based on the teacher's or evaluator's terms' and taking '. . . no account of what is to count as an educational experience or achievement in the learner's terms. This evaluation contains the implicit assumption of producing one ideal teaching treatment, which does not recognize the wide range of students' abilities and learning styles' (Morgan *et al*, 1980). While there is something in that criticism, piloting material in this way may well satisfy the demands of treatment-minded teachers.

The last of the four problems arises not from any disparity in views of what is *desirable* but from what is *practicable*. Recently, as Kirkup (1981) points out, some of the techniques of developmental testing have been transferred to a post-presentation evaluation of our New Technology Foundation Course. In that evaluation, the students' learning materials were in their final polished form; the idea was to use the first full cohort of students to identify weaknesses in the published course, with a view to revising it after two years. Unfortunately, while that methodology seemed, in the eyes of the evaluators, to provide data which was both useful and timely, it was not always the source of revisions. With hindsight, part of this can be attributed to the difficulty of maintaining teachers' commitment to evaluation and revision, over a time period at least one year longer than in the more usual piloting schemes. Perhaps as important is the great difference, not always recognized, between evaluating drafts and evaluating the final product.

For example, as Forman (1980) notes: when evaluating television programmes, for example, there can be 14 different evaluation stages for the television component alone. Evaluating the final stage — the polished programme — may be pointless if remake facilities are limited. As often demonstrated, more cost-effective is the evaluation of the final script or the rough cut: for authors and producers may then be better placed to accept as implementable the findings from a 'treatment' (or 'statement of intention') evaluation, as used for the Foundation Course's programmes.

## Mismatches

To summarize my argument so far, I have indicated a number of potential mismatches between evaluators' and teachers' conceptions of, respectively, education (eg Northedge, 1976); evaluation in education (eg Morgan *et al*, 1980); evaluation expertise (Lewis, 1980); and evaluators' findings and the options available for change (Kirkup, 1981).

I shall consider one more: conceptions of evaluation in general. According to Clift and Imrie (1980), many teachers in higher education still conceive of evaluation in terms of the congruence model, which apparently suggests to a teacher '. . . an exercise in which their performance will be rated along some continuum of effectiveness [and] . . . this current perception of evaluation [may be] . . . a major cause of resistance to and, in some cases, rejection of evaluation programmes by university teachers'. They therefore suggest a less-threatening 'intentional evaluation' scheme, which presents evaluation differently: '. . . as a learning situation in which staff and students learn how to handle and improve the contingencies of a course'. Put simply, this means involving staff and students more, so that implementation of evaluation findings is more likely. The actual mechanisms they suggest are, in my view, somewhat manipulative, but their scheme is interesting for another reason: while their data collection methods are not unusual, their description of the process of evaluation is cast in cognitive terms. By analogy with three stages of learning (apprehending, acquisition and remembering), they argue that evaluation can be viewed as apprehending, acquisition and application. They did not take that statement very far, but it has important consequences. In particular, as I shall demonstrate shortly, existing evaluation procedures might be modified to take into greater account the many ways in which individuals and groups — including evaluators — acquire and process information and make decisions.

## Information Processing

Cognitive psychology tells us that each party involved in an evaluation project — the student, the teacher and the evaluator — is prone to errors of various kinds. This will be obvious to anyone who has asked students to comment on their learning both while they study and after they have studied some material; the concurrent and retrospective data may differ, partly because forgetting can be both general and selective, but also because students may not process consistently the teaching material and questions about that material. Memory distortion and selective perception are not the only factors to influence retrospective self-reports; the basis for the students' views of themselves and their performance may be changed by the material or by being asked questions about it, leading to the phenomenon of the 'response-shift' (Howard et al, 1979). Similarly, the actual form of the questions may be a critical factor; rating scales which are labelled (eg excellent to poor) or numbered (eg 1 to 5) may be given different interpretations by different students (Frisbie and Brandenburg, 1979). Self-report measures can be made more reliable by relating them to a more meaningful yardstick (eg 'Look back to the rating you gave the last section; how does the present section compare?'), or by measuring students' intentions as an indirect measure of their feelings about the material — a 'behaviouroid measure' (Aronson and Carlsmith, 1968).

Many other familiar illustrations could be given of how the evaluation tools we use may determine the answers we obtain; I turn now to the question of how we deal with those answers. There is extensive evidence of the existence of a large number of factors which cause us to make consistent errors when we evaluate something, or when our evaluation of that something is itself evaluated by an author or group of authors. For example, we should all be aware that the sequence in which information (eg the text of an evaluation report; an audio-tape) is processed (eg studied; listened to) can influence the interpretation placed on it. Some of the influences will arise from the motives and fears of the recipient of the information, while others will be more obviously 'cognitive'. Further details can be found in books by Hogarth (1980); Nisbet and Ross (1980); and Mabry and Barnes (1980); and in papers by Shavelson et al (1977); and Mitroff and Bonoma (1978). The latter proffer one possible alternative to 'the usual approach [to evaluation which involves the author] combining . . . his own biases with the [unknown] biases of the researcher and making a decision . . . both . . . must move backward from the data to confront both their own preferred background assumptions, [and] . . . competing but plausible set of counterassumptions. Second, they must [move] forward from the data to construct a set of policy options consistent with their preferred assumptions and with the competing assumptions'. Of course, that alternative takes the data as given. Some means must also be found of communicating to an author what assumptions have been made in obtaining the data.

In so doing, educational technologists should bear in mind how easy it is for evaluators or teachers to experience: misperceptions of randomness; unrealized overdependence on data from small samples; the related 'availability' bias; 'anchoring' bias; 'hindsight' bias; and the desire for redundant information (Lefrere *et al*, 1980). Each can result in disproportionate (high or low) use of particular types of data, and inconsistent gathering of information; knowledge of how they arise might allow the criteria for reaching particular evaluation judgements to be made more explicit and less intuitive.

This brings me back to evaluators' views of education and the learner, and so to my final remarks. Easley (1977), in a paper on various possible perspectives on teaching and learning, writes of the need '. . . to alert researchers and practitioners of various persuasions to the social and cognitive phenomena in which they play a part'. This I have tried to do here, although I have not tried to identify in any detailed way, better ways of communicating with authors. Those interested in that may find the way ahead is indicated by writers such as Moxley (1979), who advises that much current educational research is made unnecessarily complex and inaccessible because we cannot see the wood for the trees (and nor either can our clients and colleagues, the authors). He uses a three-way classification ('subjective', 'individual' and 'aggregate') of the information we collect, a classification which seems capable of describing all the commonly-used evaluation models (as well as suggesting some new combinations). Translating such ideas into briefing documents for authors and evaluators might prove very useful, but I leave that to others. However, I must point out that this can lead to a change in role. I therefore close by noting the opinion of Robert Stake (quoted in Perloff, 1979). He sees a need for the professional evaluator to strive to separate his function as a data gatherer from his sentiments and values about someone else's material. Educational technologists may view evaluation differently, perhaps as just part of an educational technology service, where it is quite legitimate to attempt to improve the skills of all concerned. But in Stake's opinion: 'It is unethical to help improve the decision-making function, especially to make it more explicit and less intuitive, if accomplished under the guise of an evaluation service'.

## References

Aronson, E and Carlsmith, J (1968) Experimentation in social psychology. In Lindzey, G and Aronson, E (eds) *The Handbook of Social Psychology*, 2. *Research Methods* (Second Edition). Addision-Wesley, Reading, Mass.

Clift, J C and Imrie, B W (1980) The design of evaluation for learning. *Higher Education* 9, 1, pp 69-80.

Duchastel, P C (1976) 'TAD 292 — Art and Environment' and its challenge to educational technology. *Programmed Learning and Educational Technology* 13, 4, pp 61-6.

Easley, J A (1977) Seven modelling perspectives on teaching and learning: some interrelations and cognitive effects. *Instructional Science* 6, 4, pp 319-67.

Eraut, M (1972) Strategies for the evaluation of curriculum materials. In Austwick, K and Harris, N D C (eds) *Aspects of Educational Technology* VI. Pitman, London.

Forman, D C (1980) How to evaluate educational television. *Instructional Innovator* 25, 9, pp 39-41.

Frase, L E *et al* (1974) Product validation: pilot test or panel review? *Educational Technology* 14, 8, pp 32-5.

Frisbie, D A and Brandenburg, D C (1979) Equivalence of questionnaire items with varying response formats. *Journal of Educational Measurement* **16**, 1, pp 43-8.

Hawkridge, D G (1978) *Caricatures of Educational Evaluators* (mimeo). Open University, Milton Keynes.

Heilman, J G (1980) Paradigmatic choices in evaluation methodology. *Evaluation Review* **4**, 5, pp 693-712.

Henderson, E and Nathenson, M (1976) Developmental testing: an empirical approach to course improvement. *Programmed Learning and Educational Technology* **13**, 4, pp 31-42.

Hogarth, R M (1980) *Judgement and Choice — the Psychology of Decision.* Wiley, Chichester.

Howard, G S, Schmeck, R R and Bray, J H (1979) Internal invalidity in studies employing self-report instruments: a suggested remedy. *Journal of Educational Measurement* **16**, 2, pp 129-35.

Kirkup, G (1981) Evaluating and improving learning materials: a case study. In Percival, F and Ellington, H I (eds) *Aspects of Educational Technology* **XV**. Kogan Page, London.

Lefrere, P, Dowie, J and Whalley, P (1980) Educating for justified uncertainty. In Winterburn, R and Evans, L (eds) *Aspects of Educational Technology* **XIV**. Kogan Page, London.

Lewis, B N (1980) The professional standing of educational technology. In Howe, A (ed) *International Yearbook of Educational and Instructional Technology*. Kogan Page, London.

Mabry, E A and Barnes, R E (1980) *The Dynamics of Small Group Communication.* Prentice-Hall, Englewood Cliffs, New Jersey.

Mitroff, I and Bonoma, T V (1978) Psychological assumptions, experimentation, and real world problems: a critique and an alternate approach to evaluation. *Evaluation Quarterly* **2**, 2, pp 235-60.

Morgan, A R, Gibbs, G and Taylor, E (1980) The development of educational technology: alternative perspectives on evaluation. In Winterburn, R and Evans, L (eds) *Aspects of Educational Technology* **XIV**. Kogan Page, London.

Moxley, R A (1979) Subjective, individual and aggregate references in educational research. *Instructional Science* **8**, 2, pp 169-205.

Nisbet, R and Ross, L (1980) *Human Inference: Strategies and Shortcomings of Social Judgement.* Prentice-Hall, Englewood Cliffs, New Jersey.

Northedge, A (1976) Examining our implicit analogies for learning processes. *Programmed Learning and Educational Technology* **13**, 4, pp 67-78.

Perloff, R (ed) (1979) *Evaluator Interventions: Pros and Cons.* Sage, Beverly Hills.

Pillemer, D B and Light, R J (1980) Synthesizing outcomes: how to use research evidence from many studies. *Harvard Educational Review* **50**, 2, pp 176-95.

Popham, W J and Baker, E L (1970) *Systematic Instruction.* Prentice-Hall, Englewood Cliffs, New Jersey.

Rowntree, D (1976) Evaluation: the critical ingredient of educational technology? *Programmed Learning and Educational Technology* **13**, 4, pp 7-9.

Shavelson, R J, Caldwell, J and Izu, T (1977) Teachers' sensitivity to the reliability of information in making pedagogical decisions. *American Educational Research Journal* **14**, 1, pp 83-97.

Smith, M E (1980) How big a sample do I need for my evaluation? *NSPI Journal* **19**, 10, pp 3-10.

Stufflebeam, D I et al (1971) *Educational Evaluation and Decision Making.* Peacock, Itasca, Illinois.

Tickton, S C (ed) (1970) *To Improve Learning: An Evaluation of Instructional Technology.* Bowker, New York.

## 2.2.3 Conducting Programme Evaluations: Some Considerations

D C Moors
*Nova Scotia Department of Education, Canada*

Abstract: While most educators can suggest some reasons for, and some expected outcomes of, an evaluation of their programmes, many are at a loss for, or lack confidence in, suggesting the specifics associated with conducting the evaluative activity.

This paper will attempt to provide some suggestions for these activities as they relate to the following questions: (i) Who should be involved in directing or managing the overall programme evaluation process? (ii) How should evaluative questions be determined? (iii) What types of instruments should be used? (iv) How should the results of an evaluation process be handled? Examples of materials and suggested procedures, drawn from actual evaluations conducted by the Nova Scotia Department of Education, will be outlined.

## Introduction

Programme evaluation within an educational or occupational training context can be described as a systematic activity involving the analysis or documentation of programme-related components and processes, the measurement of variables associated with programme interests, and the elaboration of recommendations based upon a consideration of the information. This definition incorporates Smith's (1975) suggestion that programme evaluation is more than assessment, Hawkins' (1980) emphasis on programme elements during evaluation, and the systematic nature of activities during a programme evaluation as emphasized by Hyman and Wright (1967) and Stake (1967). A means of translating these concepts into actual activities has been previously described by Moors (1979).

Many who are professionally involved in the planning and delivery of education programmes recognize the value of programme evaluation. The activity provides opportunities for feedback, accountability, and cost-benefit information, to name a few. In spite of these perceived outcomes, the actual mechanics of meaningfully involving those who participate in the education activity (especially instructors) throughout a comprehensive programme evaluation sequence represents an obstacle. Educators tend to be well-versed in assessment techniques associated with their *primary* programme emphasis. For example, instructors tend to be able to assess curriculum, or administrators frequently audit their areas of programme responsibility. This in no way insures that professional educators can effectively participate in activities associated with the evaluation of a total programme, especially in those activities which relate to components and processes beyond their sphere of primary programme involvement. As educators, we tend to lack the skills associated with evaluating aspects of the system peripherally related to our primary responsibilities.

The problem is similar to the earlier dilemmas experienced by many education boards who attempted to centralize curriculum development activities. In such circumstances, those who spent extensive periods of time out of a learner environment progressively lost the ability to produce viable products for use by classroom instructors. One effective approach to solving this was to have those instructors, who were to use the product, actively participate in its development. Instructors frequently require, and are afforded, the opportunity to upgrade their curriculum development skills in order to engage in such activities. This is a normal professional responsibility, and it is now a well recognized premise of many education systems.

This same need or requirement is applicable to the development and use of skills associated with programme evaluation activities. Developing these skills among the personnel of an education system can be viewed as an innovation. To be successful in the development of these skills throughout an education system, phases associated with the continuation and diffusion of the innovation can be described. Continuation refers to the ongoing nature of activities designed to develop the skills once such programmes are initiated. Diffusion refers to the use of information associated with the innovation by other educational systems or activities.

Reilly and Starr (1980) identify factors which positively influence the continuation and diffusion of an educational innovation. The two most important factors include the support and co-operation of (i) administrative staff and (ii) instructional staff. This paper describes an approach intended to develop, among instructors and others who are involved in the educational effort, the skills associated with participating in programme evaluation activities. It is assumed that the availability of such skills will assist in the development of support for the programme evaluation process among instructors and administrators, thereby facilitating the continuation and diffusion of the innovation. It is also assumed that the support necessary for the implementation of recommendations contained in any programme evaluation report would be increased because of instructor participation in the evaluation process. While this may be true for all programme sponsors, the influences of the effort on the instructors is of prime importance.

## Who Should Be Involved?

In order to infuse and maximize the participation of instructors and other programme personnel in the complete programme evaluation process, two interacting activities occur. First of all, the activities associated with the evaluation of a particular programme, including the development of a detailed plan, are directed by an evaluation committee. Each committee is structured to reflect the sponsors or stakeholders associated with the particular programme or educational activity being evaluated. For most occupational training programmes in Nova Scotia, the committee structure begins with a representative of the funding source (Canada Employment and Immigration Commission — Regional Office) and a representative of the Nova Scotia Department of Education. Other sponsors (agencies who exercise influence over programme related activities) are invited to join the committee. While the standards or guidelines of committee membership continue to evolve, the usual procedure is to invite at least one instructor from the programme to assume committee membership.

One programme evaluation which is at present under way reflects this trend. For the evaluation of the Medical Laboratory Technology Training Programme in Nova Scotia, the following groups or agencies have been asked to name representatives to the committee:

- ☐ The Provincial Department of Education.
- ☐ The Nova Scotia Institute of Technology (where the first year of the programme is given).
- ☐ Each of the five provincial hospitals in which the second year of the programme is given.
- ☐ The Provincial Department of Health.
- ☐ The Provincial and National professional accreditation associations.

In this instance, instructors will participate on the committee as representatives of the programme delivery units. Administration involvement will occur through the Provincial Departments of Education and Health.

The second activity which insures involvement and support from critical levels is the operation of a workshop designed to develop the plan for the programme evaluation sequence. This workshop lasts over three days. The following is an example of the workshop objectives.

**Programme Evaluation Workshop (Cape Breton Regional Vocational School)**

*Objective:*

To increase the skills of a selected group of Cape Breton Regional Vocational School staff members in the activities associated with planning a programme evaluation.

Each participant will, within two months of the completion of the workshop, provide a plan that identifies the sequence of activities anticipated during an evaluation or training programme in which they professionally participate.

This plan will be rated as acceptable by the workshop participant (author), the workshop leader and the Principal of the Cape Breton Regional Vocational School.

A more specific objective associated with the development of the evaluation plan during the workshop is as follows:

Each participant will review the Moors (1979) programme evaluation model/narrative. Each participant will then suggest at least two activities for all of the model sub-systems as applied to the evaluation of their own educational or training programme.

Therefore, two products of the workshop activity can be described. The first is an increase in the level of information that workshop participants have associated with programme evaluation concepts. The second product is a detailed evaluation plan that provides the basis of all further activities associated with the planned programme evaluation. By 'front ending' each programme evaluation sequence with this workshop activity the persons who are to be involved in, and will be affected by, the evaluation sequence engage in a critical step towards eliciting their continued assistance, co-operation and support during the programme evaluation.

In summary, an important consideration in the activities associated with programme evaluation is the involvement and support of administrators and instructors. This relates to both the continuation and diffusion of programme evaluation activities, especially when the concept is at an innovative stage within an education system. Three important ways to facilitate this involvement include:

1. insuring that both groups are included on the programme evaluation committee;
2. providing persons with the opportunity to develop skills associated with conducting and participating in programme evaluation;
3. involving these persons in the development of the programme evaluation plan.

## Determining Evaluative Questions

Evaluation sequences can run astray or remain incomplete because the evaluative questions and interests remain undefined. It is reasonable to expect that the areas of evaluative questioning will reflect the programme-related responsibilities of the various sponsors. It is also reasonable to expect that further areas of interest will evolve as the various components and processes of the programme become clarified during the initial stage of the evaluation sequence. An appropriate strategy for determining evaluative questions is to store evaluative interests or areas of questioning until the descriptive information relating to the programme has been documented. Following this, each of the stored evaluative interests are retrieved and related to the defined programme objectives. This permits each evaluative interest to be refined into a specific evaluative question and stated in terms of the programme perspective. The next step is to describe the research requirements of each question and the programme implications of the possible answers to the questions. This elaboration gives decision-makers the opportunity to put in order of priority the evaluative questions — to determine if the question and the associated research are worth the investment of the research. Decisions to pursue the necessary research are then taken in light of the time and resources available and the meaningfulness or importance of the resulting information.

This approach was used during the evaluation of an academic upgrading programme for unemployed adults in Nova Scotia and permitted the general type of question 'Are the mathematics learning activity packages (LAPs) effective?' to be refined to 'Are the mathematics LAPs effective (i) as resource materials in a self-directed learning situation, and (ii) as resource materials to instructors?' The question associated with effectiveness in self-directed learning situations could be answered by examining the number of self-test tries by a student to criterion performance for each LAP. The effectiveness of the materials to instructors could be measured by constructing an instrument for an instructor rating of the various LAP sections. Elaborating on the self-directed learning questions, the evaluation committee suggested a 70 per cent successful performance level of student 'first tries' on the self-tests would mean that no changes in the LAPs for self-instructional use would be recommended. A lower success score would indicate the need for revisions. Because the programme operators intended that the instructional situation would rely heavily on self-directed learning, this evaluative question was given a high priority by the evaluation committee and subsequently pursued.

In summary, identifying evaluative questions is an important activity within any programme evaluation sequence. One useful approach is to refine general statements of interest areas to specific evaluative questions. Research and programme implications associated with the question should be clearly identified. This allows for meaningful decisions relative to which evaluative questions should be addressed.

## Instruments

The selection of instruments for evaluation purposes depends on the specific evaluative questions defined for further research. The traditional instrument categories have been outlined by Denton (1973) and are well known. These include: attitude/interest tests; criterion referenced tests; questionnaires or interviews; direct observation; and unobtrusive tests ('inference twice removed'). To these should be added the further categories of 'illuminative' instruments and check-lists. Illuminative evaluation instruments, as described by Morgan, Gibbs and Taylor (1980), have evolved because of the interest in qualitative evaluation techniques. Check-lists have become popular because of the necessity for job performance measures and include not only basic check-lists but also performance tests and observation scales. This necessity relates specifically to occupational and industry-based training programmes and has been emphasized by Forman (1980). These two types of instrumentation are relevant to the present discussion because of the information they provide to instructional staff, both during and following the programme evaluation process. In short, they provide one basis for the diffusion of an innovation.

Check-lists which are developed for programme evaluation purposes can be effectively used in subsequent instructional situations. This is especially true of instances in which an industry supervisor works with the instructor to develop the instrument.

A type of qualitative instrument has been developed and employed within Nova Scotia programmes to determine the degree to which LAPs represent an effective instructor-used teaching resource. In order to develop the instrument, a group of instructors identified the most and least preferred characteristics of instructional materials associated with the various sections of a LAP (objectives, prescriptive materials, self-tests, etc). Through a conciliation rating procedure each of these characteristics was assigned a value and a weighting factor in relation to each of the other identified characteristics. This provided a basis for a five-point rating scale associated with each of the four most important characteristics during the assessment of the LAPs by other instructors. The instrument then not only provided data for evaluation purposes. Because it reflected qualitative factors (characteristics used in instruction), it was also an effective aid in determining areas for curriculum refinements and provided guidelines for future resource development. Thus, programme evaluation activities should, where possible, select and develop instruments which can assist programme-related activities beyond the evaluation sequence.

## Handling the Results

In the final analysis, programme evaluation should provide feedback information associated with future programme direction and activities. While support and commitment for the evaluation process can be generated by treating programme evaluation as an innovation, the activities an organization initiates, based upon the recommendations of the evaluation report (ie the overall product of the evaluation process), truly determine the difference between attempts to examine quality control and efforts to maximize quality assurance. The difference in these two concepts in an education system has been identified by English (1980), who suggests that quality control is internal to the organization while quality assurance is external. Within the present context, the evaluation process represents an attempt to identify information associated with quality control. Activities based upon the resulting recommendations fall within the domain of quality assurance.

By involving all sponsors throughout the complete programme evaluation sequence, the basis of the recommendations should be understood by the agency or stakeholder to which they relate. These recommendations should be circulated, in draft form, to the sponsor agencies through their representative on the evaluative committee. Within each sponsor organization, the discussion, refinement, and confirmation of the relevant recommendations can be 'brokered' by their committee representative. This person has the advantage of being able to elaborate upon the information placing it within its proper perspective. Following this, a final or 'confirmation' meeting of the evaluation committee permits a formal opportunity to refine and accept the evaluation report. A procedure which incorporates these, or similar, activities simply views the recommendations of an evaluation report as information to be diffused, again requiring the support and commitment of programme sponsors.

## Conclusion

In conclusion, the nature of the evaluation process, to be meaningful, must establish a basis for programme sponsor support and co-operation. This suggests that activities should not be pursued which establish an adverse relationship among the participants. Rather, planned activities which are designed to involve and develop the skills of various groups associated with the programme evaluation are necessary.

## References

Denton, W T (1973) *Program Evaluation in Vocational and Technical Education.* ERIC Clearinghouse on Vocational and Technical Education, Columbus, Ohio.
English, F W (1980) A new department, a new era, a new chance to make a difference in education. *Educational Technology* 20, 4, pp 8-14.
Forman, D C (1980) Evaluation of training: present and future. *Educational Technology* 20, 10, pp 48-51.

Hawkins, C A (1980) *An Evaluation Strategy Based on Pragmatic Electicism.* O and Ovan O, RV Utrecht.

Hyman, H and Wright, C R (1967) Evaluating social action programs. In Lazarsfeld, P, Sewell, W and Lensky, H W (eds) *Uses of Sociology.* Basic Books, New York.

Morgan, A R, Gibbs, G and Taylor, E (1980) The Department of Educational Technology: alternative perspectives on evaluation. In Winterburn, R and Evans, L (eds) *Aspects of Educational Technology* **XIV.** Kogan Page, London.

Moors, D C (1979) A model for evaluating educational programmes. In Page, G T and Whitlock, Q (eds) *Aspects of Educational Technology* **XIII.** Kogan Page, London.

Reilly, D H and Starr, N K (1980) Innovative program assessment: considerations for continuation, diffusion and adoption. *Educational Technology* 20, 10, pp 13-17.

Smith, R C (1975) Program evaluation: any prime sponsor can. *Manpower.* May.

Stake, R E (1967) The countenance of educational evaluation. *Teachers College Record* 68, pp 523-40.

# 2.2.4 Evaluation Through the Aperture: An Analysis of Mediated Observational Techniques

**R M Bernard and C H Petersen**
*Concordia University, Canada*
**R D Brown**
*University of Nebraska, USA*

**Abstract:** A current conceptualization of the educational technologist (Mitchell, 1975) is one involving a multiplicity of possible roles, one of which is evaluation. Even if educational technologists are not employed as primary evaluators, they should be aware of evaluation strategies and the strengths and weaknesses of various evaluative methodologies. The purpose of this paper is to broadly sketch the potentials and limitations of data gathered through observation, with particular emphasis placed on the role of media in evaluation.

## Measurement and/or Observation

In many minds, measurement and evaluation have becone synonymous (Gardner, 1977). This may be partly due to the application of scientific research models to educational evaluation. A basic assumption is that the phenomena in question possess significant measurable attributes and that instruments can be designed which can sensitively detect those attributes. Indeed, many of the failures of the measurement approach, according to Gardner (1977) can be attributed to violations of this underlying premise.

Measurement lends itself well to evaluation-by-objective models (Tyler, 1942; Bloom *et al,* 1970; Popham, 1969) since evidence of summative output based on specific behavioural events are identified in advance and serve as the evaluative criteria. Eisner (1972) and others (eg Stake, 1975) have argued that evaluation-by-objectives and associated measurement practices tend to obfuscate potentially critical differences which may manifest themselves only during the process of learning. Also, Stake (1975) points out that certain content areas, such as the arts, are not conducive to quantification and therefore should be evaluated by employment of less restrictive models such as programme portrayal. Observational methodologies and other qualitative evidence are suggested as alternatives or supplements to objective data under such conditions.

Unquestionably, the appropriateness of any measurement and/or observational methodologies is dependent upon situational and philosophic issues, which must be resolved prior to evaluation.

## Human Observers of Human Behaviour

The prominent role of observation in inquiry has been touted in both literature and science. Sherlock Holmes was portrayed as possessing 'extraordinary powers of observation' upon which rested his 'science of deduction and analysis'. The contributions of Piaget (1926) and Gesell (1934) were founded upon observational methodologies which led, in both cases, to striking changes in our views of child development. Similarly, the sciences of ethnography and anthropology have relied heavily upon evidence collected through observation.

Human observers are, to a large extent, low fidelity recording instruments. They suffer from fatigue, expectation bias and a host of associated problems (Campbell, 1959), some of which can be corrected and some of which cannot. Even when they are highly trained, observer variability over time (Webb, Campbell, Schwartz and Sechrest, 1966) represents a major threat which is difficult to foresee. Observers may become less observant as boredom sets in, or conversely, more attentive as the task becomes better learned or provides the opportunity for participation. An extreme case of observer participation is reported by Lang and Lang (1960). During a sociological study of a Billy Graham Crusade in New York, two scientific observers became so moved by the experience that they made the 'Decision for Christ' and left their observational vantage points to walk down the aisle. While such blatant observer participation bias may not jeopardize the course of normal educational evaluation, educational technologists should be aware of the extent to which variability may influence evaluative outcomes.

When one of the more descriptive evaluative models is employed, such as the naturalistic approach(es) suggested by Guba (1978), programme portrayal (Stake, 1975), or the case study approach (Stake, 1978), data coded into nominal categories may not be appropriate or desirable. Under these conditions, observers may be asked to write anecdotal notes or in some other way provide descriptive feedback concerning the phenomenon being studied. Mediated observational procedures may be most productively employed in such circumstances. The remainder of this paper is devoted to a brief review and description of mediated observation, its potential role within various evaluative frameworks and its methodological limitations.

## Mediated Observation

It is not surprising that scientific disciplines which regularly employ observational methodologies have adopted mediated techniques (ie mechanical recording devices) to extend inquiry as well as to reduce human observational error. Collier (1967) reports that ethnographers were among the first to enthusiastically accept photographic data as the clearest evidence of a culture. Felix-Louis Renault produced ethnographic film as early as 1895 (Hockings, 1975), and Heider's (1976) comprehensive book entitled *Ethnographic Film* touches everything from the history of photographic applications in ethnography to the use of such media in teaching. Collier (1967) and Hockings (1975) also report applications of photography to anthropological research, but both note that media are used by researchers in this field more to augment traditional naturalistic inquiry than as a primary data source.

For example, mediated observation has also played a major role in a number of other contexts. Video-taping has been used extensively with pre-service teachers (Ellett and Smith, 1975; Winn, 1974) and with in-service teachers (Fuller and Manning, 1973), as well as in a host of similar arenas (such as training and therapy). The primary focus in these applications, however, is on judging or modifying individual behaviour within a given context. Since the person being observed is typically involved in review, threats to interpretation are reduced, although, as Fuller and Manning (1973) point out, under certain conditions self-confrontation via video-tape may cause more harm than good.

As a research or evaluative tool, visual media (film or video-tape) clearly can provide an advantage over human observers in certain circumstances. Mediated observational records can overcome the problems of fatigue or observer participation mentioned earlier. Once produced, these records are relatively permanent, lending themselves well to repeated viewing, editing and reproduction. Mediated records also allow flexibility in analysis and interpretation. Images can be used as descriptive evidence or can be converted into categorical data depending upon the needs of the project and the model which is being used. Finally, technological advances like stop action and slow motion can make possible the description and analysis of complex interactions which might otherwise go unobserved. In short, mediated observation can aid the evaluator or educational technologist in a variety of ways given that its limitations are understood and taken into account.

## Potential Roles of Media in Evaluation

There are a number of possible roles which media could serve in evaluation. These include (i) recording, (ii) evoking evaluative responses, and (iii) reporting.

### Recording Role

As previously mentioned, the evaluation literature is replete with evaluation models which place a high premium on observational methodologies. Guba's (1978) naturalistic inquiry approach and Stake's (1978) case study model are prominent examples which borrow heavily from the anthropological-observational research methodology. Mediated observation seems a logical extension of these approaches. For instance, where the evaluator's emphasis is on programme documentation or portrayal (ie Stake, 1975), 'portrait photography' would seem to be directly applicable. In any evaluative model employing observational methodology, Collier's book (1967) *Visual Anthropology* could serve as an excellent field manual.

Mediated recording would seem to have a use within the framework of other models as well. Evaluators (Worthen and Sanders, 1973) argue for the use of multiple dependent measures; at the very least mediated observation offers a novel and potentially valuable data source. For example, media could assist the goal-free evaluator (Scriven, 1967) in gathering evidence concerning the multiple effects of the phenomenon under study. Wide angle and zoom lens techniques would seem to be particularly amenable to the evaluator seeking a broad view of programme impacts. Media might also be employed in connection with the judicial model (Wolf, 1975) where both sides collect evidence to document and dramatize their cases, or with the more objective models (ie Tyler, 1942) in an effort to record outcomes related to specific stated objectives. Or, media might be used only during certain phases of an evaluation — such as the input and process phases of Stufflebeam's (1971) CIPP model. Regardless of the evaluation model, media applications to evaluation represent a unique data source of vast potential for recording programme events and other outcomes.

### Evocative Role

Once recorded, visual media can be used to generate a secondary data source. Seeing a photograph or video segment can serve to facilitate recall by clients and programme staff regarding the nature of events, personal reactions to those events and perceptions of the programme's effectiveness. This is not unlike the way in which photographs were used by psychologists as early as 1909 (DeBrigard, 1975), and to a greater extent by anthropologists and ethnographers (Kreb, 1975).

Researchers in teacher education have also used video records for the same purpose. Typically, representative samplings of teacher behaviour are recorded, but rather than using them to evaluate individual behaviour, the teachers themselves or panels of judges are asked to respond to the segments with descriptive and analytical comments. Thus, a new data set is created which can be analyzed separately from the original visual images.

In a goal-free evaluation (Scriven, 1967) of a student orientation programme (Petersen, Brown and Sanstead, 1979) an attempt was made to assess the impact of evocative media upon the reactions of participants and staff. The sample was randomly divided into two groups and each was asked to respond to a questionnaire concerning the programme and its effectiveness. One group viewed programme-related slides as they responded while the other group did not. When questionnaire results were analyzed across groups, no significant differences were observed. In this particular study, the questionnaire took on the structuring role for the respondents while the slides acted as supplements. However, the photographs could easily have served the same structuring role in which case different results might have been obtained.

### Reporting

Slide-tape presentations or edited video productions will probably never replace the traditional evaluation report. Yet, in cases of programme portrayal, the use of such media seems both appropriate and desirable. Recently, a study (Petersen, Brown and Sanstead, 1979) was conducted to determine if such applications can have bearing on evaluative decision-making. A judicial model (Wolf, 1975) formed the framework for the evaluation of a large university residence hall. Two teams of evaluators were employed: an advocate and an adversary, both of which took photographs to represent the environment and operating milieu of the hall. One team used an evocative approach to solicit comments of the residents while the other team supplied their own interpretations. Results from independent jury deliberations (ie administrators assigned to independent juries), one with media and one without, indicated that the use of photographs significantly affected the evaluative outcomes. The two juries reached different decisions as to the need for renovations and organizational changes in the residence hall.

Stake (1975) strongly urges the use of multiple channels for communicating evaluative results, especially when clients or decision-makers are removed from the physical setting under consideration. Media represent one means of providing concrete referents to supplement more abstract data. Though there is potential danger of media reporting becoming a multi-media extravaganza — a show with no substance — the other extreme to be avoided is the evaluator who, although he employs visual media in a recording capacity, makes no use of the medium in reporting. Even when recorded observational data are reduced to nominal categories, the actual visual images may serve as a potent methodological justification during the reporting stage.

## Methodological Issues and Concerns

There are a number of issues regarding the use of media in evaluation. These include (i) bias, (ii) obtrusiveness, and (iii) ethics.

### Bias

Subjectivity and bias are inherent risks in any observational methodology. In an earlier section, several forms of human observer bias (ie expectation, fatigue, participation) were pointed out and, to a certain extent, media applications can serve to reduce or eliminate these. However, mediated observation can introduce its own forms of bias. For instance, in representing one aspect of the visual field, others are necessarily excluded. Varying angles of view and aperture settings can give false impressions of size and depth, and still photographs are completely devoid of time referents. Close-up views may ascribe significance to the trivial, and wide-angle views may diminish the important. While the significance of these, and other, limitations may be evident to those who regularly deal with media products, uninitiated respondents and consumers should be provided with the necessary qualifications in advance.

In addition to these technical limitations, bias may be introduced through human operators. Visual media possess the potential for both recording experience and artistic expression. Photographers are often referred to as 'picture-makers' rather than 'picture-takers' since they select a particular view from an infinity of possible views, so that the product reflects the photographer as well as the pictured object (Berger, 1977). Even under the best of circumstances, media can never provide a totally true representation of reality. However, care can be taken to avoid the propensity to record the attractive or the unusual to the exclusion of other possibilities within the visual field.

In order to counteract bias, anthropologists and ethnographers have relied upon training in their disciplines to provide the necessary safeguards. Evaluation would do well to borrow some of their sampling procedures and techniques. The evaluator might also do well to borrow techniques to control observational bias from the psychologist. Base-lining, repeated measures, and time-sampling are examples of techniques which help reduce bias. Whatever approach is used, bias remains a problematic issue to be resolved whenever an observational procedure is employed.

## Obtrusiveness

A second methodological problem inherent in the mediated approach is that of obtrusiveness. Both Heider (1976) and Hockings (1975) discuss the potential impact of the camera on human behaviour. Likewise, Webb *et al* (1966) discuss the relative effects of obtrusive and non-obtrusive recording devices upon behaviour. There is little question that all observational methodologies inject an element of reactive bias into the observed setting. The Hawthorne effect is well-known and documented. However, through the use of specialized equipment (ie telephoto lenses) and appropriate attenuation and base-lining periods prior to recording, the effects of obtrusiveness can be minimized even when the most elaborate hardware set-ups are required.

## Ethics

An issue which has received relatively less attention is that of ethics. Recording the actions of others, whether through photographic or electronic means, requires participation in another person's 'mortality, vulnerability and mutability' (Sontag, 1977). In an age concerned with confidentiality and rights to privacy, there are questions of who owns the images which have been recorded, and probably more importantly, how should they be used in the course of evaluation and how should they be treated afterwards. The issue of confidentiality comes to the forefront when media are used in evaluative reporting, since it is at this point that private information is made public. Aside from the legal ramifications, it is the responsibility of those concerned to obtain consent from the people being observed and to insure that the rights of individuals have been observed and protected.

## Conclusion

The purpose of this paper was not to create yet another evaluation model, but rather to explore the potential utility of applying an existing tool to enhance and enrich the evaluation process. As with any tool, there are strengths and limitations. Mediated observation has a limited capacity to document certain cognitive events which are indicators of learning. However, in terms of observable events, media can play a direct role in recording and reporting, a secondary role in supplementing and checking other data sources, and even can be used to evoke responses for an auxiliary data set.

In illustrating potential applications of mediated techniques, at least three major issues were identified: bias, obtrusiveness, and ethics. While not unique to mediated observation, the nature of the data suggests special consideration, especially if the data are used in public reports. These issues cannot be resolved through rhetoric, but must be actively engaged through experimentation and field trials.

This paper began by suggesting that the educational technologist should become aware of and familiar with a variety of evaluation models and techniques. To a large extent, educational technologists are in a unique position to explore the utility of mediated observation, even to a greater extent than evaluators in other educational realms. Heider (1976) suggests that the best ethnographic films come from ethnographers who are photographers. Undoubtedly, the best use and applications of media to evaluation will come from educational technologists who are also evaluators.

## References

Berger, J (1977) *Ways of Seeing.* Penguin Press, New York.
Bloom, B S, Hastings, J T and Madaus, G F (1970) *Handbook on Formative and Summative Evaluation.* McGraw-Hill, New York.
Campbell, D T (1959) Systematic error on the part of human links in communication systems. *Information and Control* 1, pp 334-69.
Collier, J (1967) *Visual Anthropology: Photography as a Research Method.* Holt, Rinehart and Winston, New York.
DeBrigard, E (1975) The history of ethnographic film. In Hockings, P (ed) *Principles of Visual Anthropology.* Morton Publishers, The Hague.
Eisner, E W (1972) Emerging models for educational evaluation. *School Review* pp 573-89. August.
Ellett, L E and Smith, E P (1975) Improving performance of classroom teachers through video-taping and self-evaluation. *AV Communication Review* 23, pp 277-88.
Fuller, F F and Manning, B A (1973) Self-confrontation reviewed: a conceptualization for video playback in teacher education. *Review of Educational Research* 43, pp 469-528.
Gardner, D E (1977) Five evaluation frameworks — implications for decision making in higher education. *Journal of Higher Education* 48, pp 571-92.
Gesell, A (1934) *An Atlas of Infant Behavior: A Systematic Delineation of the Forms and Early Growth of Human Behavior Patterns.* Yale University Press, New Haven.
Guba, E (1978) *Toward a Methodology of Naturalistic Inquiry in Education Evaluation.* School of Education. UCLA, Los Angeles.
Heider, K G (1976) *Ethnographic Film.* University of Texas Press, Austin.
Hockings, P (ed) (1975) *Principles of Visual Anthropology.* Morton Publishers, The Hague.
Kreb, S (1975) The film elicitation technique. In Hockings, P (ed) *Principles of Visual Anthropology.* Morton Publishers, The Hague.
Lang, K and Lang, G E (1960) Decisions for Christ: Billy Graham in New York City. In Stein, M *et al* (eds) *Identity and Anxiety.* Free Press, Glencoe, Illinois.
Mitchell, P D (1975) The discernible educational technologist. *Programmed Learning and Educational Technology* 12, 5, pp 306-24.
Petersen, C H, Brown, R D and Sanstead, M (1979) Photographic evaluation from three perspectives: portrayal, goal-free, judicial. In *Proceedings of the Annual Meeting of the American Educational Research Association.* San Francisco.

Piaget, J (1926) *Judgment and Reasoning in the Child.* Brace and World, New York.
Popham, W J (1969) Objectives and instruction. *American Educational Research Association Monograph Series on Curriculum Evaluation* 3, pp 32-52.
Scriven, M (1967) The methodology of evaluation. *American Educational Research Association Monograph Series on Curriculum Evaluation* 1, pp 39-83.
Sontag, S (1977) *On Photography.* Farrar, Straus and Giroux, New York.
Stake, R (1975) *Evaluating the Arts in Education — A Responsive Approach.* Merrill, Columbus, Ohio.
Stake, R (1978) Case study approach. *Educational Researcher* 1, pp 5-10.
Stufflebeam, D L *et al* (1971) *Educational Evaluation and Decision-Making in Education.* Peacock Publishers, Itasca, Illinois.
Tyler, R W (1942) General statement on evaluation. *Journal of Educational Research* 35, pp 492-501.
Webb, E J, Campbell, D T, Schwartz, R D and Sechrest, L (1966) *Unobtrusive Measures: Nonreactive Research in the Social Sciences.* Rand McNally, Chicago.
Winn, W (1974) Video-taping teaching practice: strengths and weaknesses. *Audiovisual Instruction* 19, pp 18-20.
Wolf, R L (1975) Trial by jury: a new evaluation method. *Phi Delta Kappa* 57, pp 10-15.
Worthen, B and Sanders, J (1973) *Educational Evaluation: Theory and Practice.* Jones Publishing, Worthington, Ohio.

# 2.2.5 Validation Processes for Instructional Systems

M Ferraris, V Midoro and G Olimpo
*National Council for Research, Genoa, Italy*

**Abstract:** Non-traditional instructional systems, such as the ones based on distance learning or on non-conventional media, are characterized by large numbes of students and by high development costs. This implies a need for reliable validation processes.

In our view, instructional systems' validation must be aimed at (i) assuring the compliance with the stated requirements and (ii) evaluating the quality of the final products. The former function is called 'verification'; the latter one is called 'quality control' and is typically accomplished by testing techniques. In order to accomplish these two functions we define a life cycle for instructional systems. This life cycle makes explicit the phases of development and the relationship between them. Our proposed life cycle consists of five main phases: (i) requirements definition, (ii) specification, (iii) design; (iv) implementation; (v) quality control. The output of each phase is the input to the next phase. The final outputs are the validated system and the documentation of the activities performed in each phase.

## Introduction

In industrialized countries traditional instructional systems seem unable to reflect the dynamics of the society's development.

Problems which require new approaches and new tools for instruction and education are:

☐ the rising demand for education at all levels;
☐ the changing demands of the labour market;
☐ the development and dissemination of new technologies, methodologies and related methodologies pertaining to storage, elaboration and transmission of information;
☐ the rapid growth of scientific knowledge and an acceleration of the dynamics of the social need to which instructional systems are related.

To face these problems, new instructional systems have been developed to complement the traditional ones. Examples are the Open University in the UK, DIFF in West Germany, and the CAL systems developed for universities and schools. Even though these systems are quite different in their shape and content, they share several important features:

(a) they tend to rely heavily on modern communication means (TV, computer, teletext, viewdata, video-disc, etc);
(b) they are reproducible in that they may be repeated in different places at the same time;
(c) they are used by many students;
(d) time and costs for developing the instructional material are very high.

Related to these features, new problems arise. Because these systems have a large audience, poor teaching will affect many students and will be difficult to rectify. Furthermore, production costs are justifiable only if the development systems are more effective than the traditional ones. Thus, a 'reliable' control of their quality is required. On the other hand, information about the quality of the instructional process, which emerges naturally in a face-to-face situation, is not available.

Thus, as far as non-traditional instructional systems are concerned, we need more information for controlling their quality, but we are deprived of the normal information we would get in a traditional teaching situation. As a result, new methods, techniques and tools based on the reproducibility feature are required in order to evaluate them.

Up to now, many different approaches to 'evaluation' have been put forth. It emerges from an analysis of these that there is much disagreement about:

☐ techniques (what to do in order to evaluate an instructional system and how to use the gathered data);
☐ functions (why a system must be evaluated and by whom);
☐ object (what must be evaluated in a system).

In addition, the term 'evaluation' is often used ambiguously for either quality control or student assessment. In order to overcome this confused situation, we think that it is necessary to begin with a clear definition of the nature of the problem and then to derive possible solutions.

## The Nature of the Problem

In order to eliminate ambiguities, we will use the word 'validation' instead of 'evaluation'. Here, 'validation of an instructional system' is defined as a set of procedures aimed at:

(a) ensuring a compliance with specified functions;
(b) detecting the causes of deviation from the stated behaviour;
(c) identifying the activities for correcting errors and weaknesses;
(d) ensuring the compliance with needs;
(e) detecting the causes of deviation from the needs;
(f) identifying suitable modification to the system.

Moreover, since the quality of the system changes with time, an activity is required to maintain it. This activity is called maintenance.

Let us examine the consequences of these definitions, starting from a model of the instructional processes. Figure 1 shows an instructional system in operation. During an instructional process an interaction takes place between the system and a learning population that is a part of the environment of the system. The results of this interaction are a change in the knowledge state of that population (and,

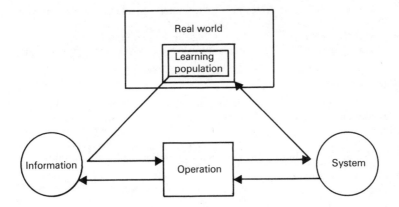

**Figure 1.** *Schematic representation of an instructional system in operation*

consequently, a change in the environment) and the gathering of data about the instructional process.

Following the definition given previously, the first function of validation is to see if the system performs the functions for which it was built. This implies that the functions of the system must be clearly and unambiguously defined before producing the system. In addition, the gathered information has to be comparable against these functions, to detect if functions are correctly accomplished, and, if deviations from the stated behaviour are detected, then suitable corrected actions must take place. This implies that the system must be produced in such a way as to be easily changeable.

Many evaluation techniques follow this scheme. In these techniques the functions are roughly identified with the instructional objectives, and information is obtained regarding the students' behaviour. Unfortunately, however, most of them fail to identify the causes of discrepancies and, what is worse, they do not indicate what must be done in order to correct the system.

Another function of validation (as defined) is to establish whether the stated functions of the system fulfil the requirements defined by means of the needs analysis.

At this stage the functions are compared with the requirements, discrepancies are detected, and functions are consequently modified. Of course, this step must precede the production of the system.

However, the quality of an instructional system does not remain the same during time, but changes continuously because — as was shown in the Introduction — the environment to which it is related changes with time. This activity of continuous change, intrinsic to the nature of the instructional system, is called maintenance.

Thus the system must be maintained and modified during its life in order to keep its quality stable. This process continues until the production of a new system becomes more profitable than the maintenance of the old one.

According to our model, validation and maintenance are strictly linked to the development process of an instructional system and they can be accomplished only if the system is developed taking them into account from the very beginning.

## Instructional System Life Cycle, Validation and Maintenance

In this section we will describe our approach to validation and maintenance. In particular, we will discuss the following items:

(a) production phases of the system;
(b) validation processes related to them which take place when the system does not yet exist (these processes are called 'verification');
(c) validation processes aimed at testing the system quality (they are called 'quality control' and take place during and after system implementation).

### Production Phases

Figure 2 shows the input and output of the production process of an instructional system. The inputs are the needs related to the environment. The output is the system, called 'gross system' because it has not been tested yet. As shown in Figure 3, this activity can be broken down into four main sub-activities or phases, namely: requirements definition; specification; design; implementation.

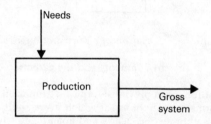

**Figure 2.** *Inputs and outputs of the production process of an instructional system*

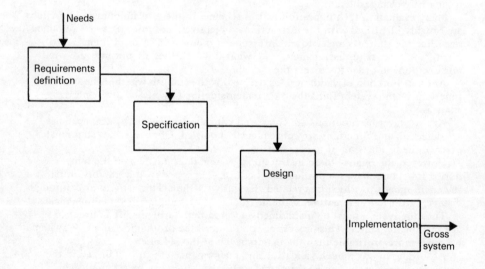

**Figure 3.** *Phases associated with the production process*

In our approach, the outputs of the first three phases have the following three main functions:

1. To set requirements for the next phase.
2. To document the production activities of each phase.
3. To supply the basis for determining whether or not each phase fulfils the requirements set by the previous one.

Let us now briefly describe each phase.

REQUIREMENTS DEFINITION
This phase endeavours to clarify:

(a) the needs for which the instructional system must be developed;
(b) the general features of the system that meet these needs, ie aims and content;
(c) available resources.

SPECIFICATION
In this stage, the system functional architecture describing all the functions to be performed by the system is supplied. We assume that the structure of these functions is isomorphic to the subject matter structure pertaining to the system. Hence this phase is mainly aimed at representing the detailed structure of the subject matter. Further activities related to this phase are the defining of design constraints (ie economic constraints, students' prerequisites, learning time forecast, and so on) and the stating of the quality measures required.

DESIGN
Based on specifications, architectural structure is developed, ie modules of which the system is made, delivery strategy, testing procedures, etc. In this phase, the detailed design of modules is also developed describing the means for presenting information, problem-solving activities; and containing AV scripts, self-instructional material, CAI dialogues, and so on. Finally, quality control procedures are defined.

IMPLEMENTATION
The design is physically carried out. Modules, assessment tests, delivery strategy and the user's manual are produced.

## Verification

Verification is strictly linked to the production process. In fact, it is an interactive process aimed at determining whether or not each phase of the production process fulfils all requirements set by the previous phase.

Initially, the requirements stated in phase 1 are compared with the needs. If they match these needs, the 'requirement document' passes to phase 2; if they do not, the requirements are changed and verified again. This process continues until they match the needs. In the same way, the specifications are compared with requirements, the design is compared with the specifications, and the gross system with the design.

Thus, verification controls the development of the production activities. It is allowed to go on to the next step only if it has been verified that the actual phase fulfils the requirements set by the previous one. In this way, errors and weaknesses are detected very early, before the system exists, and they can easily be eliminated. Thus, verification prevents building a system which deviates from the stated requirements.

## Quality Control

Quality control is a process of organized use of the system under controlled circumstances to test its quality. It takes place during and after the implementation phase. Like verification, this process is also related to each production phase.

After implementation, each module is tested to detect and correct errors and weaknesses. In the current evaluation practices of instructional systems, this process is called 'formative evaluation'.

As all tested modules become available they are assembled into a system in an integration process and a system test begins. At this stage the integration test is aimed at determining if the interfaces among the modules are correctly stated and work properly.

In the next step the system functions are tested to verify whether or not they meet the functions given in the 'specification document'.

After this function test, the system is compared with the requirements and the needs to determine if it can cope with them. Finally, an operation test is performed to detect all operational problems.

Following this stage the system is ready to be released. It is at this point, as far as quality control is concerned, that validation ends and maintenance begins.

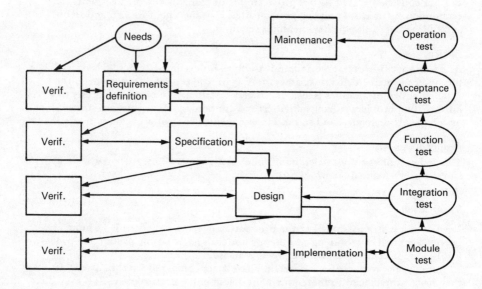

**Figure 4.** *Relationship between production, validation and maintenance*

## Maintenance

During the system operation, students learn the subject matter pertaining to the system by interacting with it. If, during use, parts of the system are found to be wrong, inappropriate, or too restricted, or if the system does not cope with the needs any more because of the changing environment, the system must then be modified.

It must be emphasized again that change is intrinsic to the nature of an instructional system because the needs to which the system is related change with time.

Thus, it must be developed in such a way as to be as easy to modify as possible. In other words, the development process must embody the feature of the system's alterability. The development of a system according to a well-defined production process and the documentation of this activity make the system changeable. Each change is brought about following the production process from the beginning.

The model in Figure 4 shows the relationship between production, validation (verification and quality control), and maintenance.

As this model shows, all these phases are strictly linked to each other. Their union constitutes the life cycle of an instructional system.

## Conclusions

In this paper we have described the nature of the problem which validation and maintenance must face. The main issue of the problem analysis is that validation and maintenance are intrinsic to the nature of the instructional systems and cannot be separated by the production process. We have discussed the relationships between verification, quality control, maintenance and the production process. Finally, we have summarized the model in a life cycle of an instructional system. In conclusion, we will make two brief remarks:

1. We have described only a general approach to validation and maintenance and not specific techniques. This reflects the fact that such techniques cannot be defined separately from the methodology, techniques, and tools related to each phase of the life cycle. Our present activity regards the definition of formal, comprehensive methodologies for carrying out each step of the stated life cycle and the associated validation processes.
2. The approach presented reflects the results of some research carried out in the software engineering field. Since a strong analogy exists between software and instructional systems regarding nature, problems and methodologies, it is possible and useful to transfer general approaches and, sometimes, specific methodologies developed in software engineering to instructional systems. The approach to validation described in this paper is an instance of how this transfer can take place.

Finally, the ideas expressed in this paper may constitute a contribution to the definition of a possible common starting point for building general acceptable paradigms for developing and validating instructional systems.

# 2.3 Evaluation of Distance Learning Schemes and Materials

## 2.3.1 Designing Evaluation of Flexistudy

P Noble
*Garnett College of Education, London*
B Green
*Book House Training Centre, London*

Abstract: Flexistudy learning systems are outlined to show how mature students are offered learning materials for home-based study, counselling, tutorial support and access to college facilities. The desirability of evaluation is explored and appropriate literature discussed.

Direct comparison with conventional courses may not be valid as Flexistudy seeks to extend further education to those who find existing provision in some way inappropriate or inaccessible. Hence, schemes should be judged on their intrinsic worth and on the opportunity costs incurred by using college resources in this particular way.

Comparison with other systems of home-based study might seem more relevant but such comparisons are vitiated by major differences between the total Flexistudy package, and broadcasting agencies and correspondence colleges which provide for home-based study. Schemes offered in Western Europe and Australia may have more similarities and evidence is offered.

A diversity of potential audiences exist for evaluation studies (eg students, course providers, the course team, college management) and the purposes of a study will determine the procedures chosen. Various possibilities are discussed in this paper.

## Flexistudy Schemes

These are operating in some 70 colleges and adult education institutes; they offer learning materials for home-based study together with counselling, tutorial support and access to facilities provided by colleges. Originating in the linked courses for correspondence students studying with the National Extension College (NEC), schemes are adapting to offer and to support other self-teaching schemes such as the NALGO in-service education programmes. By no means all Flexistudy students are preparing for public examinations even where following a GCE course; a number of the courses offered by NEC are for general interest, return to study, or for preparation for study with the Open University. Thus Flexistudy gives students a chance to discover whether they can cope with self-teaching.

Duration of study is negotiated with tutors, and students comprise largely those who could not (or would not) be drawn to day or evening classes currently offered by the institutions. Personal circumstances may mean that students spend periods 'sleeping' before resuming active study with tutorials and assignments!

Flexistudy can thus be seen to offer some qualities of 'openness' as a learning system giving discretion about course, subjects and study topics, offering choice of learning methods, command over pace and location of study, freedom to take or reject public assessment, and opportunity for students to avail themselves of counselling and guidance (Spencer, 1980). This face-to-face support is a special quality of Flexistudy.

There are inevitably variations between institutions in the quantity and extent of subject enrolments and of experience in administration of such schemes. In a study of 10 centres in 1980, we found most tutors looking after six to 20 enrolled students in their subject, most centres permitting continuous enrolment throughout the session and providing tutorials by telephone where appropriate. A few centres were able to offer practical workspace for science students. Where courses were offered by adult education centres — or adult studies departments — part-time teachers staffed the scheme; at City of Bath Technical College, the scheme was organized through the Learning by Appointments Centre which already maintained a booking service for users of the Centre.

## Evaluation

Evaluation studies could be made of any area of work in further education to appraise success in fulfilling declared intentions or effectiveness in using allocated resources; evidence from such studies would help in formulating college development plans. There would seem to be little justification for expecting greater accountability from innovative course teams than from those whose courses evolved earlier in the history of a college. Innovators themselves may, however, feel obliged to show how effectively they deploy scarce resources — and how worthwhile are the opportunities they create by the marginal shift of staff, space and facilities they occasioned.

## Audiences for Evaluation

Evaluation techniques selected for the study of Flexistudy will depend on the anticipated audiences described below, and the use likely to be made of the findings.

1. The providers of the correspondence course materials are a prime audience with an acknowledged role in improving learning materials and disseminating information through conferences and publications. Some of the knowledge and awareness might find its way back to students through the quarterly magazine from the National Extension College (*Home Study*), provided this were made available to individual Flexistudy students. A study by a local counsellor for NEC revealed problems facing many home-based students and devised some solutions (Lewis, 1980). A review of student reactions to self-teaching schemes served to point out widely reported problems of study skills that could be tackled in part by further attention in evaluation studies to the design of instructional text (Noble, 1980).

2. The course team might provide a second audience with a parallel interest in the quality of the learning materials as used by home-based students. They tend to develop instructional aids to augment, and, where necessary, compensate for, the published course materials. They are likely to have some interest in aids developed in other institutions offering the same courses, but they are hampered by the small proportion of their personal teaching likely to be allocated to any one Flexistudy course. Tutors are likely to be new to many of the processes of 1:1 and small group tutoring — and to allowing for the vulnerability of home-based students when sent marked assignments. Experience borrowed from the Open University such as MacKenzie (1976) may carry less conviction than the results of a sympathetic study of how recent students have been experiencing the courses. The course team have a third area of interest in how similar courses are administered in other institutions, a need largely met to date through day conferences organized by the NEC, Garnett College and the development work done by the NEC/CET Development Officer (Sacks, 1980). The dissemination of findings has been assisted by the Council for Educational Technology (Spencer, 1980) but we may need to discover the most effective way of disseminating ideas to course tutors.

3. A third audience comprises the senior management of colleges to assist in their overall review of resource allocation. To this end, their interest would be financial and administrative with some account of the special opportunities provided. They can derive comparative data from the studies by Spencer (1980). It will be likely that at least one member of senior management in a college is actively sponsoring the innovation and this may determine the emphasis of any report considered; the college administrative officer and librarian would need to be included in any review. As flexible learning systems develop in conjunction with TEC, BEC, NALGO and other professional bodies, the public relations role of Flexistudy will attract the attention of senior management; local press and radio have provided publicity and might be interested in the human dimension of second chance course provision.

4. A further audience for these schemes is the potential adopter in other institutions. Their interest will be in updated overviews (Sacks, 1980; Spencer 1980) and in the special local circumstances that may vitally account for a Flexistudy scheme having taken root and survived in a college. An evaluation study that aims to provide evidence through case studies has to contend with the implications of not being able to preserve anonymity for colleges and course tutors. There are political implications in such portrayals (MacDonald and Walker, 1977). A major difficulty in publishing any such account is the rate of change within pioneer institutions; any account needs frequent updating. (The 1978 Flexistudy Manual appeared in a second edition from the NEC in 1980.) A few accounts of major reconsiderations in course design and in learning materials can be found in the literature but it is unlikely that much evaluative data will derive from institutions where courses are discontinued.

## What Would Constitute Evidence in Flexistudy Appraisal?

Direct comparisons with courses offered by conventional modes of study might not be valid; such full- and part-time courses are normally time-constrained with entry to a prescribed public examination. Flexistudy seeks to extend further education to those who find existing provision in some way inappropriate or inaccessible; in many schemes, a major flexibility is seen as the right to roll onto the course at whatever point in the year suits the student, together with the right to decide what, if any, public examination to attempt. It would be difficult to cite 'wastage' or 'discontinuance' figures, as students buy the course book and opt *into* any correspondence assignments and face-to-face tutorials. Some comparison of staffing costs per unit of coursework completed might be made with an evening class group using the same learning materials, but Flexistudy yields no neat cohorts of student admissions for such comparisons. Australian experience with wholly distant learners suggests that, for those who survive, results are quite comparable with full- and part-time campus-based learners (Goodman, 1973). Further international comparisons might be made with Denmark, where 'supervised correspondence study' or 'combined education' has been offered by official schemes of study in navigation, the management of small businesses, and marketing subjects in the post-secondary sector (Nedburgh, 1973). Between 1951 and 1972, Swedish government commissions have satisfied themselves on the effectiveness of linked courses in preparing students for university entrance (Holmberg, 1973). It would not be unreasonable to assume that Flexistudy would be at least as effective as more conventional course provision; evaluation could then be seen as just a normal part of course review leading to course developments.

Self-appraisal by course participants might be the best evidence for showing what staff and students value about Flexistudy schemes — and the locus and timing of any problems encountered. Ways of supporting students in the early phases of their home study would probably emerge as greatly valued and significant in preventing discontinuance — to judge from several reports (Goodman, 1973; Lewis, 1980). There have been sufficient day conferences of teachers with experience of Flexistudy to generate a provisional check-list of issues connected with tutoring and counselling. Experience derived from work with full-time students may not raise appropriate issues. If studies by course teams are made available to outside audiences, then some measure of situational analysis would need to accompany the accounts and profiles — something of the antecedents of the students, the subject commitment and concurrent experience of the staff, the pattern of course demands, facilities available, and something of the qualitative blend of these in the college in question.

Independent evaluation might be unduly intrusive in some very small-scale schemes but there are precedents for bringing responsive and sympathetic perceptions to bear on linked courses and self-teaching schemes (Stringer, 1979; Lopez and Elton, 1980; Lewis, 1980). There is evidence that independent evaluation of learning materials can be made an integral part of following a self-teaching course (Nathenson and Henderson, 1980).

Evidence about Flexistudy could be both quantitative and qualitative though comparative data would have to be interpreted in the light of many qualifications. Evidence intended for formative evaluation, to contribute to course development, would use case study methods, contextual accounts, and responsive or illuminative procedures (MacDonald and Walker, 1977). Even for accounts of administrative procedures, context helps to interpret preferred organizational styles (Spencer, 1980).

Collecting evidence for Flexistudy evaluation would draw on an established battery of techniques. Questionnaires and attitude inventories would establish participants' experience of the course and the intensity and saliency for them of issues presented. Interviews would permit a more responsive, exploratory and open account to be built up — telephone interviews were used by Stringer (1979) and would not be inappropriate in Flexistudy where telephone tutorials are offered by tutors in a number of colleges. Repertory grid techniques have been used in eliciting attitudes to reading (Thomas and Harri-Augstein, 1980), and could well be adapted to the detailed study of course components. These techniques would be equally appropriate for use with members of teaching staff, librarians, college administrators, editors and course-writers, and students. Feedback questions have been developed for use in developmental testing of learning materials and are peculiarly well-suited to Flexistudy schemes where tutors are regularly monitoring coursework. Nathenson and Henderson (1980) publish examples of questions for use with both book and non-book materials.

## Context for Designing Evaluation of Flexistudy

College staff readily show interest in Flexistudy as is shown by attendances of 70 to 80 at information-giving conferences; there is intrinsic worth in a scheme that provides for an otherwise neglected public of mainly mature students returning to study — and that offers opportunity to continue courses that have ceased to be viable in a particular academic year. (Few colleges keep records of courses that fail to enrol viable numbers.) Most course tutors and Heads of Department are interested in administrative issues related to implementing the schemes within their institutions and to securing resources in negotiations with Local Education Authorities. Some of this information is now published (Barnet College of Further Education, 1980; Sacks, 1980; Spencer, 1980). Apart from departments of general and professional education, few will find learning materials in an appropriate correspondence format but the Polymaths course and the BBC

Living Decisions course (Noble, 1980) both show how readily resource-based courses using published materials would adapt to the Flexistudy model.

If a college were to adopt flexible learning systems over a range of courses, studies would need to be made of the scaling-up issues in connection with the college office, tutorial accommodation and the library; at present, demands are marginal to the mainstream of college activities. It is likely that course developments in connection with Technician Education Council and Business Education Council courses and with the vocational preparation of the 16 to 19-year-olds have had much more significant impact on colleges than the introduction of Flexistudy. Perhaps only in the Library and Resources Committee of a college is the relative impact of course developments likely to be monitored.

A decision could be taken to defer *any* evaluation of Flexistudy if the process of evaluation were seen to focus undue attention on a small-scale innovation without providing the essential parallel data about existing courses to assist in appraising the allocation of resources within the college. It would still be relevant to design evaluation studies by or on behalf of the team to assist with monitoring Flexistudy in operation.

# References

Barnet College of Further Education (1980) *Flexistudy Manual* (second edition). National Extension College, London.

Goodman, R D (1973) Distance education. *Epistolodidaktika* 2, pp 36-7.

Holmberg, B (1973) Supervised correspondence study. *Epistolodidaktika* 2, pp 29-34.

Lewis, R (1980) *Counselling in Open Learning: A Case Study.* National Extension College, London.

Lopez, M and Elton, L (1980) A course taught through a learning centre: an evaluation. *Studies in Higher Education* 5, 1, pp 91-9

MacDonald, B and Walker, R (1977) Case study and the social philosophy of educational research. In Hamilton, D *et al* (eds) *Beyond the Numbers Game.* Macmillan, London.

MacKenzie, K (1976) Student reactions to tutor comments on the tutor-marked assignment (the TMA). *Teaching at a Distance* 5, pp 53-8.

Nathenson, M B and Henderson, E S (1980) *Using Student Feedback to Improve Learning Materials.* Croom Helm, London.

Nedburgh, A (1973) Combined education at Norsk Korrespondanseskole (NKS). *Epistolodidaktika* 2, pp 16-17.

Noble, P (1980) *Resource-Based Learning in Post Compulsory Education.* Kogan Page, London.

Sacks, H (1980) Flexistudy: an open learning system for further and adult education. *British Journal of Educational Technology* 11, 2, pp 85-95.

Spencer, D C (1980) *Thinking About Open Learning Systems.* Council for Educational Technology, London.

Stringer, D (1979) *Make it Count.* International Broadcasting Authority, London.

Thomas, L F and Harri-Augstein, S (1980) Learning-to-learn by reading: towards a conversational technology. In Winterburn, R and Evans, L (eds) *Aspects of Educational Technology* XIV. Kogan Page, London.

*Workshop Report*

# 2.3.2 Designing Evaluation of Flexistudy

**B Green**
*Book House Training Centre, London*
**P Noble**
*Garnett College of Education, London*

## Organizers' Account

The workshop provided the opportunity for delegates to reflect on the issues involved in any attempt to evaluate Flexistudy schemes. A summary of the intentions of one scheme was made available, stressing the wish to use a carefully structured published course, and to provide full access to staff and resources in the college.

Issues were explored in small groups, each of which looked at a different aspect of the learning system: students as sources for evaluation data; ways of exploring the 'learnability' of learning materials; performance measures; the tutoring role; and the qualities and procedures of administrative support systems.

## Sources of Information

There had been some doubt in the discussion after the formal paper as to the validity of planning pre-focused evaluation studies, but workshop members agreed that objective data could usefully be collected from college enrolment and course progress records. The Flexistudy scheme was seen to provide evaluators with good contacts for studying those who discontinue or interrupt their studies. Assignments in the Flexistudy scheme are not intended to assess students so much as to assist their progress; so some thought was given to how to appraise progress, given that heavy reliance is placed on learning materials which may not match the cognitive style of the students. Asking students to envisage hypothetical alternative materials was rejected but structured interviews were favoured to encourage students to make suggestions for changes.

Some sample questions were provided that might be used in any detailed study of the match between text, learning system and learner. Members considered that a sample of students should be studied to find *how* they blended and valued the tutorials, assignments and examinations.

It was suggested that course providers might expect to allow 14 per cent revenue to cover administration costs but that in the early stages, colleges would be looking to the goodwill value of open learning systems and justify the costs in these terms. If Flexistudy schemes came to provide for more than a marginal number of students, it was envisaged that there would be a threshold beyond which the process of scaling-up would become a significant issue in terms of space, staff and procedures.

Members considered how some evaluation might be implemented using no major outside funding but harnessing the skills of the small-scale research undertaken in departments of education and colleges of education (technical).

## Appendix

Some sample questions that might be used in structured interviews with home-based students or that might be built into learning materials. (Derived from procedures described by Nathenson and Henderson, 1980.)

*Feedback questions in text*
The self-assessment questions in this unit were:

very difficult . . . . . . . . . . . . . . . . . . . . . . . . . . . . . . . .very easy

Please explain why you think the diagram on page 5 shows three heavy lines with arrows and two dotted lines . . .

Can you suggest why the author used 'evaluate' in paragraph 1, 'appraise' in paragraph 2 . . . Can you offer other words that would have been possible? . . .

*To explore the process of learning with text and tape*
Did you listen to the audio-tape recording of the interview?

If not, do let us know why . . .

Would you have preferred a transcript to read? . . .

Would it have helped to hear the interview earlier in this section? . . .

What other questions do you think the interviewer should have asked? . . .

What was your reaction to the analysis of the interview given in the text? . . .

Will you attempt the assessment for this Unit? . . . Would you explain your reply?

*To check out ways of studying where students may lack a facility for describing their own style*
I read the text and readings before starting my essay . . .

I mapped out my essay before starting the text . . .

I answered the essay question without reading the text . . .

I could follow the text but found the readings difficult and did not try the essay . . .

I wrote the essay after having . . .

*To monitor the workload*
The hours I spent on the text for this Unit added up to:

<5 . . . . . . . . . . . . . . . . . . . . . . . . . . . . . . . . . . . . . . . >20

I really needed short tutorials by phone:

. . . not at all   . . . once   . . . twice   . . . . times

I had to do extra work in the college library for this Unit . . .

## Reference

Nathenson, M B and Henderson, E S (1980) *Using Student Feedback to Improve Learning Materials.* Croom Helm, London.

# 2.3.3 Evaluation of Distance Teaching: A Criterion Sampling Approach

**M Brophy and B A C Dudley**
*University of Keele*

Abstract: The authors have been involved in an evaluation of an Emergency Science Programme (ESP), a distance teaching scheme for the in-service training of science teachers in Guyana. The study has been undertaken in collaboration with the UNESCO Institute for Education and forms part of the project 'The Evaluation of Learning in Non-Formal Educational Settings'. A number of evaluation methods have been used, of which one is the Criterion Sampling Approach (CSA). This approach involves the systematic observation, measurement, and evaluation of students' performances on standardized samples of the tasks for which they are being trained.

In the paper, the Criterion Sampling Approach to evaluation is outlined and its merits, in relation to other methods of evaluating distance teaching, discussed. An outline of the ESP programme in Guyana is given, with an account of how a CSA approach was developed for evaluating this particular project and how the results obtained by the CSA approach compare with those obtained using other evaluation techniques.

## The Emergency Science Programme

In 1976, the Science Unit of the Ministry of Education in Guyana was asked to set up a training programme to help overcome the drastic shortage of science teachers in the secondary and community high schools of Guyana. As a result, the Emergency Science Programme (ESP) was launched in 1977. This in-service science teacher education project uses a three-way distance approach; the students receive correspondence units, tapes and slides, and they attend weekly tutorial sessions and annual vacation workshops (Brophy and Dalgety, 1980). The correspondence units are prepared by local lecturers, mostly from the University of Guyana, and the regional tutorial centres are staffed, on a part-time basis, by trained graduate science teachers. In the third long vacation the students are attached for a period of work study to a local industrial or medical laboratory.

Guyana is a relatively small country with a population of only 700,000, and although almost half of the science teachers are untrained there is a need for only a small number of trained science teachers. To date, approximately 60 teachers have been recruited to follow the ESP three-year training programme. The first batch began in 1977, the second in 1978, and a third intake are currently being recruited. Twenty-nine of the 1977 intake have successfully completed training and have been awarded trained teachers' certificates which are equivalent to those awarded to students from the college of secondary education.

It is appropriate now to carry out an evaluation of the ESP programme, an evaluation which is summative in that it assesses the degree of success the programme has in training the first batch of students and formative in that it provides information on which to base improvements for future generations of students.

Many distance teaching programmes have been set up, yet we can offer little substantial evidence to show that they produce the intended results. From over 60 projects using distance teaching methods to train teachers (Brophy and Dudley, 1980) we have little more than 'circumstantial' and 'anecdotal' evidence with which we can assess them (Jenkins, 1980). A thorough evaluation of a project such as ESP would, therefore, be of benefit for those who are considering the setting up of new projects and for those who are considering modifying existing ones.

## The Evaluation Strategy

The evaluation of ESP is being carried out using a number of different approaches including:

1. A comparison of the performance of ESP 'graduates' with that of college-trained science teachers 'graduating' the same year. Points for comparison are self-image, final teaching assessment grades, ratings by headteachers and teaching style as perceived by pupils.
2. A comparison of the economic cost of training ESP teachers with that of training college science teachers.
3. An evaluation of the on-the-job performance of a sample of ESP teachers using a criterion sampling technique.

One aspect of this evaluation, namely the criterion sampling technique, will receive particular attention in this paper.

## Criterion Sampling

Two major characteristics of a criterion sampling approach (CSA) to evaluation can be deduced from its title. First, it is dependent upon criterion referenced measurement. Unlike traditional tests which use norm referencing, criterion tests assess a candidate's performance against a fixed standard and they do not judge it in relation to the performance of others. If a candidate achieves a score above the fixed, 'criterion' standard he 'passes' — irrespective of the supply and the demand for people with this 'pass' qualification. In these respects criterion reference testing involves 'quota free' selection (Hambleton and Noviack, 1973).

In traditional pencil and paper tests students gain marks by responding to stimuli which they are unlikely to encounter outside the examination hall. Pencil and paper tests require indirect, 'symbolic' responses from their candidates, responses which may have little to do with the individual's actual behaviour in the job situation. In a review of 50 years of research on general intelligence tests, Ghiselli (1966) found that the correlation between these tests and job proficiency was no more than +0.23. In a CSA evaluation, an individual is assessed by the score he achieves on a number of situational 'performance' tests, tests which reflect the real life situation.

A second traditional method of evaluation, with which most of us in teaching are familiar, depends upon the candidate being rated by his supervisor on his job performance. For example, student teachers are assessed or rated by their lecturers on their ability to teach during teaching practice. This method has the advantage of allowing assessment to take place in the job situation but has the disadvantage that it is based on unstable — high inference — observation. Supervisors' ratings can be affected by many different uncontrolled factors. The second characteristic of the CSA approach is that it can control many of the variables encountered in the real-life situation by testing the candidate's performance on a sample of the tasks he would carry out in the everyday situation. CSA, therefore, attempts to standardize the test conditions while also approaching the authenticity of real life (Fredenkens, 1975). CSA has been described as an approach: 'in which the students' performance on standardized samples of tasks for which he has been trained is systematically observed, measured and evaluated'.

The CSA approach to evaluation is at present being investigated by the UNESCO Institute for Education, Hamburg, to see if it offers a suitable method for evaluating non-formal educational programmes. Distance teaching is one type of non-formal educational programme. At the request of the UNESCO Institute, a CSA evaluation was included with the other approaches being used in the evaluation of the Emergency Science Programme. This now forms one of four case studies which are to be used for the Institute's meta evaluation, ie the evaluation of CSA as an evaluation method.

## The CSA Evaluation of ESP

In a CSA evaluation the first step is for the evaluator to identify the major goals of the project under review. For ESP this was relatively simple because the goals had been written into the original proposal for the programme as submitted to the Board of Examiners in Guyana. Its major goals can be summarized as aiming to:

> provide its students with enough theoretical and practical knowledge in science, education, earth science, English and mathematics to enable them to teach the West Indian Science Curriculum (WISC) and the community high school science programme, Secondary Departments Science Programme (SDSP).

So ESP was designed specifically to train people to teach WISC and SDSP.

The second step in the CSA approach is to determine the criteria to be used to evaluate whether or not this goal has been achieved. A CSA approach requires that we use measures of candidates' performance on a sample of the tasks for which they have been trained. The ESP evaluation required, therefore, that we determine what a teacher must be able to do to teach WISC and SDSP by answering the question: 'What are the criteria by which we judge successful science teaching in Guyana?' The answer was determined by means of a two-stage strategy. The first stage involved a thorough review of the literature to determine what competencies science teachers and science educators thought were important for science teaching. Nine such competencies were identified. A further study of the literature was then made to determine which skills were required for each competency. Eighty-eight such skills were identified. The second stage involved asking science educators in Guyana which of the nine competencies they considered to be most important for teaching science in Guyanese schools and which of the 88 skills were most important for each of the competencies they chose as being important. In this way we were able to identify both the skills and the competencies that Guyanese science educators feel to be among the most important for teaching science in Guyana.

Criterion sampling involves the sampling of the criterion behaviours for which the students have been trained. The UNESCO Institute for Education recommend that the evaluator draws up a Task by Skill matrix in which the rows represent the tasks and the columns the skills underlying the performance. This matrix can then provide the test plan from which the evaluator can draw a sample of the task skill combinations. Science teachers are required to perform an enormous range of tasks involving a great number of skills. A task by skill matrix for science teachers would contain a large number of task skill combinations, many of which would be of limited use in everyday teaching. The sampling method used for ESP, therefore, was a modification of that suggested by UNESCO. Instead of taking a random sample from the universal set of task skill combinations, it was decided to use a stratified sampling procedure. The three competencies which were rated by the Guyanese educators as being the most important were isolated. The skills rated by the educators as being most important for each of these three competencies were then listed and a random sample drawn of two skills from each of the three lists. In this way a random sample was obtained of the skills which Guyanese science educators feel are the most important for teaching science in Guyana. The six skills identified in this way were:

1. Observe safety precautions for any situation that is likely to arise in his or her teaching.
2. Use correctly all the different apparatus and materials needed for the science curriculum being used by his or her classes.
3. Guide pupils to make conclusions from their observations.

4. Encourage pupils to record what they have observed.
5. Relate new experiences to pupils' previous experience.
6. Adapt a lesson plan to suit the specific local conditions of a school.

Both the WISC and the SDSP programmes have prepared detailed teachers' guides and an analysis of these was made to identify those tasks in which these six skills were necessary. Situational tests were then designed which would test the teacher's ability to perform these tasks. Where appropriate, random selections were made of the content to be tested. For example, one of the tasks a teacher would have to perform in order to use science equipment correctly (skill 2) would be to identify the equipment. A list of the equipment needed to teach WISC and SDSP was drawn up and a random selection made of 31 of the items, a 30 per cent sample. As part of the situational test for this skill, teachers were asked to identify this sample of WISC/SDSP equipment.

The situational tests were carried out in Guyana over a three-day period in January involving 16 of the 29 ESP teachers. Criterion performance levels for each skill were determined using 'inspection-based' and consensus judgements carried out by a panel of three representatives of the Guyanese science educators.

## Results

Data from the CSA evaluation is still being analyzed but some findings are already clear, for instance 11 of the 16 teachers tested had at least minimal competence in all the six skills tested, four were competent in five of the six, and one was competent in four.

| Level of Competence | Criterion Skill | | | | | |
|---|---|---|---|---|---|---|
| | 1 | 2 | 3 | 4 | 5 | 6 |
| High competence | 0 | 6 | 12 | 8 | 7 | 13 |
| Minimal competence | 13 | 10 | 4 | 8 | 7 | 2 |
| Below minimal competence | 3 | 0 | 0 | 0 | 2 | 1 |

**Table 1a.** *Competence of ESP teachers on criterion skills*

| | Number of Skills | | | | | | |
|---|---|---|---|---|---|---|---|
| | 6 | 5 | 4 | 3 | 2 | 1 | 0 |
| High competence | 0 | 1 | 6 | 3 | 3 | 2 | 1 |
| Minimal competence | 11 | 4 | 1 | 0 | 0 | 0 | 0 |
| Below minimal competence | 0 | 0 | 0 | 0 | 1 | 4 | — |

**Table 1b.** *Number of criterion skills in which ESP teachers were competent*

As mentioned earlier, the whole study has a dual purpose — one to evaluate ESP itself, the other to investigate how effective are the CSA tests at evaluating ESP. Correlations between CSA scores and final teaching assessments were low with the only correlation above +0.1 being that between teachers' assessment grade and score on skill 1 — knowledge of safety precautions (p = 0.37). A stronger relationship might be expected between the CSA scores on the two skills related to subject knowledge and the teacher's performance on the final science examination. There was, in fact, a significant positive correlation between skill 1 scores and science examination scores (r = 0.6 p $<$ 0.01). The correlation with skill 2 — use of apparatus — was not significant at the five per cent level (r = 0.26). McClelland (1973), however, has argued that the criteria for establishing the validity of criterion referenced tests 'really ought to be not grades in schools, but "grades in life" in the broadest theoretical and practical sense'.

Accordingly the question that arises is how 'grades in life' for Guyanese science teachers can be assessed. In Guyana, as in many developing countries, headteachers tend to give the higher ability classes to the teachers in which they have the most confidence — especially with regard to their academic and subject knowledge. In Guyanese schools, a good measure of the headteacher's confidence in a teacher's subject knowledge would be whether or not he timetables that teacher to take a GCE class. Notes made of interviews with 15 of the ESP teachers' headteachers showed that 10 of the 15 taught GCE science and five taught only junior forms. In a comparison of the CSA results of the 'GCE' teachers with those of the 'non-GCE' teachers on skills 1 and 2 — those skills which related to subject knowledge — we find there is strong evidence to show that the scores of the teachers obtained via the CSA tests were consistent measures of their subject knowledge as perceived by their headteachers.

| Teaches GCE | Skill 1 | Skill 2 |
|:---:|:---:|:---:|
| + | 73 | 78 |
| + | 70 | 96 |
| + | 64 | 85 |
| + | 64 | 84 |
| + | 63 | 87 |
| + | 63 | 83 |
| + | 61 | 95 |
| + | 58 | 88 |
| + | 56 | 85 |
| + | 55 | 79 |
| − | 51 | 66 |
| − | 49 | 75 |
| − | 43 | 80 |
| − | 43 | 61 |
| − | 43 | 43 |

Correlation between skill 1 score and GCE teaching
$r = 0.83$ ($p < .001$)

Correlation between skill 2 score and GCE teaching
$r = 0.58$ ($p < .05$)

**Table 2.** *CSA scores of GCE and non-GCE teachers*

It might well appear that all we have to do to evaluate the teachers is to ask for the headteacher's opinion. However, our results show that while a headteacher's opinion correlates highly with a teacher's subject knowledge, it does not correlate at all highly with any of the other skills. So while headteachers may be choosing the most knowledgeable teacher they may not necessarily be choosing the best science teacher.

The evidence, so far, confirms that CSA testing is both feasible and suitable for evaluating distance teaching. Situational tests can be constructed to sample job tasks that the 'graduates' of distance teaching programmes are required to perform, and such tests can be accurate measures of on-the-job performance. This is not to say, however, that the CSA approach is a panacea for all problems encountered in evaluating distance teaching. Indeed, the ESP evaluation has identified a number of difficulties still to be overcome.

## References

Brophy, M and Dalgety, F (1980) Training science teachers in Guyana. *Teaching at a Distance* **17**, pp 45-51.

Brophy, M and Dudley, B A C (1980) *Patterns of Distance Teaching in Teacher Education.* Education Department, Keele University.

Fredenkens, N F (1975) Situational tests. In Anderson *et al* (eds) *Encyclopedia of Educational Evaluation.* Jossey-Bass, San Francisco.

Ghiselli, E E (1966) *The Validity of Occupational Aptitude Tests.* Wiley, New York.

Hambleton, R K and Noviack, M R (1973) Toward an integration of theory and method for criterion referenced tests. *Journal of Educational Measurement* **10**, 3, pp 159-70.

Jenkins, J (1980) Does distance training of teachers work? *About Distance Education* **10**, pp 2-3.

McClelland, D C (1973) Testing for competence rather than for 'intelligence'. *American Psychologist* **28**, 1, pp 1-14.

## Acknowledgement

The research reported here was supported by a grant from the Northern Ireland Department of Education.

## 2.3.4 Evaluating the Effectiveness of Distance Learning: A Case Study

E Scanlon
*The Open University*

**Abstract:** This paper will describe (i) the formative evaluation methods used to produce a revised version of the Science Foundation Course, (ii) the summative evaluation methods used to assess whether the revised version was an improved version, (iii) the extent to which the revised version was an improved version, and (iv) the extent to which the formative evaluation strategies used contributed to the improvement.

## Introduction

Unlike teachers in traditional universities, Open University (OU) teachers receive no direct feedback from students. In most institutions, a great deal of feedback in courses is said to emerge informally and automatically from close interaction between students and teachers. More formal methods of evaluation have therefore been given careful consideration at the OU. The University is engaged in a cycle of remaking courses and a variety of models of using feedback in the production of these courses have been tested (Nathenson *et al*, 1981).

This paper examines the evaluation history of the Science Foundation Course over 10 years. This demonstrates how feedback data can be used in the attempt to improve courses. Also, by considering the successes and failures of the remade version of the course, the contributions of the evaluation strategies to the improvements will be identified. The main conclusion is that, while the course team was able to respond collectively to large structural and content changes in the material, individual course team members did not respond appropriately in all cases to detailed feedback which dealt with individual components of the course.

# A History of the Evaluation

## The Course and its Production Process

The Science Foundation Course (S 100) was produced by a team consisting of 15 subject specialists, two editors, several BBC producers, and a member of the Institute of Educational Technology (IET). The course had four aims. These were:

1. To design an integrated multi-disciplinary course with contributions from the four disciplines (physics, chemistry, biology and earth sciences) linked together in a way which would demonstrate both the unity and diversity of the sciences.
2. To offer a course which would be both satisfying and worthwhile for students whose only contact with science it would form.
3. To teach science in its social context to bring out clearly the relationship between science and society.
4. To provide an adequate experience for students not previously exposed to experimental work in the laboratory, the practice of which is both an accepted part of the training of a scientist  and a valuable learning experience in itself.

The course consisted of correspondence texts, assignment question papers, TV and radio programmes, a summer school, a home experiment kit and some mathematical texts.

Work began on the production of the course in 1969, and production and remake activities have continued until the present day. Figure 1 summarizes the events which have filled these 12 years.

During the production phase of S 100, instructional material was drafted and redrafted several times. Each draft was scrutinized by course team members and feedback obtained through course team discussions. Some student reaction to materials was collected during this period but practical considerations made this an unsatisfactory experience for the course team as the tested materials were incomplete (Melton, 1977).

# Feedback

Once the course had been presented to students in 1971, survey data could be collected. The first survey of S 100 was undertaken in 1971 by the University's survey research department. For each unit (a week's work) students were sent an identical questionnaire to find out how difficult, interesting or helpful they had found each component of the course and the amount of work each had taken both in numbers of hours and subjectively. Students were asked to indicate their reactions to the amount of work in each unit. They complained there was much too much work in unit 10. This general survey was useful in that it helped to identify major problem areas.

The course team decided on the basis of this information to spread the load in this unit over two weeks and make the study of a later unit, unit 13, optional. The survey was repeated in 1972 and this showed that students felt less overloaded.

Where units had been identified as particularly difficult or overloaded, course team members wanted more information to help them rectify the problems. A more detailed survey undertaken in 1973 combined with reports from course tutors (part-time members of staff who give face-to-face tuition) provided this. The survey asked students for each unit to identify terms, concepts and principles they had found particularly difficult to understand. The identical questions were asked for each unit to provide a basis of comparison. Areas which authors should give most notice to in the redrafting of a unit could be identified by a rise in the percentage of students identifying them as particularly difficult ones.

However, text material is printed for four to six years and authors work on other

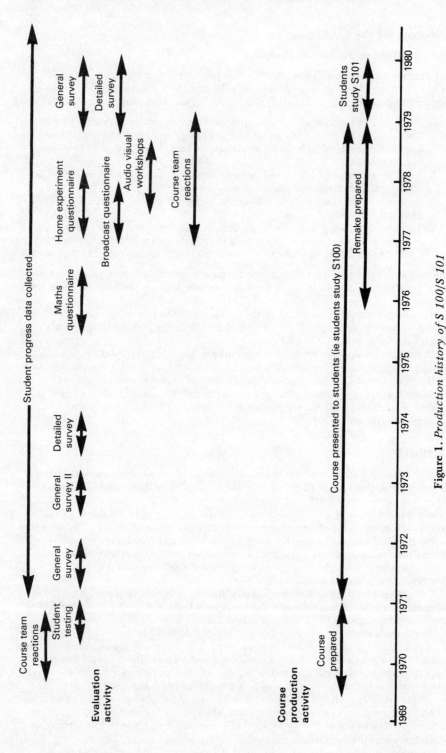

**Figure 1.** *Production history of S 100/S 101*

courses, so the opportunity and manpower to make extensive changes to the course was not present at this stage.

Also, since 1971, student progress data has been collected by the survey research department. This consists of a detailed breakdown of the students studying the course in terms of age, sex, previous educational experience and occupation. This information has been updated over the years and can be used to draw conclusions about the relative success rates of groups within a year's cohort of students.

## Decision to Remake

The original plan was to remake the course within a period of four years, but the demands made by the science courses students may subsequently study meant that consideration of what 'remaking' the course required was left until 1975. At a faculty meeting it was decided that the course content of S 100 was still appropriate, apart from the necessary updating. The majority view seemed to be that we should use what we had learned about S 100 to improve it considerably as a course and make changes with that purpose only. We wanted to develop the new course S 101 so that its educational effectiveness should be greater than that achieved in S 100, and so that dropout and failure rates become no higher than their S 100 levels.

The existence of distinct trends in the characteristics of students enrolling for S 100 had implications for this aim. The percentage of students in professional occupations was increasing and also those in manual ones. The percentage of entrants with higher educational qualifications was decreasing and that of entrants with five O-levels or less was increasing. To maintain rates of success, especially for students with minimal educational experience, without sacrificing the standards necessary for proceeding with higher level courses, was thought to be essential. A major investment of effort in the S 101 operation could produce a much-improved foundation course and, more importantly, provide techniques and procedures to facilitate future remakes.

## The Evaluation Project

A three-year evaluation project was set up in 1976. This was with the intention of concentrating attention on improving the course's educational efficiency. The aim was to devise a mechanism for ensuring that all the relevant information available was used effectively in the remake of the course. The remake team was enormous — it consisted of 45 members. Organizational structures were proposed to cope with this large number of people. This can be viewed in three ways (see Figure 2).

## Later Evidence

When the remake course team assembled in late 1976, the evaluation group began to receive requests for information. Some of these could be met by considering the feedback already available. To assist in this process, two documents were prepared for each course team member:

1. A digest of general survey data (containing overall student reaction to the course)
2. A digest of information specific to the discipline group of which he or she was a member (containing an indication of particularly difficult sections in units, objectives students felt unable to achieve, together with tutor comment on the units).

Members of the evaluation group discussed these reports with individual discipline groups to establish what other data should be collected. Several areas of interest

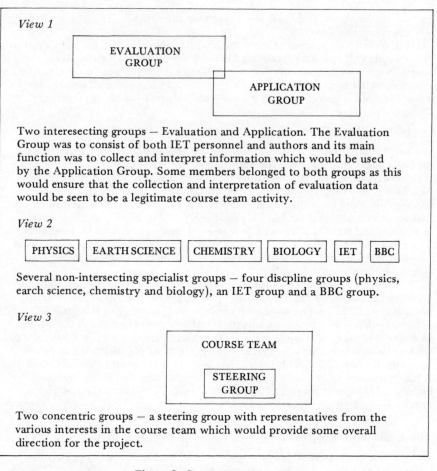

**Figure 2.** *Course team structure*

emerged: three of these were as follows:

1. *Mathematics teaching in S 100.* A detailed questionnaire on the first five units of the course where most of the new mathematical ideas are introduced was prepared to investigate student use of the parallel mathematics text, together with a survey of other OU preparatory material.
2. *Home experiment strategies.* Information was collected in 1977 by questionnaire on reasons why students were not completing the home experiments. Statistics on the cost implications of different home kit strategies were collected and guidelines for experimental work were produced.
3. *Broadcasting.* A questionnaire was sent to students on the perceptions of the usefulness of certain features of S 100 TV and radio. Workshop sessions were held with the help of the audio-visual media research group of the University, examining examples of good and bad use of television from other courses. Guidelines for the use of these media were drawn up.

## Final Structure of the Course

The final structure of the new course to emerge was as follows:

1. The number of units were reduced from 34 to 32.
2. There was a reordering of the topics covered aimed at making the more severe demands made by the course on the students appear somewhat later in the course than in S 100. The new introduction to the course conveys the relevance and utility of precise and quantitative analysis in science. The first three units of S 101 attempt to introduce students to the general ideas of the 'scientific method'.
3. A preparatory package of four booklets dealing with arithmetic, algebra, graphs and geometry has been prepared. This package, available to all students in the six months preceding the course, provides students who are uncertain of their mathematical capabilities with the opportunity of practising them before the course itself starts. Each block of work is introduced by a 15-minute television programme. As we were uncertain of the level to aim at in these programmes, and since their prime function is to motivate students, a pilot of one of the TV programmes (on algebra) was made and shown to groups of S 101 applicants. Their comments were incorporated in the final version of the programme.
4. In S 101, as in S 100, students are involved in experimental work directly with a home experiment kit. The S 100 version of this kit was criticized by students for its inconvenience, bulkiness, and the packing system which was perceived as being designed with very little attention to the convenience of the user. The new kit is dispatched in two parts, one at the start of the course and one after final registration, and the design of each section of the kit is to maximize student use. The students also criticized the consistent under-estimation of the time taken to complete the experiment component of a week's work. In S 101, introduction of a unit on experimental chemistry, where practical work is the major component of the student's workload for the week, has meant an even closer scrutiny of the times estimated.
5. A number of audio-cassettes have been introduced to replace half of the radio programmes used in S 100.

## Effectiveness of the Changes

An identical cocktail of general surveys, detailed surveys, reports from tutors and student progress data was employed to establish whether or not the changes made to the course were effective. The attempt to improve the pass rate while maintaining standards was successful.

Results from the first two years of S 101 show that the pass rate has increased slightly from 89 to 94 per cent. At the end of the year, students sat a computer-marked examination. Maintenance of standards was ensured by scrutiny of candidates' performance on selected marker questions — ie questions which had been used in previous S 100 examinations and for which item analysis data was available. The first two years' results in the course suggest that we have been successful in maintaining, and slightly increasing, the pass rate of the least qualified students.

It is too early to assess whether S 101 provides a better foundation for higher level studies in science but a follow-up study on the first two years' cohort of students is in progress. The number of students successfully completing the course has not increased dramatically. Consideration of the drop-out rates for the last year of S 100 and the first year of S 101 show a remarkably similar pattern. Since the course team's revised introduction to the course was planned to be more gentle than the S 100 early units, this result is puzzling, especially since students agreed that the early units were comparatively easy. Other studies of drop-out rates at the OU (Burt, 1976) have suggested that initial high drop-out figures on foundation courses may be due to the student's unreal expectation of the demands an OU course will make on him or her.

Workload is an area in which the changes in the course have been less successful. There is little to choose between S 100 and S 101. However, S 101 students perceive the course as considerably more interesting than S 100 students.

The mathematics pre-course package and the integration of some basic mathematics leading in the early units of the course has produced students whose performance on simple mathematics tests improves during the course and whose confidence in mathematics has increased.

Home experiments are completed by many more students and their perceptions, both of the usefulness of the experiments they have done and the importance of experimental work to a scientist, have increased. On a more particular level the remade course appears more successful. Detailed surveys of S 101 units identify areas where the teaching of particular concepts attracts more positive student reaction. The opinion of students on the teaching of elementary particle physics has increased markedly.

Not all sections of the course achieved this result and in particular the teaching of biochemistry and equilibrium in chemistry still causes students problems.

## Conclusions

My experiences on the evaluation of S 101 lead me to the following conclusions. As the history of S 100 and S 101 shows, the effort expended in remaking the course did produce a somewhat 'better' course than the original — not enormously better, as the original course was itself a successful course. Large structural changes suggested by the evaluative data had been implemented with some success. However, at the level of individual units, the feedback was useful only in identifying areas where students had particular difficulty. Alerting the authors of the new versions of the units to these was helpful, but the detailed surveys show only limited success in the attempts of the authors to improve individual units. Progressive refinement in the course design process is required.

An example of this progressive refinement is provided by the experimental chemistry unit. Owing to production difficulties with the home experiment kit, this unit was printed for one year only which allowed the author to act on the feedback collected in the first year of presentation to improve certain aspects of its teaching strategy with considerable success. This was no different from the techniques used in the unit S 100 remake process, but provided the author with the opportunity to polish the final version. Some of the remaining difficulties in the course might be removed in the same way.

But this process is dependent on the individual author's ability and willingness to respond appropriately to student feedback. He or she may be alerted to particular difficulties or confusions within the teaching text, but he or she must find his or her own solution to the problems the evaluator discovers. This process is time-consuming and, at best, the results are patchy.

On S 101, the course team was able to make large structural changes collectively with apparent success. This involved decisions about sections of work several units in length, to be studied by all students on the course. Difficulties arose where individuals had to make decisions about individual sections of work less than, or equal to, one unit. In these cases the evaluator's job becomes extremely difficult.

Effective evaluation is achieved not merely by the presentation of information in the most comprehensible and communicable form. It is vital when the decisions made are being implemented that the evaluator is available to discuss whether the action to be taken by the course team or individual author is an appropriate one in the light of the information being provided. Authors find it difficult to be objective about evaluative comment on their work. In S 101, the intersection of the evaluation and application groups was empty. No authors became involved in the collection of evaluative data. They had their own function to perform on the course team. No evaluator prepared units. To ensure that attention is paid to feedback is a difficult and time-consuming job. For an author, responding to feedback which contains only information about which sections of his or her work failed and no suggestions for possible solutions is equally difficult.

Some questions remain to be answered by our future experiments in evaluation. The two most important ones are

(a) How can the author/evaluator relationship be improved?
(b) How can the process of evaluation improve an individual author's writing skills?

A possible solution could be for authors to adopt a purely evaluative function at intervals, on material which they have not produced, to increase their experience of assessing the effectiveness of teaching strategies. Coupled with this would be the insistence that evaluators be expected to generate not only negative criticism but to present clients with positive alternatives to the strategies they criticize.

## References

Burt, G (1976) *Some Factors Influencing Dropout.* (Internal Paper) Open University, Milton Keynes.
Melton, R F (1977) *British Journal of Educational Technology* 8, 2, pp 97-103.
Nathenson *et al* (1981) Learning from evaluation at the Open University. *British Journal of Educational Technology* 12, 2, pp 120-39.

## Acknowledgements

I am grateful to R Womphrey and D Grimes for their assistance with the collection of statistics on S 101, and to T O'Shea for helpful comments on drafts of this paper.

# 2.3.5 Evaluating and Improving Learning Materials: A Case Study

G Kirkup
*The Open University*

Abstract: The Open University's foundation course 'Living with Technology' has been subjected to the largest scale evaluation ever conducted at the University. This evaluation model, known as a '2 + 6' model, entails evaluating the course during its first year of presentation, revising it during the second and presenting the revised course for the following six years. An eight-year course life is, in general, adopted for Open University courses. A team of educational technologists and members of the technology faculty are at present using the data from the first year of the evaluation, 1980, to revise the course for a new presentation in 1982.

## Introduction

Clem Adelman has written that evaluators, in their desire to have their work well received by its audience, have concentrated too much on methodology and techniques and too little on preconditions and procedures (Adelman, 1980). 'Methodology and techniques', he argues, 'are premised on preconditions and procedures'. This paper examines the procedures by which formative evaluation data (Kandaswamy, 1980) on one Open University course have been dealt with in the process of revising the course materials. It argues that these procedures have had as great an effect upon the outcome of the evaluation as the choice of evaluation model and methods.

The study is of the evaluation of the Open University's new foundation course in technology: 'Living with Technology', which, in 1980, replaced 'The Man Made World', the original technology foundation course. A detailed description of the evaluation and some of its more interesting findings are being reported in a series of articles in the *British Journal of Educational Technology* (Nathenson *et al*, 1981). A detailed description of the course can be found in the *Open University Courses Handbook* (Open University, 1979).

## Background to the Evaluation

When members of the Technology Faculty began discussing remaking the foundation course in their Faculty, it was generally accepted that the original course had been less successful than they wished, both in recruiting and teaching students. They therefore decided to begin again from scratch with a completely new course which would have different aims and philosophy. The team of academics (the Course Team) who began working on the course were enthusiastic and receptive to new ideas about teaching and presentation, as well as content. There was an atmosphere in which suggestions for evaluation were well received.

However, it is generally accepted within the Open University that evaluating course materials is 'a good thing', especially for long running courses with a large student intake. The foundation courses in the other four faculties had gone through extensive, although different, evaluations. That of the Science foundation course is described in another paper in this volume (Scanlon, 1981). It would have been difficult for the Course Team to have justified *not* engaging in some sort of evaluation. The decision was not really whether to evaluate, but what evaluation model to adopt, and the most important factor determining this was the close friendship between the Course Team Chairman and one of the educational technologists working on the course. These two travelled to work and back together every day and used that time to discuss which model would best satisfy the needs of the Course Team. The fact that the model adopted (a '2 + 6' model) was the most intensive evaluation the University has ever supported on one of its courses, was in great part owing to this friendship.

## The 2 + 6 Evaluation Model

The 2 + 6 model is one of the many variants on developmental testing used within the Open University. This is a process in which learning materials (usually in draft form) are tried out on students, and is mainly concerned with examining learning rather than content issues (Henderson *et al*, 1980). In a 2 + 6 model, a course is evaluated during its first year of presentation, revised during its second year and the revised version is presented for the following six years. It is a rigorous model, since all materials are evaluated in their final form, rather than drafts, and larger and more reliable samples of staff and students can be used. It was these factors which appealed to the Course Team. However, there are two major drawbacks to this model. First, it is very expensive since revisions must be made to printed material, broadcasting and audio-vision after they have been produced in their final form. Second, it demands a commitment from academic staff to stay with a course past its exciting production period and into the second and third year of its presentation. Neither of these factors appeared important at the planning stage but they have since had a strong influence upon the revision part of the process.

## Aims and Objectives of the Evaluation

The major aim of the evaluation was to provide the Course Team with information on which to base their decisions about revising material, and it had five objectives:

1. To identify the extent to which students were mastering the course objectives.
2. To provide quantitative feedback to the Course Team on various aspects of the course such as:
   (a) the number of students dropping out of the course;
   (b) the extent to which the materials matched the assumed entry level abilities of the students;
   (c) student workload (eg how much time students were spending on each part of the course);
   (d) students' perceptions of the relevance of broadcasting and cassette vision to the printed text.
3. To identify those parts of the course (both textual and audio-visual) which were conceptually difficult for students.
4. To try to determine the reasons *why* students were experiencing difficulties.
5. To try to elicit from students suggestions for improving the course materials.

## Evaluation Procedures

The course is divided into seven 'blocks' of materials, each based around a technological issue. This structure provided a way of organizing the evaluation data, and in 1980 data were collected for each 'block' from the following sources:

1. Item-analyses of students' assessment scores.
2. Computer-based survey data from all students.
3. In-depth feedback data from samples of students.
4. Open-ended feedback from all of the course tutors.

Short summary reports of the computer survey data, and the data from tutors, were distributed to the Course Team as they became available. However, the analysis of the in-depth student data, which was considered the most valuable and the basis for all revisions, took longer. The first evaluation report which integrated this data with data from the other sources was presented in November 1980. Reports on later blocks have been presented at intervals of four to six weeks.

During the course production stage the two educational technologists running the evaluation attended Course Team meetings and became involved with the production of the course. They also made attempts (mostly unsuccessful) to involve individual course authors more closely by asking them to identify any parts of their work they wanted given special attention. Their lack of success caused the evaluators to question the commitment of some Course Team members. The main commitment still came from the Course Team Chairman and the three course co-ordinators who, together, managed the development of the course. These co-ordinators became very involved with the evaluation and together with the educational technologists began to see themselves as a team. This team of five met regularly and produced joint authored reports and papers.

While the Evaluation Team was crystallizing, the Course Team was disintegrating. This was not unusual since, in the Open University, both resources and job satisfaction tend to be concentrated on course production rather than evaluation or maintenance (the years during which the course is presented). During the years of presentation the course team is likely to consist of one or two academics and a co-ordinator. The production period for 'Living with Technology' had been long (four years) and many Course Team members were ready for something else. Some took study leave, including the Course Team Chairman; others began working on new courses; some pursued research interests; and some left the University for new jobs. Although there was a formal commitment from the technology faculty to the evaluation it was some months before there were enough willing academics to form a Revision Course Team. During this time the morale of the Evaluation Team fell very low since it was possible that without a Revision Team the evaluation would have to be abandoned.

## The Revision Process

By September 1980, a Revision Course Team was formed. It was a mixture of some people who had been on the Production Course Team, and some new to the course, including a new Course Team Chairman. Each block had assigned to it one academic who was responsible for seeing that revisions were made to that block. Other people on the Team were evaluators, authors or monitors. The revision process could then begin.

However, from the beginning there have been pressures on the Revision Course Team both from within (because of conflict or confusion over the status of recommendations and data coming from the Evaluation Team), and from without (from the University committee structure). This external pressure was felt first through a demand, by the University, for an estimate of the percentage of revision that would be made to the course. The allocation of any resources at all for revision depended on the strength of the case presented. The Evaluation Team was therefore in the position of having, unwillingly, to produce such an estimate at a state when data were incomplete. Using a very crude measure of mastery of objectives a paper was produced which argued for revision of about one-third textual material and about one-quarter broadcasting, spread unevenly across all blocks. However, as expected, full-scale evaluation reports have contradicted this crude measure in many places, and the Evaluation Team have found themselves having to justify the contradictions. They have also had to argue against the Course Team using what was simply a committee document as a guide to revision.

Internal pressures have been reflected in both the procedure adopted for reaching a decision about revisions, and conflicts which arose within the procedure. Some structure had to be adopted so that the evaluation reports could be discussed and decisions reached, and although the Course Team is the official decision-making body on course content and teaching techniques it can be too large to debate detail. Therefore, smaller sub-groups, known as Monitoring Groups, were set up for each block. These groups would discuss in detail the recommendations in the evaluation report, decide on revisions and report their decisions to the Course Team. With Course Team approval the authors would make such revisions, and revised material would be checked by the Monitoring Group and then sent to press. Members of the Monitoring Group would be authors engaged in revising material in that block, one evaluator, and certain Course Team members called 'monitors', whose task was simply to help make the decisions. Figure 1 shows diagrammatically the membership of the different groups for any one block.

Figure 2 indicates that the Monitoring Group now controlled the revision process and the Evaluation Team functioned simply to feed in data.

The first full-scale evaluation report was produced in November 1980, and since then two others have been produced and monitoring groups on two blocks have met to discuss them. However, it has become apparent that (from the evaluators' point of view at least) there have been deficiencies in this revision model. The primary one was that no one knew who had the final say in disagreements over revisions! It had been said at the Course Team that this lay with the major academic responsible for that block who should be free to act as he thought best; which would include ignoring parts of the evaluation report if he chose. Since only one evaluator has attended the Monitoring Group's meetings he has been in a powerless

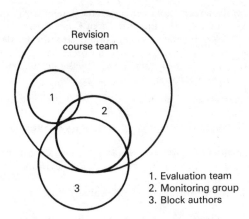

Figure 1. *Membership of groups for any one block*

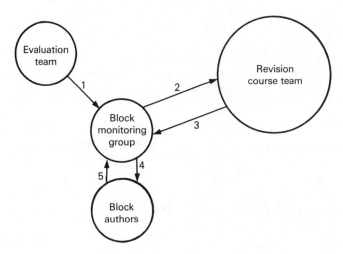

Figure 2. *Sequence of information between groups for decision-making*

position if authors refused to accept the evaluation recommendations.

Reports from the Monitoring Group to the Course Team, which has met infrequently, have been very brief and for those unfamiliar with the full evaluation report very uninformative. Therefore it has been impossible for the Course Team to engage in any extensive discussion of the revisions from this document alone, and some members of the Course Team have said they do not wish to do so since their interests lie almost exclusively with their own materials.

Authors have accused the Evaluation Team of stepping outside their brief, ie that they have recommended changes in content which they are not considered competent to do. Strictly speaking this is true, but recommendations based on learnability may often suggest changes of emphasis to, or omission of, content. It would appear that the revision process has become piecemeal, with no consistent treatment of course-wide issues, and no formal structure with which to deal with problems arising from disagreements over revisions. The experience of procedures in this one situation has demonstrated the aptness of Clem Adelman's remark given in the Introduction. Despite having an acceptable evaluation model, the preconditions of the evaluation and the revision process have changed its nature and scope, highlighting a number of questions both the evaluators and clients should have addressed in the planning stage:

1. Can the organization cope administratively with the evaluation model? (This is not a question of willingness.)
2. Should educational evaluators restrict themselves to examining issues of learnability?
3. How far should the evaluator become an advocate for his results and take part in the 'rough-and-tumble of organizational decision-making'? (Weiss, 1972)
4. Should there be an arbitrator to whom evaluators and academics are accountable?
5. How can commitment to the evaluation on the part of the academics be maintained?

## References

Adelman, C (1980) Some dilemmas of institutional evaluation and their relationship to preconditions and procedures. *Studies in Educational Evaluation* **6**.
Henderson, E *et al* (1980) *Developmental Testing for Credit. An Account of Open University Experience. (IET Course Development Paper CD9).* The Open University, Milton Keynes.
Kandaswamy, S (1980) Evaluation of instructional materials: a synthesis of models and methods. *Educational Technology* **20**, p 10.
Nathenson, M *et al* (1981) Learning from evaluation at the Open University. *British Journal of Educational Technology* **12**, 2, pp 120-39.
Open University (1979) *Courses Handbook.* Open University, Milton Keynes.
Scanlon, E (1981) Evaluating the effectiveness of distance learning: a case study. In Percival, F and Ellington, H I (eds) *Aspects of Educational Technology* **XV**. Kogan Page, London.
Weiss, C H (1972) *Evaluation Research.* Prentice-Hall, Englewood Cliffs, New Jersey.

# 2.3.6 Evaluation Methods in Distance Computer-Assisted Learning

A C Jones and T O'Shea
*The Open University*

**Abstract:** Educational materials based on computer use should be designed for continuous evaluation and refinement. Where possible, facilities for monitoring and change should be built into computer-based teaching systems. CAL tutorial packages and programming languages for novices used at the Open University are critically discussed from this point of view.

## Introduction

We would like to consider two questions in this paper:

1. How should Computer Assisted Learning (CAL) be evaluated?
2. What questions is the evaluation intended to answer?

To start with, let us take another two questions which evaluation studies often address. The first of these is: 'What is the cost of the system?', or 'How much?'. This is a reasonable question and a necessary one to ask, but it is difficult to provide a clear-cut answer and it is linked to the second question which is often asked of CAL, which is: 'Does it compare favourably with other teaching methods', or 'How effective?' The problem with this question is that this is not the right question to ask. It can be argued, in fact, that, if such a comparison can be made, then we are failing to realize the potential use of computers in education — as powerful tools for learning in ways which would not otherwise be possible. Even if, however, CAL is not introduced in such a way as to radically alter the curriculum, it rarely replaces a more traditional way of doing the same thing. The introduction of CAL is usually a new means to achieve new goals and is rarely an alternative to existing provision, and so the traditional 'comparative' statistical evaluation, where matched experimental and control groups are analyzed, becomes meaningless. There is, however, more to the argument against this sort of approach than the impracticality of standard quantitative methodology, and this is the question of the philosophy and the assumptions underlying this sort of approach, which is largely derived from the behavioural sciences, especially behaviourism with its insistence on observable outcomes and the more reactionary strands of educational psychology which emphasize psychometric testing.

## Evaluation Styles

The effect of this behaviourist tradition is for much of CAL to concentrate on *products* or *outcomes* rather than processes. This position has been attacked by protagonists of 'idiographic' evaluation such as Stephen Kemmis (Kemmis *et al*, 1979) who argues that construing learning in terms of attainment focuses attention on the content or subject matter, and the outcomes of the learning process, and away from that process itself — and from the students who are doing the learning. Thus evaluation studies concentrate on the extent to which the original objectives of the project have been met: these being, of course, the designer's objectives and not the student's, for, to return to our original questions, to answer the question 'How effective?' we need to ask 'What were the objectives — and how far have they been met?'

Proponents of illuminative evaluation (eg Parlett and Hamilton, 1977) argue that the situation into which CAL projects (or others) are introduced is very complex and is one which is constantly changing: also that it may include perspectives which the project designer is unaware of.

To try to determine whether the project has achieved pre-determined outcomes, then, has certain pitfalls:

(a) there may be features salient to the success or acceptability of the project which are never discovered, because the information to look for has already been decided at the beginning of the project in a way which excludes 'unsought' information;

(b) the situation may change so that the original questions are no longer appropriate;

(c) if an 'experimental' model is adopted it is assumed that salient variables can be identified and controlled for, an assumption unlikely to be met in a real and complex situation.

We argue that the 'How effective?' question should be replaced by one in the form of: 'How is the project perceived from the client's point of view — and what are its salient and critical features which make its acceptability and success more or less likely?'

We can then consider the first question, 'How much?', because once we know the true salient features (rather than those the designers thought were important) we can ask 'How much are they worth?' There will be no unique answer to this form of the cost question — although we can get some estimates for what CAL costs per hour to produce. (It should be noted that similar estimates for face-to-face contact are hard to come by.)

Deciding whether the project is worthwhile is very difficult and involves weighing up the costs and benefits — where costs include time and effort as well as money and some of the benefits may not be tangible.

Evaluation should provide a basis for deciding what level of trade off is reasonable and acceptable. To do this effectively, it should not be the final stage of a project which will either give it the seal of approval or 'the boot'. Instead, we argue for a process of progressive refinement, where information from the evaluation can be fed back into the system. Evaluation thus becomes part of a monitoring and tuning process: by asking, ahead of time, 'How could the situation be otherwise if the feedback I propose to collect is positive or negative?', a basis is formed for acting on that information.

Figure 1 summarizes two approaches to evaluation of CAL.

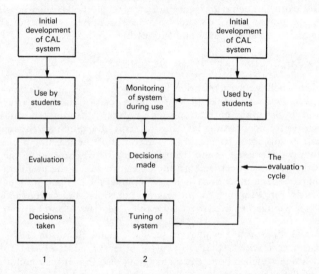

**Figure 1.** *Two 'models' of evaluation of CAL*

In the first 'static' model in Figure 1, outcomes of evaluation cannot affect the current system — although they may lead to decisions about maintaining it, dropping it or changing it. In the ideal version, 2, there is a feedback cycle based on built-in evaluation, which includes continuous tuning. To achieve this, the evaluation process should be built in to the system, which itself should itself be capable of being finely tuned. (A way of doing this is by the use of a production-rule system, O'Shea, 1979.) 1979).) In the evaluation study we will discuss here, only a small part of the evaluation was built into the CAL system and the system itself is not easily modifiable; nevertheless, we believe that by adopting an eclectic approach we obtained information which we may otherwise have missed.

## A Case Study

The CICERO computer-assisted tutorial system, which is used by people operating a range of courses at the Open University, has been described in detail elsewhere (Cooper and Lockwood, 1979) as have the various applications of CAL at the university (Bramer, 1980).

We intend to confine ourselves to discussing the evaluation of the use of CICERO on one particular course called Biological Bases of Behaviour. This study is part of a larger evaluation study of CAL in science and a full report of this particular study is available (Jones and O'Shea, 1981a).

CICERO tutorials can be used at any of the university's regional study centres which have terminals (currently 170) and are therefore theoretically available whenever the study centre is open, although students are advised to book in advance.

For each tutorial, a set of 'profile questions' relating to a specific block of the course is sent to students to answer at home: the answers to these diagnostic questions provide information about students' conceptual strengths and weaknesses related to specific objectives of the block and course. The completed answer form is taken to the study centre, the program accessed and the answers typed in. Further questions may be asked to verify the diagnosis made and, according to the students' answers, advice and remedial help may be given. So, in an interactive form, the system offers the student a means of evaluating his or her understanding and further assistance if required. For the student unable to get to the terminal, a 'postal' version is available which provides diagnostic advice based on the profile questions, but cannot, of course, enter into further dialogue. To use this a student posts the answer form and receives a print-out within a few days.

We wanted to try to answer the question we posed earlier: 'How is the project perceived from the client's point of view — what are its salient and critical features affecting its acceptability?' and to consider what changes might be required (and how to implement them) in the light of the information we would collect.

## Case Study Methodology

We were broadly following the idiographic and illuminative approach discussed earlier, which does not prescribe a 'standard methodological package'. The evaluator must be eclectic and use whatever tools are at his or her disposal which may illuminate the situation.

Our methods included:

☐ An initial questionnaire sent to students, assessing intended use, expectations and attitudes.
☐ Questionnaires *built into* interactive tutorials and sent with the postal tutorials.
☐ Interviews with staff and students at a residential summer school.
☐ A final questionnaire sent to students following up earlier open-ended ones.

## Case Study Results

Our main finding was a surprise: it seemed that the majority of factors influencing the decision to use or not to use the tutorials were not related to perceived educational benefits but turned out to be more affective in quality.

Students started off with realistic expectations of how they might benefit, and these included: diagnosing and correcting weak points, immediate feedback, remedial help, and a useful revision tool. Those who had used the system felt they had benefited in exactly these ways, yet use was low and the attrition rate high!

Seeking out students who had not used the system, we interviewed 53 students at a residential summer school. These students reported a number of 'off-putting' experiences with computers and also revealed that many of them were scared of using a terminal and embarrassed at using it in front of other students. This was followed up in a final questionnaire. Table 1 gives the percentage of respondents who reported strong agreement with the sentiments summarized in the table.

| 'Bad' computer experiences | 23% |
| Scared of using the terminal | 12%* |
| Embarrassed at using it in front of other students | 13%* |

\* Both these figures may under-represent the situation, as they only include those students who report 'strong agreement' with the statement

**Table 1.** *Negative factors in using computers*

### How Our Evaluation Study Affected Decision-Making

Although students were realistic in their expectation of how they might benefit from using CICERO, their views of the problems associated with its use were realistic too, and so take-up is low.

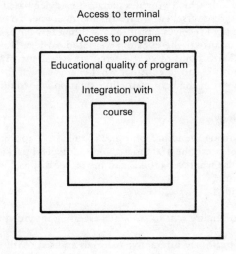

**Figure 2.** *A view of CAL as the 'Chinese box puzzle'*

The situation can be summarized as a number of barriers which students have to get through. From Figure 2 (taken from Jones and O'Shea, 1981b) we see that students must cope with access to terminals and to the programs before the quality of the program becomes a consideration. The point we want to make here is not that particular results of this study were surprising, but that some of these results would not have been obtained if a standard evaluation of educational cost-effectiveness had been carried out. For example, we discovered that some students were scared of terminals and embarrassed at using them in front of other students, by interviewing students who had not used the system. Students who did not admit to these feelings in open-ended questionnaires revealed this information in interviews. We were subsequently able to follow this up by telling students that we knew of instances of fear and embarrassment and asking them whether this applied to them.

This particular approach also reveals another aspect of our approach, which is that the discovery of widespread fear of computers cannot be acted upon by the recipients of the 'standard' evaluation study we mentioned previously, who would normally be CAL experts.

In this case what is needed is action to be taken by the Student Computing Service as a whole, and also by our regional tutors through tutorials and induction sessions. Referring back to Figure 2, we see that each box represents a problem which can be solved by different audiences. The information represented by the outer box can be acted on by university committees who can authorize expenditure on computing equipment and the organization of computing facilities at study centres or summer schools. It also points to the importance of sympathetic but competent computer induction meetings — which lies in the hands of our regional staff.

'Access to programs' — our next box — can be improved by such practices as always accessing the HELP facility in programs in the same way, and by giving users lists of options to choose from, to reduce their memory load. (The latter is usually referred to as providing MENU facilities — for obvious reasons.) These changes can be made by the Student Computing Service and some of these procedures are already, in fact, being implemented.

The inner box deals with the integration of the CAL material with the overall course and, in practise, the only group who can respond are the course team. In the past, the role of CAL in courses and in the university's organizational structure has been open to debate. Despite attempts to draw in the subject experts, both the production and maintenance of CAL lay with the CAL personnel in the Student Computing Service and this created certain problems. (This problem is not confined to CAL — Kirkup (1981) comments that the evaluation of courses is often perceived as being the sole business of the evaluator(s) as opposed to the course team.)

## Finding the Audience

However, as information from our evaluation became available and was disseminated, potential clients from a particular faculty (Science) made themselves known to the evaluators. This led to the formation of a CAL in science evaluation group which includes members from the Science Faculty, the Institute of Educational Technology, and the Student Computing Service. The different mechanisms adopted by this group for reaching different clients include: internal technical reports; workshops; and reports to the Science Faculty board and to other boards and committees.

One result of our eclectic evaluation strategy is that it has helped to establish who the different audiences in the university are, and has also led to increased awareness of the role of and use of CAL in the university.

The main virtue of the evaluation process described here is that the various audiences addressed have a much greater potential for impact on the university's total CAL provision than individual CAL authors, who are only able to improve particular CAL programs and are unable to affect other aspects of the total CAL context such as collective student attitudes and the mythology surrounding the use of computers and CAL.

## Summary

We are advocating three propositions about how CAL evaluation should be approached in distance learning.

1. CAL materials should be designed to facilitate monitoring of student use and tuning as a result of evaluation — eg the use of built-in evaluation questions.

2. A wide range of evaluation methodologies can have a useful role to play in collecting diverse information and assisting in the refinement of particular evaluation tools — eg the use of interviews to generate items for questionnaires.
3. CAL evaluators should be catholic in their choice of audiences — eg addressing both financial planners and primary producers of educational materials.

## References

Bramer, M (1980) Using computers in distance education: the first ten years of the British Open University. *Computers and Education* 4, pp 293-301.

Cooper, A and Lockwood, J (1979) The need, provision and use of a computer-assisted interactive tutorial system. In Page, G T and Whitlock, Q (eds) *Aspects of Educational Technology* XIII. Kogan Page, London.

Jones, A and O'Shea, T (1981a) *An Evaluation of Tutorial CAL at the Open University: The Use of CICERO on SDT 286.* CAL Research Group Technical Report No 5. The Open University, Milton Keynes.

Jones, A and O'Shea, T (1981b) *The Role of Tutorial CAL in the Open University.* Paper presented at CAL 81 Symposium on Computer Assisted Learning, Leeds.

Kemmis, S, Atkin, R and Wright, E (1979) *How do Students Learn?* Occasional publication No 5. Centre for Applied Research in Education, University of East Anglia.

Kirkup, G (1981) Evaluating and improving learning materials. In Percival, F and Ellington, H I (eds) *Aspects of Educational Technology* XV. Kogan Page, London.

O'Shea, T (1979) A self-improving quadratic tutor. *International Journal of Man-Machine Studies* 11, pp 97-124.

Parlett, M and Hamilton, D (1977) Evaluation as illumination: a new approach to the study of innovatory programs. In Hamilton, D *et al* (eds) *Beyond the Numbers Game: A Reader in Educational Evaluation.* Macmillan, London.

## Acknowledgements

The evaluation of SDT 286 was carried out in conjunction with Bob Womphrey and Robin Mason, and the CICERO project was directed by Aldwyn Cooper. We would also like to thank Tom Vincent, Pat Murphy, Eileen Scanlon, Liz Whitelegg, Phil Butcher and Jim Burrows for their help and support.

# 2.4 Case Studies of Course Evaluation

## 2.4.1 Integrating Evaluation with the Learning of Cashiering Skills: Problems and Procedures

**L C Barber** *Trustee Savings Bank of Birmingham and the Midlands*
**K J Adderley** *Brighton Polytechnic*
**M Randall** *Trustee Savings Bank of Birmingham and the Midlands*

**Abstract:** The Trustee Savings Bank (TSB) of Birmingham and the Midlands in 1980 launched a new scheme for training its cashiers. Early in the design stage, it was decided to run an evaluation exercise concurrent with the operation of the training scheme. This paper reviews the experience of devising and using the evaluation exercise.

# Introduction

In the last few years the Trustee Savings Banks (TSBs) have changed significantly. Small banks, taking only savings deposits, have been replaced by regional banks offering a comprehensive range of services. The TSB of Birmingham and the Midlands, created in November 1979 as part of this programmed change, employs approximately 1,300 people, serving an area of 600 square miles. One of the many initiatives taken by the constituent banks was the decision to set up the Education and Training Department in advance of amalgamation, in recognition of the importance of expanding and improving staff training. This meant a substantial financial investment, which not only demonstrated commitment to staff development, but also underlined the need for attention to evaluating training effectiveness.

After a comprehensive needs analysis, the first priority set for the department was branch clerical staff training. Proposals were discussed throughout the Bank, and the training scheme was introduced in July 1980. It spans a period of two years and combines in-branch training with tuition at the Regional Training Centre. There are three programmes based upon six stages of development ranging from simple office routines to complex counter inquiries, covering both technical and social skills.

# The Approach to Evaluation

## The Decision to Integrate Evaluation

The main reasons for evaluating the training were to check the soundness of the scheme's design, to assess the extent of the achivement of the training objectives, and to be able to report to senior management about training effectiveness. It was also deemed advantageous to be able to use both informal and formal methods to maximize data collection, to make appropriate changes as early as possible during the operation of the scheme, and to use evaluation to diversify training staff skills. For all these reasons, and taking into account the lack of data from earlier training arrangements and the impracticability of setting up control groups, an integrated approach to evaluation was chosen.

## Models for Evaluation

Much of the evaluatory literature deals either with a specific course or fails to provide practical guidelines by concentrating on such as arguing the need for evaluation, providing an overview of specific evaluatory exercises, or making theoretical observations about conducting an evaluation. This criticism does not apply, however, to evaluatory models, notably those advocated by Moors (1979) and Stake (1976) which have been of considerable assistance in designing the evaluation exercise.

Moors' model level 1, notwithstanding its emphasis on formal evaluation, was especially helpful in clarifying purposes by its systematic analysis of evaluatory interests. After slight modification its principles were used for:

☐ briefing the Trustees of the Bank of our intentions;
☐ obtaining evaluatory interests from all parties concerned;
☐ checking each stage of the procedure before going on to the next by applying the model as a 'route map'.

Stake's model, on the other hand, deals with informal as well as formal evaluation, directing attention to the need to be sensitive to unintended circumstances, activities or outcomes, and to the importance of their 'lack of congruence' with that intended. Similarly, Parlett and Hamilton (1972), in emphasizing the importance of the total 'learning milieu', influenced the adoption of a holistic approach by urging the seeking out and inclusion in the evaluation of informal comments and observations of all parties concerned (supervising staff, trainees and instructors) so that a complete record of influences is made.

## Opportunities For and Constraints To Action

Evaluation activities of the kind described in this paper are extensive and, whilst every opportunity is taken to derive benefit from the data obtained, it is accepted, for the moment, that it is relatively easy to change such things as:

- ☐ course objectives;
- ☐ the time each trainee spends on each programme to cater for individual needs;
- ☐ learning methods and materials;
- ☐ the location for learning particular topics;
- ☐ the deployment of Education and Training Department staff and, to a lesser extent, branch staff.

However, it is difficult, if not impossible, to:

- ☐ make significant changes to the intake pattern;
- ☐ expand the resources of the department in accordance with any increase in the number of entrants;
- ☐ control the quality of entrants;
- ☐ alter the flow pattern of trainees through the scheme (it being assumed that the failure rate would be negligible).

## The Evaluation Exercise

The first step was to elaborate the main evaluatory interests into a series of more detailed questions:

- ☐ What is the actual usage of taught abilities at (i) the counter; (ii) the inquiry position; (iii) the office?
- ☐ What is the difference between management's expectations and cashiers' performance?
- ☐ Are the scheme's methods — courses, workbook, visits, assignments — the most appropriate in relation to its aims?
- ☐ What difficulties do trainees have in modifying their learning style to the requirements of the scheme?
- ☐ What is the extent and effects of deviations from the planned operation of the scheme?
- ☐ How does (i) the branch environment, and (ii) movement between branches, influence the trainee's progress?
- ☐ Is the documentation adequate?

Thus a starting point for the preparation of the evaluation plan was established.

### The Evaluation Plan

The evaluatory interests outline the evaluation plan, within which the questions posed by Cranton and Legge (1978) were re-expressed and extended to describe the generation and collection of data. With such a highly structured scheme it was then easy to identify each of these processes within its operation.

The resulting evaluation plan collects data by:

☐ interviews at branches;
☐ questionnaires with a combination of open-ended and scaled questions, used during course reviews and by branch staff at pre-determined stages in the scheme;
☐ recording trainee profiles (Hills, 1980) of pre-course readiness;
☐ attainment tests prior to and during courses;
☐ observations and comments received by training staff;

so as to form a composite picture of each trainee's progress.

Those tests relating to in-branch training are marked by branch staff. The branch thereby obtains direct feedback on the trainee's progress, becoming more closely involved with the training and encouraged to comment on its relevance and effectiveness. Branch staff were also best placed to complete trainee profiles. The regular visits to branches by training officers to monitor progress and counsel trainees and supervising staff were also used for both formal and informal evaluatory activities.

## Practical Problems

### Instrumentation

With the evaluation plan finalized came the task of instrument design (Oppenheim, 1966; Edwards, 1951; Yorke *et al*, 1980). Whilst these were quickly developed, unfortunately it was not possible to pilot their use. To maximize opportunities for learning, all appropriate training staff were involved as each instrument was designed. Despite the considerable pressure this policy put on the training team, confidence and motivation grew as skills developed.

### Data Collection

It soon became evident that the collection of informal data was fraught with problems. Whilst willing to co-operate, staff experienced difficulties with recognizing relevant data and appreciating its significance and value. Regular coaching and review meetings developed their observational skills and clarified the ways data entered the records.

### Data Collation

The amount of data to be handled is large and it is crucial that the important points are identified quickly. To this end, indicators of course performance were charted in tabular form. These, together with observations made by instructors in later problem analysis sessions, were used to improve both the tuition and the evaluation procedure.

The collection and collation of formal data is relatively straightforward. Informal data, by virtue of its unstructured nature and unpredictable timing, is much more difficult, particularly in the case of opinions expressed by branch staff. A simple, but effective, solution to this problem was to list opinions from the interview schedules from which a category system was developed, which allowed frequency of opinions to be recorded with tally marks. Also, in this way, a comparison of comments from supervisors and trainees can be made.

### Miscellaneous Problems

Training courses last three or five days, and commence weekly. Sometimes courses are duplicated to match an increase in intake. It was impractical, therefore, to make changes on a weekly basis so major reviews were carried out at five-week intervals. This provided feedback from 30 per cent of the estimated total annual intake on which to base modifications of courses for the remaining 70 per cent.

Although alerted to the unexpected dimensions, via Stake (1976), the Bank's need to increase staff to service business expansion threatened to upset the operation of the scheme during its inaugural year. This change in recruitment increased trainees from an expected 150 to an actual 275. Rather than restructure the whole of the scheme, whenever possible, both group size and the number of courses were increased. This solution unfortunately reduced the available resources for evaluation, research, material design, branch visits and computer terminal practice.

## Review

Over 260 recruits have entered the training scheme to date, at a varying rate up to a maximum of 20 per week. Although a complete review will not be possible for some considerable time, the initial indications are that the basic structure of the scheme is sound and that appropriate evaluation techniques are being employed. Apart from expected teething troubles, the scheme has been introduced successfully. These early problems stemmed mainly from staff shortages in branches, rather than from non-co-operation. Unsolicited comments by branch staff to visiting training officers tend to be supportive with critical views being in the minority. Some examples, with the number of contributors in brackets, are:

☐ The scheme helps trainees to learn more quickly than in the past (14).
☐ The scheme is properly thought out (10).
☐ The scheme is not as good as previous methods (3).
☐ The training undertaken in the Training Centre and partly in-branch is the only way to train staff (29).

The evaluation exercise has been incorporated into the operation of the scheme largely as planned, although the data recording systems needed urgent and early revision to cope with the volume of data. Whilst it has provided a broad overview of the effectiveness of the scheme, particularly with regard to the thin sandwich patterns of centre and in-branch training, it has also facilitated staff development, quantified the additional work-load, and identified specific areas of training on which to focus evaluation in the future.

## References

Cranton, P A and Legge, L H (1978) Program evaluation in higher education. *Journal of Higher Education* **49**, 5, pp 464-71.
Edwards, A L (1951) *Techniques of Attitude Scale Construction.* Appleby Century-Croft, New York.
Hills, J E (1980) Educational technology helps the unemployed. In Winterburn, R and Evans, L (eds) *Aspects of Educational Technology* **XIV**. Kogan Page, London.
Moors, D C (1979) A model for evaluating educational programmes. In Page, G and Whitlock, Q (eds) *Aspects of Educational Technology* **XIII**. Kogan Page, London.
Oppenheim, A N (1966) *Questionnaire Design and Attitude Measurement.* Heinemann, London.
Parlett, M and Hamilton, D (1972) *Evaluation as Illumination.* Centre for Research in the Educational Sciences, University of Edinburgh.
Stake, R E (1976) The countenance of educational evaluation. *Teachers' College Record* **68**, 7, pp 523-40.
Yorke, D M *et al* (1980) *Evaluating Business Studies Courses: An Introduction.* Staff Development and Educational Methods Unit, Manchester Polytechnic.

## Acknowledgements

The authors are grateful to Don Moors and Jim Hills for their help with the design of the evaluation exercise and trainee profiles. They would also like to thank the Trustees of the Trustee Savings Bank of Birmingham and the Midlands for their permission to publish this paper.

# 2.4.2 Evaluation for Revision: A Case Study of a Training Programme

J M Hebein and R G Dawson
*Army Education Centre, Bad Kreuznach, West Germany*

**Abstract:** This paper presents an evaluation framework developed for a large-scale performance-based training workshop. Consideration is given to evaluation methods used during design, development, and implementation, with particular emphasis on the use of several types of evaluation instruments during the implementation phase.

## Introduction

The effectiveness of any training programme is determined, to a large extent, by the procedures employed to collect and make use of evaluation data. If provisions have been made for continuous evaluation during the design, development and implementation phases, the training will have greater likelihood for success in meeting the needs of the target population.

This paper presents a case study of the evaluation of a training programme which is based upon several key evaluation concepts. First, evaluation is viewed as decision-oriented; that is, data are collected and analyzed in order to answer specific questions and/or to assist in making particular decisions. Second, for programmes in which the outcomes, target population, content or organizational context are subject to change, the focus of evaluation is of a formative nature. Although a programme has been summatively proven to be effective, subsequent data may reveal the need for modifications. Third, multiple evaluation methods should be used to obtain information on which to base decisions regarding revisions. In this respect, both product and process can be evaluated through the use of expert appraisal and trainee performance data collection techniques. Finally, evaluation is seen as an ongoing, iterative process with data being collected during all phases of programme development and implementation. These data are obtained through measures administered before, during and after training.

## Workshop Description

The Dawson and Hebein 'Train the Trainer' workshop is designed to provide trainers and training supervisors with the knowledge, skills and attitudes needed to prepare, conduct, evaluate and manage performance-oriented training. Instruction within the workshop is performance-oriented, thereby demonstrating the training principles being presented and providing participants with direct experience in performance-oriented training.

The workshop consists of ten four-hour modules, each focusing on one aspect of applying the systems approach to training. Within each module, several performance objectives are accomplished. The topics addressed in the module are:

(a) Introduction to Performance Oriented Training
(b) Managing and Communicating in Training

(c)  Determining Training Status
(d)  Developing Performance Objectives
(e)  Preparing to Conduct Training
(f)  Selecting and Developing Training Media
(g)  Evaluating Training
(h)  Conducting Performance-Oriented Training
(i)  Gaining Acceptance for New Training Ideas
(j)  Implementing New Training Ideas.

The workshop is sequential in that the activities of one module build upon the knowledge and products developed in previous modules. This enhances the application of the systems approach to training and provides continuity to the activities of the workshop.

The topics included in the course are presented through a variety of media and techniques. The participants acquire knowledge and skills related to the use of these media and techniques in training through 'learning by doing'. Their direct experiences give them insights they would not acquire by reading or listening to formal presentations about these methods.

Evaluation is an ongoing activity throughout the workshop. Data are collected and analyzed in order to fulfil several purposes.

## Evaluation Methods

In order to determine the effectiveness of the training programme, to evaluate the performance of the participants, and to make revision decisions, several evaluation methods are used in the Dawson and Hebein 'Train the Trainer' workshop. The data from the evaluation instruments indicate training needs related to performance-oriented training before and after the workshop; participants' attitudes toward performance-oriented training; participants' reactions to the information and presentation methods of the workshop; and transfer of skills and knowledge to real-world training situations. The evaluation methods used include:

☐  Self-assessment
☐  Value assessment
☐  Content assessment
☐  Performance assessment
☐  Transfer assessment

Pre-testing of trainees to obtain entry level data on all objectives of the workshop is not practical, given the time and resource constraints of this programme. Therefore, a Participant Self-Assessment Survey is administered to determine the trainees' perceptions of their levels of expertise, as well as their attitudes and values about the topics of the workshop. This information is later compared with data from the same questionnaire, obtained upon completion of the course. The post-workshop questionnaire also requests participants to list the three topics that will be of greatest value to them on the job. Thus, this self-assessment form provides data to assess changes in perceived levels of expertise on workshop topics and in the importance of the topics to the trainees' own interests and job-related duties.

During the workshop, performance data for each participant on all objectives of the course are obtained and recorded in individual Job Books. The Job Books list all tasks required in the workshop. Participants record a 'Go' or 'No Go' upon completion of a task, based on minimum performance criteria established in the objectives.

In addition to performance data, participants also provide content assessment data during the course. The Workshop Rating Scale is completed by each participant at the end of every module of the workshop. The individual items require the trainees to react to the characteristics and elements of each module, including the objectives, activities, informational content and co-ordinators' performance. They also list any strong and weak features of the module. This form allows the participants an active part in the evaluation for revision process. This is effective not only from the perspective of the valuable data obtained but also because of the sense of influence and involvement participants feel in providing this type of feedback.

The last type of evaluation information obtained is related to the transfer of skills and knowledge acquired in the course to the real-world training environment. To determine whether transfer occurs, a follow-up Training Questionnaire is sent to participants six to eight weeks after completion of the workshop. Responses to this questionnaire are compared with pre-workshop responses to the same items. Changes in the responses indicate areas in which the workshop may have been responsible for improved training.

## Using Evaluation Data for Revisions

The approach used to analyze the evaluation data in order to determine where modifications are needed in the workshop is an adaptation of Robert Stake's matrix method (Stake, 1976). Figure 1 presents a six-cell matrix in which the two columns are labelled *intents* and *observations*, while the three rows are designated *entry conditions, training* and *outcomes*. After information is recorded in each cell of the matrix, a number of comparisons can be made which, in turn, may suggest revisions in one or more aspects of the training programme. These comparisons are of two main types. First, any one cell in the intents column can be compared with another cell in the intents column, in order to determine the match or degree of appropriateness among the intended trainees, the intended training programme, and the intended outcomes. These comparisons are qualitative in nature and are made through expert appraisal of the data during early stages of programme development. Second, the two cells in each row of the matrix can be compared in order to determine the congruence between what was intended and what actually was observed during the training programme. For example, Did the trainees exhibit the expected entry conditions? Was the training workshop implemented as planned? Were the specified outcomes achieved? Objective observational data and trainee performance and attitudinal information are needed to answer these questions. The instruments described in the previous section provide the required data.

Several specific uses of this approach, as it has been applied to the 'Train the Trainer' workshop, will serve to illustrate how revisions are suggested through an analysis of the matrix data.

During the initial design of the programme, the intended trainees were described in terms of duty titles, job responsibilities, general aptitudes and abilities, and training needs. Precise performance objectives were developed which specified the task, conditions and standards to be accomplished as a result of the training. A proposed programme of instruction which included the specific content, methods and media of instruction was also developed. The workshop developers reviewed this information for contingencies among the entry conditions, the training, and the outcomes. Additionally, several categories of experts appraised the data, among them decision-makers within the organization for which the programme was intended, subject-matter experts within the particular area of training, and individuals who were potential participants. These reviews were focused on the matches between the intended trainees and the planned training, between the intended trainees and the specified outcomes, and between the planned training and the specified outcomes. Some of the revisions which were suggested as a result of these reviews related to:

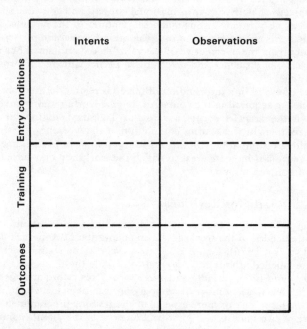

**Figure 1.** *Training evaluation matrix*

1. The addition or deletion of certain objectives.
2. The inclusion of training materials available from the organization.
3. The simplification of some content and activities.
4. The incorporation of more opportunity for practice.

During the pilot test of the workshop, and as an ongoing process in subsequent iterations, a variety of data was recorded in the *observations* cells of the matrix. Mismatches have been noted across all three rows of cells in the matrix which, in turn, have led to modifications in various aspects of the workshop.

Looking first at the entry conditions, several mismatches have indicated a need for revisions in the programme. The workshop was originally designed for a heterogeneous group of participants representing trainers and training managers. Decision-makers within the organization assign personnel to attend the workshop. Over a period of time, the participants have become more homogeneous in that they are almost exclusively trainers. The other major mismatch was related to the general ability level of the participants and their degree of motivation and attention span. It was observed that many trainees did not read as well as had been anticipated, that motivation was lacking in some, and that others had very short attention spans. These incongruencies between intended and observed entry conditions led to modifications in both outcomes and training. On the one hand, some of the original objectives were more relevant to managers than to trainers. These were substituted with outcomes more consistent with the needs of the novice trainer. On the other hand, activities within the workshop were revised, taking into account the observed ability, motivational and attention levels of the participants. For example, reading passages were shortened and simplified, oral presentations were limited, and more active participation with feedback was built into the workshop.

Mismatches between intended training and observed training were often related to incongruencies between intended and observed entry conditions. For example, a planned activity called for the participants to complete a self-instructional programmed booklet within an hour. It was observed that many trainees required assistance in completing the task, that some took much longer than an hour, and that others were not able to attend to the activity and were easily distracted. As a result, mismatches were evident between the two outcome cells; rather than being able to perform the specified objective as a result of completing the self-instructional programme, a large percentage of the trainees received 'No Go' on the task. It was obvious that changes were needed in the training activities. An audio-visual presentation, interspersed frequently with small group activities in which the task is taught in small sequential steps, is now used in place of the programmed text. The observations in terms of the trainees' performance during the activities and on the performance test are now consistent with expectations.

Discrepancies also occur between intended and observed outcomes. As previously noted, these often are related to mismatches between other cells of the matrix. A given person or group of people may not achieve the intended outcome because:

1. They do not possess the intended entry conditions.
2. The training was not implemented as planned.
3. The outcomes were not appropriate for the audience.
4. The training content, methods or media were not appropriate to teach the task.

Thus, when a mismatch occurs between the outcome cells, it is necessary to analyze the contingencies and congruencies among the other cells in order to pinpoint the reason for the difference between intended and observed outcomes and, as a result, to make needed revisions.

One example of the process used to pinpoint the reason(s) for a mismatch between intended and observed outcomes pertains to the objective which requires participants to conduct a critique of another participant's training session. Among the criteria to be met are that the critique must be positive and constructive and that it actively involves the participant-trainer in the identification of his or her strengths and weaknesses. Repeated observations indicated that these criteria were not met, although opportunity to practise and feedback had been provided. Participant-evaluators tended to focus on weaknesses, to be judgemental and to bombard the participant-trainer with a barrage of negatively-toned criticisms. The participant-trainers tended to assume a passive role and avoid responsibility for identifying their own strengths and weaknesses.

Familiarity with the organizational climate in which the participants work provided insights into the reason for this mismatch. There appears to be an institutionalized emphasis on the negative which permeates all aspects of the work and training environment. A single presentation of the guidelines for an effective critique, followed by one practice session, was not sufficient to overcome the conditioned negative approach learned through experience on the job.

Revisions include:

1. Contrasting examples of an effective and an ineffective critique session.
2. Group discussion of personal reactions to positive and negative criticism.
3. Opportunity to role-play a critique, taking alternately the part of the trainer and the evaluator.
4. Observation of the role-play critiques of other participants.
5. A constant stress, to the extent of saying the words several times during each module, on 'positive' and 'constructive'.

## Summary

The Dawson and Hebein 'Train the Trainer' workshop is evaluated for several purposes using a variety of data collection techniques. The training evaluation matrix adapted from Stake (1976) has been a useful tool in analyzing and interpreting the data. Its use, however, is limited to suggestions regarding revisions for improvement, because there are not hard and fast rules to apply in making revision decisions. The best modifications are based upon a combination of good evaluation data and creativity.

## Reference

Stake, R E (1976) The countenance of educational evaluation. *Teachers' College Record* **68**, 7, pp 523-40.

# 2.5 Evaluation Resources and Assessment Techniques

## 2.5.1 An Evaluation Resource Pack: Issues and Implications

N D C Harris and C D Bell
*University of Bath*

**Abstract:** The Evaluation Resource Pack has been developed at the University of Bath for the Council for Educational Technology. It is a collection of materials to help groups of people, or individuals, to evaluate educational courses. Also, the materials have been developed so that they are flexible enough to be used as teaching materials, if one wishes to use them in a course dealing with evaluation. As the Evaluation Resource Pack was developed to help the evaluation of educational technology courses, many, but not all, of the examples refer to educational technology courses. However, all courses and situations have many characteristics in common, and the materials can easily be used in other contexts.

This paper identifies the structure of the pack and discusses its possibilities and limitations for use beyond the target population for which it was originally devised.

## Introduction

Evaluation has always been problematic. With increasing interest being shown in institution-based evaluation and self-evaluation, both practical and theoretical issues need modifying from large-scale schemes. This paper examines these issues, and outlines attempts to overcome problems during the production of an evaluation resource pack.

## Background

In May 1979, the Council for Educational Technology (CET) invited the University of Bath to develop:

> a workshop of self-help materials for those people running long courses in educational technology. Any examples are to focus on the projects which are carried out as part of the course work.

The full brief given by the Council for Educational Technology focused on the production of materials that would help long course organizers:

(a)  improve their evaluation skills;
(b)  develop schemes of evaluation.

The materials were developed in collaboration with those institutions preparing for, or providing, courses leading to qualifications in educational technology. The field testing was in these institutions, with the University of Bath acting as a co-ordinating agent.

Long courses in educational technology were defined as those courses listed in the directory *Courses Leading to Qualifications in Educational Technology 1980-1981* (CET, 1979). In general, the courses run for a minimum of one year full-time or two years part-time. The audience was identified as those people who were named contacts in the annual CET *Directory on Courses in Educational Technology.* Many of these contacts also involved their colleagues. Altogether there are 30 institutions that run such courses, the courses being classified by qualifications and attendance. For the purpose of the needs assessment, the research degrees and the City and Guilds Certificate courses were not included: the research degree courses because they were not structured; the City and Guilds Certificate courses because of low student numbers. Some of the Master's degrees were taught courses and therefore retained.

The course organizers and tutors stated in interviews that they were concerned with their own skills and schemes of evaluation. In addition, they wanted resources to help them teach evaluation in their courses. A proposal was made for the structure of the materials and the way that the resources could be used, based on the information collected by interviews and discussions. Respondents were asked to react to the proposals by writing comments over their copy of the materials, or by comments on one side of A4 paper.

From the information collected, the decision was made to keep the dual purpose of the pack:

(a)  to improve the skills of organizers and teachers;
(b)  to allow its use as a resource pack for teaching.

More adjustments to detail were made during a small intensive weekend workshop held at Bath in December 1979. The workshop was attended by three course tutors from different types of institutions.

Further feedback was encouraged as follows:

1. *Individual comments* were made by anyone who was willing to read the resource materials in their draft form.
2. *A questionnaire* was used with 10 sets of materials which were sent to those insitutions who were willing to read them. The questionnaire included closed questions with a scale and spaces for comments. Five of the 10 were returned.
3. *A workshop,* based on the materials, was organized with the aim of:
   (a)  allowing formative evaluation data to be collected;
   (b)  simulating the planning of a small-scale evaluation;
   (c)  gaining some idea of what to put in a Users' Guide.

The first and last aims were adequately met. A wealth of constructive comment was collected which led to a revision of materials. The comments were collected by each of the three syndicates (six or seven participants) feeding back notes of their sessions, and a final plenary session during which detailed notes were made of the inter-syndicate discussion.

By this time, 21 institutions had been involved in the development in one way or another (see Harris and Bailey, 1980).

| Qualification / Attendance | Certificate: City and Guilds | Diploma: self- or locally validated* | Diploma: CNAA | Post-experience: BA degree | Master's degree | PhD | Total |
|---|---|---|---|---|---|---|---|
| Full-time | 0 | 5 | 2 | 0 | 4 | 1 | 12 |
| Part-time | 6 | 2 | 4 | 1 | 2 | 0 | 15 |
| Full-time or part-time | 0 | 2 | 0 | 1 | 4 | 2 | 9 |
| Full-time and part-time | 0 | 2 | 0 | 1 | 0 | 0 | 3 |
| Total | 6 | 11 | 6 | 3 | 10 | 3 | 39 |

* validated by local university or by the college

**Figure 1.** Long courses in educational technology offered by 24 institutions in England, Scotland and Wales

## Outline of the Product

Information collected from the formative evaluation was used to send to each user proposals outlining the changes needed to produce the final Resource Pack. The Evaluation Resource Pack (Harris and Bailey, 1980) can be used by course organizers to help them evaluate their own course and as training materials for their students.

The materials include a number of flexible units to allow the user to select materials to suit his or her own needs. The main components are:

1. *Users' Guide* combining:
   (a) outline of the materials;
   (b) suggestions for using the materials in different ways.
2. *Introduction to Evaluation* containing:
   (a) brief description of models;
   (b) brief description of techniques;
   (c) glossary of essential terms.
3. *Tool Kit* containing a number of guides to help the collection, analyzing, summarizing and reporting of evaluations. The guides cover the writing of questionnaires, interview schedules, group meetings, observation schedules, resource analysis, using assessment data, and how to summarize, analyze and organize the information for a report.
4. *Planning an Evaluation* including a guide to help select suitable techniques of evaluation. The materials take a pragmatic approach, mainly in the form of checklists and examples. The Introduction to Evaluation unit introduces some theoretical concepts and is supported by a bibliography to allow those who wish to follow up issues in depth.

A summary of the contents of the Evaluation Resource Pack is given in Figure 2.

| Users' Guide | Introduction to Evaluation |
|---|---|
| **Planning an Evaluation** | **Tool Kit** |
| Purpose of evaluation | Pencil and paper |
| Identify sponsor and audience | Talking and listening |
| Choose evaluator | Observation |
| Available resources | Sociometric |
| Context information | Assessment |
| Focus evaluation | Resource analysis |
| Choose procedures (see Tool Kit) | Curriculum analysis |
| Define responsibilities | Summarizing and analyzing |
| Timetable | Reporting |
| Report (see Tool Kit) | |

Figure 2. *Summary of the Evaluation Resource Pack materials*

## Evaluation, Self-Evaluation and Educational Technology

Educational technologists as evaluators have tended to concentrate on products rather than processes. Strategies are based on a systems view of educational technology, represented by the objectives, methods, content and output model.

Recently, increasing attention is being directed towards small-scall evaluations and self-evaluations which often favour study of the processes of education rather than the products. Reasons for this are varied, but generally centre on the need to provide information relevant to, and of practical use by, individual institutions. Such information may relate to a range of situations, from an individual teacher's professional practices to an institution's performance within the wider social context. When studying processes of education, the values and aspirations of individuals, and interactions between individuals, become important considerations. Methodologies of the systems approach, which are seen as having their roots in the 19th century view of the scientific method, are criticized for not considering these values and interactions.

Criticism has led towards a search for alternative methodologies. Such alternatives are often seem as being provided by social anthropologists, many claiming them to be in opposition to the quantitative systems approach (see Bell, 1980).

## Methodologies of Evaluation

As an aid to understanding the range of methodologies available to educational evaluators, it may be useful to study, and to classify, ways in which those engaged in evaluation are seen to work and view their work. Any number of categories are possible, but a four-fold classification maintains a manageable system, whilst overcoming some of the problems of a dichotomy. The ideas behind the following schemes originate from theoretical classifications proposed by Argyris and Schön (1974), Mitroff and Kulmann (1978), and Harris and Bailey (1980).

### Category One

This approach, based on the classical view of scientific method, strives for objectivity of results. The evaluator remains external to the situation being evaluated, and adopts a disinterested, apolitical approach. Strict boundaries to the range of inquiry are maintained, these boundaries often being agreed prior to commencing the evaluation. The evaluator is viewed as an unbiased expert. To overcome the effects of an individual's personally held values, large numbers of people are often studied using statistical analysis of collected data.

Education is seen as the transmission of organized knowledge from the older to the younger generation. Attention is focused upon the *products*, rather than the *processes*, of this transmission.

### Category Two

This approach, like the analytic, strives for an impersonal, disinterested description of the situation being evaluated. At the same time, it recognizes that the values and aspirations of the evaluator may play an important part in the way the evaluation proceeds. Unlike the analytic approach, inquiry is not seen to have strict predefined boundaries. By viewing the situation being studied from a variety of perspectives, the evaluator produces multiple, often novel, explanations to describe that situation.

Although emphasis is placed on education as being the transmission of organized and accumulated knowledge, attention is focused upon large-scale differences in products. Education as a process and the individuality of the learners is taken into account.

### Category Three

Education is seen as an essentially individual human process. It differs from the previous two approaches in certain basic assumptions:

1. It is impossible for the evaluator and those being studied to remain separate.
2. Value neutrality is improbable.
3. Those taking part have an interest in the results of the evaluation.

The main aim of an evaluation is not the production or ordering of knowledge, but the promotion of human development and growth on the widest possible scale. Individuals are helped to understand the processes in which they engage. The focus of the evaluation is on the generation of information relevant to those being studied, and to the evaluator.

The ideas of action research, and of illuminative, or problem-centred, evaluation where investigation is holistic, open-ended and accepts multiple explanations, fall within this category. As in the case of previous approaches, results of an evaluation are reported by the evaluator, and may, ultimately, be seen as judgemental.

### Category Four

An 'evaluator' adopting this approach is acting in a different capacity from those previously described. Little interest is shown in formulating general theories; the concern is to understand the uniqueness of a particular situation. Analytical or theoretical sophistication is not seen as an acceptable substitute for the presence of a participating observer who has empathy for those being observed. The 'evaluator' acts as a facilitator for the evaluation, enabling participants to gain an in-depth understanding of themselves and their situation.

Education is viewed as the personal development of the individual young becoming educated by, interacting with, and learning from, their environment.

This approach encompasses the notions of self-evaluation (Elliott, 1979; Simons, 1980) and of participant observations (Delamont, 1976).

## Implications

We do not suggest that any one approach is inherently better or worse than any other, or that the categories are mutually exclusive to an individual evaluator. Rather, we suggest an approach should be chosen to suit the situation encountered. In no way should the methodological tail be allowed to wag the evaluating dog!

The categories outlined above suggest a continuum of methodologies suited to a range of situations. Such a continuum is represented in Figure 3.

| Category One approach | | | | Category Four approach |
|---|---|---|---|---|
| Analytic | Survey | Field trials | Action research | Participant observation |
| | Large-scale (product) evaluations | | Small-scale (process) evaluations | |

Figure 3. *Range of methodologies*

In addition to certain methodologies being more applicable to certain situations, within one 'evaluation' a range of different approaches may be adopted.

The approaches of categories two and three may be useful when initially defining, and focusing on, the problem areas for evaluation.

The approaches of all categories may be useful to gather information which can subsequently be ordered and judged.

The approach of category four may be useful for the important step of increasing professional self-awareness, perhaps towards the end of an evaluation.

The Evaluation Resource Pack was designed for a specific audience, that is, organizers of long courses in educational technology. It was not designed with the view of promoting self-evaluation, but to support an individual in evaluating his or her course. As such, the Pack's philosophy falls into categories two and three of our framework of methodologies, whilst the materials offered will support those wishing to adopt the approach of categories one to three.

For those wishing to engage in institution-based self-evaluation, a new project, based at the University of Bath, funded jointly by the Council for Educational Technology and the Schools Council, is under way.

## References

Argyris, C and Schön, D A (1974) *Theory in Practice: Increasing Professional Effectiveness*. Jossey-Bass, San Francisco.

Bell, C D (1980) *Methodology and Analysis in an Educational Inquiry*. Unpublished MEd Dissertation, University of Bath.

CET (1979) *Courses Leading to Qualifications in Educational Technology 1980-1981*. Council for Educational Technology, London.

Delamont, S (1976) *Interaction in the Classroom*. Methuen, London.

Elliott, J (1979) The case for school self-evaluation. *Forum* 22, 1, pp 23-5.

Harris, N D C and Bailey, J G (1980) Technology and evaluation in the year 2000. In Winterburn, R and Evans, L (eds) *Aspects of Educational Technology* XIV. Kogan Page, London.

Harris, N D C and Bailey, J G (1981) *Evaluation Resource Pack*. Council for Educational Technology, London.

Mitroff, I I and Kulmann, R H (1978) *Methodological Approaches to Social Science*. Jossey-Bass, San Francisco.

Simons, H (1980) The evaluative school. *Forum* 22, 1, pp 55-7.

*Workshop Report*
## 2.5.2 Evaluation Resources for Teachers

**C D Bell**
*University of Bath*

### Organizer's Account

The workshop was based on new materials being produced for use by teachers in schools and other educational institutions who wish to evaluate their courses or practices. The project is funded jointly by the Council for Educational Technology and the Schools Council. (The materials are not related to the *Evaluation Resource Pack* (Harris and Bailey, 1980.)

Workshop participants were given a choice of activities, either:

(a) discussing the proposed contents of the materials; or
(b) discussing one section of the materials.

Participants chose to study contents, and then the section of materials if time permitted.

Each participant was asked to write comments about the contents. In pairs, participants identified similarities and differences in their comments, subsequently reporting to the whole group.

A number of issues were raised:

(a) Materials should be short and concise, using simple language and concepts.
(b) The need for, and utility of, evaluation and what is meant by evaluation should be made explicit.
(c) 'Accountability' and 'evaluation' should be distinguished.
(d) The materials which are being produced were thought to be applicable to training institutions. For this audience, some of the terms used may need changing.
(e) It was considered desirable that the names of the funding organizations, in particular the Schools Council, should not be too prominent on the materials.

In addition, many useful comments were made regarding specific items on the contents list and in the materials.

## Reference

Harris, N D C and Bailey, J G (1980) *Evaluation Resource Pack*. Council for Educational Technology, London.

## 2.5.3 Answers at a Distance

C Stoane
*University of Dundee*
J S Stoane
*Kingsway Technical College, Dundee*

Abstract: An important feature common to most distance learning systems is surely the provision of questions of one kind or another for the student to try to answer for himself. (This is distinguished from assignments or post-tests returned to a tutor.) On a *microscale* these may take the form of very simple one-word or phrase answers in a typical programmed learning frame. On a *macroscale* they could be lengthier, more discoursive answers to end of section or end of topic questions.

This paper investigates the various possible ways of providing the student with answers to such questions. A wide variety of alternative methods is considered, ranging from the familiar to methods probably novel to most educators; from simple to esoteric; answers on tape, paper and computer; reusable and expendable.

Two important considerations in choosing a method of providing instant feedback are: (i) When obtaining an answer the student should not incidentally obtain the answer to the next question; and (ii) Is it intended that the student should have the answer inserted in a blank place in the narrative in order to have a complete text for revision purposes? These and other points are considered for each method, along with the merits/drawbacks and suggested uses.

It is argued that careful choice of an appropriate method of providing feedback within the course material can increase considerably the effectiveness of a distance learning course.

## Introduction

An important feature of learning at a distance is the separation of teacher (tutor) from learner (Holmberg, 1981). Despite this separation it is important that a two-way communication is maintained between the learner and the tutor so that progress, problems and attitudes can be discussed. It is not sufficient to send printed materials to the learner and expect him to learn. It has been shown (Skinner, 1954; Annett, 1969; Murray *et al*, 1977) that participation on the part of the learner during the learning process makes for more effective learning.

If immediate and regular feedback is given to the learner, his retention and comprehension are tested and his subsequent ability to understand and solve problems is improved.

In distance learning programmes, it is important that an effective method of providing feedback is used as it is often the only communication the learner will have with the teacher for a period of time. Not only does a system of questions and answers help the learner to monitor his own learning, but the reinforcement gained during the process motivates him to continue learning (McGuire, 1967). A variety of techniques has been used to provide feedback in the educational setting. This paper describes:

(a) A number of techniques and some applications.
(b) The advantages and disadvantages of the methods with particular reference to distance learning.

## Techniques and Applications

1. *Answers given at the back of the book or on another page.*
This is the method frequently used, for example, in school children's arithmetic books.

2. *Answers given on the same page at the bottom of the page.*
Another standard textbook method but less common than the previous example.

3. *Answers given on the same page but printed upside down.*
Used in the 'Do You Know' corner of the children's page in daily newspapers.

4. *Answers in frames covered by a mask.*
The text is divided into frames and the answer given at the beginning of the next frame further down in the page, in the traditional programmed learning manner. This involves the conscientious reader in covering later frames with a slip of paper which he slides down as he works through the questions.

5. *Programmed text with small page format.*
A variation of the previous method. A small amount of text appears on one page with a question. The answer is on the next page and the reader overtly answers the question before turning over.

6. *Scrambled book — branching frame.*
The reader is referred to various pages throughout the book to find answers, and again, depending on his answers, will be directed to another page in the book.

Numbers 4 to 6 are variations of the programmed learning theme, but bucking the system, either intentionally or unintentionally, becomes progressively more difficult.

7. *Answers appear at the back of the book but in random order.*
By this method, questions are posed in the text. Blanks are left for the student to complete answers and the blanks given random reference numbers. At the back of the book the answers are numbered in sequence. Using this method there is less likelihood of the student seeing the next answer when looking up the current one (Tucker, 1980).

8. *Answers are printed using a 'scrambled print' technique.*
In this method the answers are printed in one colour (eg blue) and then concealed by overprinting in a second colour (eg red). The reader places a transparent red plastic mask over the scrambled print to reveal the text underneath. This method is well-known in medical education.

9. *Answers are highlighted using a pre-cut transparent template.*
The reader places the template over a set of multiple-choice answers to indicate
the correct one.

10. *Latent image printing of answers.*
This method, used extensively in medical education and now taken up by other
educationalists, is an invisible ink printing technique. A message or answer is printed
on paper, next to the question, and remains invisible until treated by a developing
pen to reveal the message.

The technique has been around since the 1940s, but the developments by
A B Dick Co in the United States have gone a long way to providing a method which
is technically reliable.

It is available commercially in two forms — one designed for use on a spirit
duplicator and the other for offset printing. Both methods use standard equipment.

SPIRIT DUPLICATING
The cheaper of the two methods, this requires a spirit duplicator, latent image
transfer sheets and latent image developer pens.

The information that is to be visible is typed or written on a carbon spirit master.
A latent image transfer sheet then replaces the carbon and the 'invisible' sections
(the answers) are typed or written on the same master. Copies (between 100 and
150) are run off from the master on a standard spirit duplicator. The answers remain
invisible until treated with the developer pen.

At Dundee College of Technology, in a distance learning course for firemen
sitting statutory promotion exams, a development of this technique has been used
(Tucker, 1980). The visible sections have been prepared by offset printing and only
the 'invisible' sections have used the spirit duplication method for applying latent
answers. (Details are obtainable from the authors — see Note on p 205.)

OFFSET PRINTING
In a similar way to the spirit duplicator process the visible information is printed
by offset and then printed again with the 'invisible sections'. Large numbers can be
run and multi-coloured printing can be used for the visible information. Adding the
latent sections is no more expensive than adding another colour.

The latent image process by offset litho is not, as yet, available commercially in
the UK. Printing must be done in the US by A B Dick Co.

It has been used at the Centre for Medical Education, Dundee University in a
series of self-assessment exercises for general practitioners (Rogers *et al*, 1979;
Harden *et al*, 1980).

11. *Cholesteric liquid crystals.*
Another method where answers remain latent until specially treated by heat, from
the hand.

12. *Scratch-off printing.*
This method is familiar in the form of instant lottery tickets where one scratches
off a silver-coloured deposit with a coin or the fingernail.

13. *Audio method.*
There would seem to be three possibilities:
  (a)  the lesson is recorded on tape. A tone instructs the student to switch off
        and write the answer to a question on a paper response sheet. He then
        switches on again to receive the correct answer.
  (b)  The lesson is presented on paper with blanks for answers to be completed
        by the student. He switches on a tape to obtain the correct answer.
  (c)  The lesson is recorded on tape. Pauses are left for the student to record his

answer on the tape, immediately followed by the correct answer on tape. This is the well-known language laboratory approach.

14. *Computer.*
Microcomputers have the facilty not only to provide answers but also to do calculations, to generate problems, and to provide the learner with appropriate *personalized* feedback. Methods of use include the following:

(a) A choice of answers of the multiple choice type is given. The letter of the answer chosen is typed into the computer. If the answer is wrong then the computer can give further guidance and the student be asked to 'try again'.

(b) No choice of answers is given. The student writes his own answer in the blank space on the question paper and then types into the computer the number of the question. He is given the correct answer and asked if he would like any further explanation in case he is wrong.

## Discussion

While all of the techniques described are valid methods of providing instant feedback, they all have advantages and disadvantages. When selecting one for use in a particular distance learning programme, it is important to bear these in mind and to select the most appropriate, and therefore the most effective, method, taking into account the style of the material and the situation of the student.

Distance learning programmes will be more effective if:

(a) Answers are provided immediately so that there is no delay for the learner between recording his own answer and learning whether he is right or wrong.

(b) Answers are provided in a way that is fool-proof, so that the reader can use the material independently without recourse to his tutor.

(c) Answers are designed so that when the reader looks up a current answer he does not see the next half dozen answers at the same time.

(d) Answers are designed so that when put into the text a continuous narrative is produced which is useful for revision purposes.

## Advantages and Disadvantages for Distance Learning of the Methods Described

1. *Answer given at the back of the book.*
This method is valid if the problem posed involves reasonably long work, eg calculations. The learner is then less likely to observe and remember the answers to the next question whilst looking up the current answer. The method can be extremely tiresome to use, however, if frequent answer checking is needed.

2. *Answer given at bottom of same page.*
This method is used as an alternative to the back of the book method and may be considered less irritating.

3. *Answers printed upside down on the same page.*
Really only a minor variation on 2, but there is less likelihood of seeing an answer beforehand. Again, it is irritating to use and not very useful as a permanent record.

The advantages of the three methods described so far are that all are reasonably easy to organize and so do not involve much extra cost. The major disadvantages are that all the methods are non-motivational and unpleasant to use. In most cases one has to be fairly blinkered to avoid seeing the next answer when looking at the current one.

4. *Answers in frames covered by a mask.*
Perhaps one of the reasons why programmed learning went out of vogue was that this method of feedback was tedious, physically cumbersome and non-motivational.

5. *Programmed text — small page format.*
This method is used particularly when simplicity is essential and motivation is necessary. The format, however, is somewhat odd.

6. *Scrambled book.*
The main disadvantage is that no permanent record is produced for revision purposes. It is irritating to use because of frequent hunting through the book.

7. *Answers at back of book in random order.*
This method is designed so that the reader does not see the answer to the next question each time he refers to the current answer. It is certainly neat and cheap to produce. It can, however, be a disadvantage in that no permanent answer appears in the text, thus providing no revision facility. The importance of the disadvantages depend on the content and uses to be made of the materials.

8. *Scrambled print.*
This method has been used extensively in medical journals. Undoubtedly the novelty wears off after a time. Unless printed very accurately the text is never completely obscured. Many people find this distracting as there is a tendency to concentrate on 'beating the system' rather than on the answer itself. As it involves two or three colour printing the method is expensive to produce. It is, however, possible to produce a crude do-it-yourself version using a typewriter and overprinting with rows of the letter 'x' typed in a second colour. The colour of the plastic must match as well as possible the second colour typing. A continuous text is provided with this method.

9. *Answers highlighted by template.*
The method can be effectively used in many learning situations where the multiple-choice question format is the preferred choice for knowledge testing. It has the disadvantage that the answers are checked one page at a time — thus there is not quite immediate feedback.

10. *Latent image printing of answers.*
A strong advantage of providing answers by latent image printing is that the method is quick and easy to use. It is well-recognized that any barriers set up between the learner and his materials will tend to decrease motivation and usage (McGuire, 1967). With latent image printing the answer is immediate and can be provided alongside the question, providing, once revealed, a permanent record. The likelihood of seeing the answer before attempting the question is less than in previous methods. As little or as much information as is appropriate in the particular learning situation can be (i) supplied by the author and (ii) revealed by the reader. This means that further explanation can be given other than the correct answer and that the reader can selectively reveal the information that is particularly relevant to him or her, and can keep a permanent record.

This method, with its flexibility and scope for individualization, is very appropriate for use in distance learning programmes. Disadvantages of the technique are concerned with the technical aspects of the process. Copies may take longer to produce, and the cost may be somewhat higher than with conventional printing. The better quality offset process is probably not economical unless large print runs are required. This must be processed, as yet, in the United States.

For small print runs the duplicating process can be used. The method is not, however, fool-proof and accuracy of register can be a problem. These materials have a more limited shelf-life than the offset printed materials, especially once the message has been revealed.

11. *Liquid crystals.*
This new method, developed in Japan, is, as yet, unknown in this country for educational purposes. It employs, on paper, the same techniques as for visual display — for example, certain types of digital thermometers. Advantages are as for latent image, with the added one that the print is revealed only for a short time. The materials are therefore reusable but there is not a permanent visible record.

12. *Scratch-off printing.*
Both the advantages and disadvantages of this method are similar to the latent image type, except that there is no do-it-yourself method. It must be processed commercially, but can be done in the United Kingdom (Pegasus Print Ltd).

13. *Answers on audio-tape.*
  (a) Lesson on tape — answers on paper — feedback on tape: a permanent record is provided on tape but the method is not fool-proof.
  (b) Lesson on paper — answers in blanks — feedback on tape: as there is no simple way of locating a particular answer on the tape it is very easy to lose the sequence of answers.
  (c) Lesson on tape — student records answers — feedback: this is the only method described which is useful for non-readers. However, the method is mechanically difficult as there is the danger of erasing the programme.

14. *Microcomputers.*
With recent developments in microcomputer technology and the lowering of costs, the technique has come within the reach of most educators. Provided that the equipment is available, the immediate feedback possible on microcomputers can be used with great effect in distance learning programmes.

This is probably the most flexible of all the methods. Not only can the correct answer, but also remedial feedback, be provided if an incorrect answer is chosen. It is probably better to present the lesson on paper as this allows for better diagrams, photographs, etc; also reading large sections of print from a VDU is tiring.

Disadvantages of the microcomputer method are:

1. No permanent record is provided.
2. The microcomputer is too expensive to provide for individual students to use in their own home. They would have to come to a local centre.

## Summary

There is a large number of methods to be used to provide answers at a distance, ranging from simple programmed learning to highly sophisticated and sometimes expensive techniques. The choice of methods is very much dependent on how important it is that the learner should not be able to see the next answers when looking at current answers, and whether or not it is important that answers inserted into the text can form a continuous narrative for revision purposes.

## Conclusions

One of the most important features of distance learning is feedback. We conclude that if appropriate and immediate feedback to the learner is provided then distance learning materials will be more effective.

# References

Annett, J (1969) *Feedback and Human Behaviour.* Penguin, Harmondsworth.

Harden, R M, Stoane, C, Murray, T S and Dunn, W R (1980) Learning at a distance: evaluation at a distance. In Winterburn, R and Evans, L (eds) *Aspects of Educational Technology* **XIV**. Kogan Page, London.

Holmberg, B (1981) *Status and Trends of Distance Education.* Kogan Page, London.

McGuire, C (1967) Simulation technique in the teaching and testing of problem solving skills. *Proceedings of the Annual Meeting of the National Association for Research in Science Teaching.* Michigan.

Murray, T S, Cupples, R W, Barber, J H, Dunn, W R, Scott, D B and Hannay, D R (1977) Teaching decision making to medical undergraduates by computer assisted learning. *Medical Education* **11**, pp 262-4.

Rogers, J, Harden, R M, Murray, T S and Dunn, W R (1979) The use of latent image printing in problem solving and self assessment exercises. *Journal of Audio Visual Media in Medicine* **2**, pp 27-9.

Skinner, B F (1954) The science of learning and the art of teaching. *Harvard Educational Review* **24**, pp 86-97.

Tucker, H T (1980) *Buildings — Their Construction and Fire Protection. Unit 1: Study Course for Module II of a Proposed Course for Leading Firemen Examinations.* Dundee College of Technology.

# Acknowledgements

The authors are grateful to the following companies for help, advice and samples

*Latent image printing*
A B Dick Company of USA.

*Scrambled printing*
Update Publications, 33-34 Alfred Place, London WC1E 7DP.

*Scratch off printing*
Pegasus Print and Display Ltd, Unit 2, Mitcham Industrial Estate, Streatham Road, Mitcham, Surrey.

*Liquid crystals*
Licral Ltd, Unit 5, Charter House Works, Eltringham Street, London.

# Note

Materials produced by offset printing and latent image applied by spirit duplication have been produced at Dundee College of Technology, Dundee. The distance learning course has been sponsored by the Home Office and the Scottish Home and Health Department.

Details can be obtained from the author (John S Stoane) at Dundee College of Technology, Audiovisual and Reprographics Unit.

*Workshop Report*

## 2.5.4 Answers at a Distance

**J S Stoane** *Kingsway Technical College, Dundee*
**D Mayho** *A B Dick Co, USA*
**C Stoane** *University of Dundee*

## Organizers' Account

The aim of this workshop was to provide participants with more details of some of the less common methods of providing feedback in distance learning materials described in the previous paper. This was to be achieved by demonstrations and by 'hands on' experience of both using and producing materials.

The feedback methods available were grouped into three categories.

1. Feedback via PET microcomputer
2. Latent image
3. Miscellaneous examples.

## Feedback Via a PET Microcomputer

Two examples were provided for participants to try for themselves on two microcomputers.

(a) (Adapted from 'IF' — a course in continuing medical education for General Practitioners.)

Participants were given a leaflet which gave a patient's case history and then they presented a variety of possible diagnoses and courses of treatment.

The user studies the case details and then rates each diagnosis or treatment on a 1-5 scale, depending on the extent to which he agrees or disagrees with it. He enters his rating of each diagnosis or treatment into the computer, one at a time. The computer then shows him the ratings given by 100 fellow-GPs and also by a hospital specialist. If the user wishes, he can ask to see a short comment by the hospital specialist and also get a print-out (to take away) from a tractor printer connected to the PET. The print-out shows his rating, the ratings of the 100 GPs and the specialist, together with the specialist's comments.

(b) (Adapted from a distance learning course in elementary chemistry for firemen sitting the station officer examination.)

Participants were given a leaflet containing an extract from the response sheet for one of the lessons. The response sheet showed two worked examples of simple calculations involving calorific values, followed by several examples to be worked by the student.

The student enters his answer to each problem into the PET which then provides him with appropriate feedback, remedial if necessary. For example, common predictable errors, such as losing a zero, dividing instead of multiplying, and getting the division the wrong way up, are recognized and the student is told what he has done wrong and is asked to try again. There are also facilities for HINT if a start is needed and HELP if the student wants to be shown how to do the whole calculation.

## Latent Image

Two types of ready-produced material were available for participants to examine and try.

In both, the visible print was by offset litho. In one, the latent image had been added by litho as well (printed in Chicago). In the other, the latent image had been added by means of a spirit duplicator. In both cases the latent image was revealed by using a developer pen.

An opportunity was provided for participants to add latent image answers for themselves to ready-prepared xeroxed sheets of questions using the spirit duplicator method.

Spirit duplicator masters for the answers were prepared in the usual way but using the special latent image carbon. These were then run off on a spirit duplicator and tested with the developer pens provided.

Of very great interest was the demonstration by Mr D Mayho of A B Dick Company of a new method of printing latent image by means of a cut stencil duplicator. This was the first time that this system had been demonstrated in the

UK. The latent image answers are typed on an ordinary cut stencil which is then fitted to an A B Dick single-cylinder duplicator loaded with the 'invisible' ink.

The superiority of this cut stencil method over the spirit duplicator method was very obvious. The reliability and quality of the latent image were vastly superior. The spirit duplicator has a run limit of about 100; the cut stencil duplicator can produce several thousand copies.

## Miscellaneous Methods

On display were examples of scrambled print, scratch-off print, and cholesteric crystals.

The cholesteric crystals took the form of small black squares stuck on the response sheet beside the blank spaces for the answers. When warmed by the finger the blackness fades to green or blue and the correct answer becomes visible. As it cools down the answer becomes obscured as the blackness returns.

The cholesteric crystals are designed to reveal the answer between $26°C$ and $33°C$. Unfortunately, the ambient temperature in the room in which the workshop was held was very high (over $27°C$) and the answers on the sample sheet were already revealed before applying the finger. (It had been found also that at ambient temperatures below about $18°C$ most people's fingers are too cold to cause the answers to be revealed.)

Before this method can be put to practical use, a lot of further technical development work is clearly required.

# Section 3:
# Educational Technology and The Learning Experience

## 3.1 The Role and Position of Summaries in Instructional Text

J Hartley and M Trueman
*University of Keele*

**Abstract:** In this paper we present the results of five experiments which examine the effects of the position of a summary (before and after) and a control condition (no summary) on the recall of a semi-technical passage. Other parameters explored are the ability of the readers (university students and secondary school pupils of different ages), the nature of the text (high and low structure), the kinds of questions asked (summary-related and text-related), and the time of recall (immediate and delayed).

The results of these experiments are presented, together with a discussion of the strengths and limitations of our approach to the problem.

## Introduction

It can be argued that summaries have two possible positions, and several possible roles. Summaries at the beginning of a text can tell readers what the text is about, they can help readers to decide whether or not they wish to read the text, and they can help readers who do read the text to organize their thoughts about what it is that they are reading. Summaries at the end of a text can list or review the main points and thus aid the recall of important points made in the text.

Summaries can be written in different ways to achieve these different goals: for instance, each chapter in *Designing Instructional Text* (Hartley, 1978) contains a different beginning and end summary.

Parker (1962) used different beginning and end summaries in his research on the effectiveness of summaries, but most investigators have used the same summary, placed either at the beginning or at the end of a text, and then have compared the results obtained with those obtained from a control text without a summary. Studies using this strategy have provided mixed results. Christensen and Stordahl (1955) found no significant effects. Vezin *et al* (1973) found a superiority for an end summary. Glynn and DiVesta (1977) found that beginning summaries aided the recall of specific facts and that end ones aided the recall of related material. McGlaughlin-Cook (1979) found that a repetitive summary led to a significant increase in the recall of summary-related items with students but not with children.

In fact, there is a paucity of studies on this topic, and the studies that have been published are themselves limited in many ways. Nearly all of them can be referred to as one-off studies (only McGlaughlin-Cook replicated his experiments) and none of them examined long-term recall.

## The Experiments

We have carried out a series of five related studies in order to try to remedy some of these deficiencies. In these studies we have sought to develop the notions we discussed in an earlier paper on the role and position of summaries in instructional text (Hartley *et al*, 1979).

Table 1 encapsulates the main parameters of our five experiments. Experiment 1 is the Hartley *et al* (1979) study. It used a semi-technical text on television viewing habits which was based on an article taken from an *Observer* colour supplement. The text contained approximately 1,000 words and was divided into 24 paragraphs. The material was fairly factual and specific, and to some extent the content was familiar to any British reader — reporting as it did the proportions of various groups of viewers watching BBC1, BBC2, ITV and certain programmes on these channels. Three versions of this text were prepared — one with a summary before it, one with a summary after it, and one without a summary. The summary was 100 words long and it summarized the main points made in the article. Each version of the text was followed by a series of short-answer questions, half of which could be answered from reading the summary and/or the text (summary-related questions) and half from reading the text alone (text-specific questions). In Experiment 1 each student reader was tested individually.

In Experiment 2 the passage was revised to make it easier to read, and the experiment was repeated in a group situation. In Experiments 3 and 4 comprehensive school pupils aged 12-13 acted as participants, and in Experiment 4 a measure of verbal ability was introduced. In Experiment 5, 14- and 15-year-old pupils participated and a measure of long-term recall was introduced as well as that of ability.

Limitations of space prevent us from discussing the details of each experiment in turn, but the main findings of the five experiments are summarized in Table 2. Table 2 shows that:

☐ In four out of the five experiments there was a significant conditions effect: participants reading summaries did better than those not reading them. The effect of the summary position was not clear. It looked as if students profited from an end summary, whereas children profited from a summary regardless of its position — but this is probably reading too much into the data.

☐ In four of the five experiments there was a significant question-type effect: participants did better on summary-related questions than on text-specific ones (whether or not they had read a summary). This finding shows that the more important material was remembered by participants regardless of their experimental condition.

☐ In four of the five experiments there was a question-type x conditions interaction: participants did better on the summary-related questions than on text-specific ones, and this difference was enhanced if they had read a summary.

☐ In the two studies that examined ability, high-ability pupils always did better than low-ability ones. In Experiment 4 the low-ability pupils profited significantly by having a summary, but in Experiment 5, although the results lay in the same direction, the differences were not statistically significant.

☐ In the last study (in which retention was also considered) the effects of the

| | Participants | Ability measures | Passage | Summaries | Immediate test | Re-test |
|---|---|---|---|---|---|---|
| *Experiment 1* | 42 university students, tested individually | (not made) | TV viewing habits c 1,000 words 'difficult' | beginning, end and control | Six summary-related questions Six text-specific questions | (not made) |
| *Experiment 2* | 49 university students, tested in a group | (not made) | TV viewing habits c 1,000 words 'fairly difficult' | beginning, end and control | Seven summary-related questions Seven text-specific questions | (not made) |
| *Experiment 3* | 89 mixed ability comprehensive school pupils aged 12 and 13 tested in groups | (not made) | TV viewing habits c 1,000 words 'fairly difficult' | beginning, end and control | Seven summary-related questions Seven text-specific questions | (not made) |
| *Experiment 4* | 120 mixed ability comprehensive school pupils aged 12 and 13 tested in groups | 11+ Verbal Reasoning Scores (two years old) | TV viewing habits c 1,000 words 'fairly difficult' | beginning, end and control | Seven summary-related questions Seven text-specific questions | (not made) |
| *Experiment 5* | 117 mixed ability comprehensive school pupils aged 14 and 15 tested in groups | Manchester Verbal Reasoning Scores (two years old) | TV viewing habits c 1,000 words 'fairly difficult' | end summary only, and control | Six summary-related questions Six text-specific questions | Six summary-related questions Six text-specific questions two weeks later |

**Table 1.** *A summary of the main parameters of the five experiments*

| | Conditions effect? | Question-type effect? | Question-type x conditions interaction? | Ability x conditions interaction? | Re-test x question-type interaction? |
|---|---|---|---|---|---|
| Experiment 1 | Yes (end summary only) | Yes (not significant) | No | — | — |
| Experiment 2 | Yes (end summary only) | Yes | Yes | — | — |
| Experiment 3 | No | Yes | Yes | — | — |
| Experiment 4 | Yes (beginning and end) | Yes | Yes | Yes | — |
| Experiment 5 | Yes (only end summary used) | Yes | Yes | Yes (not significant) | Yes |

**Table 2.** *A summary of the main findings from the five experiments*

summaries on long-term recall were negligible. There was no conditions x test-retest interaction. Initial test scores were higher than the retest ones (as measured with the same test two weeks later), but most of the differences found on the initial test tended to disappear on the retest. As an example here, on the initial test pupils scored higher on the summary-related questions than on the text-specific ones, but the difference was no longer significant on The retest.

In brief then these five experiments, taken together, suggest that with these materials and these tests, summaries aided the recall of summary-related (and hence important) material.

## Points for Consideration

Five features of our research deserve further consideration. These are problems with group methods of inquiry, the sequential nature of the research, the nature of the materials used, problems in depicting text structure, and possible future directions that research such as this might take.

### Problems with Group Methods of Inquiry

We found group methods of inquiry were to prove useful in that considerable data were collected quickly. However, we have some concern about the validity of the data that we obtained this way. Putting it bluntly, it seems to us that cheating is endemic in test situations with secondary school children although investigators may take precautions to prevent cheating (for example we varied the question order on the test sheets, and we told participants reading one version of the text that their answers to the test questions might not be the same as those given by participants reading another version). Perhaps more elaborate procedures could have been employed (eg rearranging the text and/or the questions so that different answers were indeed required), but this would have been administratively and clerically complex. Perhaps the wisest approach in studies such as these − despite the cost and the time that it would take − would be to test participants individually or in very small groups.

### The Sequential Nature of the Research

Our reading of the research literature suggested that, if work of any value was to be done on the topic of summaries, there was a need for a linked series of experiments. In such a series one would seek to modify one variable at a time and to progress steadily − as we in fact have done. We still think this is a valid procedure and one which could profitably be applied elsewhere but we would now note one particular difficulty. This is that once started, it is difficult to go back or to change course. It seems to us that people fail to recognize this when they suggest that it might be important to look at other variables, such as different texts.

### The Nature of the Materials Used

A related comment here is that the results that we have obtained are specific to the text and to the summaries that we have used. Clearly one might expect different results with different texts and summaries, and there is always a problem of choosing good examples in research of this kind. It would have been nice to work with other texts and with other kinds of summaries, but we preferred to work with the text we knew and to consider other variables first. Our plan was to progress in the manner shown, then to move on to consider different kinds of summaries (overview versus review) and finally to different kinds of text (well-structured versus less well-structured, for example).

### Problems in Depicting Text Structure

To look at different kinds of text it would be helpful if there were some recognized and easy ways for depicting their structures. Unfortunately, at present, current methods of analyzing text are too restricted for use in practical situations such as ours (Shavelson and Stasz, 1977; Macdonald-Ross, 1979). However, one can describe text in a more global manner and work within these constraints. For example, one can manipulate paragraph sequence and organization (Lee, 1965; Frase, 1969); one can measure readability (Hartley *et al*, 1980); one can introduce various 'access' structures — such as headings (Whaller, 1979); and one can use professional judgement as to whether one text is better sequenced than another.

### Future Research

Finally, we might note that some workers in this area consider that the approach we have used — of having participants read through a piece of text and then answer questions on it — to be ecologically invalid, ie they think that this approach does not reflect how people actually go about reading and learning (Macdonald-Ross, 1979). There seems to be a good deal of truth in this statement — although it is not the whole truth. Nevertheless, it does seem as though researchers in this area have generally gone in for ease in data gathering rather than for face validity. It would be interesting in future research to attempt to redress this balance. To do this we would need to do things like asking students to verbalize aloud what they are thinking about when they are reading, letting them go backwards and forwards at will, and letting them summarize in their own words what they think the text is all about. Undoubtedly such a research strategy — which is now beginning — will produce interesting findings.

## References

Christensen, C M and Stordahl, K E (1955) The effect of organisational aids on comprehension and retention. *Journal of Educational Psychology* 46, pp 65-74.

Frase, L T (1969) Paragraph organisation of written materials: the influence of conceptual clustering. *Journal of Educational Psychology* 60, pp 394-401.

Glynn, G M and DiVesta, F J (1977) Outline and hierarchical organisation as aids for study and retrieval. *Journal of Educational Psychology* 69, pp 89-95.

Hartley, J (1978) *Designing Instructional Text*. Kogan Page, London.

Hartley, J, Goldie, M and Steen, L (1979) The role and position of summaries: some issues and data. *Educational Review* 31, pp 59-65.

Hartley, J, Trueman, M and Burnhill, P (1980) Some observations on producing and measuring readable writing. *Programmed Learning and Educational Technology* 17, pp 164-74.

Lee, W (1965) Supra-paragraph prose structure: its specification, perception, and effects on learning. *Psychological Reports* 17, pp 135-44.

Macdonald-Ross, M (1979) Language in texts. In Shulman, L S (ed) *Review of Research in Education* 6. Peacock, Itasca, Illinois.

McGlaughlin-Cook, N (1979) Memory for prose: how does providing a summary affect what is learned? Unpublished MA thesis, University of Keele.

Parker, J P (1962) Some organisational aids and their effect upon comprehension. *Journal of Communication* 12, pp 27-32.

Shavelson, R J and Stasz, C (1980) Some methods for representing the structure of concepts in prose material. In Hartley, J (ed) *The Psychology of Written Communication: Selected Readings*. Kogan Page, London.Vezin, J F, Bergé, O and Mavrellis, P (1973) Role du résumé et de la répétition en fonction de leur place par rapport en texte. *Bulletin de Psychologie* 27, pp 163-7.

Whaller, R H W (1979) Typographic access structures for educational texts. In Kolers, P A, Wrolstad, M E and Bouma, H (eds) *Processing of Visible Language* 1. Plenum, New York.

## Acknowledgements

We are indebted to students at the University of Keele, and to pupils and staff at the Regis School, Tettenhall, and Clough Hall School, Kidsgrove, for their assistance in the experiments reported in this paper. The research was supported by the Social Science Research Council.

# 3.2 Strategies for the Teaching of Knowledge and Skills

A J Romiszowski
*Consultant in Educational Technology*

Abstract: A methodology for the selection of overall instructional strategies is proposed. It is shown that this methodology can be useful in the selection of specific teaching methods within the development of an instructional plan.

## Introduction

This paper develops further the approach to instructional design, based on the analysis of knowledge and skills by means of conceptual schemata. This approach to analysis was outlined at the 1980 ETIC conference (Romiszowski, 1980) and further developed into a comprehensive system for 'designing instructional systems' (Romiszowski, 1981). Space does not permit the inclusion in full, in this paper, of the schemata of learning categories used as a basis of the approach. The reader might find it helpful, therefore, to refer to one of the above-mentioned references for the necessary background.

The present paper limits itself to the proposal of a methodology for the selection of overall instructional strategies, and an indication of how this can be used to develop an instructional plan and select specific teaching methods. In order to define the terminology clearly, Figure 1 presents, in summary, a four-level model for instructional design. This paper deals with the first and, to a certain extent, the second levels of this model.

## Overall Instructional Strategies

Overall instructional strategies are the translation of a philosophical or theoretical position regarding instruction into a statement of the way in which instruction should be carried out in specific types of circumstances. We can identify two more or less opposed positions concerning the process of learning and instruction.

(a) *Reception learning.* The strongest open supporter of this position is Ausubel (1968) but the behaviourist camp also largely favours this position.
(b) *Discovery learning.* The strongest supporters of this approach are Piaget and Bruner (Bruner, 1966), most of the cognitive school of psychology and the humanists.

Both groups have tended to support their position in preference to the alternative for all, or most, of learning. Hence, they would tend to translate their view into a global strategy of instruction, to be applied whenever possible.

| Applying our: | In the light of: | Determines our: |
|---|---|---|
| 1 Philosophies and theories of instruction | ☐ Final objectives<br>☐ Target population<br>☐ Wider system | Instructional *strategies* |
| 2 Instructional strategies | ☐ Detailed objectives<br>☐ Entry skills<br>☐ Actual resources and constraints | Instructional *plans* (sets of *methods*, in sequence). |
| 3 Instructional plans | ☐ Content<br>☐ Enabling objectives<br>☐ Knowledge and skill taxonomies | Instructional *tactics* (for each step of each lesson) |
| 4 Instructional tactics | Actual practical experience in applying them to specific learning/teaching problems | Specific instructional *exercises* (in any medium) |

**Figure 1.** *Summary of the four-level model of instructional design*

| | |
|---|---|
| Impromptu discovery | Unplanned learning: no instruction involved directly (eg free use of a library/resource centre). |
| Free exploratory discovery | Bruner's approach: broad learning goals are fixed; otherwise the learner is free to choose (eg resource-based learning systems). |
| Guided discovery | Gagné's approach: objectives are fixed; otherwise learner is guided as to appropriate methods, conclusion, etc (eg typical Polya methods for problems). |
| Adaptively programmed discovery | Guidance and feedback correction is given on an individual basis (eg computer-based learning systems). |
| Intrinsically programmed discovery | Guidance and feedback according to a pre-planned programme, based on the typical student (eg some programmed instruction materials). |
| Inductive exposition | Also called 'reflective lecturing': the teacher 'talks through' the discovery process. |
| Deductive exposition | The 'meaningful reception learning' process favoured by Ausubel (mainly lectures). |
| Drill and practice | Rote reception learning: instruction demonstrates what to do and provides practice. No conceptual understanding is necessarily involved (memorization). |

**Figure 2.** *The range of instructional strategies*

An intermediate position has been adopted by Gagné and Briggs (1974) and writers such as Landa (1976), who argue that, for some types of learning, the reception learning position (leading to expositive strategies) is more effective and efficient, whilst, for other types, the discovery learning position (leading to experiential strategies) is better.

There are, of course, many variations on these two basic strategies. We can construct a continuum of discovery/expositive strategies, ranging from totally free discovery to totally controlled expositive rote learning (see Figure 2).

A course of instruction usually has a variety of aims and objectives. We would, therefore, expect to see both discovery and expositive strategies used. The question is: when is each strategy used?

There are no hard and fast rules, but, on the basis of existing research and our conceptual schemata of knowledge and skills, it is possible to establish some guidelines. We shall use the classification schemata developed by Romiszowski (1980).

## Strategies for the Teaching of Knowledge

The information to be stored falls into four basic categories: facts, concepts, procedures and principles. Remembering the definitions of these four categories (see Romiszowski, 1980), and the use that is made of these types of information in subsequent skilled activity, we can delineate the areas of application for discovery and expositive strategies (see Figure 3).

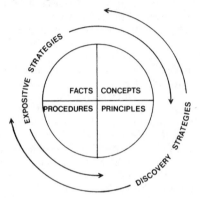

**Figure 3.** *Strategies for teaching knowledge*

The rationale for this division is as follows:

1. *Facts.* It is possible to discover facts. We discover facts of all sorts every day and this constitutes a large part of the unplanned, incidental learning that goes on throughout life. We need to know a great number of facts in order to survive. Others we do not need to know, but do need to know where to look them up when required. (Compare the need to know the meaning of road signs and the need to look up telephone numbers in a diary.)

By definition, facts do not have examples — they exist on their own. Thus, the learning of one set of facts does not greatly help the learning of some other set. There is little transfer value, and what there is relates to the development of memorization and recall skills. These are not as highly valued in education today as they used to be and still are in, for example, the Arab world where it is still common practice in education to memorize large tracts of the Koran. Much time is spent in such memorization activities, which invariably employ *expository* strategies. It is difficult to imagine a group of children being asked to 'discover' what the Koran says in its tenth chapter. Would they watch the teachers act out a charade which aims to depict the contents of Chapter 10?

2. *Principles.* Just as facts can be learned through discovery methods, principles can be learned through expositive methods. However, the evidence is overwhelming that principles learned through discovery are remembered more efficiently and applied in transfer of learning situations with more succes than when they are learned through reception learning. The price one has to pay for this is an increase in the initial learning time.

Furthermore, the principle learned through a process of discovery is more easily rediscovered if, by chance, it is forgotten through lack of use. Finally, the learning of principles by discovery (which employs the solution of problems as an instructional method) exercises the learner's problem-solving skills. In addition to mastering a new 'principle of nature' he is using and developing his 'principles of action' or heuristics. Thus he is likely to become better at the solving of other types of problems related to other sets (schemata) of concepts and principles. For all these reasons it would seem reasonable to use discovery strategies for the teaching of principles whenever this is practically possible and economically justifiable.

3. *Procedures.* By a previous definition (Romiszowski, 1980), procedures are algorithmic, composed of associations and discriminations of discrete stimulus situations. As such, they are a category of fact systems that answer the question 'how do I do it?' in a unique and unambiguous way. It would seem, therefore, that, like facts, procedures should be taught by expositive strategies. This is, in fact, commonly the case. Most industrial procedures are taught through the method of demonstration, followed by imitative practice (unstructured, as in 'sitting next to Nellie', or structured, as in the TWI method). So are most procedures in school subjects (eg long division, or the rules of grammar).

It is, however, impossible to teach procedures such as long division by a guided discovery approach, in which the teacher asks the learner to deduce the next step, by applying the concepts and principles of number and of the basic operations. Thus, the learner constructs the algorithm for himself during the learning process. Subsequently, he simply recalls the algorithm 'from store' when required and applies it mechanically. There is no long-term advantage, as far as performance of long division is concerned, so long as the algorithm remains completely remembered. However, if it is seldom used, it may be partly, or completely, forgotten with time. As in the case of principles, this is less likely to occur if a process of reflection and construction took place during the initial learning. Also, if forgotten, the conceptual schemata used in the original construction may still be 'in store', allowing the learner to reconstruct the forgotten steps. The process of construction during learning strengthens the conceptual schemata and the problem-solving schemata (heuristics) used in the proof of the algorithm. This not only aids in the reconstruction of that particular algorithm, if forgotten, but also assists in the solution of other future problems (say, the construction of the algorithm for calculating the square root of a number).

However, not all procedures are based on concepts or principles that are worth building into one's schemata and strengthening. This is the case for many administrative and bureaucratic procedures.

Thus we see that the decision between the two strategies, in the case of procedures, requires a somewhat deeper analysis of the particular case. If forgetting is likely, if the concepts and principles needed to discover the procedure in a meaningful way are already in store (or there are good reasons for wishing to put them into store), there is a strong case for the use of a discovery strategy. If the likelihood of forgetting is low, or if the concepts etc are not in store (and it is unnecessary or premature to put them there), the case is stronger for an expositive strategy. All this is tempered by the consideration that, in most cases, the expositive strategy will be more economical on time.

4. *Concepts.* These come in two forms: primary, or concrete, concepts and secondary, or defined, concepts. The situation is slightly different for each type. Concrete concepts can, up to a point, be learned without verbal communication. Animals in the laboratory can learn simple concrete concepts, such as 'red', 'circle', 'biggest', 'different from' and so on. They do not, of course, learn these verbal labels, but they demonstrate that they 'have' the concept by exhibiting correct

'classifying behaviour'. For example, the pigeon pecks at a red object but not at other colours (including near-reds such as pink or orange), or it pecks at circular objects but not at oval objects. The monkey learns to expect food under the biggest container presented, whatever its shape or colour or absolute size, or, alternatively, under the container which is a different shape from the rest, irrespective of other properties such as colour or size. The operant conditioning method used in such animal training, whilst based on the principles of reinforcement by food, is nevertheless an example of a discovery learning strategy. Mastery of the concept depends on experiencing sufficient numbers of instances of the concept to enable the learning organism to generalize the classifying principles involved.

Human beings learn primary (concrete) concepts in exactly the same way. We also learn verbal labels as we go along. This helps to define what we are about. When a child is presented with a coloured disc, it helps a great deal to establish the context of the exercise by verbal questions such as 'what is the colour?' or 'what is the shape?' (at an earlier stage of learning when the secondary, defined, concepts of colour and shape have not yet been learned, we would say 'is it red?' or 'is it round?'). However, language only establishes the context. The child needs a range of examples similar to those presented to the pigeon in order to classify red objects with precision and not include the borderline non-examples.

In the case of concrete concepts, therefore, we have no option but to apply discovery learning strategies.

In the case of defined concepts, however, the case is somewhat different. A defined concept is, in a sense, a rule for the classification of simpler concepts. Let us examine some examples.

'Red', 'blue', 'green', 'pink' and 'yellow' are examples of the concept 'colour'. It is impossible to learn this concept without first learning at least some colours and their respective verbal labels. Given that prior learning, it is possible to learn the concept of colour either by expositive means (eg by the presentation of the definition in the first sentence of this paragraph) or by discovery strategies (eg by presenting a large set of concrete examples of objects of a variety of known colours and, instead of associating the specific labels of the colours, associate the generalized label colour every time). The latter procedure will be more time-consuming and more likely to confuse the student.

## Matching Instructional Strategy to Skill Category

We will now consider a little more closely the causes of poor performance in the case of the new learner. His performance deficiency may be the result of a 'Knowledge deficiency', a 'skill deficiency' or to a combination of both. All skilled performance involves the execution of a *cycle* of activities which can be summarized as:

1. *Perception* of the relevant stimuli.
2. *Recall* of the relevant prerequisite knowledge.
3. *Planning* of the appropriate responses.
4. *Performance* of these responses (followed by *perception* of the results, etc).

Some skills are highly dependent on the *planning* element (strategy skills, planning skills, or preferably *productive* skills), while other skills involve very little original planning, requiring only the recall of a standard procedure (reflexive skills, or *reproductive* skills). Reproductive skills are thus always much the same in their execution. There is little need for further learning of *knowledge* once the basic procedure involved has been learned. These skills improve in time because of improvements in the performer's skills of perception, and of performance (dexterity, speed, precision, etc). Productive skills, on the other hand, involve an element of novel problem-solving in the planning of a response. There is a great deal of variety in the stimuli that present themselves to the performer. Although the basic principles of planning may always be the same, the examples which present themselves are always different. Thus the performer's experience grows with practice, both in terms of *knowledge* (the variety of different problems that can present themselves) and *skill* (in perceiving and interpreting the problem, deciding a course of action and executing it).

The approach suggested for matching instructional strategies to skills is based on the aforementioned consideration, and two others:

(a)  Skilled activity is useful
(b)  Skilled activity is enjoyable once a reasonable standard of performance has been reached.

One should, therefore, attempt to make the learner perform at a reasonable (not necessarily exceptionally high) standard of performance as quickly as possible. In order to achieve this, the procedure outlined below (see Figure 4 for a summary) is suggested.

|  | Reproductive skills | Productive skills |
|---|---|---|
| Imparting the knowledge content | Expositive or discovery methods (dependent on the type of knowledge) | Discovery methods (principle learning is always involved) |
| Imparting the practical application | Expositive methods (demonstration and prompted practice)<br>*Note:* Imparting the knowledge and skills content may be combined | Expositive methods (demonstration and prompted practice) |
| Developing proficiency | Supervised practice of whole task and/or special exercises<br>Continuing feedback of results | Discovery methods (guided problem-solving)<br>Continuing feedback of results |

**Figure 4.** *Instructional strategies for the development of skills*

1. Teach the knowledge necessary for reasonable performance. In the case of reproductive skills this may well be all the knowledge necessary. In the case of productive skills it will be basic knowledge required to start at a reasonable level of proficiency. The choice of strategy at this stage should be governed by the considerations presented in the previous section on the matching of instructional strategies to knowledge categories.

2. Apply an *expositive* strategy to aid the learner's initial performance of the skill (mainly because it achieves results faster). This strategy would follow a three-stage procedure:

(a)  *Demonstrate* the skill that is required, both in its entirety and in its main parts, or key points. (This may on occasions be done concomitantly with the teaching of the essential knowledge — demonstration plus explanation).
(b)  Arrange *simplified or prompted practice* of the skill by the learner. The prompting may be achieved by guidance, by simplifying the task artificially, by dividing the task into stages or parts to be practised one at a time, or by other tactics.

(c) Arrange *supervised free practice* of the complete skilled activity by the learner, supplying *feedback* in the form of knowledge of results, appropriate praise or other reinforcers. The feedback should be in a form capable of interpretation by the learner so that he may correct any errors. It should also demonstrate clearly to the learner both the usefulness and the enjoyment of the skill.

3. Once the learner is performing at a reasonable standard, the strategy will depend on whether the skill is basically reproductive or productive.

(a) In the case of reproductive skill, no third stage of planned instruction is called for, as far as the knowledge content is concerned. Often, the continuation of step 2c is all that is required for the skill to develop to the required standard. In some cases, when performance depends on exceptional levels of perceptual acuity, dexterity, strength, stamina, patience or persistence, etc, special training exercises, quite apart from the practice of the actual skilled task, may accelerate the process of skill development.

(b) In the case of a productive skill, a *discovery* strategy should be adopted in further instruction. Rather than leave the learner to develop his skill as best he can, the instructional system should:

☐ Arrange as wide a variety of problems as are likely to be encountered in real life, in the shortest possible time, thus concentrating the variety that may, in reality, be met over years into a period of weeks or months. This can be achieved by various techniques of *simulation*. (It may not be necessary to simulate reality, if the requisite variety of real-life experiences can be arranged in a reasonable period.)

☐ Arrange for the analysis of these situations by the learner, in such a way that he demonstrates the growth of his conceptual schemata to encompass the ever greater variety of problems that he has encountered. He should demonstrate that he is applying the principles he has learned and, in the light of new experiences, is modifying, complementing, or reorganizing these principles. As we are dealing here with conceptual learning, an element of verbal interaction between teacher and learner is almost inevitable at this stage, even if the skilled task itself does not call for verbal responses. The verbal communication is necessary for the learner to demonstrate to the instructor the processes of analysis (of new situations), of synthesis (of new principles or schemata) and of evaluation (of the new principles in yet further situations). The instructor, by observing the learner's performance on new and ever more difficult problems, can assess whether the learner is or is not developing his skills satisfactorily. But only through verbal interchange can he hope to get 'inside the mind' of the learner in order to assess why a skill is not developing and what should be done in order to help it to develop.

Thus, in simulation exercises (when used to develop productive skills), the debriefing or analysis session is of paramount importance. For example, a supervisor knows that he handled a simulated disciplinary problem rather badly. It is important that he analyzes why, suggests improvements, and tries them out later on, repeating the whole analysis, synthesis and evaluation cycle. Similarly, a child knows he reacted inappropriately to a simulated race relations problem. Again, it is important he should analyze why, suggest how he should have reacted, and generalize this new reaction, applying it as a heuristic in the future.

## Developing a Plan

Analysis of the task or topic leads to the development of a hierarchy of intermediate objectives, or a network of sub-topics, which allows quite detailed decisions to be made with respect to the sequence of units and individual lessons in the proposed training system. This sequence may be transformed now into a *plan* of the overall structure of the instructional system. This may be a linear, pre-ordained plan which defines the exact sequence of lessons that will be given, or it may be a flexible plan allowing for alternative routes, for student choice of certain objectives, for elective topics complementing a common core, or many other variations. A further aspect of the system that this plan would specify is the method, or combination of methods, that will be used to achieve each of the intermediate objectives.

Armed with the more detailed breakdown of the instructional objectives, a more precise idea of the necessary content and a more thorough analysis of the existing levels of knowledge and skill in the target population, we are in a position to turn our views regarding appropriate strategies into more detailed suggestions of the methods that should be adopted in order to put these strategies into operation.

The procedure we might follow is:

1. Determine, from the objectives, whether we are dealing with:
   (a) An information problem (the need to instil knowledge).
   (b) A performance problem (the need to develop skills).
   (c) A combination of information and performance problem.

Each objective should be considered in turn.

2. Consider, for each objective, the basic category of knowledge or skill that we intend to teach:
   (a) If knowledge, is it factual information, concepts, procedures or principles (or what combination)?
   (b) If skill, is it basically a simple reproductive skill or a more complex productive skill (or a combination of both reproductive and productive skills)?

3. In the light of considerations 1 and 2, decide whether expositive or discovery methods are indicated for the objective.

4. Consider now the practical constraints that have been identified as 'immutable'. These might include such factors as:
   (a) *Resources:* what is the geographical distribution of our student population, its level of study skills, social habits, etc?
   (b) *Target population:* what is the geographical distribution of our student population, its level of study skills, social habits, etc?
   (c) *Wider system:* what are the political decisions or social pressures that affect our system's design, etc?

Consider what restrictions these constraints impose on your selection of specific instructional methods.

5. Select a method (or several alternative methods) that is(are) both appropriate and viable, in the light of the considerations outlined above.

## Conclusion

Basic expositive and discovery methods have been discussed with respect to their relationship to the inculcation of knowledge and skills. This relationship is summarized in Figure 5.

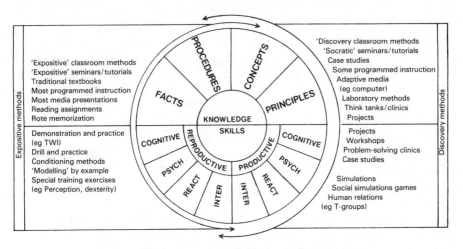

**Figure 5.** *Some basic expositive and discovery methods and their relation to the knowledge/skills schemata*

## References

Ausubel, D P (1968) *Educational Psychology: A Cognitive View.* Holt, Rinehart and Winston, New York.

Bruner, J S (1966) *Towards a Theory of Instruction.* Norton, New York.

Gagné, R M and Briggs, L J (1974) *Principles of Instructional Design.* Holt, Rinehart and Winston, New York.

Landa, L N (1976) *Instructional Regulation and Control: Cybernetics, Algorithmization and Heuristics in Education.* Educational Technology Publications, New Jersey.

Romiszowski, A J (1980) A new approach to the analysis of knowledge and skills. In Winterburn, R and Evans, L (eds) *Aspects of Educational Technology* **XIV.** Kogan Page, London.

Romiszowski, A J (1981) *Designing Instructional Systems: Decision Making in Course Planning and Curriculum Design.* Kogan Page, London.

## 3.3 Multi-Media Multi-Purpose: Is the Quality of the Learning Experience Being Well Served by the Use of Educational Media?

C F A Bryce and A M Stewart
*Dundee College of Technology*

**Abstract:** The contribution of educational technology to the quality of the learning experience can be gauged, to some degree, by the extent to which educational technology has matched the presentation stimuli and learning style to the type or types of learning being (it is to be hoped) facilitated. One of the major failures of educational technology is probably the indiscriminate way in which mediated learning materials have been applied to the learning experience. Thus, for example, tape-slide programmes are produced and expected to facilitate almost any kind of learning, although the attributes of that particular combination of media clearly are not relevant for all types of learning.

This paper describes an attempt to combine the attributes of a variety of media formats into a single presentation system and thus enrich the quality of the learning experience for the student.

## Introduction

For the past 15 years, educational technologists have been attempting to identify the characteristics and attributes of the various media available and to classify them according to the different types of learning which they facilitated or to relate the learning mode with which these media are associated to the characteristics of the individual learner.

The purpose of this paper is to review the development of theories relating media to types of learning and learner characteristics; to compare these to everyday practice; and to describe a pragmatic approach to the optimal application of media characteristics for various types of learning and learner characteristics.

## Media Classifications

Heidt (1978) has identified more than 12 media classifications or taxonomies, and has usefully reviewed the six most common. He also suggests some fundamental questions which need to be asked, in particular: 'How useful is it to attempt to develop a classification system for the scholar in the field on the one hand, and for the media producer or user on the other?'

The *Taxonomy of Communication Media* (Bretz, 1971) distinguishes between a communication medium and an instructional medium. The former is defined as: 'a system for conveying messages through reproducible and self-contained programs' and the latter is described as: 'any component of the learning environment which provides or helps to provide stimuli to learning'.

Essentially, the Bretz taxonomy concentrates on the technical aspects of communication media by classifying the media according to the kind of information they present, whether audio or visual, still or motion, and would seem to be based on the qualtity of different information a medium is capable of presenting, as shown in Figure 1. The classification is of hardware, with educational criteria seemingly ignored, so the Bretz taxonomy is not particularly helpful in relation to instructional problems.

Duncan (1969) proposed a hierarchical order of audio-visual media in an attempt to outline a frame of reference which could provide an educationally relevant order for various audio-visual aids (see Figure 2).

He draws attention, however, to the problem of conflict between appropriateness of the media for a specific task and the costs involved, and suggests the following steps in media selection:

(a) Definition of the aims of the task.
(b) Identification of the audience in terms of intelligence, etc.
(c) Selection of the method to be used on pedagogic principles.
(d) Selection/development of an aid on the basis of (i) the attributes of the equipment, and (ii) the resources available.

Again, the emphasis is on the technological description of various media, with no relationship to type of learning or learner.

One of the most frequently cited authors on the subject is Briggs (1970), who summarized the relationship between media characteristics, learner characteristics, and task requirements in the well-known matrix as shown in Figure 3.

However, it is clear that 'learner characteristics' as shown in the matrix are not really learner characteristics but, rather, categories of group size, type of stimulus, and modes of instruction, and 'task requirements' hardly relate to types of learning.

| TELECOMMUNICATION | Sound | Picture | Line Graphic | Print | Motion | RECORDING |
|---|---|---|---|---|---|---|
| CLASS I: AUDIO-MOTION-VISUAL MEDIA ||||||| 
|  | X | X | X | X | X | Sound film |
| Television | X | X | X | X | X | Video tape / Film TV recording |
|  | X | X | X | X | X | Holographic recording |
| Picturephone | X | X | X | X | X |  |
| CLASS II: AUDIO-STILL-VISUAL MEDIA |||||||
| Slow-scan TV / Time-shared TV | X | X | X | X |  | Recorded still TV |
|  | X | X | X | X |  | Sound filmstrip |
|  | X | X | X | X |  | Sound slide-set |
|  | X | X | X | X |  | Sound-on-slide |
|  | X | X | X | X |  | Sound page |
|  | X | X | X | X |  | Talking book |
| CLASS III: AUDIO-SEMIMOTION MEDIA |||||||
| Telewriting | X |  | X | X | × | Recorded telewriting |
| CLASS IV: MOTION-VISUAL MEDIA |||||||
|  |  | X | X | X | X | Silent film |
| CLASS V: STILL-VISUAL MEDIA |||||||
| Facsimile |  | X | X | X |  | Printed page |
|  |  | X | X | X |  | Filmstrip |
|  |  | X | X | X |  | Picture set |
|  |  | X | X | X |  | Microform |
|  |  | X | X | X |  | Video file |
| CLASS VI: AUDIO MEDIA |||||||
| Telephone / Radio | X |  |  |  |  | Audio disc / Audio tape |
| CLASS VII: PRINT MEDIA |||||||
| Teletype |  |  |  | X |  | Punched paper tape |

Figure 1. *The communication media (from Bretz, 1971)*

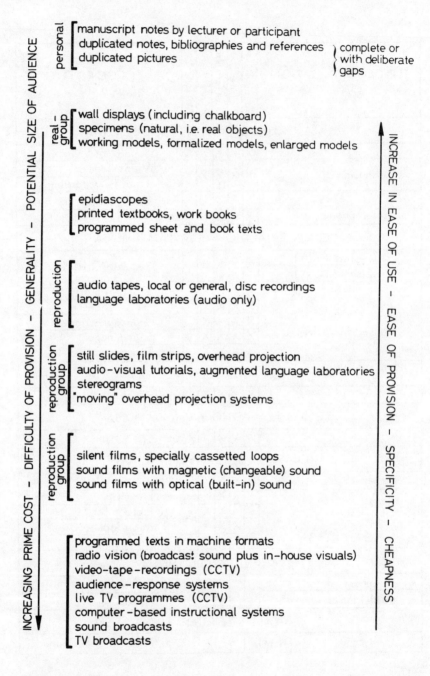

**Figure 2.** *A hierarchical order of selected audio-visual instrumental media (from Duncan, 1969)*

| IF → THEN ↓ | LEARNER CHARACTERISTICS | | | | | | | | | | TASK REQUIREMENTS | | | | | | | MATERIALS | | | | TRANSMISSION | | | | |
|---|---|---|---|---|---|---|---|---|---|---|---|---|---|---|---|---|---|---|---|---|---|---|---|---|---|---|
| | Large 100 + | Medium 20 — 100 | Small 2 — 30 | Individual | Visual | Audible | Learner Paced | Response | Self-Instructional | Motion | Time (Exp/Contract) | Fixed Sequence | Flexible Sequence | Sequential Disclo. | Repeatability | Context Creation | Affective Power | Obtainability | Reusability | Time to Obtain | Cost (4 Copies) | Simplicity (Eq.) | Availability (Eq.) | Controlability | Freedom from Dist. | Darkening not Req. |
| Real Object | | | | | | | | | | | | | | | | | | | | | | | | | | |
| Model of Real Object | | | | | | | | | | | | | | | | | | | | | | | | | | |
| Live Voice | | | | | | | | | | | | | | | | | | | | | | | | | | |
| Audio Tape Record | | | | | | | | | | | | | | | | | | | | | | | | | | |
| Print | | | | | | | | | | | | | | | | | | | | | | | | | | |
| Programmed Instruction | | | | | | | | | | | | | | | | | | | | | | | | | | |
| Chalk Board | | | | | | | | | | | | | | | | | | | | | | | | | | |
| Overhead Transparency | | | | | | | | | | | | | | | | | | | | | | | | | | |
| Filmstrip | | | | | | | | | | | | | | | | | | | | | | | | | | |
| Slide | | | | | | | | | | | | | | | | | | | | | | | | | | |
| Motion Picture | | | | | | | | | | | | | | | | | | | | | | | | | | |
| TV | | | | | | | | | | | | | | | | | | | | | | | | | | |
| Flat Picture | | | | | | | | | | | | | | | | | | | | | | | | | | |

In the matrix, solid shading means 'not applicable', partial shading means 'partially applicable', and an empty cell means 'applicable'.

**Figure 3.** *The relationship between media characteristics, learner characteristics and task requirements (from Briggs, 1970)*

The matrix is, in fact, rather disappointing and does little to help (and perhaps much to hinder) the educational media practitioner.

In another study of this problem, Gagné (1965) has listed the instructional functions of various media, but has not linked his classification of media with his hierarchy of learning types.

Again, this matrix is not really helpful when applied to a particular learning situation and it is worth noting that the table was omitted from the second edition of Gagné's book.

Tosti and Ball (1969) have identified the source of the problem as failure to distinguish between relevant classes of factors and confusion between presentational, content, and media variables, and have highlighted the distinction between medium and presentation form, both of which are regarded as being independent of content.

Essentially, Tosti and Ball's model introduces a connecting link, the presentation form, because the selection of media does not consist only of a matching of instructional functions with the medium.

Heidt (1978) argues that most media classifications are deficient in their connection with theoretical models of teaching and learning and that applicability to problems of media design and instruction are illusory.

## Learner Characteristics

It has long been recognized that learners, as individuals, differ in how they learn, and in recent years attempts have been made to relate individual differences and aptitudes to instructional presentations to determine how they interact.

| | Media | | | | | | |
|---|---|---|---|---|---|---|---|
| Function | Objects; Demon-stration | Oral Commu-nication | Printed Media | Still Pic-tures | Moving Pic-tures | Sound Movies | Teach-ing Ma-chines |
| Presenting the stimulus | Yes | Limited | Limited | Yes | Yes | Yes | Yes |
| Directing attention and other activity | No | Yes | Yes | No | No | Yes | Yes |
| Providing a model of expected perform-ance | Limited | Yes | Yes | Limited | Limited | Yes | Yes |
| Furnishing external prompts | Limited | Yes | Yes | Limited | Limited | Yes | Yes |
| Guiding thinking | No | Yes | Yes | No | No | Yes | Yes |
| Inducing transfer | Limited | Yes | Limited | Limited | Limited | Limited | Limited |
| Assessing attain-ments | No | Yes | Yes | No | No | Yes | Yes |
| Providing feedback | Limited | Yes | Yes | No | Limited | Yes | Yes |

**Figure 4.** *Instructional functions of various media*
*(from Gagné, 1965)*

Snow (1977) has indicated that 'aptitude-treatment interaction' (ATI) can be used to develop macro-adaptations of instruction assigning different kinds of students to different treatments aimed at the same goal, or to make micro-adaptations by changing aspects of one treatment so that it becomes individualized.

Heidt (1978) uses the term 'trait-treatment interaction' (TTI) and suggests that the question 'which medium (eg film or textbook) is better and more efficient than the other?' should be replaced by 'what *media attributes* are relevant for learners with what *personality traits* for what kind of *learning tasks*?' (pp 84-5).

Cronbach and Snow (1977) assert that 'the volume of research on learning instruction, and individual differences is enormous; but only limited progress has been made toward an integrated understanding of the nature of individual differences in ability to learn' and go on to assess the present state of knowledge and propose directions for further research and development.

In looking at the interactive effects of making instruction less verbal and examining claims that the addition of illustrations reduces the correlation with general ability that is typical of verbal lessons and also claims that 'spatial' ability affects learning from diagrams, they conclude that the bulk of the research evidence indicates interactions of a vaguely defined general ability with an absence of expected effects of more specialized abilities. The only helpful guidance would seem to be that there is an interaction between ability to learn from mediated instruction and pictorial/verbal presentation.

A considerable amount of research on aptitude-treatment interaction has concerned programmed instruction of various types and the most important

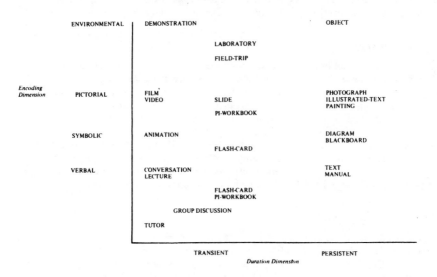

**Figure 5a.** *Media classified by encoding versus duration*

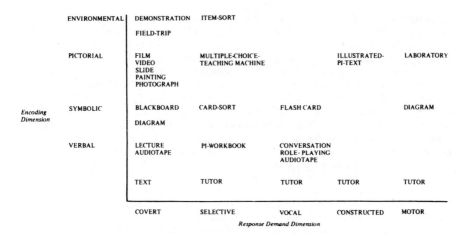

**Figure 5b.** *Media classified by encoding versus response demand*
*(from Tosti and Ball, 1969)*

conclusion by Cronbach and Snow (1977) from this research is that 'any attempt to generalize about a class of educational treatments is suspect . . . one cannot generalize about instructional techniques in the abstract'.

## Present Practices

Most of what has gone before is rather heady research material — the stuff of which PhDs are made, but how useful is it to the practising instructional designer or instructional materials developer? Is it not the case that most of this research would appear to be regarded as irrelevant or perhaps even unknown by the vast majority of teachers who have produced mediated instructional materials? Or is tape-slide really the panacea for all learning problems?

Whatever the outcome of the research referred to it must be acknowledged that no single method of instruction, no single audio-visual medium can possibly meet the widely differing demands of the many instructional tasks and multitude of learner characteristics with which the instructional designer is confronted.

## A Pragmatic Approach

It is proposed here that, given the results of research in the area and the impracticability of exactly matching the treatment to the individual learner, the best solution is to try to develop a presentational system which will incorporate the attributes of the available media and which, by requiring a variety of learning styles, will meet the learning characteristics of most learners.

In previous research, Bryce and Stewart (1978) described how they used the Philips PIP (Programmed Individual Presentation) system as it was able to combine the attributes normally associated with tape-slide, overhead projection, and film. However, there was one major disadvantage of the system: the programming had to be linear, as branching would have required a technical capability not available on the equipment.

Computer-based learning (CBL), however, does allow considerable branching but, when presented frame-by-frame on a VDU or printer, can be particularly dull and does not, of course, permit the use of other than extremely simple visuals.

Clearly, the learning experience could be enriched by bringing together the attributes of computer-based learning and a variety of audio-visual presentational devices. Bryce and Stewart (1979) described how they interfaced random-access colour microfiche with a main frame computer and outlined plans for further development. In the past year, with the assistance of a research grant from the Scottish Education Department, further developmental work has resulted in the successful interfacing of the random-access microfiche system with several stand-alone microcomputers and in the interfacing of random-access video, with the Cromemco System Three microcomputer being used for the research. Thus, the quality of the learning experience is being improved as the media relatively appropriate to the learning task are employed and the range of presentational modes and treatments accommodates a variety of learner characteristics. The structuring is done via the computer which then activates, when necessary, the presentational mode most appropriate for the content, or even using more than one simultaneously. The printer associated with the computer is used to print out a summary of the main points of the presentation and to present an analysis of the students' performance in relation to each of the objectives in the programme, together with suggestions for further study in areas of weakness.

The researchers are not entirely happy with the use of the VDU for the presentation of lengthy verbal material and it is hoped that in the near future it will be possible to interface a random-access audio unit thus further enhancing the learning experience.

Future development will be in interfacing a tape-film system with the computer and in interfacing less expensive, or more readily available, random-access audio-visual devices.

The approach being pursued is somewhat pragmatic: nevertheless it is argued that, by adopting a multi-purpose multi-media approach, the quality of the learning experience is enhanced and that is something not only desirable but essential.

## References

Bretz, R (1971) *A Taxonomy of Communication Media.* Educational Technology Publications, Englewood Cliffs, NJ.

Briggs, L J (1970) *Handbook of Procedures for the Design of Instruction.* American Institute for Research, New York.

Bryce, C F A and Stewart, A M (1978) Design and production of self-instructional learning packages in biochemistry using the Philips PIP system. In Brook, D and Race, P (eds) *Aspects of Educational Technology* XII. Kogan Page, London.

Bryce, C F A and Stewart, A M (1979) The application of random-access back projection in computer-assisted instruction. In Page, G T and Whitlock, Q (eds) *Aspects of Educational Technology* XIII. Kogan Page, London.

Cronbach, L J and Snow, R E (1977) *Aptitudes and Instructional Methods: A Handbook for Research on Interactions.* Irvington Publishers, New York.

Duncan, C J (1960) A survey of audiovisual equipment and methods. In Unwin, D (ed) *Media and Methods: Instructional Technology in Higher Education.* McGraw-Hill, London.

Gagné, R M (1965) *The Conditions of Learning.* Holt, Rinehart and Winston, New York.

Heidt, E U (1978) *Instructional Media and the Individual Learner.* Kogan Page, London.

Snow, R E (1978) Individual differences and instructional design. In Hartley, J and Davies, I K (eds) *Contributions to an Educational Technology* 2. Kogan Page, London.

Tosti, D T and Ball, J R (1969) A behavioural approach to instructional design and media selection. *A V Communication Review* 1.

## Acknowledgement

The authors gratefully acknowledge the support of the Scottish Education Department in the funding of this research.

# 3.4 The Educational Significance of Electronic Media

P Copeland
*West Sussex Institute of Higher Education*

**Abstract:** New electronic media technologies such as video disc, viewdata, microcomputers and various microprocessor-based teaching devices differ considerably in technical concept to the media technologies we have used in the past, but what do these technologies offer in terms of their capability to teach?

Those researching into educational media have often attempted to identify and classify media attributes but the models they have produced do not accommodate the display and interaction characteristics of electronic media.

This paper offers a simple 'quadrant' model which demonstrates the significance of electronic media in general and shows specifically the potential use of interactive video systems based on disc and tape.

## Micro-electronics Plus Education Equals Uncertainty

From the technologies of micro-electronics and communications have emerged pocket calculators, video discs, electronic tutors, electronic data networks, interactive cable television, videotex and more.

At the moment the educational opportunities provided by these electronic media are uncertain and will remain so until a precise functional description is available of how learning procedures will benefit.

Indeed, the differences in capability between the new electronic media and existing media are not at all clear, and already this has caused some practitioners to be somewhat sceptical about the value to education of such developments as PRESTEL and microcomputers (Howe and du Boulay, 1979; CET, 1978; Ahl, 1977).

Part of the problem seems to lie with the preoccupation with hardware-oriented descriptions of what the technology can do. While these descriptions may outline technical achievement in terms of information access-time, voice or touch-screen input, gigabyte memory and graphics display, they do not explain how any educational potential can be realized. Nor should we expect them to; the educational significance of electronic media can only be judged from an educational perspective, but it is important that this perspective takes into account the potential of the media to which it relates. In this respect, our existing educational models and theories of media do not accommodate the features characteristic of the electronic media now available.

This paper attempts to identify these features and will present a perspective from which the significance of electronic media can be examined.

## Research on Educational Media

Research on educational media is still progressing very slowly after a series of false starts. Comparisons of one medium with another dominated the field up to the early 1960s and are still in evidence today. Campeau (1967) conducted an extensive review of the literature on media experiments and concluded that the research was not asking the right questions.

Fleming (1970) identified the principal failing of the comparative research model when he suggested that the variance achieved by altering the variables within a particular medium could be greater than the variance measured when comparing different media.

This comment reinforces the view that researchers, and indeed programme makers, have not always tailored their treatment of the presented information to exploit the *distinctive* capabilities of the media they are investigating.

Consider an experiment attempting to assess the difference between learning from slide-tape on the one hand and video-tape on the other. If the information to be presented were, for example, intended to enable the learner to describe the firing sequence of the car ignition system, then the modelling animation which could be included if video-tape were used would enable a more dynamic form of presentation than the punctuated presentation characteristic of slide-tape. Because of this difference, and for this specific task, one of these media might be judged better than the other, but suppose the experiment compared video-taped slide-tape with slide-tape? The results of the experiment in this case would almost certainly be inconclusive.

The distinctive attributes of media are numerous and diverse and have been described under various labels such as 'symbol systems' (Salomon, 1980), 'media attributes' (Tosti and Ball, 1969) and 'within-media variables' (Fleming, 1970). The classification of the attributes within these labels is inconsistent between authors and unfortunately the empirical validation of this research perspective has yet to begin.

Similar conclusions are reached when comparing progress in other areas of media research. The investigation of trait-treatment interactions, for instance, in order to implement individual learner-difference theory is giving inconclusive results (Heidt, 1978). Investigations into the organization and sequencing of information are fairly recent and few in number (Pask, 1978; Allen, 1970).

Because of this diversity in approach to research and the inconclusiveness of the evidence currently available, no hard and fast rules linking media with learning procedures can be deduced from any one particular research study or promulgated theory.

Hawkridge (1973), writing on the Open University's use of media, came to a similar conclusion:

> The fact is that instructional researchers and designers have not provided even the foundations for constructing strong practical procedures for selecting media appropriate to given learning tasks.

With these remarks in mind, the 'quadrant' model which follows was arrived at by cross-fertilizing ideas from selected research in the field.

## The Media Quadrant Model

### Information Transfer

All teaching by definition requires the transfer of information. In a teaching situation the information transfer is often thought of as being one way: from teacher to learner. In fact, it is highly desirable that certain information, such as the learner's knowledge state, should be transferred to the teacher. Pask (1978) develops this notion much further in his 'conversational theory'.

The mechanism in which this bi-directional transfer operates can be, for the class teacher, question and answer; for the skill instructor, demonstration and performance monitoring; in computer-assisted learning, response frame and keyboard response.

It has been demonstrated that when the teaching agent is able to invite learner-response, the efficiency of the teaching and learning process can be significantly increased (Gropper, 1967; Campeau, 1966). When the teaching agent can *acknowledge* the response as, for instance, with the 'live' teacher or computer-assisted learning, then the agent can *adapt* the teaching to suit the learning and an interactive relationship can be established.

In an efficient teaching situation, then, exposition, the presentation of information, should ideally be accompanied by inquisition. These two elements can be positioned at the extreme ends of a continuum.

We can use the continuum to illustrate the extent to which various teaching agents extend into these dimensions by allocating them to certain positions along the continuum. If we consider the teacher and learner being in a one-to-one tutorial then this situation can provide exposition and inquisition to each extrme: not all teaching methods do. For instance, braodcast educational television, in attempting to teach cognitive skills, does not seem to be capable of inducing a high level of overt audience response (Gropper and Lumsdaine, 1960).

This could be owing to various factors, one in particular being the transient nature of its presentation which allows the viewer only a limited time to respond. Another is the inability of broadcast television to *acknowledge* any response.

The transient nature of the presentation capabilities of certain media, such as films, video-tape and slide-tape, contrasts with media which are essentially static, eg printed text, diagrams, slides, etc. We can represent this contrast by placing a visual image-change continuum across the presentation continuum.

The composite diagram given in Figure 1 can now be used to illustrate the presentation characteristics of those media which do not acknowledge learner-response.

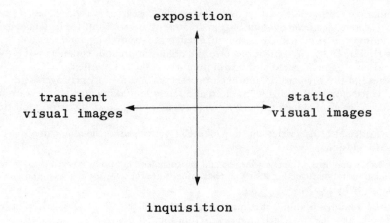

**Figure 1.** *A composite model for categorizing instructional media*

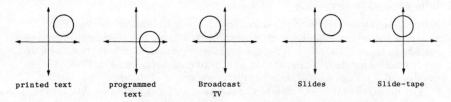

**Figure 2.** *Presentation characteristics of five instructional media*

From the diagrams in Figure 2 we can see that printed text is expository and static whereas programmed text attempts to provide inquisition. Broadcast television and cassettes which are produced with a broadcast style are situated in the exposition-transient quadrant. Slides used in their basic form are expository and static, but when used in conjunction with tape, or indeed in a lecture presentation, they become transient.

**Electronic Media**

All of the media mentioned so far could be regarded as being pre-micro-electronic and the quadrant construct has been adequate in accommodating them. However, in order to adequately situate the latest electronic media on the diagram, two feedback routes have to be added to link the inquisitional and expository dimensions. The diagram in Figure 3 can now accommodate response-acknowledging media. The feedback route which travels through the transient sector represents those responses which have to be made within a time constraint. The route through the static sector represents those responses which can be made at a time decided by the learner.

In positioning the electronic media on this diagram (see Figure 4) we see that TELETEXT is situated mostly in the exposition/static quadrant. The reason for its slight overlap into the transient area is that certain pages are presented in a time sequence. The viewer is provided with a control with which it is possible to 'hold' any page within these sequences but the cyclic nature of the presentation means the need to operate this is infrequent.

VIDEOTEX, on the other hand, has both expository and inquisitional static presentation capabilities. Its response capability enables multiple-choice and

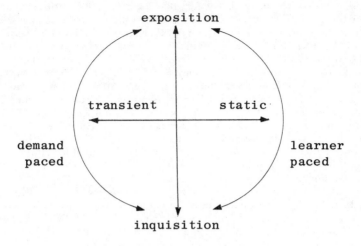

**Figure 3.** *The media quadrant model*

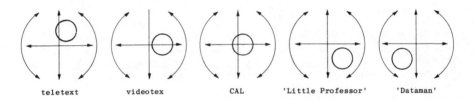

teletext          videotex          CAL          'Little Professor'          'Dataman'

**Figure 4.** *Position of five electronic media on the media quadrant model*

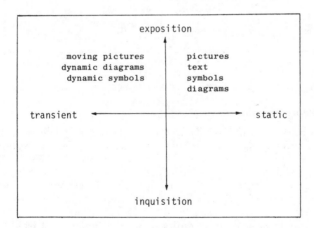

**Figure 5.** *Visual-image categories positioned on the quadrant model*

true-false questions to be asked. The fact that it can *adapt* the information being presented (ie present different pages) according to the responses being made, sets it apart from linear programmed printed text. (It could be argued that, theoretically at least, TELETEXT also has this capability but, in practice, as far as the UK's ORACLE and CEEFAX services are concerned, the limited size of the databases and the lengthy page access times make its use as a teaching agent impracticable.)

Computer-assisted learning extends into both expository and inquisitional dimensions and overlaps slightly into the transient sector. This positioning assumes that CAL generally has the capability to extend into these quadrants, although it is recognized that this capability is not always exploited. The principal characteristic of CAL which is well represented here is its highly interactive capability. Response routes can be either transient or static indicating the potential for either demand-paced or learner-paced progress. The potential for transient images is often realized in its simulation applications.

In the last two diagrams of Figure 4, two maths aids have been positioned on the model to highlight the emergence of purely inquisitional media. Both present the learner with mathematical problems at ascending levels of difficulty, but while LITTLE PROFESSOR simply waits for the learner to respond, DATAMAN actually monitors the length of time between question and response.

```
speech    -   description explanation

effects   -   cues, responses

music     -   motivation
              cues
              mood setting
```

**Figure 6.** *Audio categories*

**Analysis of Media Capabilities**

The quadrant model has successfully accommodated all the media mentioned so far, and has identified their characteristics in terms of four significant dimensions.

Acting on the advice of the research conclusions previously mentioned, the presentation capabilities of various media can now be analyzed with regard to the quadrant model. Figure 5 is a first attempt at this and shows the positions of different categories of visual image. For completeness, the table in Figure 6 lists categories of audio, and gives examples of their applications.

In order to use these analyses to optimize learning materials, it would be necessary to match learning objectives with teaching procedures and audio and visual image categories. Unfortunately, we do not, as yet, have an adequate theoretical basis for making such judgements.

Implicit in the 'multi-media' approach has been an assumption that certain media communicate certain information better than others. Whereas this might be true, it could be that it disguises the fact that media are being selected for their capability to accommodate certain audio and visual image categories and because they extend into specific dimensions of the model. Examples of this include the linking of video-cassette with textbook, slides with computer, and 8mm loop film with programmed text.

## An Electronic Super-Medium?

From the foregoing discussion it seems reasonable to suggest that an ideal medium is one which possesses the visual image categories identified, has an audio capability, and can extend fully into all the dimensions of the quadrant model (see Figure 7). It is evident from the analysis given earlier that all these capabilities exist but not, as yet, in an integrated form.

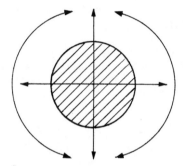

Figure 7. *Interactive video disc and tape*

Interactive video disc and tape seem to have the potential to integrate these capabilities and could well prove to be ideal educational media. Additionally, because of their response acknowledging capability, they should provide the empirical data now necessary to develop the quadrant model into a useful practical tool.

## References

Ahl, D H (1977) Does education want what technology can deliver? In Seidal, R J and Rubin, M (eds) *Computers and Communication: Implications for Education.* Academic Press, London.

Allen, W H (1970) Categories of instructional media research. *Viewpoints* 5. Bulletin of the School of Education, Indiana University.

Campeau, P L (1966) Selective review of literature on audio-visual methods of instruction. In Briggs, L J, Campeau, P L, Gagné, R M and May, M A (eds) *Instructional Media: A Procedure for the Design of Multimedia Instruction.* American Institutes for Research, Pittsburgh, Penn.

CET (1978) Viewdata not a 'teaching medium'. *Screen Digest*, p 195, October.

Gropper, G L (1967) Does programmed television need active responding? *Audio Visual Communications Review* 15, 1.

Gropper, G L and Lumsdaine, A A (1960) *Experiments on Active Student Response to Televised Instruction: An Interim Report.* American Institutes for Research, Pittsburgh, Penn.

Hawkridge, D G (1973) Media taxonomies and media selection. In Granholm, G (ed) *The Selection of Relevant Media/Methods for Defined Educational Purposes Within Distance Education.* European Home Study Council.

Heidt, E U (1978) *Instructional Media and the Individual Learner.* Kogan Page, London.

Howe, J A M and du Boulay, B (1979) Microprocessor assisted learning: turning the clock back?
    *Programmed Learning and Educational Technolgoy* **16**, 3.
Pask, G (1978) Conversational techniques in the study and practice of education. In Hartley,
    J and Davies, I K (eds) *Contributions to an Educational Technology.* Kogan Page, London.
Salomon, G (1979) *Interaction of Media, Cognition and Learning.* Jossey-Bass, New York.
Tosti, D T and Ball, J R (1969) A behavioural approach to instructional design and media
    selection. *Audio Visual Communications Review* **17**, 1.

# 3.5 Educational Films: And Now for Something Completely Different – The New Educational Video Programme

J R L Dent
*Guild Sound and Vision, Peterborough*

**Abstract:** This paper is designed to show that a new type of educational tool is available in video-cassettes. The educational film has traditionally been a passive instructional device. However, a purpose-designed video programme can be an active tool in the hands of the student, allowing interaction and self-paced learning.

## The Educational Film

As a distributor and producer of educational films, it has always struck me that very few teachers in schools, colleges and universities have any real idea how to use these films. There are, of course, many exceptions to such an observation. However, if one compares the uses made of an educational film in educational institutions with use made by training officers in industry of training films, one finds that the trainers tend to treat the use of such films far more professionally.

Consider two scenes:

### Scene One

A secondary school classroom with 25 teenagers about to start a class. A teacher enters, quells noise, deals with administrative procedures, engages two students to fetch and set up a 16mm projector, two or three others struggle with window blinds and, after some 10 minutes, a film is ready to be seen. The film will have come from the local education library and is on the subject of ancient history.

The teacher announces:

Class, we are going to look at this film 'Before the Romans'. I know we finished the pre-Roman period last term, but the film has only now arrived so do try to remember what we were studying last term. Now, as we have only 20 minutes of the class left, let us look at the film.

The film is shown and, as it ends, the bell goes and the students move out to lunch.

### Scene Two

A room in a factory administration block. The room contains tables and chairs arranged to view a screen, a projector is set up with film laced. Enter 20 or so supervisors for a training session. The trainer briefs them on the purpose of the session, introduces the film to be shown suggesting points to be noted. The lights are turned down, but not out, to allow for note-taking. The film is shown.

The trainer leads discussion. The film is shown again being stopped at points. The supervisors are split into groups and run role-playing exercises based on scenes from the film. Finally, the supervisors view the film again and either discuss or write about applications of the film's message in their own situations.

There can be little doubt as to the relative benefits gained by the two different approaches. Of course, many teachers do use film well and many trainers use film poorly. However, experience shows that the two scenes are not untypical.

From the evidence of the educational film catalogues, however, it is clear that teachers are expected to know how to use a film, to know or to find out where to stop the film, and what classroom or individual activities to set to reinforce the learning.

Many teachers and audio-visual materials producers will say that the educational film is *only an aid*. The word *only* provides the required debasement to justify showing films on days when the teacher is absent or short of ideas, or just when the film happens to be available. If it is 'only an aid', then it can be fitted in at random.

All films are expensive. In Britain in 1981, the actual release print (that is, the processed celluloid that the teacher puts on the projector) costs 12 pence per foot. Because demand per title is low, bulk purchasing is not available, and so a 20-minute film costs around £90. Shooting such a film can cost anything between £10,000 and £40,000. For a producer to recover costs of development, writing, production and negative processing, means that the price is going to be considerable even before the word 'profit' is added.

I would suggest that, for education, films can only be justified if they are cost-effective for teaching. They should provide essential elements of a course of instruction that the teacher cannot do personally or cannot do nearly as well. This means providing access to places, people and events that the class cannot otherwise obtain. Examples are of historical events, drama, micro- and macro-systems, animation, time-release photography and aerial photography.

## The Educational Video-Cassette

And now for something completely different. The video-cassette can, if the teaching and training professions allow, provide rather more than just an aid.

A noun, 'video', is actually becoming used. It is not really understood which, given its classical base, is hardly surprising. 'A video' is really a media word for a packaged television programme on cassette or, perhaps, disc. Today, it refers in almost every case to a film that has been transferred on to video-cassette to be shown on television. But this is only a film again in electronic clothing: there is no fundamental change.

Most educational television is designed to be used in the same way as educational film. A major exception is, in my view, some of the foreign language courses and in particular the literacy programmes. 'Sesame Street' and 'The Electric Light Company' were series that have shown a different technique also.

These new techniques require involvement by the listeners. If you watch an Italian language course you can hardly avoid trying to speak Italian where the programme demands that the viewer repeats the latest phrase. 'Sesame Street' demands of you to count forwards and backwards or respond to advertising commercials, eg for the letter 'P'.

By mentioning these types of broadcasting, I do not say that these are good programmes. Indeed, the British Broadcasting Corporation refused to show 'Sesame Street' because, I understand, it used rote learning methods. The element to which I draw your attention is the *active involvement* of the learner.

Learning is not passive. In almost every academic discipline, an application of thought, if not some physical effort, is required if learning is to be achieved.

Video-cassettes can be used to enable a positive learning strategy to be adopted. The change in technique appears quite simple, but in fact it requires a fundamentally different approach.

The mechanics of the video player enable the learner to control the video display. Thus the machine can be stopped or started at will. The touch of a button and the tape can be frozen to allow study of the picture. The tape can be rewound and a section played again, or the tape wound forward to skip ahead.

If, for a moment, we consider the way we all treat books, perhaps it is not so great a change after all.

Gutenberg's invention of movable type produced mass availability of books. Perhaps all the video-cassette does is to provide moveable pictures.

If we treat the video-cassette like a book, then it can provide learning at a student level and not necessarily only at a teacher or class level. For years this has been an aim of many educationalists, and now that a system is available they do not seem to have discovered how to use it.

One of the reasons why educationalists have been slow to take up video is the confusion of the technology. Video-cassettes come in a variety of formats and there looms on the horizon the video-disc. However, the domestic demand for video-cassettes has not been affected in the slightest by the various formats, and three formats are in regular use today.

Attitude to video is conditioned also by cost. It is assumed to be expensive. Today tapes are priced at between £30 and £80 for education, while film prices would be three to four times the amount. A school can realistically have its own library of tapes for access at will. Equipment costs, also, are low. In real terms the cost of a video-player has dropped significantly.

The greatest barrier is contained in methodology. Really, television viewing is a private, not a public, act. Television as a medium relies on a close relationship physically between the viewer and the screen, and this breaks up the traditional classroom style. If the student is then asked to control the video-player, the break from tradition is even greater.

Students are already good at the use of video technology, and education needs to use the available equipment to carry what may be old messages but by new methods. Much of what education offers is old (after all, experience is the result of an ageing process), but those of us who serve education have a duty to point out the new methods available.

## Using Educational Video-Cassettes

The problem with film and tape is that both are continuous pieces of material wound on to spools. It is thus not possible to look ahead or behind without a considerable pause. However, if the tape is controlled by certain electronic or mechanical systems, it is possible to index the tape and, by random access, find sections rapidly. The video disc will allow this to happen more rapidly than a tape but, in principle, there is no difference.

If we look at the sort of instructional programme that can be devised for video presentation we can see that an infinite number of options are available.

First, let us take a modern traditional approach. A video programme used in a class or group may contain the following:

(a) An introductory section giving an illustrated outline of what the programme contains, its relevance and sections that merit special attention.
(b) Instructional 'units' each concentrating on a single, or group, concept. At the end of each unit the screen might pose questions requiring answers or discussion. This would mean that the programme would be stopped and possibly the unit replayed.

(c)  A concluding section to reinforce the instruction given, possibly suggesting extensions or projects.

If this approach were adopted, an immediate factor emerges. The length of the programme is no longer relevant. The length will be in the *use*, not in the content.

If the programme does its job, then the whole programme may be used over several group sessions or classes and the value of the content extended. Also, the programme becomes less passive. By asking questions it demands a response.

Another possibility is to produce programmes that are integrated with textbooks. Thus a chapter of a textbook might have a video section to illustrate its contents in ways impossible to cover in print. The use of slow motion, microscopy, time-lapse and other techniques are obvious. Those who need 'exploded' diagrams can have then animated, providing an opportunity to make redundant those army sergeants whose methods of teaching the disassembly and reassembly of the bren gun have caused so much misery and bruised fingers.

But illustration, though valuable, is passive. Video, being electronic and thus controlled, can be totally integrated to the point where it is no longer anything but one element of a course of study. In this case it needs to be related to other forms of expression.

An example of this is in a new series on computer programming. Here, the video carries instruction while learning is practised on a computer with printed material providing a guide for both teacher and learner. In this case, the 'how to' of writing a computer program is explained and shown on video, using all the benefits that a television programme can bring but that the classroom-bound instructor lacks.

A first example of the type of programme I have in mind is *BASIC: An Introduction to Computer Programming* (produced and distributed by Guild Sound and Vision Limited). It is designed to be used either in groups or as a self-instructional course. This course is by no means the ultimate, and I expect to see a range of much more radically different courses being produced.

The course is provided on video with printed support materials. The method is for students to use the video as a source of straight instruction and to use the printed support materials to guide applications of the instruction. In this case, application is by practise of skills on a microcomputer.

The role of the teacher is as manager, planning, organizing, controlling and helping the students, who may all be at different stages of the course. The teacher's role is vital, but different from the traditional position as fountain of knowledge. Also, physically, the teacher need not always be present during the students' actual use of the course.

As said before, I believe that this methodology will continue to spread, giving us many more courses where the step-by-step approach to learning can take place. Sometimes this can be microprocessor-controlled into linear or branching programmed learning courses made more 'human' by the wonders of video technology.

## Conclusion

In summary, I am appealing to those interested in the uses of technology for education to show how video can be most effectively used. The traditional educational film was designed for the classroom or lecture hall for a captive, passive audience. There is still a place for that type of programme to be shown on video to give general information. This will be of a limited quantity and will consist largely of impressions and not hard facts or skills.

Video technology is now here, and can free the teacher and the student from the captivity of the group and class to enable self-paced learning to be managed. Video can carry out instruction in whatever length or form necessary for the learning objective, and can be used over any time period — whether that is in minutes or months.

Whatever images are put on to video, they can be chosen to enable active learning to take place. These images or messages can be programmed with built-in response demand or, less formally, be integrated with exercise/activities specified on print media.

I believe video publishing and production can lead to all kinds of cost-effective programmes being made available to enhance the role of the teacher, who can develop as a skilled and knowledgeable manager of people and resources rather than the sole source of all teaching.

# 3.6 Use of Structural Communication with Film for the Training of Agricultural Skills

P W J Howard
*Agricultural Training Board, Kenilworth*

Abstract: This paper describes how the use of the structural communication discussion method, together with 16mm film, has improved the quality of training in the specific areas of skill, knowledge and attitude change. A 'package' comprising a film, tutor's manual, course member exercises and visual aids has been used to train experienced farmers and herdspersons to interpret the signs of oestrus (heat) in dairy cattle.

## Introduction

The lecture method is commonly used to communicate job knowledge and technical information. It is, however, not a very efficient method, unless other methods are used to ensure understanding. The lack of feedback and interaction between the tutor or instructor and the learners in the lecture method means that methods such as group discussion must also be used.

This article describes how the Agricultural Training Board has developed a training package which uses structural communication techniques with 16mm film to aid communication between a tutor and adult farmers and herdspersons in short training courses. The training content deals with heat (oestrus) detection in dairy cattle; heat detection is done so that artificial insemination (AI) can be carried out at the proper time. Failure to detect heat (oestrus) in dairy cattle costs farmers in the United Kingdom thousands of pounds each year from lost revenue and increased costs.

### The Problems

The following problems existed in the training situation prior to the introduction of the package.

1. It was not possible to demonstrate the signs of heat using actual cows on the farm because the signs occur over a period of 21 days, the average length of the heat (oestrus) cycle for a cow. As a result, instruction about these signs took place verbally in a classroom or similar environment and lacked realism.
2. The method used to communicate the information about heat detection was the lecture method with some visual aids such as slides being used. Little discussion and interaction occurred and the effectiveness of the instruction was less than it should have been.

3. Although cognitive learning was an important goal, the main objective was influencing the attitudes of the farmers and herdspersons. The target population needed to be persuaded that the new procedures being advocated were better than the ones they used on their farms. There is a lot of evidence that discussion and participation are necessary if attitudes are to be changed, and that lecturing has little effect on attitudes (Hill, 1977; McLagan, 1978).

To sum up, there was a need to present the signs of heat more realistically in the off-farm situation, and some means of providing for participation and discussion was essential. Active learning methods would also assist with the learning of the concepts and information about heat detection.

## The Solution

A training package was developed for use in the small group instructional situations found in the short training courses. The tutors, who are full-time veterinary surgeons in the main, typically provide instruction on only a few days each year, so the package and the techniques had to be designed with this in mind.

The components of the training package are: a 16mm film; a tutor's manual; visual aids (overhead projector slides or charts); handouts (two discussion matrices); and a trainee guide.

The film was made for the Agricultural Training Board jointly with Bristol University to show all the main signs of heat in dairy cattle. It was made in five segments, although in practice it is shown in three parts, one per session of instruction.

The package has been used by over 40 tutors throughout the United Kingdom, and the film and structural communication techniques have been experienced by over 1,000 farmers and herdspersons during 1979 and 1980. Sales of the package to overseas countries are also being encouraged.

## Structural Communication

Structural communication is the name given by its originators to the methodology and techniques developed for group and individual instruction in the late 1960s (Bennett *et al*, 1967). The techniques have been further developed and used for supervisory and mangement training (Wilson, 1970), as well as for secondary and tertiary education (Hodgson, 1974; Egan, 1976).

### Guided Dialogue

This is the term used to describe the two-way, reciprocal dialogue that can occur between a tutor and a learner when there is some training or educational intention or goal in mind. This dialogue can be encouraged and made use of in small group instruction using special materials, or it can be simulated in the self-instructional situation by paper or computer media being used.

The intention of this guided dialogue is to ensure understanding of subject matter, and it achieves this if the following cycle of events is made to occur (Hodgson, 1974).

1. A 'directed challenge' is provided usually in the form of problems and questions.
2. A 'responsive environment' is provided by means of the discussion matrix and, in the group situation, by the tutor and other learners.
3. Finally, 'reality testing' takes place in which the tutor (in small group instruction) can probe understanding and clarify misunderstandings.

This cycle of 'challenge-response-reality test' which leads to and results in guided dialogue forms the basis of the group discussion structural communication techniques used in the training package for heat detection in cattle courses.

### The 'Matrix Method'

The 'matrix method' (Wilson, 1970) refers to the way a specially designed and prepared discussion matrix is used by the tutor and the learners to help create the guided dialogue. The use of the discussion matrix and other materials will be described in following sections.

## The Training Package

As described above, the training package consists of materials that provide the tutor and the learners with the means to engage in a form of guided dialogue after a part of the film has been viewed.

### The Instructional Sessions

There are three instructional sessions catered for by the training package; the film is shown in three parts, one part per session, with group work and discussion afterwards. The three sessions were designed as suggested by Hodgson (Hodgson, 1968) and take the following form.

1. *Introduction.* This corresponds to the 'intention' which is the term used by the originators (Egan, 1976). The objectives and importance of the session are outlined, and an 'advance organizer' (Ausubel, 1963) may be used to advantage (Weil and Joyce, 1978).
2. *Presentation.* A part of the film is presented to provide a basis for the subsequent exercise and discussion. Tutorial input may or may not be provided depending on the tutor and the situation.
3. *Exercise.* In this stage the course members use the discussion matrix to answer problems, the directed challenges, by working together in small groups. No direct tutorial input occurs at this stage.
4. *Discussion.* The tutor diagnoses any misunderstandings, using the answers to the problems, and also questions the course members and clarifies any misconceptions. Group discussion about the new ideas and information is also permitted and encouraged.
5. *Conclusion.* This corresponds to the 'viewpoints' stage described by the originators (Egan, 1976). A summary of the key ideas and main points from the preceding presentation and discussion is provided, and an overview is used to ensure that the overall message is grasped clearly.

For reasons that will be discussed shortly, the first instructional session has a combined exercise and discussion. Two techniques were developed to allow the tutor to create the guided dialogue: the dynamic summary technique and the guided discussion technique. These two techniques are outlined below.

### The 'Guided Discussion' Technique

This technique is used in the second session. It is, in most essentials, the same as the discussion unit method of using structural communication described by Egan (1972) whose procedures were adopted when first developing the training sessions and package materials.

This technique creates the conditions required for the guided dialogue in two separate stages: the group exercise stage and the guided discussion stage as we called them. The first stage is learner-oriented with minimal tutor input and intervention during the exercise, whereas the second stage is mainly tutor-directed when the reality testing and discussion takes place.

In the group exercise stage each course member is required to think about and answer two problem questions using items from the discussion matrix. Then, with other course members in small groups of about five in number, each course member discusses his choice of items from the matrix, and agrees a 'consensus' answer for the group as a whole. Items from the matrix are referred to by number once the meaning of each item has been grasped; this means that the matrix items act rather like a form of verbal 'shorthand' making thinking and formulating responses easier.

In the guided discussion stage at the end of the exercise, the tutor first writes each group's answer to each question on a flipchart or a board for all to see and compare with their own answers. Then the tutor quickly diagnoses misunderstandings in the various answers by noting matrix items wrongly included or items omitted that should have been included. A discussion guide assists the tutor in this task which is really quite straightforward and presents no problems for the tutor in practice. The tutor then starts discussion about items that should or should not have been included in the different groups' answers, and clarifies where necessary or provides further explanation. In many instances, the course members of the different groups can be made to clarify misconceptions without much, if any, explanation from the tutor.

This technique is most effective in actively involving the course members in the teaching/learning process. Its use by part-time tutors with the given target population of non-academic farmers and herdspersons was, in over 90 per cent of the courses, most successful and effective. In those instances when it was not successful it is unlikely that any other techniques would have worked either, for example when the course members had been sent on the course by their employers against their wishes. The vast majority of the tutors welcomed being able to use the techniques and thereby involve the course members in meaningful discussion.

## The 'Dynamic Summary' Technique

After a number of tryouts, it became clear that the first session did not require the guided discussion technique — a briefer version was required. The reason for this was that the film communicated effectively, yet the tutors tended to discuss and review the content too fully. This was encouraged, if not caused, by the use of the guided discussion technique when what was really required was a briefer check on understanding.

To overcome this tendency to labour the points already made clearly in the film, while still using the guided dialogue process, the exercise and discussion stages were combined. Course members have to think out their answers to the problem questions but there is no group work or discussion in separate, small groups as in the guided discussion technique. The tutor then uses what we called 'question and answer dialogue' to diagnose misconceptions that course members may have so that they can be clarified. Some group discussion is usually permitted to allow course members to release tension and help to obtain acceptance for the new ideas and recommendations.

This technique is much more tutor-directed than the guided discussion technique, yet the course members are actively involved most of the time in discussion or answering questions. One other important function is also performed by the dynamic summary technique: it introduces the course members to the 'matrix method' which is almost always unfamiliar when first tried. The course members can then do the exercise in the second session with few, if any, problems.

## Evaluation of the Training Package and Sessions

The main source of data for evaluation purposes of the structural communication techniques comes from the answers to the problems, the numbers of the items selected from the discussion matrix, and from the reactions to the film and the techniques.

### Reactions

As mentioned previously, both tutors and course members have, in almost every instance, welcomed the use of the structural communication techniques and found them useful for ensuring understanding and aiding communication.

### Learning

Achievement of the cognitive objectives can be measured during the sessions due to the feedback provided by the answers to the problems and to questions later on. Early on in the tryout stages a short true/false item test was given before and after the three sessions to measure cognitive learning. This was discontinued because it takes time that cannot be spared, and provides less feedback than can be gained from the answers to the problems. What is understood and retained after the sessions is greater than before the introduction of the training package materials and techniques.

### Performance

This relates to the attitudinal objective, that is: are the course members accepting the new ideas and are they motivated to use them on the farm afterwards? No data are available about this question, except from informal interviews of a small percentage of the course members after the courses. We are sure, nevertheless, that acceptance and motivation to action are very much better with the film and structural communication techniques than they were beforehand.

## Conclusions

The use of structural communication with film has been effective in improving communication and increasing interaction between tutor and course members. The two discussion guidance techniques enabled the tutors, almost without exception, to use guided dialogue to improve understanding, gain acceptance for the new ideas, and ensure that the course members leave the course motivated to use the information and adopt the recommended heat detection procedures on the farm.

The Agricultural Training Board is now extending the use of structural communication in courses where information transfer and conceptual understanding are major objectives, or where attitudinal objectives are important. The use of audio-visual media, including a 16mm film about ploughing faults, is continuing to be developed, since this appears to be an effective way of structuring sessions without unduly limiting the tutor.

## References

Ausubel, D P (1963) The Psychology of Meaningful Verbal Learning. Grune and Stratton, New York.
Bennett, J G et al (1967) Structural communication. Systematics 5, 3, December.
Egan, K (1972) How to use structural communication discussion units to improve group discussions. The BC Teacher, November.
Egan, K (1976) Structural Communication. Fearon, Belmont, California.

Hill, W F (1977) *Learning Thru Discussion.* Sage Publications, Beverly Hills, California.
Hodgson, A M (1968) Structural communication — a new automation aid. In Davies, I K and Hartley, J (eds) (1972) *Contributions to an Educational Technology.* Butterworths, London.
Hodgson, A M (1974) Structural communication in practice. In *APLET Yearbook of Educational and Instructional Technology 1974/1975.* Kogan Page, London.
McLagan, P A (1978) *Helping Others Learn.* Addison-Wesley, Reading, Massachusetts.
Weil, M and Weil, J B (1978) *Information Processing Models of Teaching.* Prentice-Hall, Englewood Cliffs, New Jersey.
Wilson, J C (1970) *Structural Communication in Management.* Structural Communication Systems Ltd, Kingston-on-Thames.

# 3.7 Questions About the Uncontrollable Element in Audio-Visual Communication

R N Tucker
*Scottish Council for Educational Technology*

**Abstract:** This paper is intended to raise a number of questions about the function of the visual images that we use in education. Those who originate or select these images know what they want to convey. Many test to discover whether they have been successful in that transfer. This paper raises questions as to whether we have successfully tested whether the learner, in addition to absorbing that which we wished to convey, has also learned something that we cannot easily control, by adding to the presented image, associations founded in personal experience.

## A Media-Based Society

We now live in a society in which we are assaulted by visual media to the extent that it is very difficult to escape from man-made messages and simply view the world around us. Whatever we think of the writing and sayings of the late Marshall Macluhan, he did at least force us to recognize that we receive far more visual information of a constructed kind outside the formal learning environment than in it. The child of today arises listening to the radio, breakfasts with this and the newspapers, travels to school past seemingly endless advertising boards and, having spent a relatively protected day in school, goes home past the same bright stimuli to become the willing recipient of vast arrays of information flooding from the television set. We may debate the quality of what is recieved but we cannot deny the quantity.

Education has in some measure followed the trend of increasing the use of visual carriers of information. Perhaps we are just beginning to catch up with Jan Amos Komensky who, in 1632, advocated: 'let it be given unto the children into their hands to delight themselves with the sight of pictures'. This is not the place to enter into any philosophical debate as to the pedagogical virtues of 'delight', but it is undeniable that there has been for at least 10 years a concerted movement within education to shift the basic carriers of content towards audio-visual resources.

Resource-based learning exists in a strange sort of limbo. On the one hand it is recognized that the use of resources is in keeping with the contemporary world and that it has much educational support as an approach to learning. On the other hand there is still the persistent view that audio-visual learning materials are useful as lecture or learning support but that if one really wants to get at 'facts', at material of real value, then one has to turn to a book (preferably a hardback) or to the teacher in person. There are many reasons why this view should persist and why what are seen as audio-visual *'aids'* can be perceived of as a threat by those teachers who prefer to work in a more traditional role.

The supporters of resource-based learning argue that the increase in the variety of materials and methods is a natural move to cope with the different learning patterns and abilities of the pupils. Some might be so bold as to argue that resource-based learning is better than traditional methods. I have a personal belief that resource-based learning is better, but find it hard to define that 'better'. Helen Coppen, in all her researches, could not show that any one method of learning was more effective than any other within a 5 per cent probability error, as long as the assessment method was related to the method of learning. My belief in the usefulness of visual images in conveying messages is in all probability founded on the way that I personally find it easiest to learn. Like many others I will turn to the figures that we receive about 80 per cent of our sense data through our eyes and only about 11 per cent through our ears. Armed with this I will question the way that many teach, but cannot trace the originator of these oft-quoted figures. I also believe, with the same lack of experimental data, the figures that are quoted in Karch's manual that we can remember about twice as much of what we see than that which we hear and when we both see and hear something we are likely to remember about twice as much again.

Whatever sources we claim for the effectiveness of the power of sight we cannot easily argue that we actually *learn* more by this method. What can be argued is that some things are better conveyed in visual terms. Resource-based learning has, if it has not improved learning, opened up a greater number of possible teaching and learning strategies. The point that should perhaps be questioned is whether it is ever worthwhile to try to prove that visual means are better than any other *in general*. Learning is so dependent upon the individual variable that is the learner that one must raise doubts about any conclusions on comparative methods unless they can show replicated findings with many individuals.

For most teachers, the way that they teach will be a combination of those techniques that they observed during their formation as teachers and their personal predelictions towards the oral, the literal or the pictorial. We as teachers tend to choose the method which best suits our talents and gives us the greatest sense of security. If we are highly motivated we may be fortunate enough to motivate our students and thereby prove to our own satisfaction that the method we have chosen is effective.

Many teachers have proposed the use of pictures in the learning process. Many curriculum packages incorporate visual material. The teams that developed these packages would readily claim that the materials had been validated. But I would like to question the way in which this validation has been carried out — in fact I would like to throw a question towards almost all the experimentation that I have so far read about or seen which seeks to discover whether students have learned effectively from visual sources.

In order to make this point I would like to examine, albeit briefly, the way that we perceive two-dimensional images, how these images are used in the commercial world as opposed to an educational context, and finally how education chooses and manipulates images.

## How We See

Stanley W Hayter quotes experiments conducted at the New School in 1940 and 1941 which demonstrated that all people, when presented with a plane image, scan it left to right (no matter which way they read and write) and that as a result a diagonal line from the bottom left to the top right will appear to be a rising line and that the mirror image — the line from the top left to the bottom right — will appear to be a falling line. Having been discovered, it was obvious that this was a principle on which the breakthrough of Renaissance painting was founded centuries before. One only has to look at a mirror image of many of these paintings to understand the way in which they are structured.

The left to right scan is reflected in the language we use. In most languages the word for right is equated with the good and with justice, whilst the word for left is often taken to mean awkward or clumsy. Which mathematician would draw a graph with the positive values on the left and the negative on the right?

The way we scan a picture within a frame allows the artist in a painting to place the subject or subjects in certain ways which will make the viewer perform a number of complex operations. Relating the size of objects, as represented, to our knowledge of the world we will impose on the flat surface notions of Euclidean space and deduce perspective. We cannot have a world in which lampposts in one street are of progressively smaller size, so we interpret this information as depth and distance.

The extent to which we need to have some knowledge against which to compare our sense data has been argued about extensively (Panofsky, 1939; Gombrich, 1960; Gombrich, 1969). It may be true that we change the way we see the world once we have seen it represented in a different way by an artist. It is not known how people saw the world before the painters began to struggle with painted perspective on a flat surface. What is known now is that we do not need to have first-hand experience of one thing in order to make sense of representation of a similar object. A child who has never seen a skyscraper can make immediate sense of a distorted view of New York through the experience it has had via photographs and television. This relationship between the flat image/experience and perception has been explored in a number of articles in Educational Broadcasting International (1979 and 1980) in the context of creating learning materials for use in Africa. These articles tend to reinforce the view that, though we see in the same way no matter what our cultural background, we have to learn some skills, such as the judging of perspective, when we view a representation.

## The Image Makers

The more we understand of the ways in which we interpret plane images, the more the image makers learn how to *make* us see what they want us to see. The Surrealist painters understood that the marks made by the painter on a flat surface are not what they represent. René Magritte painted an almost photographic representation of an apple and then wrote above it: 'Ceci n'est pas une pomme' to remind the viewer that it was paint, not a real apple. (See the development of this in Doelker, 1979.) Whilst we might accept the distinction between the medium and what is being represented in the case of a painting, we are perhaps less ready to do this in the case of photographs and moving pictures. Yet these are simply chemical marks in which we see configurations of light and shade that we can take for reality.

The painter can establish by position within the frame, the order in which we see the elements of a picture. The same is true of the photographer. The image maker makes for us, the viewer, that image which will convey a particular message — or at least that is what is hoped for. The message may ostensibly be very simple: 'this is a baby on a lawn' or it may be very complex: 'if you use this type of cosmetic this is what is likely to happen to you as a result'.

The makers of film or video can control the meaning of the image even more than the creator of the still image, for they can control the element of time that the viewer has to absorb the data. The dynamic nature of the film image allows even greater control through selective focus and changes of lighting and point of view. The image maker selects from reality carefully judged moments of time and selected views. In this respect film and photography are not reality, but someone else's creation. The image maker must be able to manipulate pictures, just as the writer can manipulate words. We are all familiar with press photographs which have given radically different interpretations of particular events. These are representations of reality which have been passed through the filter of an editorial perspective (see Bachy, 1979; Evans, 1978 for differing views on this subject).

The image maker can alter the apparent meaning of a picture by changing the information that is given to the viewer. An interesting experiment is to take a street scene at random and then provide the viewer with fabricated information about the people. For example, one only has to suggest that one of the people in the frame is a detective in plain clothes and that one of the others is suspected of criminal activity, and immediately the viewer establishes relationships between these people within the frame. Change the information and the dynamics of the frame will change. Sometimes, all that is needed is the change of title to a picture to completely change the viewers' response. More obvious effects can be achieved by changing the music and sounds that go with a motion picture. Hitchcock, the master of suspense, was a genius not only at creating mood through the use of sound but also by giving the audience information that the characters in the film did not have. If we see a bomb being placed under a table at which the unsuspecting hero and heroine then sit, our reactions tend to be predictable: we are held in suspense.

## Images as Signals

No image has any value in itself. It can only be said to exist when it is being perceived, and therefore an essential part of its existence is the viewer. It is the process that the viewer uses in comparing an image with prior experience that largely conditions the meaning which that image will have for that person. The process is complex, but, in essence, two things are happening. The viewer, in making sense of the marks or alterations of light that are presented, is coding the data against internal templates and coming up with the answer: 'that is a so-and-so'. The primary qualities of position and extension in space are combined to give the viewer the *denotation*, but it is only from the viewer's own experience that the *connotation* can be added. Some images call forth connotations that are stereotyped within a particular society. A picture of a baby has a range of stock connotations, but a picture of a knotted sheaf of grass would carry little extra meaning unless one were Japanese and recognized it as a boundary marker. Connotations can, however, be suggested — if they could not then those who make the images, both moving and still, for commercial advertising would not be able to do their job with such penetrating social effect.

## Images in Education

We know that the film maker and the commercial photographer can control the associations that we bring to an image to a very large degree, and it might be thought strange that we should be concerned about this in education. It might be stated that in education we use images to convey facts, not to attack the murky subconscious of the student. But the fact remains that, whether we like it or not, the student looking at the images that we present will bring to them something over which we have no real control. We might equally argue that a picture of a plant or a slice through a liver, a diagram of vectors, or a graph of steel production do not call forth associations and it is true that they are not normally considered in this way. Nevertheless, we ought to be aware that each viewer might well be adding to the learning process something for which we had not calculated.

In the early days of cinema, Eisenstein and Pudovkin demonstrated that the juxtaposition of images creates in the mind of the viewer an association between the images which might not originally have been there. In an experiment which the author conducted at Bristol University, it was shown that a film in which every effort had been made to remove logical connections between sequences still received remarkably consistent responses within certain age bands. We cannot remove all the signals from an image but at the same time we can do little to control the random associations.

If we present a picture of a family, say, within a lesson about society, who is to know that one particular viewer has not already made the link between one of the people and the grandmother who died last year at whose funeral there was a good meal which will not compare to the meal to be had that evening . . . and so on? In seconds, the associations can have led away from the subject in hand. Now this might be simply a wandering of attention but it could equally be a valid part of the learning if an association is clear and strong.

Admittedly, the vast majority of images that we use will be unlikely to give rise to any problems but since it is possible that the irrelevant will be learned with equal force along with the relevant, then we should be on our guard. If we only test for the internalizing of the denotation then we might well be missing a great deal of what is actually being learned. One has, then, to raise questions about some of the research that has been carried out on the effectiveness of learning through various visual media. There is no evidence I have found yet to suggest that any serious account has been taken of this hidden area of learning that takes place, or to what extent this might vary with different methods. If the professional photographers and film makers have learned how to tell controlled 'lies' with their pictures, and persuade the viewers of particular messages of the truth, is it not time that the makers of the educational media, the evaluators of its effectiveness, and the teachers who select and use these images took some notice and began to use the same skills more constructively? Why should the devil have the best pictures?

## References

Bachy, V (1979) A propos de la photo de presse. In van Aelbrouk, A (ed) *Information et Media.* Huitieme Recontre des Chercheurs en Communication Sociale, Brussels.
Doelker, C (1979) *'Wirklichkeit' in der Medien.* Klett and Balmer, Zug.
Evans, H (1978) *Pictures on a Page.* Heinemann, London.
Gombrich, E H (1960) *Art and Illusion.* Phaidon, London.
Gombrich, E H (1969) Visual discovery through art. In Hogg, J (ed) *Psychology and the Visual Arts.* Penguin, Harmondsworth.
Panofsky, E (1939) *Studies in Iconology.* Oxford University Press, Oxford.

# 3.8 The Role of the Educational Technologist in the In-Service Training of Teachers in the New Micro-Electronics-Based Techologies

C Neville and R F Windsor
*Council for Educational Technology, London*

**Abstract:** As part of the national micro-electronics education programme (MEP), CET has been monitoring and managing a group of training activities, some for teachers, some for advisory teachers and some for advisers, to explore the training implications of introducing the new, micro-electronic-based technologies into schools and colleges. The courses mounted have variously dealt with aspects of teaching method, curriculum content, learning and resource management, and support services, as affected by the introduction of microprocessor-based techniques.

The paper attempts to identify the wide range of training courses being run within the MEP and the overall strategy, as well as the differences between the training needs for the new, and for the older, audio-visual technologies, drawing on the evidence of the many courses overseen by CET. Strategies for meeting these needs are proposed.

## Introduction

The current demand for the in-service training of teachers in various aspects of the newer micro-electronics-based technologies, notably the use of microcomputers, appears to stem from three widely held assumptions. These may be stated briefly as:

1. The new technologies will change the structure of society, particularly the patterns of work and leisure, access to information and the means of interpersonal communication.
2. The industrial survival of developed countries depends on the rapid acceptance of the new technologies and their introduction into industrial and commercial practice.
3. The school system has a major role to play in preparing the next generation to live within, accept and contribute to the radically changed society which will emerge.

All three assumptions can be questioned, but since they underlie the current demand for in-service courses of the kind which will be discussed in this paper, and the political promotion of a national micro-electronics education programme (MEP) within which many such courses are being, and will be, operated, no attempt will be made to refute them in this paper. The paper will instead attempt to identify the relationship of the educational technologist to the kinds of INSET courses running and proposed, and his role in INSET in this area generally. In so doing, the authors can only draw on experience gained from the courses and projects with which they are directly involved through the Council for Educational Technology (CET) and the MEP. However, they are of the impression that these activities are typical of many being organized throughout the country by local education authorities and other INSET providers.

## Examples of Courses and a Discussion of Issues

One course, a course for advisers, was a project proposed and now run by CET and was accepted by the Department of Education and Science (DES) as one of the 31 projects that it approved for funding during 1980/81 before a director of MEP was appointed. In a completely separate role, CET has acted as an agent of the DES in drawing up the contracts on the other projects. Whilst CET was not involved in selecting these projects or the terms of contract, it has enabled CET to gain a wider perspective of the work going on within MEP. The programme will spend £9,000,000 over four years on the development of micro-electronics in schools and colleges for England, Wales and Northern Ireland. This programme of work is quite separate from the Scottish Microelectronics Development Programme, on which £1.3 million is being spent over a similar period of time.

It is first necessary to distinguish between two broad categories of course: those aimed primarily at curriculum development and those concerned primarily with teaching methodology. Broadly speaking, the first group aims to improve teachers' ability to teach *about* the new technologies, while the second group is concerned to encourage teachers to teach (any subject) more effectively *with* the new technologies. Of the courses with which the authors are involved, 20 per cent might fall into the first group, 50 per cent into the second, and 30 per cent contain substantial elements of both groups.

Now it might be argued that if the aim of INSET is to help teachers to prepare pupils for the new society, then the direct approach of teaching about the influential technologies should be the more effective. Thus, courses should be mounted to help teachers teach micro-electronics (within physics courses), computer science and control technology to potential specialists, and computer literacy to the generality of pupils.

These may need to be preceded by efforts to persuade those who effectively control the overall curriculum content of the importance of such studies.

However, in a decentralized educational system it is difficult to introduce quickly major curriculum changes, and in such circumstances it is tempting to resort to an indirect approach. This is based on the assumption that learning anything through the new technologies will achieve the same longer term effect of fitting pupils to cope with the new technologies in society. This strategy throws emphasis on the training of all teachers to make effective use of the new technologies while teaching to the 'old' curriculum. This is the strategy being adopted in a majority of MEP courses.

There is little evidence to show that 'learning through' is an effective substitute for 'learning about' the new technologies. For example, work by the Minnesota Education Computing Consortium, using the Minnesota Computer Literacy and Awareness Assessment, indicates that computer literacy improves less for groups whose only experience in school with computers is as an aid to learning in other subject courses, than for those who receive some form of direct teaching about computers and computing. In fact, there are indications that 'learning through' computers can develop antipathetic attitudes to computers, which courses in computer science or computer studies do not.

It may be, therefore, that the currently adopted strategy of encouraging INSET in methodology rather than curriculum development is unsuited to achieving longer term aims of preparing pupils for a changing society. The proper role of the educational technologist in these circumstances should be to establish whether this is so, and, if so, design alternative strategies to achieve the aims. The fact that the changes in society, and so the impetus for curriculum change, happen to be linked with a piece of technology, gives the educational technologist no more (and no less) right than others to try to prescribe the curriculum change.

Yet, as will be seen from the courses to be described, a majority are concerned with methodology and are aimed at the generality of teachers, not specialists or policy makers. At a time when, except in this one area, opportunities for INSET are diminishing, surely educational technologists, to whom methodology is of central professional concern, cannot afford to dissociate themselves because the reasoning leading to the courses may be suspect?

The greater danger would appear to be that of becoming associated with courses devoted to the promotion of a single, hardware-oriented, method, particularly microcomputer-based techniques. A number of courses being run currently show alarming parallels with those in the early 1960s on programmed learning. Those courses were not, however, subject to the kind or degree of political and popular pressures which exist today.

The similarities and differences with programmed learning are indicative of the kinds of problem which are arising in obtaining effective use of microcomputers in schools. First, it must be said that the microcomputer is a vastly more versatile piece of hardware than the teaching machine. As well as being used for computer-assisted learning (CAL), it can be used in school management, it can provide certain teacher support services such as record keeping, it can contribute to the management of complex learning programmes, and it can be used as a teacher classroom aid (for example, as a responsive display device for running simulations and for demonstrating computing and control applications). It can also be a learner's tool, providing calculating power, practice in programming and access to special techniques such as word processing. Simply because of this enormous versatility, microcomputer hardware is potentially more cost-effective than teaching machines could ever have been.

However, in common with the teaching machine, the microcomputer is useless without its software, and what it achieves is only as good as the quality of the software allows. As with programmed learning the key question will be: 'Who can, and who should, produce software quickly which is of the quality, content and acceptability to ensure its use by teachers?' The answers implicit in the content and recruitment of the courses and activities with which the authors are associated range from 'the individual classroom teacher' to 'the national curriculum development body', with various compromises in between. The parallel question for educational technologists is: 'To what extent should we be involved in teaching programming, and to whom?'

A second parallel with programmed learning concerns the perceived role of the new technologies in the classroom. Both the computer, used for computer-assisted management of learning (CAMOL) and CAL, and, say, PRESTEL or other means of searching information banks, can be seen as threatening to take over two roles central to many teachers' sense of identity; manager of learning and controller of information. To counteract reactions of this kind to any medium or technique, past experience suggests starting from a problem recognizable to the teacher and only proffering the medium or technique when it genuinely presents a practicable and acceptable solution. Many of the current courses smack of the 'solution in search of a problem' approach. There is one notable exception to this: in education for the severely handicapped. Teachers here have immediately seen the potential of the microcomputer which, with specially designed learner-computer interfaces, can enable the severely disabled child to communicate, and interact with information, with a flexibility and control not previously available. Problem-based courses in this area are leading already to very exciting developments in special schools.

However, in general, the government plans that there will be a microcomputer in every school before most schools have had an opportunity to frame an answer to the question 'what for?'. There is a clear role here for educational technologists in helping teachers to decide 'what for?'.

This role is reflected in the CET-managed and MEP-sponsored courses for LEA advisers. These six-week full-time courses are designed to provide the advisers with sufficient background knowledge to make reasoned decisions about the introduction of the new technologies to schools. As a result, the advice given to individual schools, and, in some cases, even the LEA's policy of installation of equipment, is showing a shift of emphasis, generally away from CAL and towards control applications and computer studies.

The other MEP courses sponsored so far demonstrate the current indecision on who needs to be trained to obtain the maximum impetus for change and with whom should the considerable technical expertise (programming, control applications, design) associated with the new technologies lie — with the generality of teachers, with specialist teachers, with advisers, or with support staff?

The West Midlands scheme for micro-electronics education (MACE) is the biggest and most expensive project taking place in 1980/81. Fifteen teachers from 11 LEAs have been seconded to the University of Birmingham for a one-year full-time course. Its aim is to produce teachers who, in their own and neighbouring schools, are able to promote both 'teaching with' and 'teaching about' micro-electronics. It is intended that on their return to their posts they will be released for 50 per cent of the time for this purpose. Within the project there was provision for Awareness Sessions for the headteachers of the 11 authorities, as well as meetings for representatives of the advisers from the authorities to prepare a receptive medium for the return of the secondees. While the cost of the exercise and the strategy of giving a small number of teachers an advanced course might be questionable in the short term, the associated longer term production of training materials could be very cost-effective for MEP as a whole. The materials developed for the course at the University are copyright of MEP and are being fed into a word processor to enable widespread distribution to take place.

The College of St Mark and St John in Plymouth has attempted to train six teachers, who are already competent programmers, as advanced program designers within an educational environment. These courses will build upon the considerable experience and expertise that the College has gained from the ITMA project, which is concerned with the effective integration of microcomputers into classroom teaching. Again, the intention is for each teacher to spend at least 20 per cent of his or her time on return to post in development work. St Mark and St John are also running a course for three Teacher Consultants who will already have been involved in school computing activities. This group will be trained in a promotional role as disseminators or consultants or in-school course organizers. A third aspect of this project is the awareness courses for headteachers in the authorities close to the College. The scheme outlined above therefore attempts to cover both teaching with, and about, micro-electronics but by a quite different strategy from the MACE course. If the strategy used by the college is intended to dovetail, so that programmers, consultants and heads all act as change agents, then the co-ordination of the three aspects will be most important. A valuable aspect of this course could be making the programmers aware of the consultants' problems when back in the classroom. This would enable the programmers to produce software that is possible to teach with a particular program.

Programming courses for teachers as an introduction to microcomputers do seem to be useful as awareness raisers, but pose other questions such as:

- ☐ How far can you teach teachers about microcomputers by such methods?
- ☐ With the technology advancing so rapidly, how quickly will programming skills, as we know them, become redundant?
- ☐ Is it not possible to undertake training in programming skills at a distance? For example, the National Extension College (NEC) is producing a course on programming in BASIC — a 30-hour course for correspondence, flexistudy or individual study.

Nevertheless, Thames Polytechnic is running courses for teachers from ILEA, and five London boroughs, on programming skills. These teachers, during their term's course, undertake fairly ambitious software development projects. Yet the intention is that, on their return, for 20 per cent of the time they will develop the awareness of teachers in their school on both the problems of teaching with, and teaching about, micro-electronics and then advise on designing the programs that those teachers wish to develop. The work of programming will be carried out, not only by these teachers but, by full-time programmers in the employ of the authorities. ILEA already have them available. The trained teachers will be concerned with the design and structure of the program, not the programming. If and when programming skills become less important with the advent of such packages as 'The Last One' or new hardware attachments, the skills of design will still remain important.

## Conclusion

A survey of the activities and courses sponsored by the MEP during its first year, including others not described in this paper, indicates, therefore, that as yet there is no clear agreement among trainers as to who will need training in the new skills associated with the new technologies, and to what level. Nor are there yet positive indications as to whether 'learning through' or 'learning about' the new technologies will be the more successful strategy for preparing pupils.

As MEP moves into its second, more co-ordinated, phase under its appointed director, funding will be largely diverted from direct training, which will become the responsibility of LEAs. They, presumably, will exhibit the same degree of indecision on these matters by the variety of courses they will mount. The educational technologists associated with these courses will, therefore, have a number of roles to play.

In the area of curriculum development and course design for teaching about the new technologies the educational technologist's role will be no different from that in other curriculum areas, namely that of the 'content free' member of the curriculum development team. He may find himself, perhaps unwillingly, advising on the choice of hardware to support the courses, not as a teaching aid but as the subject of study. This should properly be the subject specialist's decision. The educational technologist can help the designers of in-service training to define the long-term aims of INSET, and to prepare training strategies likely to achieve them.

Through research and evaluation he can give guidance on the proper target audience for training, identifying the key agents for change and the respective levels and kinds of competence each will need.

Lastly, the educational technologist himself will be offering training in new areas of methodology. His success in this, his major contribution to the introduction of the new technologies into education, is likely to depend on the speed with which he can design a problem-solving form of training which integrates the new technologies with the old.


*Workshop Report*

## 3.9 Computer-Based Learning: What Will We Teach the Teachers?

N J Rushby
*CEDAR Project, Imperial College, London*

### Organizer's Account

The introduction of computer-based learning (CBL) has traditionally been seen as a chicken and egg problem: there was no need for large-scale staff development, because the computing equipment was not widely available, but the expensive equipment could not be provided until teachers were trained to use it. Now, as microcomputers have become more widely available in educational institutions, the possibilities for using them in teaching grow and the focus of the problem has changed.

It must be stressed that computer-based learning and micro-electronics are not synonymous, although they are often confused by many people. There are already a number of computer and micro-electronics appreciation courses which deal with the way in which computers work, how they process information, how they are programmed, and their impact on society. These are primarily concerned with teaching *about*, rather than teaching *with the aid of* the computer, and are not designed to help teachers to make informed decisions about whether, and how, to use computer-based learning (CBL) in the classroom.

Publishers have already started to market CBL materials to schools and to higher education (and to domestic consumers too). It is essential that teachers are adequately equipped to make their own decisions about the worth of these materials, to adapt them to meet their own needs, and to develop new materials for their own use. Good CBL materials can make a valuable contribution to their students' learning — but only if the teachers know how to use them appropriately.

There is a need for courses at two levels. At the first level there is a general need which could be described as computer literacy. At the second level there is a need for a course which can build on this basic level of computing, to provide teachers with an appreciation of computer-based learning as a medium for teaching and learning, and to introduce them to the basic skills needed to use the medium effectively.

To meet this need, a consortium of institutions comprising the CEDAR Project at Imperial College London, the London University Teaching Methods Unit, the new University of Ulster Education Centre, Bradford College, and the Learning Systems Group at Middlesex Polytechnic, has embarked on a project to develop and pilot a course on 'The Use of Computer-Based Learning' (Rushby et al, 1981). Its aim will be to consider the impact of computer-based learning on teaching methods and on curriculum, rather than to concentrate on the computer as an object of study.

An important feature of the course will be to get teachers to think about the ways in which they could use this new medium in their own subject areas. In the case of staff working in teacher education or in training development, this should provide an effective strategy for introducing their own students and other colleagues to computer-based learning.

The proposed course is to be highly flexible so that it can be used effectively in a variety of different ways. It is envisaged that it will consist of a structured set of materials, covering about 30-35 hours of study, that can be used either as a complete package or piecemeal by an experienced course leader, and for both local and distance learning. The study may be in a wide variety of forms, for example compressed into a two- or three-day intensive workshop, or spread out over several months. Although there are obvious problems in designing materials which can be used successfully in such a variety of environments, we believe that sufficient flexibility can be provided by a modular set of resources that can be selected from, and combined in, different ways to meet different needs.

The central feature of the course will be a number of case studies built round CBL packages to illustrate why and how CBL can be used in support of learning in different subject areas. These will provide worked examples of the impact of CBL on curriculum and method, enable the participants to gain a 'feel' for the use of the medium, and provide examples to try with their own students. Since it is vital that the case studies should be seen to be relevant, they must cover a range of subjects and levels of teaching. To ensure ease of use in a wide range of institutions, the computer-based materials will be written in a subset of BASIC and will be available for all common microcomputer systems.

The project will also study the feasibility of using computer-managed learning (CML) to support distant and independent study of the course materials, and the materials will be designed so as to facilitate their later use in this way.

During the development and trial phases, the project team is studying the problems posed by implementing these materials in different environments and for different audiences. While the development, which is to be carried out in diverse settings, can be expected to produce a series of course guides recommending different ways of adapting the course, it is probable that the exercise will need to continue beyond the two-year timescale of this project, to extend the versatility and area of implementation of the modules.

The main part of the workshop was concerned with the content of such a course and was an accelerated rehearsal of the design process undertaken by the course team during the first phase of the project. Starting with a long list of possible topics which had been produced by the course team, the workshop participants were asked to decide which of these *must* be included in the course, which *should* be, and which *might* be included if time and circumstances permitted. They were encouraged to think of additional topics, to rephrase topics, and to eliminate some of those on the given list. A snowballing technique was used to bring the individual participants together.

From the start, it was clear that the relatively unstructured nature of the task and the plethora of possible topics was bewildering. This paralleled the experience of the course team. However, during the debriefing, three competing aspects emerged. The course had to strike a balance between the computing aspects, the educational theory and hands-on experience of CBL. In each case it was necessary to decide whether the student needed an awareness, a familiarity, or mastery of the subject. Different participants struck the balance in different places, but were generally in agreement with the course team that the computing aspects were less important than the student learning aspects, and that practical experience was essential.

Some doubt was expressed as to whether sufficient flexibility could be built in to cater for the wide range of intended audiences who would start the course with very different knowledge and skills.

One dissenting note was struck by a group concerned with teacher education who felt that the aim of 30 to 35 hours of study was unrealistic and outlined a four-hour course with a strong practical content.

The session closed with a brief discussion of some of the design decisions taken by the course team, and an outline of the course that is now under development.

## References

Rushby, N J, Anderson, J S A, Howe, A, Marrow, F and Warren Piper, D (1981) *A Recursive Approach to Teacher Training in the Use of CBL.* IFIP Elsevier (in press).

# 3.10 Computer-Assisted Training in Practice

**D Wright**
*Mills and Allen Communications Ltd, London*

**Abstract:** The National Development Programme in Computer Assisted Learning (NDPCAL), which ran from 1972-1977, was predominantly concerned with the application of computer-based techniques to learning in the education sector. In 1978, the Manpower Services Commission began funding a three-year development programme to explore the current use and potential of such techniques in industrial and commercial training. This paper discusses aspects of the programme's activities.

## Background

Over the last decade we have witnessed in the UK significant (though some would argue still inadequate) developments in education about computers and the use of computers as an aid in the process of education. Recently, the government has launched the £9 million Microelectronics in Schools Programme to promote each of these aspects (Scotland has its own corresponding programme). Prior to this, the five-year National Development Programme in Computer Assisted Learning (NDPCAL) had spent £2.5 million supporting a wide range of projects and feasibility studies specifically concerned with the use of the computer as a medium for instruction and as a manager of the learning environment.

The industrial and commercial training world has not, however, been significantly affected by these substantial investments. Apart from a number of applications in the Armed Services, only three of the NDPCAL development projects were concerned directly with vocational training applications. Roger Miles, NDPCAL's Assistant Director, concluded in a future study report that:

> ... CAL (computer-assisted learning) is as yet a minor activity and low priority in industrial training circles. Unless there is a dramatic change in the present situation, the 1980s will find industrial training lagging far behind education and military training in computer applications ... there are good grounds for believing that computers could and should play a more important part in industrial training in the future.

Taking note of such views, the Training Services Division of the Manpower Services Commission (MSC) initiated a further three-year development programme in computer-assisted training (on a somewhat more modest scale, costing £100,000). Late in 1978, Mills and Allen Communications were contracted to investigate the use of computer-assisted training (CAT) in the UK and to support, with the programme resources, a limited number of pilot CAT developments. A major part of the programme was to disseminate to the training world the knowledge and experience gained, in order to highlight the possibilities of CAT and the ways in which it might be carried forward.

## Progress in CAT

First I will briefly mention how we found the state of CAT after the MSC programme began. From a widespread survey questionnaire which received a good response we discovered that very little was happening. Only six organizations responded that they were using CAT techniques on an institutional basis. Another 30 or so were actively experimenting or looking at CAT.

The six major users of CAT were all large, computer-orientated companies (such as financial institutions), typically using mainframe machines for teaching computer-related topics. The reasons for this picture were not difficult to analyze:

- ☐ The organizations had large numbers of dispersed trainees making decentralized and individualized training very attractive.
- ☐ Existing in-house computers had spare capacity.
- ☐ Software systems for the development and delivery of training material were available for their computers.
- ☐ There was a general familiarity with computer equipment within the organizations.

Undoubtedly there were many other organizations to whom this description could be applied, but who were not using CAT. Such companies must be considered the most likely sites for new applications of CAT. However, a number of developments over the last few years have meant that CAT can, or must, now be considered by a wider range of organizations. There has been a significant increase in:

- ☐ The availability of low-cost computer hardware.
- ☐ General familiarity and use of computer equipment (particularly microcomputers).
- ☐ Pressures for training/retraining.
- ☐ Organizations offering CAT systems and services.
- ☐ Publicity and information on CAT (through such programmes as those run by the MSC, the National Computing Centre and CEDAR).

Nevertheless, the high development costs of CAT, and the fact that the development systems available are still predominantly large machine systems, have tended to constrain the progress of CAT.

## Some Current Developments (Five Case Studies)

A number of trends in CAT are illustrated by the current developments described below, starting with three microcomputer applications.

### Fault-Finding Training

Inefficient fault-finding can cost an organization large sums of money each year, yet there are few feasible ways of setting up and monitoring fault-finding situations to assess a particular technician's abilities. As one of the pilot developments within the MSC/CAT development programme, and with the help of the Chemical and Allied Products Industry Training Board, Mills and Allen have developed a training package to develop and test the fault-finding skills required.

The training package instructs on the logic of fault-finding and sets up simulations of fault situations which the trainee must work through. The program analyses the fault-finding approach adopted and gives the trainee immediate feedback on performance. The programs were written in BASIC for a Commodore PET microcomputer to provide maximum accessibility to the material and flexibility of use.

### Simulating a Production Line

Ford's at Dagenham are using a PET to simulate the operation of sections of the car production line. It is essential for efficient operations that buffer stocks are maintained at the correct levels so that, in the event of a failure in one part of the production line, the rest can carry on working normally.

With considerable enthusiasm, trainee foremen have been using the material competitively in small groups, attempting to maximize production on the simulated production line under circumstances of varying difficulty.

### Critical Incident Training

Another development within the MSC programme is yet again a training package based on the use of a computer simulation. In this development (which is not yet completed) Wessex Regional Health Authority personnel will be trained in dealing with 'critical incidents' (eg major rail disasters). A number of disaster 'models' have been constructed which will test the decision-making skills of the personnel who make up the incident control teams.

This application of CAT will involve training, training which at the moment is inadequate. A microcomputer solution has again been chosen to enable the training package with hardware to be transported from hospital-to-hospital.

### Office Practice Training

Moving on to a more ambitious development at Speedwriting Speedtyping Ltd, a London-based secretarial college, a minicomputer system with 14 terminals has been installed in a classroom set-up to provide basic training in office skills.

With support from the MSC development programme, Speedwriting commissioned the production of an authoring system which would allow their own tutors to develop training material without the need of complex programming skills.

The first CAT material to be produced was a series of lessons in keyboard skills. In these lessons, each student is presented with appropriately graded exercises which appear on a terminal screen. The student's typed attempts are automatically analyzed for speed and/or accuracy, an immediate feedback on performance is given, and further exercises are set as appropriate.

This use of CAT to provide self-paced learning has significantly reduced the training time required. At the same time, through a comprehensive computer-management system, the tutors are provided automatically with detailed student and course records.

## Sales Training

Lastly, turning to mainframe applications of CAT, it should not be ignored that this provides the easiest and most effective use of CAT for many companies. Organizations such as Barclaycard and British Airways, who have been using CAT on their own large IBM computers for some years, are continuing to develop and use new training material successfully.

One organization to adopt a slightly different approach is Smith Kline and French, a pharmaceuticals company, who are using Control Data's PLATO bureau service to provide training for their sales force. The excellent graphics facilities of PLATO allowed Smith Kline and French to develop training material in human physiology and the effects of drugs. Although the development and PLATO terminal costs have been very high, the training has proved extremely effective with significant savings in course duration.

## Trends and Persisting Problems

We can see, partly from the case studies described, the directions in which CAT is moving — albeit rather more slowly than some of us would like. There is a generally increasing commitment to CAT which tends to be moving away from the 'traditional' approach of using a time-sharing mainframe system. Many training departments are 'experimenting' with microcomputers, and some are committing themselves to larger systems dedicated to training use.

The number of organizations offering CAT bureau services is expanding and this will provide an easy, though sometimes expensive, entry for many companies. However, although this reduces or removes the need to purchase dedicated CAT hardware, it is unlikely to provide an acceptable long-term solution for those organizations developing any sizeable commitment to CAT.

Despite this increased availability of low-cost computer hardware and powerful CAT authoring systems, problems in the way of CAT progress persist. Perhaps most significantly there are still very few software aids for those wishing to develop CAT for delivery on microcomputers. In addition, there is a general lack of expertise in developing good CAT courses, resulting in rather a lot of poor material being produced. Unfortunately, there is no indication that any organizations are willing to invest the considerable sums of money required to produce high quality CAT courses which could be made commercially available.

The cost of CAT course development continues to be a significant issue. The debate over the last few years has concentrated on arguments concerning the CAT development ratio — the number of development hours required to produce one hour of training. A ratio of 100 to 1 is an often quoted 'average', but proponents of CAT authoring systems claim to be able to reduce this figure considerably. Such arguments are usually unproductive since the variability in complexity of CAT material which can be developed is immense. To produce simple textual material can be extremely easy, especially when using an authoring system. However, to produce sophisticated CAT material using, say, simulation techniques and complex graphical presentation, can be far in excess of 100 to 1, even when using a powerful authoring system.

I believe that most such arguments are conducted on the wrong basis, with the defendants of CAT attempting to reduce the development costs to something comparable with the production of printed material. In trying to achieve this in practice, trivial and ineffective CAT material often results. In fact, CAT offers training methods which, in many cases, are significantly more powerful than the printed page. Comparison of CAT development costs with those of video-tape production would be far more appropriate!

## 3.11 A Trial Course in Basic Programming and Mathematics Using CAL for a Group of Maladjusted Boys

M J Cox
*University of Surrey*

**Abstract:** This paper describes the activities of two groups of 14-year-old boys taking part in an introductory CAL course initially aimed at teaching the group BASIC programming.

### Development of the Course

The first group of nine boys from a CSE class visited the CAL laboratory in the Institute for Educational Technology at the University of Surrey once a week for a term. The second group of eight boys used CAL packages in their maths class at school on two microcomputers. Because of the serious social problems which these boys suffered, their knowledge of mathematics was very severely limited. This lack of a good grounding in mathematics resulted in a very slow progress of the boys' learning BASIC.

After four weeks of concentrating on the BASIC programming language with the first group, using a series of Teach Yourself BASIC programs, the students were able to write simple programs themselves, but were limited in their choices by their lack of mathematical knowledge.

It was decided to use the second half of the term to teach some simple mathematics to the students, using CAL packages, instead of attempting to teach more advanced programming techniques.

Throughout the first course, the students were assisted by their own maths teacher and by three of the CAL staff at the University. It was impossible at that stage to assess the educational and social contributions to the course from the use of computer-assisted learning and from the large amount of individual help given by the staff present. However, their mathematics teacher considered the benefits of CAL to be 'enormous'.

> In just a few weeks the boys have actually increased their knowledge and understanding of many mathematical concepts. Their imagination has been extended and they are slowly developing a more questioning approach to (at the present time) the mathematical world around them.

### Effects of the Course

Although this CAL course was the first one experienced by these students, and it would be premature to draw many conclusions from it, the changes observed in the students during the course strongly indicate that CAL had a beneficial educational effect on the group. One of the problems associated with severely maladjusted students is their difficulty in communicating with their teachers and colleagues. This was apparent when the students were required to work in pairs at the terminal and with the staff supervising in the laboratory. The interactive nature of the terminals helped to overcome this communication problem and gave pleasure to the students, keeping their interest throughout the course. Each session finished late because of the reluctance of the students to leave the terminals even after one-and-a-half hours of use. It was obvious that these students could relate with less fear and apprehension to the terminal than they could to some of their colleagues. It is possible that this 'friendly' aspect of CAL may have important implications for teaching students with special problems.

We also observed the change in the students' ability to work in pairs and the captivating effect of the computer during the course. By the end of the course they were willing to discuss the work to some extent with their partners, and this had not been possible at the beginning.

## Conclusion

The eagerness of these students to continue with CAL work suggests that CAL could play an important part in the education of children who, until now, have shown little enthusiasm for school work.

*Workshop Report*
## 3.12 Mentor – An Unstructured Mechanism for Lesson Development, Delivery and Management

T Stirk
*PMSL Computer Services, Halifax*

### Organizer's Account

A soft CAL system has the advantage of tailoring the mechanism for lesson development and delivery to the needs of the organization or instructor within the constraints of a given course programme. It is neither necessary nor desirable for teachers to become programmers, nor for programmers to become teachers, and by presenting a friendly trainer-computer interface, together with a flexible structural mechanism for development, this need not be a problem.

The aim of the workshop was to show that 'bespoke' courseware is not difficult to achieve using MENTOR and that instructors could create non-linear CAL material within hours.

The specific objectives of the workshop were:

1. To use existing MENTOR quasi-courseware to demonstrate some of the facilities and techniques available at delivery stage, with special emphasis on analyzing student responses.
2. To discuss briefly the CML facilities available under MENTOR, including management information and control sub-systems.
3. To give participants the opportunity to create and subsequently edit courseware, using both conversational and author modules.

(The equipment used was an emulating Univac U100 VDU on-line to the MENTOR mainframe in Halifax.)

After a brief introduction which outlined the format of the workshop, the participants were told how MENTOR grew out of the in-house training requirements of our parent group (Provident Financial Group), especially in distance learning.

It was also stated how MENTOR is attempting to reverse the time ratio development: student $\approx 18:1$, and has actually achieved this at a certain college which is using a specially designed music terminal. However, at present, this seems only to be possible in drill and practice learning situations, by designing a structure which enables variable input in non-programming language by an instructor.

An example of a form-filling exercise was demonstrated and this included many of the control facilities available under MENTOR (ie full screen control, protected fields, partial erasure, and cursor positioning).

Some time was devoted to analyzing student alpha responses. We looked in detail at exact, word (strings of characters bounded by spaces), string, string n (n out of a string of m > n characters), string order and phonetic matches.

(It was not considered appropriate at this time to give details of other alpha matches available, nor the various numeric, nor cursor matches.) Participants seemed to be particularly interested in the phonetic match and associated algorithm.

During the remaining time, workshop members were given the option of either discussing with MENTOR staff any queries or points needing further classification, or forming small working groups with the aim of devising short units of interactive CAL, using both conversational and author modules.

The organizers feel that the objectives were achieved, but that there are problems in expecting participants to think of lesson material at short notice.

# 3.13 'Graph-It' – A Package for Teaching Graphical Skills

W P Race
*The Polytechnic of Wales*
R Vaughan-Williams
*South Glamorgan Institute of Higher Education*

**Abstract:** The authors recognized that many students throughout the disciplines of science and engineering show undue difficulty in their graphical handling and interpretation of experimental data. The need exists for rapid yet thorough training of students in graphical techniques, and this applies to students on courses ranging from honours degree level to technician levels. Since there is rarely much tuition time available to provide such instruction, it was recognized that there was a need for materials to enable the required tuition to approach the self-instructional mode, while still providing the student detailed feedback about his performance.

The paper describes the conception, design, trials and adjustment of a short series of objective-based completion-type units, intended to advance the average student to a quite sophisticated understanding of graphical methods in about four hours of work, while allowing those students who were already either advanced or retarded in the skills and understanding involved to assimilate the material at their own pace. The authors paid particular attention to eliciting feedback from the students during initial trials of the materials with students in three sectors of higher education. Modifications made to the materials as a result of the trials and feedback are described.

It is believed that the general approach adopted in this work may have relevance in many other subject areas, where it is necessary to advance students' skills and comprehension in peripheral areas, without the availability of timetable hours to match those that would be needed if appropriate conventional tuition were to be provided.

## Introduction

Many courses in higher education require students to be able to handle data graphically. Such courses include all the science and engineering disciplines. Increasingly, however, the need to be able to interpret visually-displayed data extends over a broader spectrum of curricula. Students entering higher education show a wide range of ability regarding graphical skills, ranging from the highly competent and well-practised to the virtually inexperienced. The difficulty in catering for such diverse background levels has been described (Zepp and Selwyn, 1980), and the suitability of workbooks providing individualized learning has been recognized. As long ago as 1968, it was proposed in a survey of sixth-form mathematics teaching that:

> the multiplicity of syllabuses, the differing depths of study in various topics, the conflicting methods of teaching certain basic concepts, the compulsion of examination syllabuses as a whole on schools to do too much too quickly over too wide a field . . . produces chaos in institutions of higher education. (James, 1969).

Recently, among the aspects of mathematics singled out requiring special attention, was 'graphical skills including those of accurate drawing of data and function graphs, and sketching function and relation graphs' (Knowles, 1980).

There is seldom time to mount tuition specifically to enhance students' graphical skills in higher education, particularly when for some students such tuition would be unnecessary. This results in those students lacking the required skills spending inordinate amounts of time and energy when they encounter graphical difficulties; they may develop such a lack of confidence that they avoid all graphical questions in examinations. The difficulties of such students are further compounded in science and engineering laboratory classes, where graphical handling of experimental data is frequently required.

At its most severe, a student's difficulties with graphs can cause him to be so preoccupied with his problems that he misses much of the real significance of the data being analyzed, or even becomes disillusioned with his choice of discipline. Even for the average student, considerable difficulties may arise when meeting logarithmic graphs, and logarithmic graph paper, for the first time.

The authors, through contact with students across a broad spectrum of higher education, recognized the need for suitable self-instructional materials to be available to help students acquire the required skills and understanding. The present paper is an account of the development, testing and modification of a pilot scheme, using students from three sectors of higher education: a university, a polytechnic, and a technical college.

There are already in existence many good mathematics texts including sections about graphs (Nelkon, 1978; Buckwell and Ball, 1978; Tabberer, 1978; Leaver and Thomas, 1974; Macpherson and Jones, 1974; Schofield, 1975; Davies and Hicks, 1975). An extended and very interesting treatment is included in the Open University preparatory mathematics material for students about to start the Science Foundation Course. Here, the material is largely self-instructional, with extensive practice exercises and with the addition of a computer-marked assignment from which the student gains a measure of feedback about the strengths and weaknesses of his graphical skills. However, such feedback is not necessarily comparable to direct tutor-comment about the actual drawing of graphs, and, furthermore, the time delay in the provision of the feedback means that the student will be immersed in a different branch of the subject when the feedback arrives. He is then unlikely to give serious reconsideration to the areas of weakness diagnosed if the general standard of the answers was deemed satisfactory. In addition, the Open University material does not go as far as logarithmic graphs, but concentrates on establishing a thorough understanding of the more basic aspects.

Even when suitable material exists to which students having difficulties could be referred, students are already under so much pressure within their main disciplines that the luxury of spending time reading peripheral material can rarely be afforded. The students who are already low in motivation (and may well need the help most) are very unlikely to use published material in their own time. In any case, the required skills are developed much faster by direct experience than by reading about them.

Therefore, the required materials need to be capable of being used by the student on his own, but with the incentive of the provision of feedback to him about his strengths and weaknesses. If the graphical work is to be submitted for marking, the student will complete the tasks required, rather than give way to the temptation to stop when he *sees how* to complete them. The capable student can proceed through the material at a rapid pace, while the inexperienced student can spend as long as necessary studying and practising the elements new to him, and find how successful his work is.

## Content of the Course

Most students have already had experience of handling data giving straight line graphs and smooth curves. However, it is surprisingly common to find such inadequacies as: poor choice of scales; lack of precision in determining gradients; and inability to *calculate* the value of a remote intercept.

Some students even show difficulty in locating the co-ordinates of points accurately. Their understanding of how to treat data showing 'scatter' is often poor, particularly in the estimation of the error limits to be given to a gradient of a line through scattered data.

More general difficulties emerge when students encounter logarithmic graphs — particularly when negative logarithms are involved. These problems seem to be amplified when natural logarithms are to be used, even though most students own a calculator providing both kinds of logarithms and the need to use tables is avoided. Very few entrants to higher education seem to have used logarithmic or semi-log graph paper, yet they are likely to find that such paper is very useful indeed, saving considerable time and effort, once they understand when and how to use it.

Even with students who can competently follow instructions and use logarithmic graphs, there is surprisingly often a lack of any real appreciation as to *why* such a graph is being employed; the distinctions between different common equation forms are not clear to the students.

To identify the main topics to be included in the present course units, the authors first built up a list of objectives arising from the sort of difficulties mentioned above, then grouped these objectives into sets around which the intention was to design course units which would take the average student about one hour to complete successfully. The result was a set of four units, and for each of these completion-type handout was designed, suitable to be handed in and assessed. The title 'Graph-It' was chosen for the series of units, and the front page of each handout contained the list of objectives after the statement: 'When you have completed this unit, you should be able to . . .' As well as accuracy, speed is mentioned in some of the objectives, particularly those of a more basic nature. This allows the capable student to view the materials as a challenge to his speed as well as his competence. A list of the initial unit titles is shown:

Unit 1. Straight Line Graphs
Unit 2. Adaption, Scatter and Curves
Unit 3. Log Graphs
Unit 4. Graphs Using Logarithmic Paper.

The choice of about four hours' duration for the complete course was not based on the authors' estimation of the time needed for students to fully familiarize themselves with the topics chosen; as expected, the latter takes much longer. Four hours was chosen primarily because this was recognized as the maximum amount of time that may reasonably be asked for when approaching course leaders about 'borrowing' their students to test out some exploratory material.

## Operation of the Course

It has already been explained that self-instructional capability is envisaged for students approaching the materials eventually. However, in the pilot stage described here, the authors wished to gain as much feedback about the strengths and weaknesses of the materials as possible, and to give the students direct help and feedback where necessary. Therefore, the handout materials were issued to small classes of students, with a preliminary explanation about the intentions, and the students were then told to proceed with the work as though it were purely self-instructional, but to seek advice if any aspects were found particularly obscure or difficult. The authors observed the most common difficulties the students faced and covered those problematic areas by conventional tuition. The students were asked to give frank comments (either directly or anonymously in writing) about the materials, particularly about whether the materials were satisfactorily enabling the objectives to be achieved. The completed materials were assessed and returned to the students some weeks later, when the students' reactions were again sought.

## Evaluation and Modification

The materials were well received by the students in general, and the feeling was that the course provided both well-needed practice in basic principles and a stimulating introduction to the newer concepts and practices. Examples of student comment are:

> First question needed some thought, and showed the pitfalls of rushing into a question without thinking. Rest of tasks were fair, and there was substantial but not laborious theory in all cases.
> I have picked up the basis of log-log and semi-log graphs, but I feel more practice would be beneficial.

However, the authors found much room for modification, based on the more prevalent errors made by students and on the time taken to complete the units. For example, Unit 1 was found to be taking up to two hours in its original form, and was shortened considerably.

Other factors arising from the evaluation of the original materials were that, while the units seemed to be very successful in persuading the students to choose the most appropriately sensitive scales for their data (ie not starting the axes at the origin if the origin itself was remote from the spread of data points), they then unexpectedly showed difficulty in the *calculation* of the (remote) intercept — some opting to revert to drawing a graph including the origin (at the expense of precision in both the gradient and intercept values). It was therefore felt that there was a need for a supplementary unit concerning remote intercepts on both logarithmic and linear scales.

Also, a number of occasions were recognized where, by the addition of a further short task, a student could check that his work thus far was in order. For example, having determined the equation of a graph, the student can be asked to determine $y$ for a given value of $x$, and then check the value with that actually on the graph.

## Proposals for Further Development

The authors believe that the present pilot study has confirmed the following:

☐ The need for instruction in graphical skills in most higher education science and engineering disciplines.
☐ The nature of many of the specific problem areas.

☐ The difficulty of persuading those in charge of courses that tuition time should be allowed for the required instruction.
☐ That feedback to the student about his performance is essential and that for optimum value such feedback needs to be much more specific than could be achieved by computer-managed systems.

It is planned to develop the materials in the following ways. A series of complementary units, providing background material for those students particularly inexperienced and practice material to consolidate the learning achieved, is being developed. These additional units are intended to be used when necessary (for example, when a score of less than 60 per cent is attained on a 'core' unit).

The mode and nature of the feedback to the students requires further thought and exploration. Perhaps the inevitable delay produced by tutor-marking would be partially avoided by issuing the students with a set of 'correct solutions' to the tasks when they hand in their attempts. Perhaps also it would be profitable to devise sets of follow-up problems specific to certain subject disciplines (for example, 'Graphical Problems for Chemical Engineers') so that the relevance of the learning to the students' principal disciplines could be reinforced. The problems could be issued with lists of 'solutions and clues', so that the students were in a position to use these independently.

The original intention of developing self-instructional materials has not been abandoned, though the advantages to the students of receiving directly relevant feedback have somewhat diminished the importance of trying to achieve the required learning entirely without tutor support. However, it seems worthwhile to continue to devise completely self-instructional versions for those circumstances where no tutorial support is forthcoming. It seems more worthwhile, though, to concentrate on producing materials which can be marked by a 'non-expert' on graphical methods by devising a rigorous marking schedule (which could also be used directly by sufficiently motivated students on their own).

The production costs of the handout materials remain satisfactorily low, involving mainly offset lithographic duplication, including that of the various kinds of graph paper. The expense of tutor-time is also minimal, as the scripts can be marked almost on a correspondence basis, without the necessity of the tutor's own presence when the work is done by the students.

## Conclusion

The work described in this paper does not exploit the 'technological' dimensions of educational technology. Rather, it is hoped to be an example of the way the philosphy of educational technology may be applied; the diagnosis of a need, the design of materials appropriate to the need, and the testing and evaluation of materials designed to accommodate the need. Although it requires considerable time and patience to produce optimum educational materials, the economics remain very favourable as the product is basically duplicated handout material. The authors feel that the question of graphical skills illustrates a widespread problem: that of the lack of essential skills or understanding. Tutors in many higher education courses have to assume that students have already acquired the requisite practice and experience, as there is not the tuition time to spare to devote to such preparatory or remedial instruction as may actually be necessary. In such situations, if educational technology can be used to boost the production of low-cost materials, which can still achieve the required learning objectives, without the need for lengthy formal tuition, the reputation of educational technology, among those whose primary function is teaching, may be improved.

It is to everyone's benefit if the term 'educational technology' becomes less associated with the sophisticated instrumentation of the microprocessor age and more closely linked to the choosing of the most appropriate and simple means of meeting educational needs.

## References

Buckwell, G D and Ball, A D (1978) *Maths for Today.* Macmillan, London.

Davies, H G and Hicks, G A (1975) *Mathematics for Scientific and Technological Students.* Longman, London.

James, W L (1969) *The Interdependence of Sixth Form Mathematics and the Mathematical Courses of Universities and Colleges of Education: A Survey.* The University of Newcastle-upon-Tyne, Newcastle-upon-Tyne.

Knowles, F (1980) Core syllabuses and A-level mathematics. *Mathematics Teaching* 90, pp 40-3.

Leaver, R H and Thomas, T R (1974) *Analysis and Presentation of Experimental Results.* Macmillan, London.

Macpherson, I S and Jones, B R (1974) *The Interpretation of Graphs in Physics.* Hutchinson, London.

Nelkon, M (1978) *Basic Mathematics for Scientists.* Heinemann, London.

Schofield, C W (1975) *Mathematics for Construction Students.* Arnold, London.

Tabberer, F (1978) *Mathematics for Technicians.* Butterworths, London.

Zepp, R A and Selwyn, J B (1980) A course in essential mathematics. *Mathematics Teaching* 92, pp 26-30.

## Acknowledgements

The authors thank many students from the Polytechnic of Wales, University College, Cardiff, and the South Glamorgan Institute of Higher Education for their participation in the trials of the course materials, and Professor J Beetlestone and Dr R A Sutton of University College, Cardiff, for their interest in the work.

*Workshop Report*

# 3.14 Reappraisal of Graphical Learning Techniques

**B Alloway**
*Huddersfield Polytechnic*

## Organizer's Account

This workshop set out to explore one aspect of the conference theme 'Educational Technology and the Learning Experience' — namely, how graphical techniques can be reinterpreted to emphasize learning strategies, and by so doing seek an improvement in some types of learning performance.

## Background to the Workshop

How significant are the now traditional areas of educational technology as new systems, techniques and media emerge from the widespread contributions of research and development? The author has attempted to include both ancient and modern elements in a designed course structure, offering individual course members individual course variables. This system attempts to meet the current requirements of a range of professions in education, training, information and communications services. Experience of organizing and conducting such variable courses based upon individually selected elements (called 'modules' in the course description) has now been gained over five academic sessions.

One of the 21 educational technology modules that make up the course provides an exploration of 'Graphical Media in Visual Communication' and the inspiration for this conference workshop stems from the implementation of the following 'course negotiation document'.

## Visual Communication: Graphical Media

GENERAL AIMS

(a) The heightening of awareness of the value of visual communication as used normally and as employed to a reasoned design in the classroom.

(b) An exploration of commercial and purpose-made software items of graphical media for visual communication.

(c) Theoretical and practical familiarization with selected items in the graphical media range.

(d) Task explorations and exercises relating to specific learning needs covering 'design, production, class use and/or commercial selection, acquisition, class use' sequences, together with some methods of evaluation.

STUDY QUESTIONS

1. Can the chalk element of the 'chalk and talk' method of classroom communication be significantly improved by an analysis/synthesis study?

2. What are the relative advantages and disadvantages of each graphical medium of communication in the classroom?

3. From where can commercially available visual material be obtained on loan, hire, or to purchase?

4. Which production techniques are most efficient when making materials for each of the media, and how do you evaluate their effectiveness for classroom use?

ITEM BANK

Graphical, pictorial and language image representation — real world and conceptual images — vision and visual perception — illusions and abberations — implicit and explicit visual communication — design criteria for graphical media — chalkboard — wall chart — flannelgraph — plastigraph — magnetic board — displays and exhibitions — individual and group paced work — textbook illustrations — task sheets — study documents — handouts — response sheets — assessment documents — graphical design components — lettering — captions — drawing techniques — representing quantity — design dimensions — integration of graphical media with traditional and innovative teaching methods.

OBJECTIVES FOCUS

Although the areas of graphical visual communication can be represented by the simplest non-projected visual aids, much work has been carried out on design, production, uses and evaluation of these media. In consequence, study techniques can range in complexity from the improvement of chalkboard presentation to the co-ordination of photographic, reprographic and typographical developments with designed learning intentions and measured learning results. The previous knowledge, working environment and course intentions will all determine the style of objectives best suited to the study of this module.

ACHIEVEMENT TIME

*One day:* to cover aims (a), (b) and (c) with emphasis upon the practical teaching needs of the study group.

*Two or more days:* to cover aims (a) to (d) with the implementation of project work to cover a selected subject theme. This to be consolidated by a short report, including bibliographic references and a thoughtful conclusion.

## Workshop Activities

Eighteen conference delegates from seven different countries came to the workshop session when a range of explorations were presented. Participants carried out the following tasks and contributed to the workshop discussion after each graphical learning technique.

The first activity was the design and use of handouts requiring completion by using information obtained from adjunctive sources. (In the first handout examined, a cross-section of human skin was represented together with 17 numbered arrows, each requiring the addition of the correct biological notation.) The discussion on this technique considered how and when such devices were of value in support of learning. Used as pre-lesson activities (possibly as library or homework tasks), or as a shorthand journal record as teaching or laboratory demonstration progressed, the graphical display provides reinforcement to the cognitive demand upon the learner. The most widely used technique amongst members was as an 'end test' including as an examination question. This would demand recall skills predominantly, although some higher levels of learning might be employed through the association of ideas.

Applications of programmed learning response, using activity handouts, were next introduced through an example in which a series of technical diagrams required annotation from another sector of the handout, together with questions and response blanks. To add an element of self-direction to the example, each member of the workshop was asked to estimate his or her own completion time, and then to work fast yet accurately on the handout and compare the real-time result. (This type of 'choice reaction time experiment' is studied in more detail in the module 'Ergonomics in the Classroom, Laboratory and Workshop' — another of the 21 modules mentioned above.) In the discussion after this exercise, about 70 per cent of the group had under-estimated their time and had perhaps concentrated on a measure of understanding. Those who had completed the handout in a faster than estimated time admitted to the thrill of the race. The workshop again attempted to identify the types of learning experience gained through this technique. Limiting the response time and indicating specific response spaces was thought to be stimulating if used in moderation, constraining if excessively imposed, and counter-productive in motivation if used as the only response mode.

The third graphical exploration used a chart presentation of teaching, learning and testing information. Assuming that the map of learning many subjects requires the sequential, hierarchical or inter-relationship order of facts (which can, in a majority of cases, be learnt as key words or key statements), then such criteria should be an important part of designed strategies for learning. Following the examination of some of the work done in this area at Huddersfield Polytechnic, each member of the workshop set up a subject learning list. In most cases these were numerically sequenced. As in previous experiences, the author was impressed with the wide variety of subject themes which were treated by this technique. In this case they included:

1. Logging into the Open University computer.
2. Production of a response booklet.
3. Budding a rose tree.
4. Drawing a straight line graph.
5. Design of a tape-slide unit.

6. Starting a car.
7. Acquiring training aids from a military stores system.
8. Scientific decision-making.
9. A system for peeling potatoes.

The teaching side of the charts were then drafted with the correct learning sequence on that side, for example:

*Scientific Decision-Making*
1. Specify system boundaries.
2. Specify aim of system.
3. Specify system parameters.
4. List alternative courses of action
5. Set up a scale of values in terms of system aims.
6. Evaluate each alternative.
7. Pick alternative with highest value.
8. Compare alternative with next highest value.
9. Check sensitivity to system parameters.
10. Recommend decisions.

On the reverse side of the chart, the items in each workshop member's sequence were again set out but here in a randomized order, thus producing a recall testing sequence. A sliding indicator was introduced which could cover the correct order or be moved to show the right item sequence after a test of learning from the opposite side. Discussion of the technique included the possibility of various time spans between the teaching and testing activities with the charts, how much emphasis should be placed upon exact recall, and the possibility of 'beating the system'.

The final workshop exercise explored the use of graphical decision algorithms and their relationship to computer programming and how they might be used as learning techniques in their own right. An example was developed, showing the decision stages in 'organizing a learning project' using giant flow-chart symbols, OHP transparencies, and lengths of pre-printed flow-chart paper. The workshop found (as with all sequential programming) that there were a variety of decision routes possible when allowed outcomes included alternatives. In the example developed, the organization of a learning project could, for instance, include journal record, audio-tape interview, photograph, quotation, etc as permissible study evidence. In discussion, the group considered that, by using such a graphical technique at the beginning of a learning activity, students would be able to take early consideration of the overall study demands of a learning programme. This could save frustration and wasted effort, especially where time was short in a demanding curriculum.

## Conclusions

It was agreed in discussion at the end of the workshop that attempts to identify learning strategies using graphical techniques indicated the close relationship of many different areas of human knowledge. This transcended the traditional parameters of subject disciplines and opened up new systems of learning. Numeracy, literacy, spatial relationships and psychomotor skills were interdependently related in the graphical learning techniques considered by the workshop. A willingness to at least consider interdependence may lead to a greater understanding of learning achievement — if this occurs, then the consideration of graphical learning techniques in relation to this understanding has a significant role in the future.

# 3.15 A Method for Teaching the Deaf to Read and Write

**R Phillips**
*Glasgow College of Technology*
**J Stirling Phillips**
*University of Strathclyde*

**Abstract:** Deaf children can normally learn words that stand for objects or observable actions, but they have considerable difficulty with the grammatical structure of the language. We have thus represented the various parts of speech with different shapes. A noun is always presented on a square piece of card, a verb on a diamond shape, an adjective on a circle, and so on. As the child puts sentences together he or she can actually *see* the grammar involved in terms of a sequence of shapes.

The lessons are laid down in a specified order so that the child's progression is not an *ad hoc* process of picking up this and that, but a logical cumulative sequence with new learning building on the old. Piaget's notions of assimilation and accommodation underlie this structure with vocabulary being equated with assimilation and grammar with accommodation.

A pilot study has been carried out, with promising results.

## Introduction

There can be no doubt about the disadvantages suffered by the deaf with regard to reading and writing. A study carried out by Conrad (1979) showed that the 16-year-old deaf adolescent can only be expected to reach a reading level equal to that of a nine-year-old hearing child. Some people would, perhaps, argue that this is inevitable. We believe, however, that the scheme which we have devised for the teaching of reading and writing can go a long way to reducing or even eliminating this disparity. We have been very fortunate in getting a local school for the deaf to carry out a pilot study and, although the scheme has only operated for a relatively short time, the results we have obtained have more than come up to our initial hopes.

The scheme has two main features:

(a)  A method of communication.
(b)  A highly structured teaching system.

## The Method of Communication

The deaf child has no great difficulty in naming objects or observable actions, but he does have trouble in understanding and using the network of rules and exceptions-to-the-rules that we call grammar. So the basic problem, as we saw it, was to communicate clearly to the child the structure of language.

This we have done by representing every different part of speech — noun, verb, adjective, etc — by a specific shape. Thus nouns are presented on pieces of square-shaped card, verbs are presented on diamond shapes and adjectives on circles, etc. When a child sees a sentence spelt out, he not only sees the vocabulary, he also *sees* the grammar. Syntax is expressed quite visibly as a sequence of geometrical shapes. Hence we call the scheme Grammar Shapes.

The sentences shown in Figure 1 have the grammatical form:

definite article    +    noun    +    copula    +    verb

The child sees many instances of these presented to him as captions to pictures, and from these he abstracts their common feature — the grammatical structure.

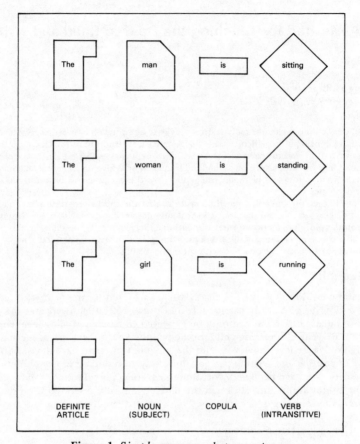

**Figure 1.** *Simple grammar shapes sentences*

Some examples of other structures are given in Figure 2. These include the adjective, the preposition and the noun used as object as well as subject. It can be seen that they increase in level of complexity. This is the way they are gradually introduced to the child.

## The Structure of the Teaching System

In general, we try to initiate each lesson with error-free learning; that is, we try to prevent the child from making mistakes so that he does not have to unlearn them. When he appears to have grasped the essentials, however, we wean him into the more normal trial-and-error situation. We maintain motivation by treating each lesson as a game and we vary the game as much as possible.

To get the child to pay attention to the words we begin with a pre-reading scheme in which he learns to respond to actions such as JUMP, RUN, FALL, SLEEP, etc, written out on large flash cards. In other words, he has to show that he understands what the cards say. Once he realizes that these squiggly things, which we call words, carry meaning, we are ready to begin.

In lesson 1, the child learns to discriminate and associate. First of all, he sorts out pictures of men and women into the two sexes and this is followed by shapes for MAN and WOMAN. Once he has achieved this discrimination we get him to

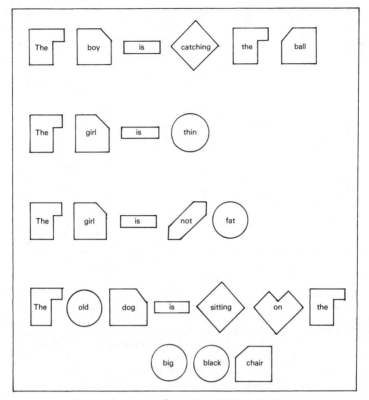

**Figure 2.** *More complex grammar shapes sentences*

associate the word with the picture: he learns to put the pictures of men under the word MAN and the pictures of women under the word WOMAN.

The people in the pictures are either sitting or standing. We then take the picture of men and sort these out into those sitting and those standing, so we next introduce the words SITTING and STANDING. So under the heading MAN, the child sorts out the pictures and places them against the words SITTING or STANDING. The child's attention is drawn to the difference in shape between noun and verb and then the word WOMAN is brought back and the pictures of women are sorted out and placed against the words SITTING and STANDING too.

Now for the definite article and the copula. THE is introduced to the child as the verbal equivalent of pointing (at the noun) and IS as a sort of joining word indicated by a clenching of hands. THE MAN and THE WOMAN is assembled down the side. This gives a 2 x 2 matrix and the child has to place the pictures in the correct intersection of the article + noun and copula + verb. This is shown in Figure 3.

The next step is to give the child individual pictures and to get him to assemble the correct description — in grammar shapes — under them as captions. Under the picture of a woman sitting, for example, he has to spell out THE WOMAN IS SITTING.

From THE MAN/WOMAN IS SITTING/STANDING we progress to THE BOY/GIRL IS WALKING/RUNNING. (This, in the study we carried out, took much less time than the first lesson.) The child now has 16 sentences at his command which he can put together without being able as yet to write.

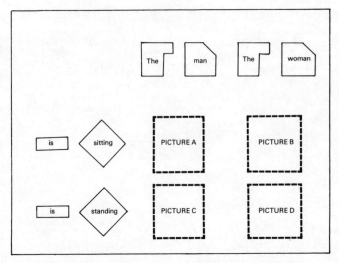

**Figure 3.** *Sorting matrix for learning the first sentence*

The next stage is to extend vocabulary. The first lessons use intransitive verbs. We now introduce verbs that can be either intransitive or transitive in anticipation of the next grammatical structure to be learnt. So the verbs EATING, DRINKING, PUSHING, PULLING, CATCHING and THROWING are brought in and the child learns sentences such as THE BOY IS EATING, THE WOMAN IS THROWING, etc.

We now extend the grammar a little: we add another definite article and a noun. The child learns sentences such as THE GIRL IS EATING THE APPLE, THE MAN IS PUSHING THE PRAM, and so on. He now has acquired the structure:

definite article + noun (subject) + copula + verb + definite article + noun (object)

This is followed by an extension of vocabulary to include CAKE, MILK and BALL.

Next comes the adjective. Instead of locating it in front of the noun, however, we simply substitute it for the verb in a structure the child already knows. We present sentences such as THE MAN IS FAT, THE MAN IS THIN, THE GIRL IS SHORT, THE GIRL IS TALL, etc. The transformation from this structure to the form THE TALL MAN, etc, comes later. We introduce the adjectives in pairs of opposites so as to aid comprehension. This also allows us to bring in the negative NOT. The child goes on to learn sentences such as THE MAN IS FAT, THE MAN IS NOT THIN, and THE WOMAN IS OLD, THE WOMAN IS NOT YOUNG.

This is the level we have reached in our pilot study. We have produced a very full and detailed textbook of instructions for the teacher, stating exactly what to do and when. We have given a lot of consideration to the material chosen to be presented and the order in which it occurs, as well as the way in which it should be taught.

For example, we have chosen to begin with the present continuous tense, partly because the -ing ending acts as a cue and partly because it stays consistent when the tense changes as, for example, THE MAN IS WALKING, THE MAN WAS WALKING and THE MAN WILL BE WALKING. We have designed the course so that the information load on the child increases gradually. He or she begins with a simple sentence with an intransitive verb and no object, then proceeds through sentences with an object, with an adjective and an object, and with an object with a preposition and an indirect object. We are attempting to create a logical, systematic, cumulative programme.

When the school year ended four-and-a-half months after the study began, the children had the ability to use four grammatical structures, a vocabulary of at least 30 words, and the capacity to generate a great number of sentences. Once they began to show some facility in the use of Grammar Shapes they were given lessons in writing. This added interest, and helped to consolidate their knowledge of language. We observed too that the children tended to vocalize as they manipulated the shapes. We had not expected an increase in vocal skills but we are now hoping that this will be a consistent effect. The children range in age from four-and-a-half to five-and-a-half; three are profoundly deaf and one is severely deaf. They can read and write sentences such as THE BOY IS CATCHING THE BALL, THE GIRL IS NOT FAT and a variety of others. This, perhaps, is a better performance than many hearing children may achieve at that age.

## Reference

Conrad, R (1979) *The Deaf School Child.* Harper and Row, London.

## Acknowledgements

We must express out thanks to Miss M Burton, the headmistress of the Gateside School for the Deaf in Paisley, for the enthusiastic welcome and encouragement that she gave us, and to Mrs Joyce MacFarlane, the teacher of the deaf, who showed as much patience with us as she did with the children she taught. We must also express our gratitude to the Renfrew Division of the Education Department of Strathclyde Region for the support we have obtained from them. Without the involvement of all of these, Grammar Shapes would still be an unrealized idea.

# 3.16 'Help Yourself to Success' — Improving Polytechnic Students' Study Skills

W P Race
*The Polytechnic of Wales*

Abstract: This paper outlines the initiation, development, operation and evaluation of a study skills course at the Polytechnic of Wales.

Despite the proliferation of study skills literature, the author contends that most students are too preoccupied with their main disciplines to spontaneously seek to update their study skills. The need for some 'live' interactive guidance was identified, and the paper describes the design and operation of a 'taught' course aiming to meet the needs of students in a variety of disciplines. The paper also describes the way student feedback was gathered, and discusses the provision of such study-skills help in terms of timetabling, flexibility, and costing.

## Introduction

This paper examines a facet of the main theme of the ETIC 81 Conference — 'Educational Technology and the Learning Experience' from the viewpoint of the learner's *own* requirements to optimize his learning experiences. The learner needs to be equipped with 'tools' from educational technology appropriate to his requirements. Some of the most valuable of these tools may be categorized as 'study skills', and they are at least as important as the 'teaching strategies and skills' more commonly identified as part of educational technology.

In any educational system, nothing is more important than students' success. In the present economic climate, where cost-effectiveness has become a pass-word, student drop-outs and failures are recognized as representing serious wastes of resources. Even more tragic than this is the personal devastation which may be suffered by any student who is unsuccessful: shattered confidence, time wasted, and apprehension (even revulsion) at the thought of any further study.

Many educational institutions offer their students a measure of support, and much has been published on the subject of study skills. However, even if each student is provided with an excellent book, or manual on study skills, it is found that the chance of his using it spontaneously is small. Syllabus content is demanding and courses are intensive. With the additional pressures on a student's time and energy posed by the social dimension of student life, is it surprising that he will read that which is directly relevant to his discipline before taking 'time off' to update his learning strategies?

## Study Skills Publications

The present paper is primarily a case study about the development and operation of a particular study skills course. However, having already stressed the point that the less motivated students will be unlikely to take advantage of even the most excellent materials already published, it is fitting to examine briefly the range of the relevant literature.

There are a number of excellent texts. Cassie and Constantine present a very digestible, non-patronizing account extending far beyond study skills, written in an engaging, humorous manner (Cassie and Constantine, 1977). Buzan provides one of the most detailed expositions of the visual aspects of memory, and note-making (Buzan, 1974). Maddox provided one of the first widely read texts (Maddox, 1967), while Rowntree's *Learn How to Study* is probably the most distinguished work of its kind (Rowntree, 1976). A number of texts focus on particular aspects or disciplines, such as examinations (Erasmus, 1978), memory (Hunter, 1964), and there are several more general guides (Burnett, 1979; Parsons, 1976; James, 1967).

A package comprising an audio-cassette and workbook sets out to meet the needs of students entering any sector of higher education (Haynes *et al*, 1977). Various publications have surveyed whole courses, strategies, or selected topics (Hills, 1979; Howe and Godfrey, 1979; Rees and Reid, 1977). Finally, a large number of papers have appeared in the literature in the last few years, many from the United States; a selection of the details of papers has been collected (Race, 1981a).

## Why Should Students be Helped to Acquire Study Skills?

A surprising question, perhaps, but course leaders are often reluctant to allocate a few hours for this purpose. They welcome the provision of evening sessions for students to attend voluntarily, but any 'invasion' of sacred schedules must be rigorously justified. To convince polytechnic lecturers that their students may indeed need study skills help, it has been found useful to pose the following comments and questions:

- ☐ In a non-university educational establishment, most lecturers are themselves university trained; is it not then possible for the needs of the students to be somewhat different from each lecturer's memories of his own needs as a student?
- ☐ A lecturer is a student who *did* succeed; is he in danger of underestimating the needs of students whose success is not as certain?
- ☐ For some lecturers (particularly those holding principal posts) many years have passed since their student days. Have such lecturers always a realistic appraisal of the needs of the modern student?

☐ In scientific and technological disciplines, the pace continues to accelerate. Students need to be equipped to acquire much greater flexibility and adaptability than those of previous generations. New graduates of today will have to learn new 'tricks' several times in their later careers.

## Identification of Students' Needs

The author, while lecturing in physical chemistry full-time, was warden for eight years of a student hall of residence. Living under the same roof as 100 students enabled the author to pinpoint many of the causes of students' anxiety or difficulty. Students are naturally unwilling to alter their long-standing strategies (which, after all, have thus far served them successfully) unless they can see rewards to be gained, such as:

☐ A more 'normal' life style when preparing for exams.
☐ More effective use of study time, producing more free time to be spent with an easy conscience in social and extra-curricular activities.
☐ A greater belief in the probability of success.

It is also possible to identify certain categories of student, each posing particular needs, such as:

☐ Students learning in a foreign language.
☐ 'Slow-but-sure' students — too easily examination casualties.
☐ Over-anxious students, requiring primarily increased confidence in their own abilities with improved study strategies.
☐ Students who leave serious work too late, needing help in using to best effect the time remaining.
☐ Mature students, usually high in motivation, but with dated study techniques, inappropriate to modern requirements.

Therefore, the course design has to accommodate three general requirements. It has to:

(a) be short enough that lecturers may be prepared to spare the time;
(b) be seen by the students to offer tangible benefits;
(c) cater simultaneously for each of the main categories of students needing particular help.

## Content of the Course

The following general topics were identified as capable of satisfying as many of the needs as possible in four to six hours' tuition time:

☐ Writing effective lecture notes.
☐ Compiling better laboratory or field work reports.
☐ Revising and learning efficiently and methodically.
☐ Developing examination technique.

However, the pressures on students extend further as they plan ahead to the start of their careers. It was therefore found appropriate to round off the course with help and advice relating to:

☐ Dealing with complex application forms.
☐ Writing a *curriculum vitae*.
☐ Improving interview performance.

It was found suitable to divide the course into four one-hour sessions (ideally with a further half-hour available for discussion) and preferably to run at weekly intervals as follows:

*Unit 1*    Effective Study
*Unit 2*    Revision
*Unit 3*    Examination Technique
*Unit 4*    Job-Hunting

and the title 'Help Yourself to Success' was given to the course as a whole. Detailed discussion of the exact content of the course is beyond the scope of the present paper (though the author will supply a detailed analysis of the content on request [Race, 1981b]). The remainder of the present paper is devoted to discussion of the mode of operation of the course and plans to develop the work further.

## Mode of Operation of Course

Each session is run using a handout of five to seven pages. The author has previously considered the advantages of the use of a completion-type, objective-based handout design (Race, 1979) and this was found ideally suitable for the present course. The student fills into suitably spaced blank areas those points he finds most relevant and useful, while the printed sections of the handout set the scene, or give additional detail.

The style of writing of the handout material is informal, often humorous where appropriate. A particular feature adopted throughout the course is extensive posing of questions, both in the handouts and orally to the class. The students learn much more by thinking for themselves about such questions then they would if the answers were simply given to them. Indeed, many of the questions have no definitive answers; instead each student needs to determine the most appropriate response suited to his own personality. Figure 1 shows a typical introduction section from one of the handouts.

The course as a whole has been operated as 'open runs' (during evenings or lunch-times) with students from a wide variety of disciplines attending on their own initiative. Increasingly, however, the course has been adopted by most departments in the polytechnic as an integral part of first-year courses; this brings the help offered directly to those students who most need it — those lacking the motivation to attend a voluntary course.

## Flexibility and Costing

It was recognized from the outset that, if the course was to be widely used within the institution, it had to cost little to mount and be easily brought to large or small groups of students — preferably on their own familiar 'learning territory'.

At the same time, the author is committed to colourful visual presentation to accompany the completion-type handouts. Therefore, the overhead projector was chosen as the visual aid, rather than slides, so the course could be run in even the smallest, most poorly equipped rooms. The advantages of sequential display of transparencies, and use of overlays, were exploited to the full in the design of transparencies. The material shown on the transparencies was divided into two broad categories:

☐ 'Setting the scene' material, objectives, humorous comment.
☐ 'Key information and suggestions' suitable for students to insert into suitable blank areas of their handout copies.

Therefore, the costing was in fact very low, only amounting to the offset lithography in producing handouts of five to seven pages; these costs are minimal when the materials are prepared in batches of about 200.

The ready availability of handouts, the visual aids and a portable overhead projector mean that any session from the course can be mounted virtually at a few

**Examination Technique**

*Introduction*

You may be one of the fortunate people who have never had to give exam technique a conscious thought — but then you probably would not have come along to this session. To have qualified to enter higher education your examination technique must have been at least satisfactory, but perhaps that may not be enough for your next exams. In any case, you can do no harm by analyzing your way of doing exams. All too often, even in higher education, much depends on a few vital hours at the end of a course or term; even when your performance has been 'continually assessed', there is usually some form of exam where 'more-marks-are-gained-or-lost-per-minute' than at any other time. Almost all candidates who end up 'on the borderline' in an exam could have easily cleared the passmark if they had slightly altered their way of going about certain parts of the exam.

Ask yourself a few questions:

    Have you ever experienced 'blind panic' during an exam?
    Does your memory sometimes go blank?
    Does your pen sometimes shake so much you can't write?
    Have you had to 'take something' to keep going?
    Would you rather have gone to the dentist?

If you have answered 'yes' to some of these questions — congratulations, you belong to the human race! Every successful person has at some time had a 'hard time' in exams, but usually has found how to come to terms with the root of the trouble.

**Figure 1.** *Part of the Introduction from one of the handouts*

minutes' notice — though the demand for it has grown, so advance bookings are now needed!

## Obtaining Feedback

This is crucial, if the course is to develop optimum usefulness to the broad spectrum of the student population. Each of the four handouts ends with a detachable 'five-minute questionnaire', to be filled in and returned at the end of each session. Frank comment is encouraged, and the student is left free to remain anonymous if he wishes. The response to the questionnaires has been most useful, and the course has already been improved greatly by due attention to the feedback gained. The questionnaire used in the 'Examination Technique' session is shown in Figure 2.

When describing the 'before the exam' and 'after the exam' time periods with classes, it was stressed that the suggestions offered were of much less importance than those directly concerned with exam performance. However, actions immediately prior to an exam can affect the mental state of students at the start of the exam, and also behaviour patterns after an exam often affect performance in the *next* exam. For some students these effects can be significant, and this was reflected by a surprisingly high proportion of students ticking the 'very useful' boxes on the questionnaire. The relevance of the 'essays versus problems' discussion was soon found to depend primarily on subject disciplines and was dropped from the session when inappropriate. However, in science and engineering subjects it was usually graded 'very useful'.

The feedback was more useful in 'compulsory' runs of the sessions than in voluntary ones. In the latter sessions, students already display motivation by their presence, and are less likely to admit that what they came for proved 'not useful'. However, they are usually quite expansive on ideas and comments. With class-time runs of the sessions there is always a small proportion of students who have no intention of changing their to-date-successful strategies, and the proportion of 'not useful' gradings is a little higher.

Ultimately, however, the author derived satisfaction as long as *each* sub-topic was found very useful by *some* of those present, and this was taken as justification for continuing to include the topics, though the actual presentation of topics was continuously adjusted in response to comments, criticisms, and the gradings.

It is planned to attempt a statistical analysis of the responses to the questionnaires, though it is recognized that various factors make the situation complex, such as:

☐ Differing disciplines produce different patterns of 'usefulness'.
☐ Variation of motivation between voluntary and class-time runs.
☐ Variation in length of experience in higher education from a few days (induction period runs) to several terms.

Quite apart from the aspects mentioned above, the use of questionnaires is seen to have value in the following ways:

☐ The receptiveness and motivation of the students are enhanced by their realization that their own views are being sought and will be valued.
☐ The activity of grading topics in terms of usefulness involves the students quickly reappraising the material, thereby helping establish the ideas in their thinking.
☐ Students *like* to have the opportunity to make comments and criticisms. It is often useful to discuss some specific reactions arising in the response at the start of the following session in the course.

**Examinations Techniques**

*Five-minute Questionnaire*

1. Which of the following adjectives apply to you on average when doing exams?

   confident          tense          panic-stricken          disorganized

2. How often have you left an exam before the end, without re-reading your answers?

   never          sometimes          usually

3. Indicate how useful or otherwise you found the advice offered on the following aspects of examination technique:

| | *very useful* | *quite useful* | *not useful* |
|---|---|---|---|
| Before the exam | | | |
| The first 10 minutes | | | |
| Writing answers in general | | | |
| Essays versus problems | | | |
| The last 20 minutes | | | |
| After the exam | | | |

4. Write any points which you think should be included in this part of the course (in addition to those already covered).

5. Any other comments or criticisms?

   Name (if you wish) . . . . . . . . . . . . . . . . Course . . . . . . . . . . .

Figure 2. *Example of a Questionnaire*

## Conclusions

This paper has described what amounts to a 'one-man stand' aimed at satisfying a major student need in one particular educational institution. To do this successfully obviously requires considerable enthusiasm and commitment, but the author hopes that the above account may interest more academics in trying to ensure that their students are *helped* to get the most from the learning experience.

## References

Burnett, J (1979) *Successful Study: A Handbook for Students.* Hodder and Stoughton, London.

Buzan, T (1974) *Use Your Head.* BBC Publications, London.

Cassie, W F and Constantine, T (1977) *Students' Guide to Success.* Macmillan, London.

Erasmus, J (1978) *How to Pass Examinations.* Oriel Press, Stocksfield.

Haynes, L J, Groves, P D, Hills, P J and Moyes, R B (1977) *Effective Learning: A Practical Guide for Students.* Tetrahedron (40 Hadzor Road, Warley, West Midlands, UK).

Hills, P J (ed) (1979) *Study Courses and Counselling, Problems and Possibilities.* Society for Research into Higher Education, Guildford.

Howe, M J A and Godfrey, J (1979) *Student Note-Taking as an Aid to Learning.* University of Exeter, Exeter.

Hunter, I M L (1964) *Memory.* Penguin, Harmondsworth.

James, D E (1967) *A Student's Guide to Efficient Study.* Pergamon, London.

Maddox, H (1967) *How to Study.* Pan, London.

Parsons, C J (1976) *How to Study Effectively.* Arrow, London.

Race, W P (1979) An objective approach to teaching physical chemistry. In Page, G T and Whitlock, Q (eds) *Aspects of Educational Technology* **XIII.** Kogan Page, London.

Race, W P (1981a) Monitoring. *Programmed Learning and Educational Technology* **18,** 3.

Race, W P (1981b) *Helping Polytechnic Students Acquire Study Skills.* Learning Resources Centre, Polytechnic of Wales, Treforest, Pontypridd, UK.

Rees, L and Reid, F (1977) *The Development and Evaluation of Study Skills Courses for Students in Higher Education.* SCEDSIP, Petras, Newcastle-upon-Tyne Polytechnic.

Rowntree, D (1976) *Learn How To Study.* Macdonald and Jane's, London.

# 3.17 Cybernetic Principles in the Education of Educational Technologists

G M Boyd
*Concordia University, Canada*

**Abstract:** Certain cybernetic principles and methods can be very helpful to instructional designers, managers, and consultants in the educational and training technology field. Consequently, Educational Cybernetics has been a core course in the Concordia University graduate programme for a decade now. Some of the key concepts and most important topics which have proved to be intelligible and useful to educational technologists are enumerated and exemplified. In particular, the process of modelling high-level communications and control behaviour, the problems and opportunities related to feedback loops, and the necessity of providing three types of Requisite Variety are discussed.

## Introduction

If an educational technologist is to be able to help solve education and training problems which have proved intractable to others, then one needs not merely some new tools but rather a radically different perspective. Cybernetic systems theory is such a perspective. It is radical in that it requires that the complex 'messes' be

# CYBERNETIC PRINCIPLES IN EDUCATIONAL TECHNOLOGISTS' EDUCATION 285

modelled and resolved in terms of different boundaries and different kinds of concepts than conventional perception and wisdom deal with. It is also unitary in that it includes the practitioner in his or her own models and explicitly takes the environment as well as the whole system of interest into account.

This is not, it must be admitted, what the ordinary teacher imagines when he or she encounters the term 'cybernetic system'. Popular associations seem to be with computers, the management of massive projects and behaviourist manipulation of people. A cybernetic systems perspective can be used in an exploitative and dehumanizing manner just as murder can be done with a hammer. Any powerful tool can be readily abused, but this does not mean that we should ban all powerful tools from our schools. The moral is rather to make sure the people to whom we give such tools share our concern for the autonomy of others. This is part of the professional responsibility of an educator, and has been so since at least the time of Hippocrates. Unfortunately, it is a form of responsibility which contemporary 'open access rhetoric' deprecates.

The cybernetic systems theory which is advocated here is a form of Paskian self-producing (Pask, 1980) Conversation Theory which explicitly includes the personae of the designer or consultant using the theory in the model. Morally this amounts to a sort of exemplification of the 'do-as-you-would-be-done-by' rule. Of course, the theory cannot prevent its own abuse; that is up to the practitioners of our profession.

## Key Concepts

The seven key concepts in cybernetic systems theory which are most important for educational technologists are:

1. The concept of the (five) inclusively hierarchical levels of communication and control (Ackoff and Emery, 1972; Weltner, 1973; Boyd, 1980).
2. The concept of system 'integrity' (ie requisite internal signal-to-noise ratio) (Goode and Machol, 1959; Klapp, 1978).
3. The concept of feedback, both deviation-limiting *and* deviation-amplifying (Mayr, 1970; Mitchell, 1975).
4. The concept of procedures, both algorithmic (Landa, 1976) and heuristic (Papert, 1980).
5. Ashby's Law of Requisite Variety (Ashby, 1956).
6. Self-productive conversation (MacMurray, 1961; Pask, 1980; Maturana and Varela, 1980).
7. Prescriptive positive-sum n-person Game Models (Rapoport, 1970; Boyd, 1976).

While any of these concepts used in isolation can provide valuable, counter-intuitive insights, it is only when all are used together to model a situation or project that the greatest benefits accrue. The way in which these concepts depend on each other is somewhat complicated, and depends on the backgrounds of the learners and the nature of the task at hand, as well as upon logic (Boyd, 1981).

If the cybernetic systems perspective is to be a valuable part of the training of an educational technologist, he or she must use it to analyze, and if possible solve, meaningful problems. But to do that one first needs familiarity with the seven key process concepts and with procedures for combining them to model and perhaps to simulate an actual system.

Three classes of system are considered:

1. The individual learner qua system.
2. Conversational teaching and learning systems.
3. Resource and staff management systems.

The first involves a cybernetic approach to psychology, the second a cybernetic pedagogy, the third cybernetic management science. At Concordia University this is accomplished mainly in four courses: a foundations course in educational cybernetics, and two more advanced courses, one on instructional systems analysis, the other on educational systems analysis, and a course in CAL from a cybernetic point of view. Some students also do systems analysis or development thesis projects, and they are the ones who most clearly vindicate this approach to educational technology training (Bettman, 1980; Pastrana-Alvarado, 1980).

## Textbooks

As yet there are no educational cybernetics textbooks which cover all the key concepts and all of the main areas (management, public communication, instruction and autopoeisis) which are important to graduate students in educational technology.

There are four good books in print for introducing the subject. They are Norbert Wiener's *The Human Use of Human Beings*; John MacMurray's *The Self as Agent*; Gordon Pask's *An Approach to Cybernetics*; and Stafford Beer's *Designing Freedom*.

Useful cybernetic models of the individual learner are provided by William Powers' *Behaviour: The Control of Perception*; and Gordon Pask's *The Cybernetics of Human Learning and Performance*. (The formalizations of the latter do, however, pose real difficulties for many students.) Both should be studied with the philosophical perspective of MacMurray's Gifford lectures borne in mind.

Cybernetics applied to the instructional process is handled in a very practical way by Landa in his *Instructional Regulation and Control*.

Stafford Beer's *The Heart of Enterprise* gives the best overview of cybernetics applied to management. But Schoderbek, Schoderbek and Kefalas' *Management Systems* gives a more detailed coverage of the theoretical and practical knowledge needed.

The educational cybernetics of public media and communication networks is well introduced by Orrin Klapp in his book *Opening and Closing*. On the formal and technical side we have found John Warfield's *Societal Systems* to be very useful, although it tends to be rather technocratic in tone and perspective. Systems should be designed by insiders *with* each other, not by outsiders for someone else.

## Learning Activities

Three video-tapes have been produced at Concordia for this course and are used to introduce some of the main concepts and relations among these concepts. The video-tapes are: *Systems Perspective* (1979); *Feedback: Bomb or Balm?* (1978, remade 1980); and *An Introduction to Cybernetic Theory in Management* (1980).

Graduate students working in pairs then present seminars on selected classic papers, applying the key cybernetic systems concepts to educational processes.

All students undertake a project to model some learning process, or instructional system, or some managerial system which they have worked in and know personally.

Students also prepare their own short annotated bibliographies of 'most helpful papers' and exchange these.

If educators are to assimilate the cybernetic systems paradigm to their work, it is essential that they have guided project experience in doing so. If it is possible for pairs or teams of graduate students to work together they should do so, not only because real tasks in all their complexity require a lot of work but also because the supportive and critical dialogue which ensues greatly enhances the work.

A very wide range of projects has been undertaken by our students. For example N Blass, as part of the Quebec Ministry of Education project 'Integration', for

Grade One curriculum, prescribed a quasi-cybernetic system for classroom use involving multi-media documents, lesson-game protocols, and a special piece of furniture called 'Philodor' which provided for images and sound and participation by the children in educational performances. In experimental use the Integrative curriculum system resulted in highly satisfactory learning gains (Blass, 1973).

In another direction altogether, Pastrana-Alvarado constructed an educational programme evaluation guide on the basis of a cybernetic systems model of a school system. She compared the systems model-based evaluation approach with three other models: the goal attainment model; the judgement-oriented model; and the decision facilitation model. She was able to revise the systems model to incorporate their strengths and circumvent their weaknesses (Pastrana-Alvarado, 1980).

Many projects have modelled various existing individualized instruction programmes, extending from very ambitious multi-media collegial programmes (CEGEP Montmorency) down to minimal training programmes for immigrants (COFI) and for mentally retarded adults. These models have shown that everywhere the cost and structures required to provide a requisite variety of instructional conversations, to meet the variety of needs and capabilities of the learners, is underestimated and underfunded.

## Difficulties

Three difficulties arise. First, some students are unwilling to try out the radically different point of view implicit in 'conversational' (Paskian) educational cybernetics. (This may be partly due to a reluctance to think abstractly and holistically.)

Second, pre-conceived notions of the meaning of words interfere with the introduction of new concepts labelled with old words (eg system, noise, feedback, information, hierarchy, integrity, control all have everyday denotations and connotations which are at variance with their usage in cybernetics).

Third, the successful application of cybernetic systems analysis modelling and world re-making is usually a long and complicated job, involving two or more (often many more) people functioning together in a mutually supportive fashion (Beer, 1975). Although such an approach may offer the only realistic possibility for development, it may appear quite overwhelming to the novice educational technologist. He or she may prefer to do something small and safe, which at best amounts to merely strengthening an already strong link in the chain, or at worst may be 'acceptable' activity which is utterly useless and perniciously wasteful.

## Progress and Prospects

Gordon Pask (1961), Lawrence Stolurow (1965) and Helmar Frank (1962) were the first to refer to, elaborate on, and teach cybernetics applied to educational training technology. To my knowledge, the Sir George Williams (now Concordia) University graduate course in educational cybernetics which I started in 1969 was the first formal course entirely devoted to the qualitative cybernetic modelling of educational and instructional processes to be offered anywhere. It continues. Brunel University and the University of Montreal also offer educational cybernetics courses, and many other universities and colleges (eg OISE, Surrey, MIT) use a cybernetic systems perspective in educational technology and artificial intelligence, applied to instructional courses.

The spread of this approach to educational technology has been slow because workers in the field are, perhaps rightly, sceptical of theory, and particularly theory of a mathematical nature whose origins in engineering, biology and philosophy make it doubly suspect.

Recent developments with VLSI microprocessors and associated equipment enable qualitative cybernetic models to be realized as interactive simulations with graphical displays which are very attractive to learners and managers of learning alike.

Gordon Pask (1980), Mildred Shaw (1980), Alfred Bork (1980), and Seymour Papert (1980) among others, have been building and promoting such systems for some years, but it is only now that cheap personal computers are becoming available that a widespread realization of the importance of this perspective is imminent.

In some senses people have always used regulative feedback, requisite variety, and cyclic spatial and temporal openings and closings to control each other and to make our world, but the intuitive and/or non-conscious use of cybernetic principles in small-scale personal situations is very different from their conscious conversational use in the public educational communication system of this little planet. Whether education will outpace vivicide (the collective suicide of mankind) remains an open question.

# References

Ackoff, R and Emery, F (1972) *On Purposeful Systems.* Aldine, Chicago.
Ashby, W R (1956) *An Introduction to Cybernetics.* Chapman and Hall, London.
Beer, S (1974) *Designing Freedom.* Canadian Broadcasting Corporation, Toronto.
Beer, S (1975) *Platform for Change.* John Wiley, London.
Beer, S (1979) *The Heart of Enterprise.* John Wiley, New York.
Bettman, B (1980) *Goal Priorities in a Jewish Day School: Systems Approach.* MA thesis, Concordia University, Montreal.
Blass, N (1973) Private communication. Concordia University, Montreal.
Bork, A (1980) Preparing on-line quizzes. *ACM SIGCUE Bulletin* 14, 4, pp 2-16.
Boyd, G M (1976) Developments in individualized learning at Concordia University. In *ACIT Proceedings of the Second Canadian Symposium on Instructional Technology.* NRC, Ottawa.
Boyd, G M (1980) Essential elements of prescriptive cybernetic models for educational operations. In Trappl, R (ed) *Proceedings of the Fifth International Meeting on Cybernetics and Systems Research.* Hemisphere Publishing Company, New York.
Boyd, G M (1981) Systems and cybernetic theory as a core-component in the education of professional educators. In Reckmeyer, J (ed) *Proceedings of the 25th Annual North American Meeting of the Society for General Systems Research with the American Association for the Advancement of Science.* Louisville, Kentucky.
Frank, H (1972) *Kybernetische Grundlagen der Padagogik.* Agis-Verlag, Baden-Baden.
Goode, H H and Machol, R E (1959) *Systems Engineering.* McGraw-Hill, New York.
Klapp, O E (1978) *Opening and Closing: Strategies of Information Adaptation in Society.* Cambridge University Press, Cambridge.
Landa, L N (1976) *Instructional Regulation and Control: Cybernetics, Algorithmization and Heuristics in Education.* Educational Technology Publications, Englewood Cliffs, New Jersey.
MacMurray, J (1957) *The Self as Agent.* Faber and Faber, London.
MacMurray, J (1961) *Persons in Relation.* Humanities Press, New York.
Maturana, H R and Varela, F J (1980) *Autopoiesis and Cognition.* Reidel Publications, Dordecht.
Mayr, O (1970) *The Origins of Feedback Control.* MIT Press, Cambridge, Massachusetts.
Mitchell, P D (1975) The discernible educational technologist. *Programmed Learning and Educational Technology* 12, 5, pp 306-26.
Papert, S (1980) *Mindstorms, Children, Computers, and Powerful Ideas.* Basic Books, New York.
Pask, G (1961) *An Approach to Cybernetics.* Hutchinson, London.
Pask, G (1975) *The Cybernetics of Human Learning and Performance.* Hutchinson, London.
Pask, G (1980) *Developments in Conversation Theory, Part I.* Academic Press, London.
Pastrana-Alvarado, N (1980) *An Educational Evaluation Guide.* MA thesis, Concordia University, Montreal.
Powers, W T (1974) *Behaviour: The Control of Perception.* Wildwood House, London.

Rapoport, A (1970) *N-Person Game Theory: Concepts and Applications.* University of
   Michigan Press, Ann Arbor.
Schoderbek, C G, Schoderbek, P P and Kefalas, A G (1980) *Management Systems.* Business
   Publications, Dallas.
Shaw, M L G (1980) On becoming a 'personal scientist'. In Gaines, B R (ed) *Computers and
   People Series.* Academic Press, London.
Stolurow, L M (1965) A model and cybernetic system for research on the teaching-learning
   process. *Programmed Learning* 2, 3, pp 138-56.
Warfield, J N (1976) *Societal Systems Planning, Policy, and Complexity.* John Wiley,
   New York.
Weltner, K (1973) *The Measurement of Verbal Information in Psychology and Education.*
   Springer Verlag, New York.
Wiener, N (1950) *The Human Use of Human Beings: Cybernetics and Society.* Avon Books,
   New York.

# 3.18 An Analytic Model and Instructional Paradigm for Training 'Soft Skills'

R R Begland
*US Army Exchange Officer to the Royal Army Educational Corps*

**Abstract:** Regardless of the systems approach to training (SAT) model used in any training
developments effort, the traditional focus or starting point has been the definition of the
real-world performance requirement as ascertained by a front-end analysis. Varied organizations
have committed themselves to the *sine qua non* of an empirically-based job and task analysis.
Yet many organizations have discovered that the traditional analysis procedures do not
adequately address a substantial percentage of the tasks identified during a front-end analysis.
These tasks are difficult to define, and more difficult to analyze. Traditionally, these tasks or
functional areas have been referred to (both affectionately and euphemistically) as 'soft skills'
and intentionally avoided as too difficult to analyze. This difficulty is attributable to the
variability in conditions and standards. For this reason, the traditional Magerian task
definitional format and SAT analytic procedures have proved to be inadequate. This paper
presents a model for the analysis of soft skills and describes in detail the empirical basis and
research relating to its derivation.

## Introduction

The analytic approach to soft skills suggested in this paper is the result of
continuous research started by the author in 1979 while assigned to the Training
and Doctrine Command (TRADOC) Headquarters, US Army, Fort Monroe. The
technique suggested is the product of several seminars, symposia and consultant
contributions.

## Historical Perspective

The American Army adopted the concept of a systems approach to training (SAT)
as early as 1967. Although the early 'systems engineering' of training met with
limited success, later broad scale implementation of the interservice procedures
for instructional systems development (IPISD) model realized the potential
inherent in SAT based training.

   The American Army presents a challenge to its senior Training Managers in
terms of its scope of training. The Army has 23 major service schools, nine training
centres and a variety of training related commands and organizations all over the

world. The Army has an annual training requirement of approximately 70,000 active duty soldiers. Yet if you look at the role of a peace-time army as training, this figure quickly jumps to approximately 773,800, the size of the active Army.

In terms of a financial investment, the Army spends approximately $3,296,000,000 annually on individual training of its active duty soldiers. The scale, scope, complexity, and difficulty of managing such a training requirement cannot be fully grasped from a written description such as this brief overview. Yet it is important to realize that this challenge is the goal, mission and responsibility of the commander of TRADOC. To achieve the benefit of standardization and systematization, in 1975 the Army adopted the IPISD model.

This model has give distinct phases that describe the training development and management process used in the various training establishments. These five phases are: analysis, design, development, management/conduct, and evaluation.

## Analysis Phase

This paper is primarily concerned with the analysis phase of the IPISD model referred to, and the product of analysis influences all subsequent training efforts. Recognizing the legitimate differences that exist between service arms, eg infantry, medical corps, transporation, maintenance, military police, etc it was *not* intuitively obvious to the training managers that these different arms might require different analysis data or employ different analysis techniques to collect the important front-end analysis data. Eventually, this important fact became apparent and the subsequent analysis guidance produced by TRADOC attempted to accommodate these differences. The traditional analytic techniques and procedures available were described in detail in TRADOC publications and accompanying self-paced training modules were developed to be used as on-the-job training materials. Nevertheless, it became obvious that the techniques and procedures suggested were not adequate for a variety of the 'soft-skills' present in the Army. The procedures were adequate for analyzing procedural tasks; they just did not feel good for those 'soft-skill' areas.

## Soft Skills

Over the years, a variety of analytic models have evolved. This list represents a selection of the more well known.

| Author | Analytic model |
|--------|----------------|
| Fine | Functional job analysis |
| Miller | Task analysis (man-machine systems) |
| Foley | Analysis of procedural tasks |
| Mager | Goal analysis |
| Gagné | Hierarchical analysis |
| Scandura | Rule analysis |
| Resnick | Information processing analysis |
| Pask | Entailment meshes |
| Gilbert | Practical analysis |
| Mechner | Behavioural analysis |
| Smith, E | Content, task, skills analysis |
| Merrill, M D | Content analysis |
| Smith | Critical incident analysis |

These various analysis techniques were developed to help the practitioner ultimately conduct more accurate and realistic training. Yet not one of them was sufficient to deal with the dilemma created by soft skills. The research issues of what precisely is a soft skill?, how best do you analyze it?, how best can you train it?. and how do you evaluate it? had not been resolved.

Soft skills have been called by a variety of labels, and have taken many forms: *soft* — unduly susceptible to influence, *skill* — the ability to use one's knowledge effectively and readily in execution or performance, . . . a learned power of doing something, . . . a developed aptitude or ability. Practitioners have labelled soft skills as:

☐ Part of supervision and/or management.
☐ Tasks that do not involve equipment.
☐ Tasks that no one knows how to train.
☐ Tasks that do not have a prescribed procedure.
☐ Tasks that require cognitive skills.
☐ Tasks that are situationally dependent.
☐ Tasks that must be subjectively evaluated.
☐ Tasks that cannot be taught!

Even the uninformed could recognize that confusion reigns in the soft skills area. Yet from the confusion emerged the truth. There were skills out there that were soft, and they had practically nothing in common, yet collectively they could be analyzed using the same model. The reason for this unity related to the nature of each task. These soft skills were all tasks:

☐ for which there were at least two approaches for performing the task, and
☐ for which following a set procedure that would yield the desired result in certain situations would not yield the desired results in another situation, *or*
☐ for which two or more set procedures may yield the desired results for a single situation.

It was this theme of *variance* in the accomplishment of the task that operationally defined a task as a soft skill. The essence of the problem became clear: 'How do you analyze, write training objectives and train for tasks when it can be performed in a variety of different ways depending upon a variety of conditions?' The concept of task variance is such that a given task may well be performed in a variety of different ways, depending upon the conditions (situational variance) and the person doing it (performer variance).

If a task has little or no situational or performer variance, then it is considered to be a procedural task. A procedural task is a task:

☐ for which there is a set procedure for doing the task;
☐ for which, if one follows that procedure the desired result will occur every time; and
☐ for which, if one does not follow the procedure, the desired result will not usually occur.

If a task has substantial situational and/or performer variance, then it is considered to be a 'transfer task' and a candidate for a slightly different analytic approach, training objective specification and training technique. There is an asymtotic point where the amount of situational and performer variance changes a task from being a multiple procedural task to being a transfer task. This subjective determination is a function of the analysis time available and the subsequent training time available.

A logic tree approach to distinguishing between a procedural and a transfer task, and the subsequent analysis technique to apply, is shown in Figure 1. If a task is a procedural task (or a transfer task with a relatively small number of branches) then a procedural task analysis technique is recommended. If, however, the task is a transfer task then an extended task analysis technique is suggested. This extended task analysis procedure is required because of the substantial variance in the

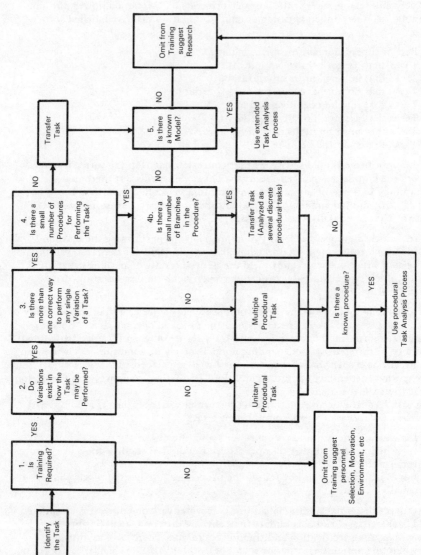

**Figure 1.** *Logic tree for distinguishing between a procedural and a transfer task, and subsequent analysis procedure*

performance of the task. Thus the analysis technique has evolved to accommodate the 'soft' nature of the task.

The focus of the analysis effort, and the key to training our transfer tasks, is found in the definition of the rules that support performance and the creation of the cognitive strategy that tells the performer when to apply which rules. It is through the identification of these rules and their hierarchical relationship that the instructional designer for soft skills is able to achieve a training capability and degree of efficiency not achievable by traditional analytic and design models. The function of the cognitive strategy is of equal importance in that accomplished performance is achieved, not just by an understanding of the rules of performance but also by an understanding of when to apply them.

The issue of training transfer tasks is not how to train a given task, but rather what to train. We have never had problems defining what transfer tasks were, or of providing examples. The problem has been related to the lack of transfer of proficiency when a person has been trained on a specific instance and his behaviour did not generalize to a related instance. Because of the variance implied in a transfer task, the training must focus on the acquisition of the rules that define the performance, and upon the decision points that allow for the how, where, and when, application of the said rules.

## Methodology

The actual procedure for analyzing a transfer task is composed of a series of related steps. These steps are slightly different from the previous analysis models, yet represent only an extension of these techniques. None of the ideas are new. It is the integration of these steps that facilitate the analysis and subsequent training on transfer tasks. The procedure is basically as follows:

1. A task has been identified as a transfer task.
2. Identify the set of behaviour from which the transfer task has been taken.
3. Identify related but different examples of the transfer task.
4. Verify the behavioural set and the examples.
5. Extract the rules that are used during performance of the task to control or define the performance.
6. Identify any official, accepted set of rules that specify acceptable performance.
7. Continue the extraction of the rules, striving to describe the higher order rules that tend to control or operate upon the lower order rules.
8. Consolidate the lower order rules and group those that are similar.
9. Establish the hierarchical relationship of rules.
10. Verify the rules and the hierarchy.
11. Define the conditions and cues that are present prior to, during, and after task accomplishment.
12. Develop the cognitive strategy (decision model) that tells the performer which rules to apply, how to use them, and when to do it.
13. Verify the decision rules as to adequacy, accuracy and efficiency.
14. Validate the rules and cognitive strategy by application to a set of transfer tasks on previously non-used examples from the behaviour set.
15. Revise or modify the rules, hierarchy and cognitive strategy based upon validation.

## Summary

The ultimate goal of a training programme in the Army is to achieve a level of confidence, whereby the trainer and commander are sure that the graduate (soldier) is capable of performing those tasks for which he was trained and designated as proficient. Concerning transfer tasks (soft skills), it is suggested that the optimal sequencing of instruction will capitalize upon the hierarchical relationship of the rules, wherein competence at or understanding of a higher order rule will transfer to and facilitate acquisition, understanding and application of a lower-order rule. In this way the starting point of instruction is not the performance specified in a traditional Magerian task statement, but rather the higher-order rule, followed by lower-order rules and examples of each instance and application.

The most difficult phase of developing this analytic technique was in identifying what soft skills were.

Once we had decided what a soft skill was, the remaining pieces fell into place, for as Confucius once said:

> The beginning of all wisdom is to call things by their proper names, for if things are not called by their proper names, then what is said is not what is meant, then that which might ought to be done is left undone.

By labelling tasks as transfer tasks, the entire focus and training development efforts changed. The proposed procedure is an attempt to deal with the inimitable variance that has confounded the analysis and training of soft skills for many years.

# 3.19 A Cross-Cultural Study of the Teaching Effectiveness of the Case Method Versus the Lecture Method of Teaching in Lecture-Orientated Environments

E A Stuhler and S Misra
*Technical University of Munich, West Germany*

Abstract: In most German universities many management education students are exposed to about 25-30 hours of lectures per week during a four-year training period. Two resulting problems are: (i) the required period of training is very long and very expensive, and (ii) the significant gap between economic theory and principles as taught in the universities and real life problems.

To address these problems in management education, an experiment has been set up to investigate the effectiveness of the case method as a teaching tool. This paper discusses the experiment.

## Introduction

Transmission of knowledge in a manner which the recipients are able to assimilate and, to some extent, identify with is one of the main determinants of the effectiveness of any educational and/or training programme. Another major purpose of training programmes is to stimulate development of skills which would equip the learners to meet the needs and demands of their occupations. However, there appear to be both substantive and qualitative differences between the knowledge transmitted by the teacher and the knowledge and skills acquired by the students. This is a matter of common experience. Although factors such as the ability of the teacher and the abilities and prior educational background of the student are important in the teaching/learning process, equally important is the particular teaching method practised for imparting educational training deemed conducive to real life problem-solving.

Imparting knowledge and skills primarily through lectures is prevalent in centres of higher learning throughout the world. This is particularly so in social sciences.

For several years now, some teachers, students and professionals in the field have expressed dissatisfaction with the time-honoured lecture method. This has probably led to supplementing lectures in the classroom with a variety of other educational technologies, eg audio-visual aids, role-playing and computer-assisted teaching. However, barring a few exceptions, most universities have not substituted any other method of instruction for the lecture method. The Harvard Business School appears to have been the first to substitute the case method for the lecture method in its Master of Business Administration and Management Development programme.

The phenomenal success of the management programmes at Harvard, as shown in industry confidence, has been partly attributed to the case method of teaching/ learning. While there are detractors of the case method, other American, European and Asian schools of management have satisfactorily adopted it for management training. However, scant empirical evidence is available to support the many positive results of training which are attributed to this method.

The purpose of this paper is to describe an ongoing study which examines the comparative effectiveness of case versus lecture method. In four different universities (three West German universities and the University of the Philippines), teaching effectiveness is being evaluated in two main areas: cognitive and affective. In addition, it is of interest to measure the differences between the actual process of conducting case discussions and lecturing at various sites.

It is necessary to clarify two important points in respect to this study. First, the study was conducted in environments where the lecture method is used almost exclusively and both teachers and students have longstanding experience with it. Second, the case method was used for certain groups of students as a substitution and not as a supplement. For instance, if a course in business administration were to use the case method, the entire course material and each of the topics within the course were dealt with through cases accompanied by relevant technical notes. In contrast, the same course taught through the lecture method covered the syllabus but did not use a single case study.

## Objective of the Study

The main objective of the study is to determine the comparative effectiveness of the case course versus lecture course for the development of the specific knowledge, skills and relevant attitudes conducive to the application of those skills and knowledge to decision-making in problem-solving situations.

## Method

The basic features of the research design were as follows:

1. The total number of students attending a particular course at each of the universities mentioned above were divided into two groups. One group attended the case method class and the other the lecture method class.
2. As far as possible, efforts were made to attain maximum similarity of composition in the two groups with respect to prerequisites (entry knowledge) for the course. This was achieved by administering an 'entry knowledge' test to individuals in each group.
3. In the middle and at the end of each course, students in each group were individually tested with respect to knowledge gained in the subject matter areas of the particular course. This was one major dependent variable.
4. In addition, the students' attitudes towards the course subject matter and their learning effiency were measured.
5. In order to compare the actual process of teaching through both methods at the different sites, Flanders' Interaction Analysis was used. This was done to

enable us to compare the process whereby the case and lecture methods of teaching were actually conducted in different universities and across cultures.

## Preliminary Findings

It is not yet possible to make any definitive statements regarding the outcomes of the study. However, some speculations are in order.

The cases used in the three German universities, as contrasted with the cases used in the University of the Philippines, are lengthier and have incorporated a good deal of uncertainties into the decision-making situations. The cases used in the University of the Philippines, in retrospect, appear to be more like 'exercises' than 'cases'.

With respect to the results so far obtained in the German universities, one of the questions that remains open is whether the effectiveness of the case method can be ascertained over the short period of one year. The long-term effects of case courses can perhaps be better examined through longitudinal studies, wherein the synergetic effects of the case method of education or training may demonstrate clearly positive results.

# 3.20 Programmable Pocket Calculators as Didactic Aids in Italian Upper Secondary Schools

**R M Bottino**
*National Council for Research, Genoa, Italy*

**Abstract:** This article describes work being carried out in Italy based on the educational potential of programmable pocket calculators for mathematics teaching in secondary schools.

## Introduction

My research concerns the teaching of mathematics in Italian upper secondary schools (ages 14-18). It may be useful here to describe briefly the Italian educational system. Italian schools are divided into:

(a) primary schools (ages 6-11);
(b) lower secondary schools (ages 11-14); and
(c) upper secondary schools (ages 14-18), which themselves include different types of school, such as high schools, technical and professional schools etc.

While a reform in 1962 introduced significant changes in the lower secondary schools, unifying them to one curriculum of studies, the reform for upper secondary schools has not yet been accomplished. This has meant that the curricula in upper secondary schools have remained virtually unchanged for about 50 years.

## The Research

Attempts are currently being made to adapt and update the curricula in upper secondary schools. For example, several groups are involved in research into possible new teaching programmes in mathematics. The overall aim is to make the subject more integrated with the present-day world, and in so doing to take advantage of the potential offered by recent technological developments in education. The research in which I have been involved has been centred in Genoa, Italy and involves a series of classroom experiments based on the use of programmable pocket calculators in mathematics.

There are both technical and educational reasons for investigating the potential use of such calculators in schools. Because they are now widely available in Italy, we consider it very important that schools should supply the necessary training in using them correctly and efficiently. In addition, we wish to consider the possibilities for innovative teaching which they allow. After a first group of experiments, where programmable pocket calculators were used to introduce and develop subjects connected to the traditional programme of mathematics, our emphasis has been directed towards mathematical areas which could be considered of interest in a social, economic and cultural context, and which could make effective use of such calculators.

At present, we are working in the area of economic concepts. Programmable pocket calculators are used to introduce these concepts and to develop the numerical calculus involved. For example, often 'per cent differences' are the first approach to many economic phenomena which, in turn, are well represented in terms of 'constant per cent differences'.

The study of frame references which show up the invariance of per cent differences leads students 'to discover' the logarithms family as the set of solutions. The development of this particular area also involves the use of differential equations and definite integrals.

It has been found that programmable pocket calculators can encourage the introduction of some fundamental areas of calculus which are otherwise 'left out' or are developed only in the final year of upper secondary school. Students learn to see that the importance of such mathematical areas goes well beyond the examples which motivated their introduction.

# Section 4:
# Reports on One-Day Symposia

## 4.1 Information Retrieval in Educational Technology

**E B Duncan**
*Robert Gordon's Institute of Technology, Aberdeen*
**R McAleese**
*University of Aberdeen*

### Introduction

This is a summary of events which took place during a one-day symposium on Information Retrieval, held on 1 April, during ETIC 81. The Proceedings of the day are being published separately.

Thirty-three delegates, with varied background interests, listened to and discussed papers ranging from information-seeking behaviour of educational technology users, through present provision of information services, to possible innovations in relaying of information to users. The theme of the day's discussions was the variety of means by which one can convey information from source to user and consideration of ways in which information might be packaged or filtered to achieve this most effectively.

Educational technology as a subject is an area in which there has been a great deal of controversy in identifying who the users really are. It is an area in which resources are scattered, due to its disparate nature, and access to them is difficult. It is therefore important that both the users and their patterns of information need are clearly identified.

The format of the day was that of a structured seminar, that is, the presentation of five papers, each followed by a formal, prepared reply. The objective of the reply was to stimulate discussion and to pose a contrasting view. The presentation of papers was preceded by a small information-gathering exercise or task completed by delegates. The day concluded with the formation of three Working Groups discussing separately three topics isolated as being of direct current interest. Each of the three groups reported back to the symposium before further discussion took place.

### Task

The information need problem was explored in a practical exercise or task. Participants were asked to complete, in a space of 10 minutes, a set of questions aimed at identifying individual needs in information retrieval (see Figure 1). They were asked to identify a recent instance where they had needed to find out something relating to educational technology, and to indicate from a list of

**Task:** Identifying individual needs in information retrieval

Please complete the following to the best of your ability using an instance from your own experience, if possible.

*Name:*

*Organization:*

*Task:*

Think of a recent instance where you have needed to find out something related to educational technology.

   Would your need have been met by having one of the following solutions suggested to you: (Mark with a * any which seem appropriate to your situation.)

   (1)  An introductory work or textbook                                    ( )
   (2)  A background review article                                         ( )
   (3)  Someone who knows something about the subject                       ( )
   (4)  Someone who knows something about the literature of
        the subject                                                        ( )
   (5)  An organization where the subject is being studied                  ( )
   (6)  Courses or conferences which might be relevant                      ( )
   (7)  Software or other AV materials as well as literature                ( )
   (8)  A selected list of literature and/or software to suit
        your needs
        (a)  selected to two or three items                                 ( )
        (b)  selected to 30 items                                           ( )
        (c)  selected to 100 items                                          ( )
        (d)  a complete list of all published material                      ( )
   (9)  Names of professional bodies in the subject area                    ( )
   (10) Any other solution — please specify:                                ( )


Mark the most important with an extra *

Make a brief note of what the topic was: (eg distance learning — recent research — UK only)

**Figure 1.** *Task questionnaire*

10 possible courses of action which would seem the most appropriate. Results from this instant assessment were tabulated and used in discussion later in the day (see Table 1).

## Summary of Task Responses

From the tabulated responses, it is clear that most users were looking either for someone who knows the subject, or for a background review of the subject. Is information provision too abundant? Are filters needed? Compare these categories with the fact that very few people wished to be given a list of more than 100 bibliographic items. Is the most popular category really the most needed, or is it

|  |  | Score | Rank |
|---|---|---|---|
| (1) | An introductory work or textbook | 8 | 8 |
| (2) | A background review article | 20 | 2 |
| (3) | Someone who knows the subject | 30 | 1 |
| (4) | Someone who knows the literature | 17 | 3 |
| (5) | An organization in the field | 17 | 3 |
| (6) | Courses or conferences | 9 | 7 |
| (7) | Software or AV materials and literature | 10 | 6 |
| (8) | Selected list of literature and/or software | | |
| | (a)  selected to two or three items | 4 | 10 |
| | (b)  selected to 30 items | 14 | 5 |
| | (c)  selected to 100 items | 2 | – |
| | (d)  complete list of all published material | 4 | 10 |
| (9) | Professional bodies in subject field | 5 | 9 |
| (10) | Other solutions | | |

|  |  |
|---|---|
| Committees | 2 |
| Personal files | 1 |
| Abstracts | 2 |
| Workshops | 3 |
| Trade literature | 5 |
| Popular press | 1 |
| Interview/questionnaire | 2 |
| List of research projects | 1 |

**Table 1:** *Tabulated responses to task*

the most frequently thought of? It is difficult to identify on such a brief response whether the replies referred to 'need' or 'use', but a similar, informal survey carried out by the Qualified Citation Indexing Project of approximately 25 potential users from differing educational experience (unpublished) gave an almost parallel pattern of response (see below for details of the paper on qualified citation indexing).

## Presentations

The presentations consisted of two general papers on information needs and possible solutions. These were followed by reports on two working information systems, and finally, a report on a new form of information retrieval in educational technology — qualified citation indexing.

### Information Needs

The present information-seeking behaviour of users, as displayed by a small group of American university lecturers, was presented in the first paper of the day, given by Professor Donald Ely of Syracuse University (Director, ERIC Clearinghouse on Information Resources). Professor Ely's paper was on 'Educational Technologists as Consumers of Educational Information', and described the information-coping strategies of educational technologists, the types of educational technologist, and the purpose of seeking information. He emphasized in particular the danger of designing complex systems for non-existent people in hypothetical situations with unknown needs. The ideal is not to aim for one universal system but to identify, co-ordinate and communicate the information options already in existence, and make them available to the individual user.

In reply, Mr N Rushby of Imperial College, London, emphasized the need for identification of real users. There is a possible confusion in people's minds between need and use. He asked to what extent participants considered that users' needs are shaped by what is available. Points raised in discussion reinforced the connection between users' needs and environment, and emphasized the difficulty of communication of need. Intermediaries were considered to be important, a point which was also brought out by the task results, as discussed earlier. The question of what people want is often a function of the way in which the question is asked. People like problems — few like solutions.

Possible solutions to the information-handling problem were described in the paper given by Miss Jane Hustwit of the Council for Educational Technology. Miss Hustwit outlined some of the work of the Council in investigating problems surrounding and blocking access to information. In particular, she emphasized the role of the Council in the development of experimental information services and the investigation of the application of new technologies to these problems. The main theme of her paper, however, was a brief description of the CEDAR project on educational computing, centred at Imperial College, London, and a detailed account of Contact, the Council's information service on teaching and learning methods. The background, structure and operation of Contact were described in full, together with a description of some of the problems encountered in its operation.

Mr M Head (RGIT, Aberdeen) in reply to Miss Hustwit's paper, emphasized the value of personal contact in information transfer. This point was also made by Professor Ely, and identified in the task results. Several doubts remained, however, on the basic structure of the information held, and therefore of the efficiency of search strategies, in terms of controlled vocabulary, definition of subject coverage, and identification of user group.

Discussion centred very much on practical operating details of the system described, and as such, indicated a great deal of interest being shown in the concept of a personalized information system. Evaluation of the system by user feedback was considered, by some participants, to be a point which had been underestimated as a controlling factor in the development of the system.

## Working Information Systems

Two working information systems were described by the next two speakers, Mr W J K Davies and Dr D Bligh (the latter paper presented by Miss J Claridge, in the absence of Dr Bligh).

QUERY, developed at Hertfordshire County Programmed Learning Centre, as described by Mr Davies, is a system designed for classroom teachers. Mr Davies emphasized that, with a computer-based system, a clear layout of complex information is most important for the user. He pointed out various limitations of the present QUERY system, such as sequential searching, which makes response times relatively slow, and various restrictions on record length and layout. Systems designed for microcomputers tend to suffer from similar restrictions. There is, apparently, a new, improved QUERY in preparation, although not yet available. It will still essentially be a locally based system, since Mr Davies believes that individuals or groups may usefully develop their own data retrieval systems with their own local idiosyncracies in preference or in addition to using national systems.

This last point was taken up by Mr L McMorran of Aberdeen College of Education Library, in reply. Mr McMorran emphasized the value of local systems for local needs, and specifically for changing needs, but pointed out at the same time that many of the advantages of sophisticated search strategies, and rapid access and interaction for users, at present taken for granted in large systems, are not available to small systems. There is a danger of producing a multiplicity of isolated systems using different programs and thereby becoming incompatible, either with each other or with a national system. Systems like ERIC, while perhaps not ideal for local needs, do at least have the advantage of a carefully constructed thesaurus of controlled vocabulary terms and relationships. As Mr McMorran indicated, terms with vague and ambiguous meaning are not uncommon in the free language of education or educational technology.

TEARS, developed at Exeter University (The Exeter Abstract Reference System) is, like QUERY, essentially a local system for higher education. Three problem areas in higher education were identified by Dr Bligh as areas in which an information retrieval system could play a part: the system could identify relevance, ie delineate the field; it could establish authority for included items; and it could direct or assist in mapping the research field. The implications of an information retrieval system can be much wider than the relaying of references, and supplementary services such as an 'interest bank' of research or interest profiles could act, not only as a search or alerting service but as an exchange arena for teachers with similar interests. In the paper, Dr Bligh described the operation of TEARS and the type of record it contains. Complex logic is used in search strategy, but questions remain relating to the amount of information to include, from what sources, and overall evaluative questions of cost and charging. User consultation and user evaluation were mentioned, as was the importance of personal contact to user satisfaction.

In reply, Mr Martyn Roebuck of the Scottish Education Department endorsed the belief that a system to be used must be accessible, and must be needed. In practical terms, the cost of a system must compare favourably with other means of retrieving information perhaps more familiar to the user. Problems of recall or precision, and of scale, were referred to briefly as worthy of consideration in designing systems. Doubt was cast on the idea of having a universally acceptable thesaurus or map, since from experience Mr Roebuck had found that the self-correcting hierarchy or concept map was perhaps more flexible.

## Qualified Citation Indexing

The concept of citation indexing may be relatively new to the field of educational technology, but it is well-established in other fields. Science Citation Index, Social Sciences Citation Index, and Arts and Humanities Citation Index, all published by the American Institute for Scientific Information (ISI), each run to several large volumes per year of very small print. The theme of the paper on qualified citation indexing, presented by Mrs E Duncan (RGIT), was that citation indexing techniques are particularly appropriate for educational technology because of the wide spread of subject interest, the difficulty of identifying a user population, and the ambiguities of an international terminology. A qualified citation index, in which relationships between published works would be specified and described by a qualifying term or phrase, is being developed in prototype on a DEC-20 computer at RGIT. Phrases, such as 'similar research' or 'methodology', indicate the context in which a reference has been quoted. The project is sponsored by the Scottish Education Department and run jointly by Dr R McAleese of the University of Aberdeen and Mr D Anderson of RGIT.

Mr L Corbett of Stirling University Library, in reply, emphasized the size of files necessarily created by citation indexing — manual handling is impracticable, and output includes much 'noise'. Qualifying of citations therefore would appear to be helpful. Other techniques, such as 'cycling' have been used by ISI for similar purposes. Difficulties remaining for the project, and for citation indexing of educational technology are, in Mr Corbett's view, those of subject definition, and of understanding the reasons an author has had for quoting a particular reference — these are not always clear or meaningful!

**Working Groups**

Three working groups will consider the following topics:

1. The usefulness of published resources.
2. Mapping educational technology concepts.
3. Citation indexing.

*Group 1*

This group will consider whether existing resources in educational technology meet the needs of individual users

— identify the range of resources available;
— classify the resources into a framework that places similar resources together, eg books, journals etc;
— agree on reasons where existing resources do not seem to meet the conditions you expect;
— report on some suggestions as to how resources might be made more useful.

*Group 2*

— identify an important concept in educational technology;
— list 11 related concepts;
— construct a 'map' of the concept identified, ie indicate the relationships between the prime concept and the related concepts;
— report on how the mapping technique may be usefully applied to other areas.

*Group 3*

— undertake a citation search on the QCIP citation data base;
— list the ways in which the retrieval system can help the user;
— report on the ways in which the system could be improved.

**Figure 2.** *Working group instructions*

## Working Groups

Participants were asked to join one of three groups given the remits shown in Figure 2. The overall aim of the working groups was to identify ways in which information needs may best be fulfilled in the three areas specified.

Group 1 discussions centred on the relative importance to users of the centralization of information resources or level of support. Questions raised by the group were whether centralization implies control, how immediate are most information needs, and how difficult it is to identify the searcher and thus match needs to sources.

Group 2 produced a visual map of the topic 'independent study' with indications of relationships between the concepts displayed. Comparisons with construction of a linear theasaurus were made, and ideas on variation in interpretation of 'level', 'timeliness' and 'value' discussed. It was felt that the graphical technique could be applied very usefully in other subject areas as an aid in identifying relationships between parts of subjects and evaluation of the importance of some subjects in relation to others.

Group 3 concluded that citation indexing could be a helpful approach to an information query, since often the query begins with knowing people or authors working in an area. It could be used as a way of seeing how ideas recur in the literature and could be helpful in solving unformulated queries. Again, discussion took place on who the user community might be.

## Issues

From the variety of presentations during the day — the papers, the task, the working groups and the discussions — a number of issues emerged. These issues are important as they indicate the problematic nature of educational information retrieval, and perhaps provide indicators to the future. In summary the issues were:

1. *Who* is the searcher? It is important to begin with the searcher — after all no system would be needed if there were no inquirer. Is it an experienced research worker, or is it a student learning the subject and the language of the subject? Different searchers need different facilities and different types of information.
2. *Level of support.* Where is the information to be located? Will the focus be local or national or international? A local information retrieval system has very different characteristics from those of an international facility. A good comparison to make at this point would be the Exeter system — TEARS (described by Bligh) and ERIC.
3. *Immediacy.* How soon does the user need the information? Will tomorrow be too late? What do we know about the 'intellectual windows' where researchers and thinkers need to know that missing piece of information immediately before they can continue with their creative thinking? Does one need on-line search facilities or will a postal retrieval system meet the needs of most users?
4. *Presentation.* Is it good enough to see the information on a VDU screen, or does the searcher need the hard copy of printed text? The ergonomic, as well as social and psychological issues with regard to user interaction with data are far from clear. Can systems be made user-friendly for the interactive and mediated searcher?
5. *Is there a need for intermediaries?* Is there a role for the information scientist to counsel the searcher and identify profiles and user needs? Who is best qualified to make the intervention — librarians, information scientists, or subject specialists?
6. *Are there limits to technology?* Can the technological answers provided by large computer-based systems get in the way of the searcher? Are we in danger of looking for elegant technical solutions when the searcher needs the feel of a few back copies of a journal, or an hour browsing from shelf to shelf in a library?

The symposium did more to raise to the surface some of the issues than to provide solutions. Perhaps the model of the symposium, in which some of the thinking was left to the participants, is one which the information scientist must consider when designing information systems. An ideal solution is often one where some of the decisions are left to the searcher and where most of the hard drudgery of searching is removed. By the time the Second Information Retrieval Symposium is held in 1982, some further issues will emerge and perhaps some clarification may be made on the information needs of educational technologists.

# 4.2 Microcomputers and Scottish Education

J Megarry, *Scottish Microelectronics Development Programme*
N Smart, *Aberdeen College of Education*
C Tomasso, *Secondary Schools Computer Administration and Management Project*

## Preface

This is the report of a one-day workshop conference mounted by the Scottish
Microelectronics Development Programme (SMDP) in association with the main
conference, ETIC 81. There were three sessions presenting diverse material mostly
on microcomputers in schools, followed by an open forum. Over 50 delegates
attended the workshop, most of whom had come in for the day from local schools,
colleges and Grampian Region Education Department; a minority were ETIC 81
international delegates. Thus, although the main workshop input related to
microcomputers in Scottish secondary schools, the discussion broadened the issues
to micro-electronics generally, to other sectors in education, and to developments
outside Scotland. This report follows the timetable of the workshop in outline and
has been edited from the various authors' contributions as follows:

□ *The Scottish Microelectronics Development Programme* (Jacquetta Megarry)
□ *Microcomputers in the secondary school curriculum* (Norman Smart)
□ *SCAMP: Secondary Schools Computer Administration and Management
   Project* (Carlo Tomasso)
□ *Open Forum* (reported by Ian Graham, SMDP programmer)

## The Scottish Microelectronics Development Programme

### Phase 1

The Scottish Education Department (SED) has funded this programme through the
Scottish Council for Educational Technology, in whose Glasgow premises the team
is based. The present £1m funding lasts until April 1984 and is the second phase of
an equipment loan scheme under which hardware worth £320,000 was allocated
to 68 project centres throughout Scotland. This scheme was launched in November
1979, when it was estimated that around 100 micro-systems existed in Scottish
schools; bids exceeded funds by a factor of over 6:1 and equipment was loaned to
a variety of educational establishments:

| | | |
|---|---|---|
| (a) | Primary schools | 3 |
| (b) | Secondary schools | 26 |
| (c) | Further education | 15 |
| (d) | Higher education | 11 |
| (e) | Supporting agencies | 3 |
| | | 68 |

These Phase 1 project centres were scattered throughout the Regions of Scotland.
The applications suggested covered the full range of subjects taught in schools and
colleges, from predictable ones like maths, science, engineering and technical
subjects to less obvious ones like social work, careers guidance, social subjects and
music, with application in geography, home economics, farm management and
business studies somewhere in between. Delivery and installation of the equipment
was carried out by David D Walker on secondment from Perth College of Further
Education and by Tague McFadden on secondment from the Scottish Education
Department, with some secretarial assistance, from April 1980.

## Phase 2

It rapidly became clear that educational establishments badly needed support to get the most out of this equipment. In order to provide support for these projects, to help to exchange and develop software, to provide information and to establish helpful contacts, a second phase (entitled SMDP) was announced. By Autumn 1980, David D Walker had been appointed as Director, and Jacquetta Megarry as Deputy. Tague McFadden remained as SED Co-ordinator and a support staff began to be appointed. By the time of the conference, the Technician, the Information Officer, two secretaries and five of the 10 programmers had been appointed and most had taken up duties.

SMDP policy is determined by a Steering Committee representing the Scottish Education Department (SED), the Convention of Scottish Local Authorities (COSLA), and the Scottish Council for Educational Technology (SCET), with observers from the Department of Education and Science, SED, SCET and SMDP.

Responsibility for independent evaluation of the Programme has been accepted by the Department of Education, Edinburgh University. SMDP has a continuing commitment to all the Phase 1 projects but it has also identified a smaller number of Phase 2 development centres from among them.

## Aims

Having identified the projects with which SMDP is concerned, its main aims can now be identified. These apply to all the Phase 1 project centres (including the Phase 2 development centres) and only incidentally may be realized elsewhere in Scottish education.

The initial objectives stated were:

- ☐ the promotion of general awareness of the implications of micro-electronics among pupils, students and staff;
- ☐ the production of materials and the provision of practical experience for those who will conduct teachers' pre-service and in-service courses in the application of micro-electronics in various subjects;
- ☐ the use of microcomputers in a curriculum context for learning and for assessment purposes;
- ☐ the production of curriculum materials to enable pupils/students to learn about and gain experience in the use of microcomputers;
- ☐ the exploitation of micro-electronics to assist pupils/students with special educational needs, particularly those suffering from sensory loss;
- ☐ the application of microcomputers to management in school and post-school education.

These initial objectives have been supplemented by a further four because of developments since 1979:

- ☐ the application of microcomputers to community education and for general awareness in association with the Scottish Council for Community Education;
- ☐ the development of ways and means of promoting joint industry and education micro-electronics projects in association with the Microelectronics Educational Development Centre (MEDC) based at Paisley College of Technology. (MEDC has a remit to encourage micro-electronics courses in further and higher education and to ensure an adequate supply of manpower for Scottish industry in this field.);
- ☐ the development of a central software and information service in association with selected colleges and Regional authorities;
- ☐ the dissemination, collection and exchange of information with other agencies and projects in the UK and abroad.

## Activities

### SOFTWARE LIBRARY

SMDP is in the process of establishing a national software library under Phase 2. The intention is to allocate resources — notably programmer support for working groups of teachers — to centres chosen on a number of criteria, including the likelihood that they will produce software of potential value elsewhere. Of all the needs SMDP is trying to meet, this seems the most pressing. All over Scotland, the same picture emerges — commercial software is usually found to be gimmicky, badly documented or inappropriate. It is difficult to find out what other educational establishments have produced materials, and much of it is designed for American high school curricula or English A-level courses. Few teachers are able to write their own programs, and those few who are skilful have little time free from teaching duties to produce software. The rationale for the pump-priming model is thus simply the severity of the software 'drought'.

The SMDP national software library contains materials of varied provenance — purchased, distributed under licence, donated, home-grown, and home-converted from other versions. It is organized on two levels, with lower-level packages freely available and freely donated but with no guarantees issued for quality. To qualify for promotion to the upper level of the library, a package must not only be technically competent, but also educational valuable and adequately documented.

### PERIODICAL

SMDP launched its illustrated quarterly periodical *Phase Two* in February 1981. This gives regular news of activity, ideas and developments in educational computing, carries reviews of books and software, and has articles describing work in SMDP projects and elsewhere. It is distributed free to projects and is available to anyone interested, on subscription.

### DISPLAY AREA

At its base in Dowanhill, Glasgow, SMDP has a large display area in which all the popular microcomputer systems in use in Scottish education are available, together with appropriate software and peripherals. As the equipment also functions as workstations for programmers and is sometimes moved away (eg for conferences such as ETIC), visitors are entertained by appointment only. There is also a reference library of books, periodicals and audio-visual resources.

### INQUIRY SERVICE

The SMDP information service deals with inquiries not only from visitors but also by post and telephone. Queries are often from potential or impending purchasers of micro-systems and software and SMDP tries to give impartial advice about the choices. It also receives inquiries of a general nature, and attempts to keep in touch with other information services, eg CEDAR, the Council for Educational Technology, and the Microelectronics Education Programme for the rest of the UK.

In all of the above activities, the primary objective is to assist the original 68 project centres, though SMDP obviously hopes for spin-off benefits to the rest of Scottish education and to some extent to interested people outside Scotland.

## Future Developments

Much of the work mentioned above is still in its early stages. Signs are already emerging from the projects that equipment was being put to uses not originally anticipated. For example, the Apple II system at Tain Royal Academy, Ross-shire, was not only being used for maths and business studies but also for careers guidance, and in the evenings the school was being kept open for evening classes in which oil workers from Nigg pursued studies on the Apple. Outreach of the educational potential to the community will perhaps be a growing feature in the Scottish scene, as is already happening in the United States.

### SCAMP and SCEMP

Two acronymic (and easily confusable) projects were associated with SMDP. The SCAMP project in school administration is covered by a later section, but the SCEMP project should be mentioned briefly here. SCEMP is the Scottish Community Education Microelectronics Project and has been funded over three years by the Scottish Education Department through the Scottish Council for Community Education, who are developing the project in close co-operation with SMDP. Within the field of community education, two areas in which microcomputers can have a major impact have been identified:

    (a)  information storage and retrieval;
    (b)  the provision of individualized learning opportunities for individuals and groups.

One of the difficulties of any inquiry service lies in the lengthy and tedious business of checking through files for appropriate information and the corresponding difficulties of maintaining up-to-date records. The use of computers to ease this burden and ensure a more effective updating system and search of the files is an obvious one, especially in the case of telephone inquiries where time spent waiting is costly. The Scottish Telephone Referral Service will be equipped with Cromemcos and data-base software under SCEMP.

In the area of individual tutorials, many programs have been developed but mostly for schools and colleges. Very little work has been done in the development of programs useful to individuals and groups in an informal or community setting. SCEMP will explore how such facilities could be used, for example in:

□ personal problem-solving
□ child development and education
□ home information systems and word processing
□ community councils and local organizations
□ library and job-finding data banks
□ demonstrations for small companies and individuals
□ educational and recreational activities.

## Microcomputers in the Secondary School Curriculum

This session consisted of an illustrated presentation and demonstration by Norman Smart, followed by a solid opportunity for all the delegates to get 'hands-on' experience with a variety of machines and software, most of which had been developed in Aberdeen College of Education and associated schools on SMDP equipment. As this was mainly in a variety of secondary subjects, he touched first on the role of the computer in the primary school, where a lot of interest is being expressed.

The versatility of the microcomputer combined with the more flexible, open-ended, individualized or small group approach makes the microcomputer an ideal resource for the primary school teacher. Fortunately, the interest in secondary schools also shows great promise of exciting teaching techniques based on microcomputers. Undoubtedly there are problems: lack of time; the microcomputer is two floors down, three blocks away; how can 20 to 30 pupils use one machine?; the software is not quite good enough; it can be done better by conventional techniques; and so on. Even better, cheaper, more portable machines will appear.

We must therefore put up with shortcomings at present and look to the possibilities of the mid-1980s and the 1990s. Teachers should not leave it to the commercial firms. Surely teachers have always been 'software writers' — it is only the medium that is different — albeit a more exacting one for those new to it.

Possible modes of use were discussed and it was pointed out that the Aberdeen College of Education/Grampian Region project had adopted the deliberate policy of coping with the pupil/micro ratio by attempting to create, at the lowest level, a high quality animated overhead projector (electronic blackboard) to perform tasks which could not be undertaken as well by conventional techniques. Successful material can then form the basis for expansion by introducing teaching notes, exercises, assessment for computer-assisted instruction or data, graphics, etc for computer-assisted learning tasks.

The versatility of the Apple II Plus was then demonstrated using programs from physics (diagnostic assessment on second-year electricity using graphics techniques for circuit illustration), technical subjects (3-D package, program for estimating centre of gravity using games paddles), music (synthesizer — composition using paddles to build up the score and playback), geography (general graphics tablets applications and use of effective colour maps created from Ordnance Survey map extract using the tablet with automatic calculation of grid references, distances and area).

For an hour after the presentation, delegates circulated round a number of microcomputers for 'hands-on' experience and demonstrations in mathematics, physics, music, languages, geography and remedial education.

## SCAMP: Secondary Schools Computer Administration and Management Project

### Origins

The emergence of SCAMP in 1978 can be attributed to a variety of pressures built up over a period of years, summarized as follows:

1. Management at all levels within education and particularly within the schools needs increasingly more accurate information in order to make better use of manpower and other scarce resources.
2. Information required from the school can often be difficult to obtain, since it either exists in a form which is unsuitable or is difficult to collate in time to be of use, or it cannot be assembled at all due to the inordinate amount of time and effort needed to provide such information.
3. If developments in computer administration were to continue to expand in an *ad hoc* manner and on a piecemeal basis from one school to the next, either within a single Region or across Regional boundaries, a state of chaos would ensue that would counter many of the potential benefits of a fully integrated compatible system of information processing for all schools.
4. In the mid-1970s the Computer and School Administration project COMSAD) in Central Region highlighted the value of building up main files from which many different school reports could be produced.

In 1977, Central Region, Fife Region and the Scottish Education Department agreed to co-operate and SCAMP began work early in 1978. The Project is directed by a Steering Committee comprising representatives of the two Regions and the Scottish Education Department. The development work is in the hands of a Project Team consisting of a systems analyst, two computer experts and two assistant headteachers. Although initially piloted in two schools (one in each of the two Regions), numerous schools in both Regions were consulted before details of the Phase 1 applications were agreed.

SCAMP Phase 1 has received considerable funding from SMDP, and its somewhat ponderous title is now 'SCAMP in association with SMDP'. The SED's view is that this Project is one of major importance which could point the way ahead for school administration for the next two decades.

## Aims

To tackle the pressures and problems outlined above, SCAMP's major aims are:

(a) to examine the total information requirements for secondary schools, taking into account SED, Regional and Divisional requirements;
(b) to design a computer-based administrative support system to meet the information needs in a way which is both self-contained and interlocking.

## Sub-Systems

A close study of the main ingredients of a total information system suggests that the set of necessary sub-systems would include: organization definition; admissions; staffing; careers; guidance; class/course allocation; assessment; resource management; timetabling aids; library; finance, etc.

In seeking to enlist the assistance of schools in piloting the initial system and demonstrating quickly the major advantages in adopting an integrated approach to computerization of school administration, the sub-systems selected had to be aimed, in the first instance, at the needs of the senior administrative team in the school. To accommodate all these requirements, SCAMP identified the three main areas developed in Phase 1 of the Project. These sub-systems are:

SYSTEM INITIALIZATION SUB-SYSTEM
This is to identify and define all aspects of the organization which, in general, remain static throughout the school academic year. This sub-system is of fundamental importance to the checking of all data entered into the system.

ADMISSIONS SUB-SYSTEM
This caters for all new entrants to the school, be they primary intake or secondary transfers. This sub-system also encompasses all leavers, whether they transfer to other secondary schools or out of the system altogether.

CLASS/COURSE ALLOCATION SUB-SYSTEM
This provides facilities to form mixed-ability classes or streamed classes based on school-supplied criteria and pupil performance for first-year primary intake. In addition, it caters for rolling forward the entire school without loss of information — an annual requirement in every school — keeping track of class and curriculum changes for each and every pupil.

ASSESSMENT SUB-SYSTEM
This caters for the administration needs of all examinations/assessment diets within the school and extends to cover a comprehensive marks/grade processing, recording and reporting capability.

## Main Characteristics of the System

Irrespective of who benefits most at first, the overall benefits of the above lie in the techniques employed to solve both general and specific problems which exist in traditional school administration. The techniques which characterize the system include:

- ☐ sufficient flexibility to permit a school to impose its own identity on to the system;
- ☐ user-control in driving and over-riding the system processes;
- ☐ easily-used report requisition facilities;
- ☐ single-entry, multiple-use economy throughout;
- ☐ use of turnaround documents wherever possible;
- ☐ checking digiting used where appropriate;
- ☐ maintenance of data integrity at all times.

## How the System Works

The system is specified in such a way as to be independent of the hardware since it is recognized that:

(a)  there is no such thing as a truly transferable program or set of programs;
(b)  different authorities may wish to implement the system using a range of different hardware approaches dependent upon their existing or planned resources.

It is emphasized that, whatever solution a particular authority chooses to adopt, the system should appear to the user to be no different from its implementation elsewhere, ie the input/output forms, reports and procedures remain identical.

Possible hardware implementations might include:

BATCH MODE
Operating in this mode, a school need have no computer equipment whatsoever. All computer processing would be done at a central site to which the school would send all input documents and processing requests. The central site would maintain all the school's records and supply the school with all requested lists and reports.

The main advantage in adopting this approach is one of cost — batch processing is the cheapest solution. To the school, the disadvantage is the unavoidable turnaround delay incurred in getting data and reports to and from the external site. Two factors which tend to aggravate this delay are errors on input documents sent from the school for processing, and the bottle-neck effects at the central site which are usually caused by several schools using the SCAMP system requiring to be serviced simultaneously, eg examinations and the processing of marks tend to occur in most schools at or about the same time. Records are held outside the school on the batch facility, and, if it fails for any reason, all schools using the facility are brought to a halt until the fault is remedied.

SEMI-BATCH MODE
This mode of operation requires that the school has some computer equipment, consisting of at least a central processing unit with a floppy disc, a reasonably fast printer, and a keyboard input device. Using this kind of equipment, the school would input and vet its own data to provide 'clean' data on floppy disc. The disc would then be physically transported or posted to the central site for batch processing, as described above, where the 'clean' data is processed as required. Having performed the necessary processing, the centre would send all output lists and reports derived from the processing back to the school on floppy discs, whereupon the school would off-load the information on the school printer.

This has the advantage that all data preparation is done within the school at its own pace and under its own control. Errors can now be corrected at source and potential delays are drastically reduced. Bottle-neck problems become surmountable since the centre only processes 'clean' data and is not involved with data preparation or the printing of reports — both of which can be very time-consuming. The disadvantage is that the cost is higher than a purely batch solution since it requires equipment to pre-process the data in order to eradicate input errors and off-load returned lists and reports. Further, the school's master records are located outside the school itself at the central site and, as above, if the central facility develops a fault, then all schools using the machine are brought to a halt until the fault is remedied.

ON-LINE MODE

This mode of operation is essentially the same as the semi-batch mode of operation, the difference being that no physical transfer of discs takes place. Indeed, 'clean' data is transmitted directly to the batch facility over the Post Office telephone network, as is all processed output returned to the school.

The advantage is the reduction in the turnaround time while still avoiding the bottle-neck problems outlined in the strict batch approach described above. If the floppy discs are used to accumulate 'clean' data and returned output from the central site, then efficient 'bursting' of data over the telephone network could well reduce the telephone element of the total cost. Because the school is on-line, the potential for direct access to its own records becomes a distinct possibility and opens up scope for a host of useful on-line inquiry applications. The disadvantage is that the cost is higher than the previous modes of operation, owing essentially to line charges and equipment charges. Finally, as with the previous modes of operation, if the central site fails for any reason, then all schools networked to the system fail.

STAND-ALONE MODE

In this mode, the school has its own computer facility with a definite requirement for a large capacity disc (possibly 20-40Mb) to hold all its own records, so that all processing requirements can be achieved without relying on a batch processing central site facility at all.

This approach has all the advantages of the on-line mode of operation, together with the fact that both master records and processing arrangements come under the direct control of the school. Additionally, since the school has its own master records on site, all the benefits of on-line inquiry accrue. Unfortunately, hardware costs rise sharply, principally due to the expense of a hard disc requirement. As these devices become more common, costs can be expected to drop, thus making the stand-alone mode of operation a much more attractive proposition.

## Progress to Date

So far, although the two Regions have co-operated in specifying the overall system and in the design for records, they have taken different approaches to the hardware. Central Region has adopted a data entry system, on-line to the mainframe computer at Falkirk College of Technology, whereas Fife Region is using a school-based microcomputer with a view to assessing the performance of its 'stand-alone' processing capability. Once the comparative merits of these arrangements in the two pilot secondary schools have begun to emerge, it will become easier to chart the way forward for computer-based school administration and management.

## Open Forum

In the closing discussion, a number of questions were directed at controversial aspects of SCAMP. The issue of security was raised, especially if the system were to be run on a stand-alone basis. The desirability of locking the equipment way to prevent unauthorized access was put forward. Mr Tomasso suggested that the temptation to re-use the same hardware for computer-assisted learning on an individual or classroom basis should be resisted. If the same microcomputer were used both for computer-assisted learning and for computer-based management, the classroom demands would always prevail over the administrative need in the event of a conflict.

Some questioners were critical of the extent and scope of the data collection which SCAMP was apparently proposing. Mr Tomasso emphasized that the system was simply designed to make existing practice more efficient, not to advocate new practices, though he admitted that it afforded the possibility of swift and accurate answers to questions not previously posed. Jacquetta Megarry linked this possibility of the technology affecting the goals of the exercise to the complex issues about who should have access to the information stored and hence to the ethical and political implications of the whole exercise. The Scottish Education Data Archive Collaborative Research Programme at Edinburgh University was cited as a relevant example of how computer-based data banks *could*, in principle, be used to *de-restrict* access to information and to bridge the information gap between pupil, teacher, parent, administrator and professional researcher by encouraging and training different interest groups to interrogate the data bank.

A number of questions related to the morning's session and the problems of software; questioners with PET s wanted access to Apple programs and vice versa. Jacquetta Megarry said that transferring programs from one micro to another was just the sort of task which is done more efficiently centrally — but that whether SMDP would in fact convert a particular program depended on its value and the demand for alternative versions. The long-term solution might well be through mainframe computer programs to carry out the transfer automatically. However, the greater the extent to which a particular program capitalized on the facilities of a particular machine, the harder it was to transfer the program fully and satisfactorily.

A questioner asked about SMDP's level of interest in the use of microelectronics for interfacing with science experiments or for control devices. It was pointed out in reply that about 10 of the SMDP projects involved these aspects; the role of the MEDC at Paisley College of Technology (see *Aims* section of SMDP paper) was also mentioned in this connection. Part of SMDP's display area is to be set aside for physics and engineering control techniques. However, SMDP's main interest was in computer-assisted learning in all subjects.

In answer to a question from Leslie Gilbert of the Council for Educational Technology, Jacquetta Megarry spoke about the relationship between SMDP and the Microelectronics Education Programme for the rest of the UK. The two programmes have been involved in informal contact — and perhaps also friendly rivalry — from the start. SMDP has purchased a Diamond word processor so that it could participate in the UK distribution network. The aim is that software and documents will be downloaded directly into various microcomputers, thus facilitating the sharing of ideas as well as software between the two programmes. Although they share similar aims, it should be remembered that there are points of contrast. MEP has no central team of programmers, has not lent out hardware, is working through a regional network, and is heavily committed to teacher education. SMDP, as perhaps befits the more centralized Scottish educational system, is attempting a more centralized strategy and is only supporting teacher education through the Colleges of Education and Regional Authorities, into whose remit the task fell. Nevertheless, there is much to be gained by co-operation, and everything to be lost on either side of the border by squandering further effort on reinventing irregular wheels!

## Further Information

For more details about developments in educational computing in Scotland, please refer to the SMDP quarterly periodical *Phase Two*.

For more information about SMDP's policies and activities, refer to SMDP's *Strategy and Implementation* paper and other literature. All are available, from:

> The Information Officer
> Scottish Microelectronics Development Programme
> 74 Victoria Crescent Road
> Glasgow G12 9JN
> Scotland.

# The 1981 Agecroft Trophy Competition

**H I Ellington**
*Robert Gordon's Institute of Technology, Aberdeen*

## Introduction

Between 1973 and 1975, a team of Aberdeen teachers, lecturers and educational administrators developed the POWER STATION GAME — a physics-based simulation exercise concerned with the planning of a new power station (Ellington, Langton and Smythe, 1977). The game was published by the Institution of Electrical Engineers (IEE) in 1976, and has since been used in schools, colleges, universities and training establishments in all parts of the world (Ellington and Langton, 1979).

Shortly after the publication of the exercise, the Agecroft Training Centre of the Central Electricity Generating Board presented the IEE with a specially-made trophy in the form of a power station (see Figure 1), a trophy that was to be competed for annually by teams playing the POWER STATION GAME. The first competition for the Agecroft Trophy took place in Aberdeen in 1977 during the 1977 SAGSET Conference (Ellington, Langton and Smythe, 1978), and similar competitions have since taken place in other parts of Britain. The 1981 Agecroft Trophy Competition, which was held during ETIC 81, is described below.

## The POWER STATION GAME

Before describing the actual competition, let us briefly examine the POWER STATION GAME itself. This is a manual simulation game designed for use with physics pupils in the upper forms of secondary schools and with junior science and engineering undergraduates. It is based on the assumption that a decision has been reached to build a 2,000 MW power station in a certain (hypothetical) area, the object of the game being to determine which type of station to build (coal, oil or nuclear) and where to site it. The participants (optimum number 18) are divided into three equal groups, each of which has to make the strongest possible case for building one particular type of station. The exercise is described in more detail elsewhere (Ellington and Langton, 1975; Ellington, Langton and Smythe, 1977).

## Preparation for the Competition

In the autumn of 1979, when it was definitely decided that the 1981 AETT Conference would be held in Aberdeen, discussions took place between myself and Mr M E Smythe (the IEE's Director of Professional Services) regarding the possibility of holding the 1981 Agecroft Trophy Competition during the conference. Agreement was subsequently reached between RGIT, the IEE and the Royal Bank of Scotland whereby the latter two bodies would provide money for prizes and contribute to the general expenses involved in running the competition.

In September 1980, I approached Mr K Duncan, Adviser in Science for Grampian Region, asking him to suggest suitable schools for the competition. It was agreed that one of the three schools should be Inverurie Academy (who had won the original Agecroft Trophy Competition in 1977), and Mr Duncan subsequently selected two Aberdeen schools (Aberdeen Grammar School and Linksfield Academy) to make up the required number.

In January 1981, I visited each of the three schools in order to meet the teacher who would be in charge of their team and to brief him on the rules of the

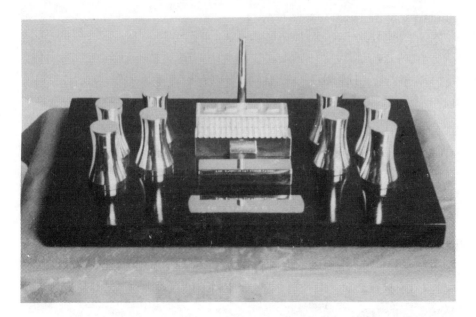

**Figure 1.** *The Agecroft Trophy*

**Figure 2.** *The Inverurie Academy team carrying out their technical calculations*

**Figure 3.** *The Linksfield Academy team presenting the case for an oil-fired station at the plenary session*

**Figure 4.** *Mr J G Graham presenting the Agecroft Trophy to Aberdeen Grammar School*

competition. Each school was asked to select a mixed team of fifth- and sixth-form pupils with a sufficiently wide range of disciplinary backgrounds to play the game effectively. The team was to be issued with copies of a background booklet on the electricity generation industry, and could be given any general coaching and background teaching thought necessary, provided that they were not allowed to see the actual game documents.

## The Competition

At 2 pm on the afternoon of 1 April (the second day of ETIC 81), the three teams assembled at the conference centre, where they were given a short introductory talk and allocated the type of station for which they had to prepare and present a case; this was done by drawing lots. The teams were then shown to their respective work rooms.

During the remainder of the afternoon, the whole of 2 April, and the first part of the morning of 3 April, the three teams worked on the preparation of their cases under the supervision of Mr G Ritchie, the teacher in charge of the Inverurie Academy team. (He had run the POWER STATION GAME before, and had agreed to stay with the teams throughout the competition — help for which the competition organizers were extremely grateful.) First, each team had to carry out a testing set of technical calculations on their station, working out (among other things) its annual fuel and cooling water requirements (see Figure 2). Next, they had to choose the best site for their station, plan its layout, and determine the capital and operating costs. Finally, they had to decide how best to present the case for their station at the plenary session that would constitute the climax of the competition. Each team was provided with an OHP and a supply of blank acetate sheets and felt pens in order to help them prepare visual support material. The conference delegates were invited to 'drop in' on the teams during the above work, and several of them in fact did so.

At 11 am on the morning of 3 April, the final day of ETIC 81, the teams assembled in the Main Hall at the conference centre in order to present their case before the conference delegates. Each team was given 15 minutes to present its case (see Figure 3), after which it was cross-examined by the other two teams. The session was chaired by Mr J G Graham, Grampian Region's Senior Depute Director of Education — one of the team who developed the POWER STATION GAME.

All previous Agecroft Trophy Competitions had employed a panel of judges to decide which team presented the best case. At ETIC 81, however, it had been decided to let the conference delegates judge the competition themselves. Each delegate was therefore provided with a marking scheme in his or her conference booklet in order to help him or her do so. Somewhat disappointingly, only about 40 delegates attended the final session of the competition, but those who did so were given a convincing demonstration both of the power and potential of simulation/gaming as an educational technique and of the almost frightening ability, sophistication and self-confidence of the modern sixth-former (see also 'Final Thoughts' by J G Morris). Our schools may lack some of the academic rigour that is supposed to have been present in earlier, grimmer days, but those who witnessed the performance of the three teams in the 1981 Agecroft Trophy Competition can surely be in no doubt that this has been more than compensated for in other areas.

## The Results

When the votes of the delegates were counted, it was found that Aberdeen Grammar School (who presented a case for a nuclear power station) had just stolen the verdict from Inverurie Academy (who proposed a coal-fired station). Subsequent discussions with delegates showed that it was the former's brilliant team work that decided the issue, there having been no significant difference in the quality of the arguments presented by the two schools. The winning team were presented with the Agecroft Trophy by Mr Graham (see Figure 4), and were also given a permanent trophy and a cheque for £50 (for their school) and £4 book tokens (for themselves). The members of the other two teams received £3 book tokens.

## References

Ellington, H I and Langton, N H (1975) The POWER STATION GAME. *Physics Education* **10**, 5, pp 445-9.

Ellington, H I and Langton, N H (1979) The POWER STATION GAME project and its aftermath. *Bulletin of the Scottish Curriculum Development Service — Dundee Centre* **15**, pp 11-18.

Ellington, H I, Langton, N H and Smythe, M E (1977) The use of simulation game in schools — a case study. In Hills, P and Gilbert, J (eds) *Aspects of Educational Technology* **XI**. Kogan Page, London.

Ellington, H I, Langton, N H and Smythe, M E (1978) The POWER STATION GAME competition for the Agecroft Trophy. *SAGSET Journal* **8**, 2, pp 56-62.

# Closing Address

## Final Thoughts

**J G Morris**
*Scottish Education Department*

All of you will agree that it is fitting that I should pay tribute to the tremendous work done by Henry Ellington and the committee under Professor Langton. The quality of the organization has been superb, a matter which is fitting as the theme of the conference has been *quality* in educational technology. Earlier conferences have considered progress, and this conference is on experience in learning which must imply quality. In some ways there is a paradox, because so much stress is being put upon efficient systems of teaching that the learner tends to be left out of the reckoning. I am glad that the stress has been on *learning*.

A Celt from west of Offa's Dyke says, 'to begin at the beginning'. We had an overview by John Nisbet from an ancient university in a city which, at one time, had two universities when the whole of England and Walea also had two. He recalled the Aberdeen Teaching Machine. Some of you may remember it. It had an anti-cheat device, whereby if you rolled the programme back in order to make a change a small pin sprang up and tore your paper. The machine also used the window approach where only the matter in hand was exposed at any one time. Our relations with learners are now better and we do not exercise ourselves about cheating. It is also important to realize that pupils learn what they choose to learn. In the case of this machine, which is now a museum piece, they learned how to beat the anti-cheat device!

The evaluation system in use was the gain/ratio technique which now appears rather old-fashioned, showing that we have progressed even further in our attitude towards learning. The advantages of this system were that it insisted on clarity of objectives and could be called a resource-based systems approach. The disadvantages were, to a degree, that it was innovation without change. Probably education is such a huge curmudgeon that it is changeless. The metaphor of those days was 'grafting on'. One wonders why another metaphor of dilution by additives until there is a new solution was not used.

With regard to change, John Nisbet identified three features. Education seems to deal in threes. There was the three-card trick of Spens; the post-war three levels of secondary education; and now the total innovator, the 20 per cent innovator and the softly-softly innovator.

A lesson of history to be disregarded at our peril is that innovators must look for allies and the one on offer was the cognitive psychologist. I was relieved to find that the old cliche that 'we don't know how children learn' was not used. We know a vast amount about how people learn, or at least the evidence is there if we are prepared to work it up.

The final call from John Nisbet was in the form of a question, 'Who wants your solution?' It was a rhetorical question but at least the person asking the question should be able to answer that he wants the solution himself. My only disappointment in this paper was that there was no comment about the post-school scene.

The next keynote paper, and it is appropriate that I deal first with keynote papers, (otherwise why call them that?) was from David Butts. He gave us a short trot from the cheap and nasty 19th century correspondence schools to the up-market distance learning mode of teaching. It is difficult to determine why educational technology exponents bid so hard for having distance learning within their orbit. It may be because they are team workers, or it may be simply territorial acquisition. They certainly worry about whether the students learn and to that extent quality is a built-in feature, but they have logistical and psychological problems from working in a team. In the current terminology they would be called structuralists. The Open University has raised the quality of lecture material because the peer-group of the various lecturers see the material.

There was little mention of costs from David Butts but distance learning is certainly not cheap. As befits an ex-producer from the BBC he saw broadcasting as a great delivery system with the good fairy of micro-technology making it more possible. By this I mean that material could be stored on tape and used when most appropriate. This view is regularly expressed but time is a finite commodity and the question arises when the material would be played back. Those who have recently purchased a video-cassette recorder for the home to avoid family fights will be aware that it does not really avoid the problem, because when the person who has a cassette wishes to use it there is something else on television which some other person wishes to look at. I have not even mentioned human frailty yet which will still be around regardless of technology and copyright problems, and saving of someone's time at the expense of someone else's time always leads to trouble. Even in School Broadcasting Council circles today it is difficult to persuade broadcasters to provide for what is now being called 'narrow-casting'.

The next keynote speaker was Tony Becher who came in by Dan Air to give us a structure for evaluation. If Sussex had not been close to Gatwick Airport would it have been different? He is an old ed tech man, a former director of NCET, the predecessor of CETUK.

We had two sets of concentric rings for forms of educational technology and forms of evaluation. Tony said that he felt by now we would all be tired of overhead projector transparencies and so we could imagine them. Some of the best visual aids of the conference resulted from this imagination! I assimilated mine into a set of rings and a set of squares.

Evaluation is like religion. Everyone believes that it is a good thing — for others. You must pay lip-service to it. I have heard it claimed that Schools Council began it. This is improbable. It, too, is a militarist metaphor or analogue. De-briefing; reporting back; analyzing — all have a familiar ring in military circles. We could compare the Battle of Britain figures for aircraft shot down and published at the time with the actual figures provided some 30 years later by the records. There was a factor of three in the errors. People are friendly to themselves.

Tony Becher did not speak about the great problem of evaluation, as I see it, which is how the evaluator makes close relations with the working group of teachers and taught, but at the same time maintains his independence. He is sucked into the working group or else he stays so far from it that he misses a great deal and is thrown back on to the arid comparison of performance before and after. This is the computer model of input-process-output which works fine as long as we do not examine the process. The other possibility is to write the history of the failure. Neville Henderson with his book *Failure of a Mission* in

1939 about his failure as Ambassador to Germany is in the classic mould of deploying the only exact science — hindsight. Evaluators themselves have the usual jargon terms for their activities and we tend to accept them in two categories: that of formative and that of summative. Having classified them thus we then proceed to criticize both types.

The second set of rings (my square ones) listed psychometrics, illuminative and organo-systemic activities. Tony Becher seemed rather kind to those who scorn the first. The real reason is that we are a non-numerate society so the vast majority of people have a vested interest in decrying any psychometric approach.

Illuminative evaluation makes the best reading material and the evaluation of the National Development Programme in Computer Assisted Learning is an excellent example of it. It is fine bedtime reading but nobody wanted to publish it. Such material can be resisted on the grounds that it is a value judgement. Could anything be more ridiculous? Value judgements of people fit to make these judgements are probably the most effective way of reaching a conclusion about anything.

We then went through the matches and mismatches of these two groupings on a 3 x 3 grid, with each member of the audience supplying his own in imagination in front of him. This is probably the cheapest way of obtaining colour graphics! I agreed with the conclusion reached by Tony that process-oriented evaluation was the best buy and the flavour of the month, but not with how he arrived at the conclusion. I would prefer to say that quality *of* learning produces quality *in* people. This is another of the prepositional juxtapositions which Martyn Roebuck parodied in his opening remarks as chairman. A good person can do process-orientation but it may not be a marketable product as I have indicated above regarding the NDPCAL document. Of course, I am preaching elitism which is acceptable in sport, business, politics, marriage and other games of chance, but is unacceptable in education. I would not wish to confuse judgement with performance, but both exist in the example which I will take to make the point. If, when you board the aircraft tonight, you find that a vote is being taken on who is going to be pilot, get off and go by train.

I have spent much of this closing talk on the three keynote papers, which seems to me appropriate. Also it would be impossible for one individual to cover all the sessions which were in parallel. However, there were some moles out in the field in the shape of my colleagues Martyn Roebuck, Leslie Hunter, Mary Hope Johnston and Sonia Morgan. Only the first two are still with us, as the women have been 'sent back to do the clearing up' in male chauvinist porker style. We cannot preach elitism and talk about equality. Between us we covered every session. In general terms, there were certain workshops which were clearly not workshops, and the besetting sin of all conferences occurred in that some speakers just grabbed the ball, ran off with it, and would not give up. Both of these forms of activity annoy, but nothing can be done about it except to complain at the closing session when the organizers ask for advice for future conferences, and to know that at the next conference in a year's time the same will happen again. It does mean that with workshops where there are restrictions on numbers some people make the wrong choice and are cut out of other papers and workshops.

Otherwise, my colleagues tell me that there was plenty of hands-on experience and also a chance to look at and interact with teaching and learning. An unusual example of the latter was that of the final of the Agecroft Trophy competition, in which three schools from the Grampian Region stated and defended their case for choice of fuel for a power station, and the audience determined the winner. I am bound to say I was rather annoyed that it took so long for most of the audience to reach the auditorium. Many of the adults present who made up the audience would have been very critical of such tardiness in young people. There is always a risk in putting on a live performance, but fortunately some 40 people eventually attended the competition and were rewarded with some excellent speaking and arguments.

There were some straight papers of work in hand, such as that of Gaye Manwaring on distance learning, Jim Hartley on typography and the McIntyre and Richardson paper on school broadcasting. These worked very well with a high information output. Other papers of the bridging type were that of Phillips and Phillips on reading for the deaf, with much practical information on a more tenuous theoretical base. There were also some straight theoretical papers suffused with all the tedium and bumps of a long train journey with nothing to read. The audience at ETIC conferences is a cross-section and theory loses them or else makes them a very cross section.

Strangely enough at this time I attended an *ad hoc* meeting of the Editorial Board of *Programmed Learning and Educational Technology*, the journal of AETT. We discussed articles and domestic matters of editorship. There is still a belief that theoretical papers in our Journal lend tone, credence and academic respectability. The question of whether they are read by anyone other than the typesetter does not seem to matter. I am not making that false dichotomy between theory and practice, as I believe that there is nothing as practical as a good theory, but I am saying that any short theoretical paper is bound to be in the high risk category at a conference unless it is an equation, and then it would require much explanation.

My impression of the audience was that the trainers are conspicuous by their absence. Those who came spent most of the time in the workshops and the practical side of these conferences has advanced hugely since the first ed tech conference put on a session called 'Simple Skills for Simple People'. We progressed through sessions at other conferences listed as 'Idiots' Guides', and now we have a very good range of worthwhile activities. My impression also was that very few people used the hardware which was available such as the banks of microcomputers when unguided. This also happened in 1976 at the ETIC conference in Dundee where the choice was given of do-it-yourself or go to a lecture-cum-discussion session, and the vast majority plumped for the latter.

There were also whole-day sessions. I sampled two of these, the Information Retrieval Symposium (with not a drink in sight) and the SMDP (Scottish Microelectronics Development Programme) session. The first one was very good but in a navel-contemplating mode, as tends to happen to all in-groups. Please would people who use runs of letters and acronyms say what they *mean* when introducing them — even the best of us forget. It seems that we have too many small systems and I was reminded of the story of the man standing at the traffic lights watching a line of 50 cars, one behind the other waiting for the lights to change and each with one occupant. He thought there would be advantage in taking the engines out of the rear 49, putting a bigger engine in the front one, and linking them all together. He had invented the train. It is a matter of fine judgement whether one big system can do the work of many small systems which may have very limited audiences, but it would certainly help if smaller systems could relate to one another. The technology is available but perhaps the will is not. Information explosions like other explosions cause trouble. There is far too much information around and it would help to have bio-degradable or other forms of self-destruct systems as silting up takes place, whether in manilla files, card indexes or VLSIC (very large scale integrated circuits).

The SMDP session (see above) was like some of the other workshops, a conference within a conference, with most of the participants not delegates at ETIC. It was over-subscribed but hardly anyone from outside of Scotland was present. There were two notable exceptions to that and all honour to them. I found it an excellent day, with a good team led, on this occasion, by Jacquetta

Megarry. Despite the Dismal Desmonds in our midst, I was surprised at the amount
of Applications software which was already available and there was a good supply
of applications software which was already available and there was a good supply
Oxford's answer to the microcomputing world, was not much in evidence. Was
Oxford the home of lost causes? Probably the difficulty lay in the fact that the
supply line was too long and the company had no service base north of Oxford,
which, I understand, is a town somewhere in the deep South.

In closing, let me recall the after-dinner thoughts of Peter Clarke, Principal of
our host college — Robert Gordon's Institute of Technology. He struck two
serious notes. The first was that it is nonsense to separate training and education
other than for administrative convenience. Let us not drift back to that period
where we co-existed in a state of mutual contempt. The second note was to run
the gamut of the emotions in any major new development. He classified them as
enthusiasm, doubt, panic, searching for the guilty, punishing the innocent and
rewarding those who had nothing to do with it.

Perception is selective. These are my perceptions.

# Keyword Index